Studies in Diplomacy and International Relations

General Editors: **Donna Lee**, Senior Lecturer in International Organisations and International Political Economy, University of Birmingham, UK and

Paul Sharp, Professor of Political Science and Director of the Alworth Institute for International Studies at the University of Minnesota, Duluth, USA

The series was launched as *Studies in Diplomacy* in 1994 under the general editorship of G.R. Berridge. Its purpose is to encourage original scholarship on all aspects of the theory and practice of diplomacy. The new editors assumed their duties in 2003 with a mandate to maintain this focus while also publishing research which demonstrates the importance of diplomacy to contemporary international relations more broadly conceived.

Titles include:

Christer Jönsson and Martin Hall
ESSENCE OF DIPLOMACY

Donna Lee
MIDDLE POWERS AND COMMERCIAL DIPLOMACY
British Influence at the Kennedy Trade Round

Donna Lee, Ian Taylor, and Paul D. Williams (editors)
THE NEW MULTILATERALISM IN SOUTH AFRICAN DIPLOMACY

Mario Liverani
INTERNATIONAL RELATIONS IN THE ANCIENT NEAR EAST, 1600–1100 BC

Jan Melissen (editor)
INNOVATION IN DIPLOMATIC PRACTICE

THE NEW PUBLIC DIPLOMACY
Soft Power in International Relations

Peter Neville
APPEASING HITLER
The Diplomacy of Sir Nevile Henderson, 1937–39

M.J. Peterson
RECOGNITION OF GOVERNMENTS
Legal Doctrine and State Practice, 1815–1995

Gary D. Rawnsley
RADIO DIPLOMACY AND PROPAGANDA
The BBC and VOA in International Politics, 1956–64

TAIWAN'S INFORMAL DIPLOMACY AND PROPAGANDA

Karl W. Schweizer and Paul Sharp (editors)
THE INTERNATIONAL THOUGHT OF HERBERT BUTTERFIELD

Paul Sharp and Geoffrey Wiseman (editors)
THE DIPLOMATIC CORPS AS AN INSTITUTION OF INTERNATIONAL SOCIETY

Ronald A. Walker
MULTILATERAL CONFERENCES
Purposeful International Negotiation

A. Nuri Yurdusev (editor)
OTTOMAN DIPLOMACY
Conventional or Unconventional?

Studies in Diplomacy and International Relations
Series Standing Order ISBN 0–333–71495–4
(*outside North America only*)

You can receive future titles in this series as they are published by placing a standing order. Please contact your bookseller or, in case of difficulty, write to us at the address below with your name and address, the title of the series and the ISBN quoted above.

Customer Services Department, Macmillan Distribution Ltd, Houndmills, Basingstoke, Hampshire RG21 6XS, England

First published in 2008 by
PALGRAVE MACMILLAN
Houndmills, Basingstoke, Hampshire RG21 6XS and
175 Fifth Avenue, New York, N.Y. 10010
Companies and representatives throughout the world.

PALGRAVE MACMILLAN is the global academic imprint of the Palgrave
Macmillan division of St. Martin's Press, LLC and of Palgrave Macmillan Ltd.
Macmillan® is a registered trademark in the United States, United Kingdom
and other countries. Palgrave is a registered trademark in the European
Union and other countries.

ISBN-13: 978–0–230–21059–2 hardback
ISBN-10: 0–230–21059–7 hardback

This book is printed on paper suitable for recycling and made from fully
managed and sustained forest sources. Logging, pulping and manufacturing
processes are expected to conform to the environmental regulations of
the country of origin.

A catalogue record for this book is available from the British Library.

A catalog record for this book is available from the Library of Congress.

10 9 8 7 6 5 4 3 2 1
17 16 15 14 13 12 11 10 09 08

Transferred to Digital Printing 2009

Contents

Part III Targeting the Policy Arenas of Interaction

Part IV Restrictive Dichotomies and Open-Ended Trajectories

List of Tables

List of Figures

Acknowledgements

This edited collection derives from papers presented at two conferences, the first at the Asia-Pacific College of Diplomacy (March 2006), and the second at Wilton Park (June 2006). The conferences brought together experts on diplomacy and global governance, two areas that have been traditionally cordoned off from each other both in their conceptual and operational dimensions. Although the reasons for and the consequences of this disconnected image remain at the centre of the thematic structure of the book, much of its innovative quality is a reflection of how, where, and why this siloed condition has eroded. Intellectually and practically, the standard assumption that diplomacy and governance exist as 'Worlds Apart' can no longer be simply taken as a given.

Although The Centre for International Governance Innovation (CIGI) took the lead role in this project, it did so in partnership with the Asia-Pacific College of Diplomacy at The Australian National University, and Loughborough University in the United Kingdom. The first conference benefited from the outstanding organisational skills of Andrea Haese, the Executive Officer of the Asia-Pacific College of Diplomacy, and Kaye Eldridge, the Project Officer of the College. Much of the administrative preparation for the second conference was undertaken with great competence by Carina Gerlach, then a research student at Loughborough University.

We benefited at both conferences from the presence not only of an array of knowledgeable academics but also a number of experienced current and former practitioners. These included David Allen, Karen Banks, Jozef Batora, Frank Brennan, Michael Carrel, Felix Dodds, John Eddy, SJ, Alexander Evans, Carlton Evans, Frédéric Grare, Klaus-Peter Klaiber, Sarah Kline, Bernard Kuiten, John Hemery, David Hendon, Ross Hornby, Geoffrey Brahm Levey, David Lovell, Tony McGrew, Paul O'Callaghan, April Palmerlee, Tony Payne, Nana Poku, Pallavi Rai, Haider Reza, Peter Rodgers, Carne Ross, Michael Reiffenstuel, Ralph Seccombe, Tim Shaw, Major-General Michael Smith, AO, Koichiro Tanaka, Ronald Walker, Ali Wardak, and Geoffrey Wiseman. Ambassador Muhammad Shaaban provided a very informative dinner speech at the Wilton Park conference.

At CIGI, Kelly Jackson's role was crucial for the successful running of the two conferences. Andrew Schrumm smoothly managed the process for delivering the completed manuscript. David Yoon provided a creative template for the cover design.

As in other projects John English, the executive director, and Daniel Schwanen, the chief operating officer and director of research, created an environment amenable to productive research. CIGI was founded in 2002 by Jim Balsillie, co-CEO of RIM (Research In Motion), and it collaborates with and gratefully acknowledges support from a number of strategic partners, in particular the Government of Canada and the Government of Ontario.

Le CIGI a été fondé en 2002 par Jim Balsillie, co-chef de la direction de RIM (Research In Motion). Il collabore avec de nombreux partenaires stratégiques et exprime sa reconnaissance du soutien reçu de ceux-ci, notamment de l'appui reçu du gouvernement du Canada et de celui du gouvernement de l'Ontario.

The final thanks are for the professionals at or associated with Palgrave Macmillan Publishing. Gemma d'Arcy Hughes commissioned and effectively ran the project to completion. Vidhya Jayaprakash did a very able job of copy-editing. Donna Lee and Paul Sharp, as co-editors of the Palgrave Studies in Diplomacy and International Studies series, provided an excellent platform to showcase this work.

Notes on Contributors

Ivan Cook is Director of the Lowy Poll Project at the Lowy Institute for International Policy. Mr. Cook holds a Bachelor of Arts (Honours) from the Australian National University and a Masters Degree in International Studies from the University of Sydney. His current research focuses on public opinion on international policy issues.

Andrew F. Cooper is the Associate Director and Distinguished Fellow at The Centre for International Governance Innovation (CIGI) and a Professor in the Department of Political Science at the University of Waterloo, where he teaches in the areas of International Political Economy, Comparative and Canadian Foreign Policy, and Global Governance and the Practice of Diplomacy. Dr. Cooper's other research interests include international institutional reform, diplomatic innovation and practices and celebrity diplomacy.

Megan Davis is the Director of the Indigenous Law Centre at the University of New South Wales where she is also Senior Lecturer in the Faculty of Law. Ms Davis's research includes critical analysis of Indigenous public law issues with particular interest in constitutional reform and democratic theory and governance as well as Indigenous people's rights in international law. She is also an Australian member of the International Law Association's Indigenous Rights Committee.

Bruce Gregory is Director of the Public Diplomacy Institute at the George Washington University and a research professor at the University's School of Media and Public Affairs. He was a member of the Defense Science Board's 2007 and 2004 studies on Strategic Communication, and is a member of the Council on Foreign Relations Task Force on Public Diplomacy, the Washington Institute of Foreign Affairs, and the Public Diplomacy Council where he served as executive director from 2001–2004. Mr Gregory's expertise is in public diplomacy, strategic communication, national defence and the media.

Jorge Heine is Chair in International Governance and Distinguished Fellow at The Centre for International Governance Innovation (CIGI). Dr. Heine served as Ambassador of Chile to India and South Africa, as well as non-resident Ambassador to Mozambique, Namibia, Swaziland, and Zimbabwe. He was a member of the Executive Committee of the International Political Science Association (IPSA), as well as professor of Political Science at Diego Portales University. He is an expert in Latin American politics, multilateralism, and transitional justice and democracy.

Brian Hocking is Professor of International Relations in the Department of Politics, International Relations and European Studies at Loughborough University. He has taught and held visiting fellowships at universities in Australia, the USA and Europe specialising in the interaction between domestic and international forces in the conduct of foreign and foreign economic policy and the impact of globalisation on diplomacy.

Christer Jönsson has been a Professor of Political Science at Lund University since 1989. His field of specialisation is International Politics. Professor Jönsson's main research interests are international negotiation, diplomacy and the role of transnational networks in international cooperation.

Jovan Kurbalija is the founding director of DiploFoundation. His professional and academic background is in diplomacy, international law and ICT. In 1992 he left the Yugoslav diplomatic service and established the Unit for IT and Diplomacy at the Mediterranean Academy of Diplomatic Studies in Malta. Since 1994 Mr Kurbalija has been conceptualising and directing a course focusing on the impact of ICT/Internet on diplomacy.

Martine Letts has served as Deputy Director of the Lowy Institute for International Policy since January 2005. She also served as Secretary General (CEO) of the Australian Red Cross following a 17-year career with the Government of Australia's Department of Foreign Affairs and Trade. She has served as Australian Ambassador to Argentina, Uruguay and Paraguay, as well as Deputy Head of Mission and Australian Deputy Permanent Representative to the International Atomic Energy Agency (IAEA) in Vienna. Ms Letts specialised in arms control and disarmament on postings in Geneva, Vienna and as a policy officer in DFAT.

Franklyn Lisk is a Professorial Research Fellow at the Centre for the Study of Globalisation and Regionalisation (CSGR) at the University of Warwick. He has also held the position of Professor Extraordinary at the Africa Centre for HIV/AIDS Management at Stellenbosch University, South Africa. From 1974 to 2005, Prof. Lisk held various positions within the International Labour Organization (ILO) including Director and Representative to the United Nations ILO Liaison Office and was Founding Director of the ILO Global Programme on HIV/AIDS and the World of Work, as well as being the ILO Global Coordinator for UNAIDS.

William Maley has been Foundation Director of the Asia-Pacific College of Diplomacy since 2003. He was a professor in the School of Politics at the University of New South Wales' Australian Defence Force Academy. Prof. Maley is also a Barrister of the High Court of Australia, a member of the Executive Committee of the Refugee Council of Australia, and a member of the Australian Committee of the Council for Security Cooperation in the Asia Pacific (CSCAP). He is a member of the Order of Australia.

Iver B. Neumann is an Adjunct Professor in the Department of International Politics at the Norwegian Institute of International Affairs (NUPI) and was NUPI's Senior Research Fellow and Head in the Department of Russian Studies. He is also a professor in the Department of Literature, Area Studies and European Languages at the University of Oslo. Professor Neumann has served as a Senior Advisor to Norway's Ministry of Foreign Affairs and Ministry of Defence.

Shaun Riordan served in the British Diplomatic Service for 16 years until he resigned in 2000. He has served in New York and Beijing and in the Foreign and Commonwealth Office as Head of the Middle Eastern Section of the Counter-Terrorist Department. He also served as Head of the Policy Section of the Yugoslav Department during the war in Bosnia. His final posting was as head of the Political Section and Political and Press Section of the British Embassy in Madrid.

Raymond Saner is Director of Diplomacy Dialogue, and Co-founder and Director of the Centre for Socio-Economic Development, based in Geneva. He also teaches at Basle University and Sciences Po in Paris. He has been a consultant to European and Asian governments, multinational companies and international organisations, including the United Nations Development Programme, the World Trade Organisation and the European Bank for Reconstruction and Development.

Jan Aart Scholte is a professor in Politics and International Studies and Director of the Centre for the Study of Globalisation and Regionalisation (CSGR) at the University of Warwick. He also holds a part-time appointment as Centennial Professor at the London School of Economics. Prior to his appointment at Warwick, he worked at the University of Sussex, Brighton and the Institute of Social Studies, The Hague. His research focuses on questions of governing a more global world, with particular emphasis on democracy in this context.

David Spence is First Counsellor for Security and Disarmament at the European Commission Delegation to the United Nations in Geneva, Switzerland. His previous responsibilities in the Commission include work on terrorism, enlargement, European Security and Defence Policy, and general security issues. He has also been head of training for the Commission's External Service and was Secretary of the Commission's task force for German Unification. He has lectured at the Sorbonne, the Ecole Normale Supérieure, and the Institut d'Etudes Politiques in Paris, and is a graduate of Sussex, Oxford, and Nice Universities.

Shankari Sundararaman is an Associate Professor of Southeast Asian Studies at the Centre for South, Central, Southeast Asian and Southwest Pacific Studies of the School of International Studies at Jawaharlal Nehru University. Her research interests pertain to politics and security in the Asia–Pacific region with a special emphasis on Southeast Asia, particularly on Indonesia and Cambodia. Dr Sundararaman has also worked as a member of the research faculty of the Institute for Defence Studies and Analyses (IDSA).

Ramesh Thakur is a Distinguished Fellow at The Centre for International Governance Innovation (CIGI) and Professor of Political Science at the University of Waterloo in Canada. Dr. Thakur was Vice Rector and Senior Vice Rector of the United Nations University as well as Assistant Secretary-General of the United Nations from 1998–2007. He serves on the international advisory boards of institutes in Africa, Asia, Europe and North America. He is an expert in the United Nations, peace operations, arms control and disarmament, and the international relations of Asia and the Pacific.

Rorden Wilkinson is a Professor of International Political Economy at the University of Manchester. Prior to Manchester he was an assistant lecturer at the University of Auckland. He is a member of the executive committee of the British International Studies Association (BISA); he has served on the editorial board of the international public policy journal *Global Governance*; and he is past-convener of the International Political Economy Group (IPEG) of BISA. His research interests include international trade, the World Trade Organisation, development, globalisation, international labour standards and Small States.

Samina Yasmeen is Director of Centre for Muslim States and Societies and lectures in Political Science and International Relations in the School of Social and Cultural Studies, the University of Western Australia (UWA), Perth. She is also a Co-Chair of the Discipline of International Studies at the UWA. She works closely with the West Australian Government on issues affecting Muslims and is a Vice-President of the Australian Institute for International Affairs and a member of the Red Cross WA International Humanitarian Law Committee.

Lichia Yiu is President of the Centre for Socio-economic Development, based in Geneva. She holds a doctorate in psychology from Indiana University, she completed a post-doctoral fellow at Columbia University in organisational psychology, and is a former Associate Professor at Chinese Culture University, Taipei. Dr Yiu has over 20 years of experience as an advisor to governments and international organisations on organisational development and reform of public administration. She has consulted to the United Nations Development Programme, the government of Slovenia, as well as to private-sector organisations. Her current research focuses on global leadership, learning and development management, and HR governance.

Introduction: Diplomacy and Global Governance: Locating Patterns of (Dis)Connection

Andrew F. Cooper, Brian Hocking, and William Maley

This book examines the relationship between diplomacy and global governance. While diplomacy is a well-established topic for study, global governance, conceived broadly as a pattern of transparent and inclusive processes to address complex transnational collective-action problems, is a relatively new arrival on the conceptual landscape of global politics. At first glance the two – whether interpreted as academic concepts or operational patterns – exist in separate worlds with little or no engagement between scholars of diplomacy on the one hand and of global governance on the other. And even in recent work dealing with these two areas, there is often a substantial silence about the significance or even the existence of the other (Ba and Hoffmann, 2005; Berridge, 2005). In practical terms, the functions of diplomacy and global governance can be portrayed as distinct and in opposition to one another. Thus diplomacy is sometimes viewed as a guild activity, with well-placed insiders distinguished from excluded outsiders (Henrikson, 1997; Ross, 2007). Through this lens, diplomatic skills are a type of knowledge possessed by a particular set of professionals and handed down via a long apprenticeship. Global governance, by contrast, is an open-ended way of looking at and navigating in the world, with a high degree of inclusiveness about whom and what is included in its machinery and agenda.

Any analysis of the relationship between diplomacy and global governance must look therefore at the source and significance of such disconnections: discerning the location of these barriers to communication is a pre-condition for any serious, nuanced analysis of the relationship. Furthermore, the extent of these barriers should not be exaggerated. If the starting point of this book emphasises the walls between diplomacy and global governance, the contributions to it reveal myriad points of contact between them. Nor do these emergent components of contact only signify the stretching of the conceptual imagination, although this trend is significant in itself. It is the co-existence between diplomacy and governance on the front lines of issue-specific policy and process that is most compelling.

Why a disconnection?

The causes of the tension between diplomacy and global governance, hinted at above, need to be elaborated if the full extent of the separation is to be understood. At the most fundamental level, understanding the presence or absence of dialogue between diplomacy and governance is rooted in contrasting understandings of the nature of contemporary world politics. This point is made in greater depth later in this introductory chapter, but it is worth stressing here that the diplomacy-governance relationship rests on such disputed issues as the nature of globalisation and the role of the state in the twenty-first century. As with the more general debate on the significance or otherwise of diplomacy, this can easily become a more rarefied manifestation of key debates about the character of the discipline of International Relations, what is important within it and how it should be studied (Clark, 1999; Hocking, 1999a; Lee and Hudson, 2004; Jönsson and Hall, 2005).

More specifically, the disconnection between diplomacy and global governance is underpinned by stylistic differences (see Keohane and Nye, 2001). In form, a strong image of hierarchy, and of command and control, hangs over the world of diplomacy. In terms of intensity, the preference is for concentrating on what is doable – the choice of the possible over what is 'right'. Ends are shaped by a cautious sense of pragmatism, with acute recognition of the boundaries of action. Emotionalism, along with transparency, is subordinated to patience and discretion. The attention Sir Harold Nicolson gave to 'social trust' and keeping confidences remains highly salient (Nicolson, 1939; Drinkwater, 2005).

Global governance in contradistinction is pluralistic or multi-layered with a variety of actors in the mix (Rosenau, 1992; Muldoon, 2004: 7–10). It embraces civil society as well as the state. As Marie Claude Smouts puts it: 'First and foremost, governance places emphasis on the multiplicity and diversity of the actors' (Smouts, 1998: 84). Time sensitivity is at the core of the dynamic, with a sense of immediacy running through the entire ambit of activity. The possibilities in terms of re-shaping the agenda are limitless, with a discourse highlighting the transformative or transfigurative nature of the project. Rights and wrongs should be publicised, with offenders called out. Secrecy of negotiations – by design or by stealth – is taken to be an excuse to restrict participation and avoid opening up the parameters of discussion.

A focus on the substantive differences between diplomacy and global governance stretches the range of disconnects still further. In its essential structure, international diplomacy remains state-centric. Advocacy is performed for the advance of the 'national interest'. And state officials, if not always sent to 'lie abroad' for their country (in Sir Henry Wotton's famously-ambiguous formulation), use manipulation as a vital and ongoing component in their tool-kit. Given this traditional attitude, there remains as well a pre-occupation in diplomacy (and among diplomats) with status in regard to representation and authority. Albeit commonly acknowledging that state officials no longer have an absolute monopoly over the negotiation of the global agenda, these actors still work to retain their relative hold on this dynamic, on the assumption they alone have the credibility and the capacity to speak and act for their national constituents.

Proponents of global governance prefer the moral high ground. Their concern is with extending the ambit of rules and regulations on a global basis. Their normative map is far more ambitious both in terms of criteria for activity and scale of coverage. The diplomatic preference for order and stability is replaced by a concern for equity and justice. The temporal timeline is re-jigged away from an instrumental concern with the here-and-now to a futuristic outlook. As one author describes it, global governance is conceived as an ongoing project that 'may well come to resemble a societal fabric through which the global system is governed' (Clarke, 2004).

Evolving connections

Yet, amidst all of these embedded disconnections, there is evidence of emergent connections taking shape between diplomacy and governance, which the academic world is sometimes slow to recognise. Diplomacy, like global governance, is a highly-contested project with a huge debate opening up about whether it is capable of undergoing change or not (Hoffman, 2003; Riordan, 2003). Many critics do see it in static terms. Indeed, Lipschutz (2004) notably depicts diplomacy as being: 'Trapped in past ways of doing things [with] no reason to think that [its] practices will change at any time in the foreseeable future.'

Other observers point alternatively to the imaginative qualities available to diplomacy. Some issue-specific areas of state-based diplomacy have taken on a just-in-time quality, pushing for advances in an expedited and often emotional fashion. In other areas, diplomacy (and diplomats) can take on the role of norm-entrepreneur with tremendous insight and consequences for the practice of governance. If still lagging behind the rules identified with a sovereignty-free world, the tone is distinctly progressive, with real possibilities for re-defining the rules in components of global regulation.

The template for these changes has been established in well-known cases such as the campaigns against landmines and for the International Criminal Court. However, as many of the contributions highlight, these cases do not exhaust the possibilities where innovation is an option (Cooper et al., 2002; Cooper, 2004; Thakur et al., 2005; Cooper, 2007). But alongside such adaptive processes, the structures of traditional state-based diplomacy are undergoing changes of which academic observers often appear to be unaware. Irrespective of how sceptical one might be regarding the motivations for such change (after all, diplomatic services are organisational entities geared to self-preservation) it is nonetheless the case that significant changes are occurring that reflect the demands of global governance agendas.

Not least of these is the redefinition of the stakeholders, both domestic and international, with whom Ministries of Foreign Affairs (MFAs) need to engage, and the development of structures for such engagement. These embrace more traditional interlocutors such as the business community, but also a growing range of civil society organisations amongst which non-governmental organisations (NGOs) assume a major place. In organisational terms, then, there is recognition that global challenges require domestic responses on the part of the state and its agents, of which the MFA, despite challenges to its role, remains a significant part (Hocking, 1999b; Hocking and Spence, 2005). Understanding organisational change within the state and at the points where it engages with its international environments thus forms a key dimension of the spectrum of relationships between governance and diplomacy.

If diplomacy has engaged the practices of global governance by segmented design, global governance has been re-cast in a more pragmatic guise because of a number of apparent contradictions in its elevated form. In conceptual terms, global governance has fallen short of its ambitious goals with regard to transparency and accountability on a number of counts. But there has been a backlash as well in regard to its abstract orientation and/or divorce from an engagement with a concrete agenda (Murphy, 2000).

Nor has the global governance project achieved primacy in the vast majority of the policy struggles. By placing such considerable emphasis on norms and values – most notably justice and equity – the project lost its appreciation of the power dimension in world affairs. A huge gap exists between the professed goal of global governance and modes of credible operational commitment.

While it can remain tempting for the proponents of global governance to advance a maximalist approach, they are often confronted by a choice of getting something instead of missing everything. To get this something, however, requires a willingness to cut corners, to compromise, to temper strident voices and to negotiate on details – that is to say, to act rather like skilled diplomats.

Such signs of engagement – whether by design or ambiguous default – inform much of the discussion central to this book. Is such engagement intellectually viable with students of diplomacy and global governance speaking across an entrenched divide? In policy terms, what difference does such an engagement make? Are there some areas where a blending of diplomacy and governance is more viable than others? And what does a revisionist governance agenda look like on an operational basis?

Contextual challenges

A logical starting point for locating the interface between international diplomacy and global governance is in the contextual challenges they both face. A common assumption is that the multiple and diverse forces of globalisation have thrown the practice of diplomacy into crisis (Hamilton and Langhorne, 1995: 231–245). Through one prism, globalisation can be taken to have raised the disconnection – or even the process of estrangement – between diplomacy and society to a more pronounced stage. Through another prism, many of the traditional bureaucratic advantages enjoyed by the state diplomatic apparatus have been thoroughly eroded.

Iver Neumann's Chapter 1 showcases how globalisation has accentuated the dysfunctions of diplomacy cast at least in its Westphalian image. For the de-territorialisation impulse at the heart of globalisation is a fundamental threat to the centralised, hierarchical and state-bounded ethos of modern diplomacy. Contributing to the impact of this process of change comes the sheer volume (or density) of these pressures.

This pivotal representation is juxtaposed, though, with Neumann's backward-looking glance at modes of pre-modern diplomatic behaviour. What stands out through this portrayal is the connection between these earlier diplomatic practices and current images of governance in terms of the space for a multiplicity of actors, the blurring of the domestic and the international, and the bending of sovereign representation.

Both Neumann and Jönsson pinpoint technology and information as the cutting edge of this contextual challenge. Diplomats may still prefer to use secrecy and manipulation. But their opportunities to utilise such methods have become much more circumscribed under conditions of globalisation. Advocacy by societal forces – together with investigative journalism – is therefore a trigger for a re-thinking and re-calibration of public diplomacy into more sophisticated and diverse forms.

Jönsson embellishes these themes in Chapter 2 with a particular focus on how the information technology revolution has influenced diplomatic practice. Increased resort to new communication techniques in some ways exacerbates the sense of crisis within the practice of diplomacy. Public diplomacy in its basic form uses standard branding techniques, very different from the traditional methods in which differentiated messages were aimed at different audiences. An emphasis on public diplomacy (or strategic communication) also signals the sheer complexity of current diplomatic demands, with potential concerns among both national and transnational audiences about a massive variety of policy arenas.

If the reaction of diplomacy to global governance – and to the pressures of globalisation – is becoming better understood, the adaptation of global governance to diplomatic practices has lagged behind. The global governance project is intended to counter all sorts of problems, such as those surrounding human rights and the environment. But at its core is a reaction to the neoliberal strategy of globalisation with its accelerated agenda of economic interaction, liberalisation, deregulation and privatisation (Richardson, 2001). The holistic menu presented by the global governance project is an attempt to manage, if not reverse, the self-consciously economistic, rationalistic and homogenising thrust of the globalisation challenge – through checks on the hyper-competitive ethos and challenges to the sharp distinction between winners and losers. This may account for some of the opposition which the global governance project has encountered (see Rabkin, 2005).

The first part of Jan Aart Scholte's Chapter 3 is an artful rendition of this ambitious project of global governance. As in most general renditions, Scholte gives ample attention to the capacity of governance as a global-scale regulatory apparatus. He provides a nuanced interpretation through both his allowance for the application of this model through a wide variety of dimensions and his appreciation of the normative and technical test to implement this agenda. Still, the major source of innovation – and glue – for this book is in his willingness and capacity to examine what the role and interface of diplomacy will be vis-à-vis global governance.

Authority beyond the state

At the core of the distance between diplomacy and global governance is the issue of authority. Do state officials retain a privileged status in representative and functional terms? Or has the push towards multilevel governance raised other sites to competing status? Some of the most innovative recent work on International Relations has been driven by the significance of these very questions (Barnett and Finnemore, 2004; Slaughter, 2004).

The European Union's (EU) dual function in expanding the terms of diplomatic representation is innovative to the point of being sui generis. With its post-modern characteristics, the EU has legitimised the claims of a wide number of non-state actors in the diplomatic process in an unprecedented fashion. At the same time, the EU's unique form of supra-nationalism has provided its own diplomats with a degree of recognition unavailable in other regional groupings. The EU – jumping ahead to another key dichotomy assessed in this book – has traits that mark it off as both a traditional club and an evolving network.

David Spence is fully aware of the gaps within the system of EU governance, especially with respect to the problems of legitimacy in terms of the well-known democratic deficit (Keohane, 2006). Nonetheless, he is equally conscious of the enormous potential that the EU possesses for advancing a very distinctive type of global governance that may well have serious impacts beyond Europe. As Spence puts it neatly, 'Diplomats worldwide cannot remain unaffected' by these trends within the EU, 'even if they may sometimes appear unconcerned.'

Spence's Chapter 4 rehearses in finer detail a good many themes key to the emergent connection between diplomacy and global governance: the enormous strains on the Westphalian state; the focus of diplomacy on laborious, technical, and complex issues far from the traditional preserve of state diplomats; the multi-layered look; and the deep connection between diplomacy and policy-making pertaining to regulatory activities, together with the pervasive concern with normative attributes in governance developments and diplomatic 'soft power' (see Nye, 2004b).

Whereas the EU dynamics add to the layering in an often vertically-composed inter-governmental fashion, the space opened up to non-state actors adds to a horizontal layering of diplomatic practices. As Raymond Saner and Lichia Yiu suggest, much of this activity has another form of duality affixed to it: an image of both competition and cooperation. From one angle, both business/corporate groups and NGOs lay very different claims to state officials about efficiency and legitimacy. From another angle, state and non-state actors have numerous incentives to work at least on a tactical basis with each other.

The two case studies that Saner and Yiu develop in their Chapter 5 reveal the mixed results of trying to push global governance-oriented diplomatic initiatives. One severe test continues to be the stretch in technical competence necessary for implementing these initiatives. Another pertains to how multi-stake governance/diplomacy is to be operationalised in practice with due consideration to power differentials.

New forms of competition and cooperation not only impact on state diplomats; indeed, NGOs and all non-state actors are also affected by the crowding of the field of activity. The chapter by Ivan Cook and Martine Letts (Chapter 6) analyses the manner by which the International Committee of the Red Cross (ICRC) has adapted to the dilemma of vying for public attention with other actors within the parameters of a culture that acknowledges the sensitivities of public advocacy.

A good deal of the successful adaptation by the ICRC has hinged on its own unique comparative advantage blending diplomacy and governance: its role as 'repository and guardian of international humanitarian law' with particular reference to the Geneva Conventions. The ICRC has continued to concentrate on humanitarian diplomacy, but its distinctive 'quiet' approach has morphed over the last decade. Whereas it has shied away from public campaigns in the past – most unfortunately and detrimentally to its reputation staying quiet on its knowledge of the Holocaust (Favez, 1999; Forsythe, 2005) – both the landmines and Abu Ghraib cases disclosed the extent to which the ICRC was prepared to go public. Even if a certain mythology has grown around this case, the break from its traditional ways of doing things is striking.

The novelty of the Cook and Letts chapter comes in the way that they trace the combination of altruistic and opportunistic motivations behind this change. Recognising the intersection of diplomacy and evolving rules of governance – as well as avoiding any activity that smacks of cooptation by member states – the ICRC has steered a committed albeit delicate course on issues such as campaigning against terrorism. However, Cook and Letts position some aspects of this shift as part of a new convenient strategy on the part of the ICRC: in effect relocating itself in an increasingly challenging environment for not only policy space but also publicity and fundraising.

An excellent illustration of the intrusive quality of new actors is captured by Shankari Sundararaman's Chapter 7 on Research Institutes as Diplomatic Actors. Until recent years, the activity of this type of actor has been cast as complementary to that of state-based officials, the most common example of which is depicted as Track-II initiatives. Increasingly, though, research institutions have been recognised not as part of the mainstream but as a source of considerable innovation across a wide spectrum. In advancing positive expressions of a normative global governance agenda, research has the intrinsic ability to become 'a moral force' (Duffield, 2001: 259).

Notwithstanding these strengths, the diplomatic credentials of research institutes have been criticised for being too geographically confined to the North/West. As witnessed by Sundararaman's chapter, however, this image has become diluted. Political restrictions may still constrain the work of research institutes. But paradoxically, systemic shocks – viewed as undercutting the status of diplomacy and state diplomacy – may be a catalyst for giving added credentials to research institutes in the South generally – and as she demonstrates, in Association of Southeast Asian Nations specifically – in that these actors have a comparative advantage in 'the planning of policy initiatives based on the trends that are likely to emerge.'

Targeting the policy arenas of interaction

One of the primary boundaries in the search for connects between diplomacy and governance is an issue-specific one: the impression that the main sites for this type of interaction are in areas of 'low' policy. With this delimitation in mind, Shaun Riordan's Chapter 8 provides a valuable rejoinder. Riordan gives particular weight to the challenges imposed on state diplomats by security threats beyond the contours of state relationships. On many of these different threats, traditional modes of operation are simply ill-suited. Command and control must give way to facilitation – with diplomats nudging and cajoling a variety of non-state actors to take the lead on issues that are more readily defined through a governance framework. The timeline must also be expanded. Instead of maintaining 'short-termism' as the standard repertoire for diplomats, Riordan sees strategic creativity as the key to problem solving, not only to meet the enhanced demands but also to ease the crisis of confidence in state diplomacy.

Riordan admits that a shift along these lines is full of risks. Opening up the message and the type of messengers has the potential for reinforcing the image that the traditional diplomatic corps is in over its head in terms of an increasingly complex agenda. But for Riordan these risks go hand in hand with opportunities, as it is only through such innovative practices that the importance of diplomacy and diplomats will be embraced through the political system.

The chapter by Franklyn Lisk (Chapter 9) provides detail of the type of site that is a centrepiece of this expanded security agenda. Elaborating on an arena to which Riordan devotes some considerable attention, Lisk's chapter examines one vital component of health security: HIV/AIDS. Both directly and indirectly this disease has a massive negative impact on security as well as social and economic governance capacity in the global South generally and southern Africa more specifically. It is arguable that on no other issue is the requirement for a new architecture of global governance more vital. Nor is there a greater demand for making the connection between governance and diplomacy more tangible and sustainable. The words uttered at a host of high-level summits through the United Nations, the G8 and others must be translated into deeds when it comes to governance regimes. This forging of a nexus along these lines is of particular import in terms of the content of the delivery from the international financial institutions and the World Trade Organization (WTO).

Rorden Wilkinson attaches a personal behavioural analogy to the pattern of disconnections/connections located in the WTO negotiations as a whole. As in private family dramas, the image of the cause and effect of WTO diplomacy and system of governance produced thereby is one in which dynamics are shaped according to a standard script. The key ingredient here is a particular process of institutional development – with a considerable asymmetry of opportunity built within – that is highly resistant to fundamental change.

Yet drama does not mean immobilisation. Wilkinson contends that even with all its many crises, the WTO has not become inert. 'Suspension' of talks leads to reflection and a return to negotiations. The question posed by Wilkinson, nonetheless, is whether or not this sort of dysfunction can continue to go on or whether there is a need and the means to break out of this family drama?

The proclivity for drama of a related kind extends to Jovan Kurbalija's exploration of the diplomatic/governance nexus at the site of the World Summit on Information Society. The diplomacy related to this issue-area clashed with sensitive areas of global governance, above all human rights and intellectual property. As in other arenas, diplomats tried to negotiate where the scope, form and intensity of the issues before them moved in unanticipated directions. The 'Internet community' provided one unique element on top of the activity by states, NGOs and the business community. E-diplomacy provides an interesting twist to the potential of virtual diplomacy.

Restrictive dichotomies and open-ended trajectories

It is easy to see established disconnects between diplomacy and governance morphing into newer, albeit more refined, forms of restrictive dichotomies.

One dividing element is the distinction between the types of audience targeted by various forms of transnational activity. Do they focus on élite or mass opinion? Is that audience at one or multiple sites? Another is the difference in styles of approach. Does it have a technical or emotional bias? And finally, in terms of the temporal conditions, does the focus have a one-off appeal or is it sustained over time? If the former, is the focus exclusively one of achieving some measure of diplomatic success? If the latter, how is this effort translated into a global governance-oriented agenda?

As in many other research projects, the circular imagery created by Keck and Sikkink (1998) is compelling. Through her examination of the manner by which Indigenous peoples have lobbied the United Nations, Megan Davis' Chapter 12 is illustrative of these powerful trends. In common with the NGO community, the main strategy has been to go around the national state and appeal to this international forum directly. On the one hand, the United Nations created attractive institutional vehicles through which Indigenous peoples could work. On the other hand, the time was ripe for this outlet as both the skills and the demands – while increasingly available – had become frustrated with using other routes of action.

In making use of the United Nations, various adjustments had to be made about what was possible versus what was right. The focus was increasingly directed towards negotiations conducted at a highly-technical level, under rather rarefied conditions in Geneva and New York. Principles remained important but so did expertise. The goal was both to score diplomatic points and to obtain reform in governance structures within member states. And patience has been a strong virtue, as much of the success of Indigenous transnational advocacy has come through the exchange of ideas and networking, not through tangible delivery.

Samina Yasmeen's Chapter 13 on the Danish cartoon controversy turns the transnational advocacy described by Megan Davis on its head. Instead of being the culmination of a long diffuse process, this episode burst out quite suddenly. Instead of pushing out into one technically-oriented United Nations forum, mass opinion was mobilised through the Muslim world. And instead of having to work awkwardly with 'like-minded' countries on the rights of Indigenous peoples, diplomats from a variety of Islamic states lent vigorous and continuous support.

A second dichotomy pushes across the boundaries from transnational advocacy to public diplomacy. Megan Davis' chapter is at one end of this spectrum with its concentration on how Indigenous peoples lobby the United Nations. No mention is made about how the states under pressure in this issue-area attempt to brand or re-brand themselves via public diplomacy. Samina Yasmeen's chapter extends this framework to include state-based diplomacy, but again this focus is largely subordinated to an analysis of the tactics and impact of this novel campaign of transnational advocacy.

In some ways, Bruce Gregory's Chapter 14 reinforces the notion of public diplomacy as simply the mirror-image of advocacy. Whereas society groups attempt to use lobbying to influence states and public opinion, states reverse the process by mobilising a variety of techniques as part of an increasingly well-publicised mode of public diplomacy to try to shape global publics.

Yet, elevating the level of discussion, Gregory demonstrates that this dichotomous approach is too rigidly dualistic. Significantly, for Gregory the pattern of public diplomacy needs to be located not just as a means of image-building by states (let alone as an instrument of propaganda), but as an instrument of global governance. Furthermore, he argues that public diplomacy is no longer the exclusive preserve of statecraft but a terrain that non-state actors have also penetrated both in tandem with, and in parallel fashion to, national governments. And he provides a number of compelling snapshots where this type of activity can be witnessed.

The open-ended trajectory of these processes is accentuated by Gregory's discussion of the power of dialogue and the logic of the network society. Both concepts break down the rigidities in thinking and action. Indeed, in an extension of Brian Hocking's own work, Gregory uses these concepts to expand on why the future of diplomacy must be associated with 'boundary spanning' as opposed to 'gate-keeping', with hierarchal-oriented diplomats adopting more flexible characteristics in such areas as knowledge-sharing (Hocking, 2005a).

In a similar fashion, Andrew F. Cooper's Chapter 15 shows both the presence of what appear to be rigid dualities and the possibility of some merger of trajectories. On first impression, there is a massive distance – or chasm – between the top-down coalitions of the willing epitomised by the US-led intervention against Saddam's Iraq, and the bottom-up coalitions as featured in the campaigns against anti-personnel landmines and for the establishment of the International Criminal Court. A good deal of Cooper's chapter is devoted to accenting these differences in criteria related to diplomacy as well as practices devoted to global governance.

While manifestations of divergent world views, however, these models of mobilisation not only interact but also blend into each with respect to intensity and some elements of form. Instead of being cast therefore as simply polar opposites, a more subtle rendition is offered.

Jorge Heine's Chapter 16 expresses the strain between rigidity and flexibility in a comprehensive number of ways. Many of these are familiar reprises with echoes from the other contributions in this volume: the push and pull of established diplomatic practices on one side and the normative development of global governance on the other side, in the context not only of the blurring of what constitutes the international and the domestic but also the challenge from globalism together with a 'rising' global South in terms of ideas as well as material wealth.

Heine reinforces the notion that a transition from the 'club' model to a networked approach is vital if the duality between diplomacy and governance is to be broken (see also Cooper and Legler, 2006), and that buying into the new flatter and more flexible model is an advance not only for the global governance project but also for the practice of diplomacy itself. Instead of redundancy – or disenfranchisement – of diplomats, such adaptive practices according to Heine open up the prospect for greater access and leverage. Amidst all the challenges commonly ascribed to an inexorable sense of decline, the future of skilful 'networked' diplomats is deemed to be a bright and sustained one.

Overall, as Ramesh Thakur's concluding chapter shows, at both the analytical and the practical level the contributions to this book reflect a transformative international order, the precise contours of which remain indistinct. In this context, the agendas of diplomacy and global governance should not – and indeed, do not – exist in separate boxes but rather serve to inform one another. It is important to recall that diplomacy – as several authors in this volume note – is not the preserve of the 'Westphalian' international order but has a pedigree that precedes it and is, equally, capable of transcending it. In doing so, however, some of the key features of the state-centred diplomatic order that have been familiar to us are being challenged by the demands of a more complex environment, which the logic of global governance seeks to address. Hence the emphasis on flexibility and adaptability of policy networks is set against the traditional hierarchical and relatively closed forms associated with diplomacy.

One conceptualisation of this changing, polycentric order is presented in terms of 'multistakeholder diplomacy', wherein the demands of tackling complex global agendas are met by the construction of processes that link actors representing differing interests and possessing distinctive skills (Kurbalija and Katrandjiev, 2006). Such experiments, however, are not without significant challenges. The 'rules' that govern the workings of the diplomatic community are rooted in sets of cultural norms and values that differ markedly from those of other stakeholders in the governance processes. The test of success, then, becomes one of establishing effective 'rules of engagement' through which the traditional norms of the corps diplomatique and those of other key stakeholders adapt to each other's demands in management of global issues. Critical to this process is an engagement of ideas and information and it is towards such an exchange that the chapters in this book make a significant contribution. For if understanding the nature and complexities of global governance is a critical task in interpreting the character of contemporary world politics, equally – as Scholte suggests at the end of his chapter – 'the study of diplomacy…has arguably never been as important'.

Part I
Contextual Challenges

1

Globalisation and Diplomacy

Iver B. Neumann

When I was about 15 years old, I asked my godfather, a palaeontologist, whether he thought global warming was a man-made or a natural phenomenon. He replied that however substantive the changes wrought by human beings might be, there was no way we could have substantially affected the cycle of global warming that has covered the billions of years over which the earth had existed. When I pointed out that the time span that I had in mind was less than 20,000 years, during which human societies had been sedentary, he remarked that such periods were simply too short to be of interest to a palaeontologist and that was the end of the discussion. There is a lesson here. Without specifying a time interval, little of interest may be said about questions of newness. What is new about globalisation and what is relevant to diplomacy depends on your time perspective. I will begin by tracing the phenomenon as changes in the way space, time and density mould global politics. I will go on to argue that globalisation has a forerunner in internationalisation, and discuss some key changes that internationalisation brought to diplomacy. I will then proceed to ask whether there are ways in which the changes in diplomacy that characterised internationalisation are now being further intensified, whether there are new factors afoot, and whether we are looking at changes that cumulate to a major change in diplomatic practices overall. First, the phenomenon of globalisation.

Space

If diplomacy is defined in a wide enough manner, say as the mediated exchange between polities, then globalisation does not necessarily emerge as a vital challenge to modern day diplomats, and the changes that it brings to diplomacy appear inconsequential to its practice. In the extant literature, we have an early example of this approach in Adam Watson's work. Watson (1982) was primarily interested in changes in international systems as they have unfolded over the last five thousand years. When confronted with a new issue area such as human rights, he rested content with the assertion that time-honoured practices would take care of it.

If, however, we define diplomacy as the written exchange of documents between states, where 'state' is understood to be the kind of centralised, hierarchical and bounded polity that has emerged in Europe and then spread across the globe over the last five centuries or so, then globalisation is a key challenge to the practice of diplomacy. The reason is spatial organisation. The state is a polity based on a particular territorial mode of organisation. Weber saw it as a claimed monopoly on the use of physical force. Schumpeter saw it as a claimed monopoly on taxation. Durkheim saw it as a nexus of domination between a power élite and a spatially bounded society. In any case, we are talking about a spatial area that at any given time remains the same, and that is clearly delineated for all involved. The delineations may vary over time and they may at any given time be contested, but the principle of delineation is of the essence. Globalisation inherently involves deterritorialisation, hence it is an *ipso facto* challenge to the state.

It may be argued that we have been here before. For example, during the Middle Ages, spatial organisation was fluid. Not all polities were bounded, and different polities faced different challenges. This made for a plethora of diplomatic practices. Let us take the 1240s as an example. Certain realms were fairly centralised, particularly in the North of what had sometimes been called Europe some four hundred before and was to be known by that moniker again within some two hundred years. The people who were sent on the drawn-out expeditions which went by the name of embassies, however, were not specifically trained to deal with foreign kings. They were the same people that the king used to deal with his nobles. There was no such thing as foreign policy personnel whatsoever, for the simple reason that there was no division between 'foreign' and 'domestic' policy (Neumann, 2007). The same went for the pope's *missi*: these messengers were used for dealing with people of power regardless of where these people fit into spatial organisation (Der Derian, 1987). We have a survival of this practice in the etymology of the term 'exequatur' for the agreement of a polity's head to allow someone to serve as a consul to another polity. Furthermore, even if the *missi* were seemingly specialists in diplomacy, there was no guarantee that they would head up diplomatic missions. For example, of the three missions sent by the pope to meet the invading Mongols at this time, none seems to have been manned by *missi* (Ruotsala, 2001). Furthermore, the fact that diplomats often hailed from the same polity as the one they represented was largely due to convenience. This discussion of diplomacy in the 1240s demonstrates that deterritorialised politics is not something new, and that diplomatic functions can reflect this kind of spatial organisation.

Time and density

Simply because the deterritorialisation of politics is nothing new does not mean that globalisation is not a new challenge for diplomats. In fact, globalisation entails two more crucial factors in addition to space. The first of these is time. The speed with which information and, in a slightly lesser degree, material objects can travel is rapidly increasing. Again, it may be argued that the challenges posed by this shrinking of response time to diplomacy are not new. For example, if one compares the response of diplomacy to the advent of the wire (cable-based telegraphy) from the 1860s onwards and the advent of the Internet over a century later, there are obvious parallels to be drawn. In both cases, the changes were driven by soldiers and merchants, and resisted by diplomats, who were reluctant to use this technology when it was introduced. Of course, it soon became an indispensable tool for diplomats (Nickels, 2003). In both cases, the reasons for the reluctance can be attributed to a fear of compromising secret information and of letting underlings into the heart of the organisation. This pattern may in a lesser degree be found where all new technology is concerned (for an additional example, one can consider the telephone). Historically, diplomats seem to be particularly petrified by social change, but eventually they, like everybody else, are forced to respond. Whereas in the case of space, the changes are to do with the recurrence of a pattern; where time is concerned, the changes are to do rather with an intensification of a pattern.

The second factor, density (as coined by John Ruggie, 1993), is also associated with intensification. The density of flows of everything from persons (tourism, migration) to information (TV programmes, Internet home pages) to goods (electronics, bottled water) is higher than ever. A crucial precondition for this was the decreasing cost of communication. For diplomacy, one obvious consequence is that consular work has exploded and its potential tasks are literally infinite. True, in the late nineteenth century the flow of goods was intense and increasing rapidly, but the relative flows of persons and information were partial. Furthermore, the total global population was significantly lower (something in the order of one in every ten human beings who has ever lived has done so in the post-Second World War period). A global population of six and a half billion need not be more restive than one of three billion for the flows to increase; the mere fact of increased numbers will increase the flows as well. Both in relative and absolute terms, the contemporary flows of persons and goods are absolutely unprecedented. This density has effects that are not only quantitative, but also qualitative, for it challenges the very 'boundedness' of the state. A polity may only be called bounded if a set of boundaries exists between it and other polities that are important in a sufficient number of contexts. Therefore, there is a threshold for how large the flows of information and material objects may be perceived to be before the polity is no longer thought of as bounded. Once the density of communication exceeds this threshold, the polity is no longer clearly territorialised.

The flow of immigrants into the United States is substantial, as is the flow of information and material objects in and out of that state. The US government has reacted by thinking about territorialisation in a new way. For example, it is taxing certain goods and services at the source and insisting on American jurisdiction over companies that are noted on American stock exchanges, regardless of their physical location. The US government, as well as a number of their business organisations, are also imposing a certain number of deterritorialised practices, such as email surveillance. We would, nonetheless, hardly conclude that the United States is a deterritorialised state. But the changes are of such a magnitude and are increasing at such a pace that we may easily conceive of a situation in which the 'density threshold' is perceived to be surpassed.[1]

In sum, the deterritorialisation of politics which is at the heart of globalisation is nothing new. There are precedents. But the degree in which time and density have intensified is indeed new. Everything moves faster, more often, in more directions. Taken together, the reconfigurations of space, time and density make for a new global constellation. The globalised world is indeed a new world.

Internationalisation

As noted earlier, we have seen intensification in time and density before, in the process that began to accelerate somewhere around the Seven Years' War (1756–1763) and that gathered momentum around the time of the First World War. Let us call it internationalisation and it is a phenomenon that foreshadows globalisation. Then, too, the key changes were to do with intensifications of time and density. New technologies played a key role (the telegraph, the wire, the telephone) and there was a considerable time lag before diplomats were forced to implement changes that were already well under way in other parts of the political world. Internationalisation eventually brought about key changes, including mounting pressure for accountability, widening in recruitment patterns and multilateral diplomacy. It is instructive to briefly consider how diplomacy was changed by these developments, because it suggests ways in which diplomacy is challenged by globalisation as well.

Where accountability is concerned, diplomacy did not need to change its working methods radically in order to stand up to parliamentary scrutiny. The foreign services could leave it to their top politicians to groom, handle and stonewall the foreign policy committees that appeared first in Britain, and then throughout the industrialised world. The other way foreign services met the challenge of accountability from society, was to thicken their interface to the press and the media. First, foreign services added on press offices which in some cases were even secret, then these offices were made public, and then they grew into fully-fledged information handling departments. We are talking about a build-up of outer bulwarks in the organisation, typically called Press and Information Departments that were low in internal prestige, and whose job it was to serve and stall journalists. In this way, the information flow was contained at least in principle, and a time lag was created in which most of diplomacy's business could go on as before without the intervention of journalists. The upshot was that the closer to the public a diplomat works, the less important he or she tends to be.[2]

Widening in diplomatic service recruitment patterns started with a change from the aristocracy to the bourgeoisie (typically at the end of the nineteenth century), continued with women (typically sometime around the Second World War), and went on to encompass new social groups (with class and ethnicity being particularly important). The overall trend here was the same as in the case of technology: diplomats lag behind soldiers and merchants, but before very long they mimic the changes that have taken place in these spheres.

Fairly quickly, the new institutional form of permanent multilateral diplomacy that was to be found in The League of Nations went from being the preserve of politicians to being the preserve of diplomats. Furthermore, it fell to foreign ministries to man the offices of the League, and they generally did so by drawing on people from their own ranks (including the diplomatic services). As the number of International Organization (IO) employees increased, fewer entered it directly from the diplomatic services, but recruitment remained in a very high degree the preserve of the world's foreign ministries. We are talking about delegation of key functions under the guidance of a foreign ministry-based cadre (Weiss, 1975).

It has been observed that some of the key effects that were expected to flow from internationalisation did not happen. First and foremost among these was the predicted fall of permanent representations. Pointing exactly to the ever-increasing density of international and transnational relations, analysts like George Modelski predicted the demise of the state's permanent representation. With tongue in cheek, Modelski suggested that the whole institution be substituted by a ship afloat on some world ocean, with one ambassadorial cabin per state, where the ambassadors could conveniently pay calls on and sit down to supper with one another.

Modelski's comment is not much more than an elegant way of pointing out that the ambassador's function of representation had become less important. But there is enough of this function left for the ambassador still to be necessary on these grounds alone (in addition, he or she fills other important functions). Even between pairs of states where the density of contacts has been extremely high for decades (e.g., Scandinavia, Canada–United States) or in countries engaged in an advanced state of supranational integration (e.g., the original EU six), the resident ambassador holds sway. Internationalisation brought new practices to diplomacy, but much like new technologies, they did not supplant old ones, but added themselves nicely to their number.

More of the same

With globalisation, there has been a further increase where the pressure for accountability, the widening in recruitment patterns and multilateral diplomacy are concerned.

The pressure for accountability has not first and foremost taken the form of further calls for parliamentarian control. It is true that parliamentary foreign affairs committees take intermittent interest, and in Europe, integration makes for more parliamentary involvement. This amounts to little more than a tentative intensification of well-established practices, however. The key change seems rather to concern relations with the media. Half a century ago, Marshall McLuhan (1962: 41) pointed out that compression in time and space put speed of information at a premium and changed our ways of understanding the world: '[When] a new technology extends one or more of our senses outside us into the social world, then new ratios among all of our senses will occur in that particular culture.' It is comparable to what happens when a new note is added to a melody.

It is journalists who are the principal narrators of globalisation. Gone are the days when journalists respectfully approached diplomats in the hope of picking up some treasured comment.[3] Journalists and diplomats are mutually dependent on one another, but in recent decades, the power relation has been turned around. *Ceteris paribus,* it is the journalists that set the pace by breaking the news, and the diplomats who react. In the Norwegian Foreign Ministry, morning meetings address the question of how to respond to headline news. Furthermore, the media regularly decide to cover the same news or feature story for days in a row, and frequently succeed in forcing the Ministry into a defensive posture. The reverse is rarely the case. It is the media which are the prime agenda-setters. We should, of course, not totalise this trend. Any foreign ministry may still withhold information from the media that it deems to be particularly sensitive, and will continue to do so. During the Thatcher years, the Foreign Office was able to play favourites with the journalists, and often denied access to overtly critical journalists to its daily briefings. Still, the trend remains clear and ubiquitous; the level of access for journalists which is considered 'normal' by all parties is rising. All this happens in the name of transparency. This norm is part and parcel of the state-society model that is presently spreading across the globe, which means that as long as ministries and politicians do not take active measures to halt or reverse the trend, it is set to continue.

Since people like Benjamin Franklin and Tom Paine played a role in internationalisation by casting themselves as diplomats of mankind, much has been made of the importance of 'world society' and 'world opinion.' While world opinion is a social fact, it remains unclear how it should be conceptualised. Furthermore, it is not evident to what degree world opinion impinges on foreign policy outcomes. National public opinions are multifaceted and blurry as well, and we have endless examples of how political outcomes may run against them, but that does not stop them from acting as very real parts of any politician's equation. For diplomats, who deal in changing peoples' impressions of countries and of events, world opinion is of importance and it looms larger as space is compressed.[4]

Globalisation means that the question of information becomes a question of proliferating target groups. Where the diplomatic function of information used to concern gathering information and presenting it to politicians, the circle of relevant takers has increased. Public diplomacy, once trail blasted by Soviet diplomats bent on using it to ripen the world for revolution, has now changed irrevocably. It no longer targets the downtrodden masses, but rather the domestic media. There are, however, other targets as well. More resources are being spent on entertaining foreign journalists. It is not unheard of for ambassadors to write letters to the editor or even appear on TV in their host countries. The Canadian innovation of staging town hall meetings has begun to spread. Utilising interactive arenas for discussing foreign policy on and off the Internet is increasingly common and expected. Since it is hard to see how Internet discussions could be limited to citizens, the nature of that medium may further open up space for non-citizen voices and so further blur the distinction between citizens and foreign nationals. Malleable geographical boundaries go together with malleable social boundaries. Briefly, the deepening and widening of accountability experienced by diplomats means that the area of validity for the old adage 'never apologise, never explain' is diminishing, and the cost of following it is increasing.

Societal and political pressure on diplomatic services for widening their recruitment practices is also increasing. Since globalisation involves migration, and since ethnicity remains a key principle of social organisation throughout the globe, countries that are experiencing widespread immigration are also experiencing a push for more diplomats with an ethnic minority background. This is an old hat in immigrant societies like the United States, Israel and, more recently, Canada, but it makes for increasing tension in states and diplomatic services with a longer history. The gains to diplomatic services of having personnel with diverse linguistic and cultural skills are tangible. Knowing a culture is similar to knowing a language in that everyone who starts young is fluent, whereas most of the latecomers have a certain cumbersomeness about them. There is a difference here between being and doing which gives the native the upper hand. The flip side of this cultural effortlessness is that, in an age of nationalism and, seemingly, also of postnationalism, it invites questions of clashing loyalties to the diplomat's country of birth and his or her adopted country.

So far, pressure for more diverse recruitment has concerned citizens. Given the nature of globalisation, however, it would not be surprising to see a return of the once quite established and non-controversial practice of using non-citizens as regular diplomats. After all, this practice survived until well into the eighteenth century and would in a number of ways signify a historical normalisation. We see a special case of this already in the regular exchanges of diplomats between foreign ministries; French diplomats serve in the Foreign Office, Hungarian diplomats in the Norwegian Ministry of Foreign Affairs (MFA), and so on.

New factors

Novelty is relative. If we ever find ourselves (or land ourselves) in the situation of having to establish diplomatic first contact with aliens, some researcher is certain to write a piece on how first contacts between ancient cultures may be seen as a predecessor. Every Jesus has his John the Baptist. So if it is assumed that the exchange of diplomats between diplomatic services is following an established historical pattern, whereas co-opting diplomats from the NGOs is not, this distinction in the final analysis is arbitrary. Nonetheless, when, on Robin Cook's behest, the Foreign Office recruited Amnesty International's former parliamentary officer to advise on human rights, and a member of Save the Children to work on the rights of children, Cook went from soliciting advice to headhunting people. If that is not totally new, there is certainly a novelty to his reverse move, which was to second people from the Foreign Office's own human-rights department to Article 19 and to the Minority Rights Group (*The Economist*, 6 March 1999). During internationalisation, diplomats took on the new register of working for international organisations. Now, they are also increasingly expected to work not only with or for, but actually *in* non-governmental organisations. These movements of people between the state sector and NGOs add themselves to a certain increase in movement between a state's ministries (Cooper and Hocking, 2000). There is of course large variation between services when it comes to the level of diplomatic exclusivity associated with their recruitment and training patterns. In France, state officials are educated *en bloc* and the best tend to choose employment in the Ministry of Finance, whereas the runner-ups go to the Quai d'Orsay; in the United States, there is an open exam, in Norway, there is application followed by a two-tiered exam system. The more closed the system, the larger the shock of having to migrate to NGOs. Furthermore, in states such as the United States that avail themselves of the spoils system for ambassadorial posts, the *problematique* of the closed system is valid only for the levels of the organisation up to the ambassadorial level. We may add that diplomats throughout the twentieth century went on leave to work as judges, business analysts etc., only to return to their service; so whatever the degree of professionalisation, diplomacy was never an entirely closed system. Nonetheless, it is a fact that the *ésprit de corps* amongst diplomats has been due to common training, the feeling of belonging to the chosen few, and common nomadic professional experience. By 'taking people in from the street' as the saying goes, this principle is put under strain. It is also challenged when diplomats are put to work if not on the street, then in (other) non-traditional settings. If diplomats were always nomadic, there is something new about being a nomad between an MFA and NGOs rather than between MFAs and postings abroad, or MFAs and IOs. Changes in recruitment patterns mirror changes in other diplomatic practices. The explosion in multilateral diplomacy is being followed by a widening of the kind of entities between which diplomats mediate.

Here, we have arrived at a logical consequence of globalisation. If transcendence of boundaries is the essence of the phenomenon and this means that the state system must increasingly be seen as only one part of the global political system, then it stands to reason that the state's diplomats must sooner or later take cognizance of the other kinds of polities that exist within the system. If negotiation and, more widely, mediation is a key diplomatic function, then the work of the state's diplomats increasingly involves mediating not only between states, but also between states and other polities. Neither is it surprising that the question of whether these other polities may be called 'domestic' or 'foreign' is not necessarily of the essence. The domestic/foreign distinction is correlated to state boundaries. If state boundaries are relativised, so too is the domestic/foreign distinction.

Again, one may argue that this development is nothing new by pointing to the already widespread proliferation in state agencies that pursue diplomatic practices. Students of diplomacy have covered this well. Beginning in the late 1960s, the 'comparative foreign policy' school detailed the challenge that other ministries posed to diplomatic services (Rosenau, 1969; Hermann et al., 1987). Beginning some twenty years later, a modest literature on sub-state diplomacy emerged (Michelmann and Soldatos, 1990; Hocking, 1993a; Neumann, 2002). It is also the case that, throughout the European Union (EU), the prime minister's offices have played an increasingly important role in the shaping of diplomacy. Furthermore, the explosion in so-called summit diplomacy may be seen as a case of non-diplomats availing themselves of the shrinking of space and time to take matters in their own hands. But the people involved are by definition top politicians, usually heads of state, and those always had the last word in affairs diplomatic. By rushing things to the top, summit diplomacy may serve as shorthand for the kind of possibilities that globalisation opens up, but it does not involve a radical reshuffling of diplomacy.[5]

All these trends are well covered in extant writings on diplomacy. But where is the literature on the diplomacy of state-NGO relations? For example, although states are the standard targets for the work of what Keck and Sikkink (1998) refer to as transnational agency networks, there is little literature on state responses. These responses make up a growing part of diplomacy, and should therefore be examined.

The increasing significance of other kinds of polities (migrants, business and activist networks, regions, cities) is a potential challenge to the exclusivity of the state's diplomats. Since every polity needs diplomacy, there is an increasing number of groups that look like functional equivalents of diplomats. They are sometimes even referred to as diplomats – even in the academic literature (Stopford and Strange, 1991). At this state, it seems infelicitous, for the simple reason that the tasks undertaken by any one of these people do not generally add up to the tasks of a diplomat. The three key functions of diplomacy are often said to be: information gathering, negotiation and communication (Wight, 1977: 115–117). Bull (1977: 171–172) adds 'minimisation of the effects of friction' and 'symbolising the existence of the society of states'; this can be called smoothing and representation.[6] Typically, the groups of people outside the diplomatic services that carry out functions equivalent to these do not handle the full gamut of these tasks. For example, any transnational firm of some size will have people working on information gathering and communication as well as employing negotiators, but typically, these are different people. Again, travel bureaus will have offices overseas representing them, but the people working there will be different from those who do their information gathering and their negotiation. It would be a mistake to maintain that even the most central diplomat encapsulates all five functions at the same point in time; nonetheless, so far, state diplomats seem to combine them in a qualitatively higher degree than do representatives of other kinds of polities (see Table 1.1).

As an example, consider expatriates working for development NGOs. This may be the one group of non-diplomats that comes closest to combining the traditional functions of diplomats. They are still a far stretch from doing it in the same degree as traditional diplomats though. Moreover, foreign ministries have thus far been able to control these groups fairly effortlessly. Where NGOs are concerned, the pattern is that foreign ministries tend to co-opt NGOs once they have reached a certain mass and turn them into Quasi-Autonomous Non-governmental Organisations (QUANGOs). For example, in Norway, there are five large NGOs working in the field of development, two of which are detachments of transnational outfits (Red Cross, Save the Children). All five receive more than 90 per cent of their financial budgets from the Norwegian state, as administered by the Norwegian MFA. Diplomats remain in control. So far, there are very few examples of developmentalists (or 'well-diggers', to use diplomatic jargon) taking over traditional diplomatic functions in such a degree that the resulting policy looks qualitatively new, but plenty of examples of the reverse.

Table 1.1   Some relevant social group scores regarding key diplomatic functions.

	Information	Negotiation	Communication	Smoothing	Representation
The Diplomat	X	x	X	x	X
The Developmentalist	X		X		X
The Academic	X		X		
The Spin Doctor	X		X	x	
The Politician	X	x	X	x	X
The Soldier	X		X		X
The Merchant	X	x	X	x	X
The Activist	X		X		X

Note that representation is scored regarding to the group's self-perception and may vary; in the case of the diplomat, the most obvious object of reference is the state, whereas for the journalist, it will probably be public or even world opinion.

There is an outright exception to what has been said, and that is the politician; but heads of state and government, foreign ministers and the like have always been the diplomats' bosses, so this is nothing new. The challenge to diplomats is, therefore, the same as the challenge to the states for which they work, namely to deal with globalisation's new polities and their personnel. If the state and the diplomats maintain traditional working methods, their importance must be expected to wane. The less change, the less chance that diplomacy will be able to maintain its present social and political relevance. If diplomacy transforms to handle the new networking tasks and networking working methods, however, it is not a foregone conclusion that diplomacy's relative importance will diminish as a result of globalisation.

The circle of what may be called the diplomat's *relevant others* – those other social groups with which the diplomat has to work – is widening. So far, however, no other group has personnel that come as close to embodying the whole range of relevant functions that the diplomat does. An interesting trend, however, is the growing use that other actors make of former diplomats (pensioned or otherwise). There is a large literature on the importance of privatisation in the area of security and the role played by companies such as Sandlines, Executive Outcomes and Blackwater. The use of former diplomats by transnational corporations and other polities is growing, and needs to be studied.

Conclusion

In conclusion, it may be asked which transformations are necessary for state diplomats to maintain their importance. The key challenge springs from the very nature of globalisation. Density makes new polities possible, and the reconfiguration of space and time increases the viability and reach of these new polities within the global political system. As diplomats' circle of relevant others widens, they are faced with the challenge of mediating more types of relations than ever before. The first challenge is to acknowledge this transformation. This may sound obvious, but it is important in identity politics for a group to acknowledge its relevant others, wherein the 'we-group' is dependent on this acknowledgement. The fact that diplomacy's circle of relevant others is widening does not mean that diplomacy's circle of recognition is widening as well. Diplomats and diplomatic services continue to seek recognition primarily from other diplomats and other diplomatic services. When diplomats effectively come to understand that they are actually dependent on the recognition of other social entities, they will be forced to review and improve upon their traditional methods. I will name two: hierarchy and *modus operandi.*

Hierarchy is a cherished principle of diplomacy, and in a number of ways, it is unavoidable. Clear communication of intent is a key diplomatic task which spells coordination, and coordination spells some kind of hierarchy. However, the stronger the hierarchy, the more cumbersome the chain of command and the longer the reaction time. This means that globalisation, which compresses time, is a direct challenge to hierarchy. New technologies also favour hierarchy – emails may be used for commands, and electronic texts make it easier for the top of the hierarchy to trim information right before it is released. At the same time, these technologies have contributed to the density of flows that put hierarchy under attack. We may look to the Danish diplomatic service for one type of response, namely to increase the number of interfaces between diplomats and their environment. During the 1990s, the Danish MFA simply decided that any diplomat should be empowered to answer a wide range of questions from outside and take a wide range of new initiatives on their own. This did not change the principle of hierarchy in any way – people who are out of line still get slapped down and the insubordinate are disciplined just as they used to be – but the subject matter to which hierarchy is applied shrunk dramatically. If an organisation may speak with a thousand voices on a number of issues, on which it used to be able to speak with only one, it spells increased action capacity. The network organisation is simply a much more efficient model for fulfilling the key diplomatic function of information collection and information dissemination under the conditions created by globalisation than is the old megaphone model. It also gives the Danish MFA the upper hand over other diplomatic services that still do not trust their employees to speak on their behalf on quotidian business, and therefore deem it necessary to handle all kinds of queries from the very top.

A second consequence stemming from the range of polities is a proliferation of sources of information. As a result, the public struggle for defining reality intensifies and diplomats have certain disadvantages in this respect. Since journalists specialise in speed and academics specialise in adding social and historical context, diplomats will tend to lose out to these relevant others on both breaking news and on analysis. For decades now, diplomatic services have compensated for this by co-opting journalists and academics. Diplomats have nonetheless maintained their *modus operandi* of reacting to others rather than initiating action themselves. The advent of globalisation has put this principle under increasing pressure, for with the mounting speed of information and density, the advantages of having the communicative initiative are forever growing. The Canadian Department of Foreign Affairs and International Trade (DFAIT) has experimented with changing the *modus operandi* from being reactive to being proactive, or, to use their jargon, from being backward leaning to being forward leaning.[7] Increase in efficiency where carrying out the function of communication is concerned followed immediately. This type of proactive track allows DFAIT to take a hand in building the playing field, giving them a home turf advantage they would not otherwise have. It means that they are ready with their version of reality at an earlier stage than they would otherwise have been, making it more likely that their version will mould and crowd out other versions. It lends to

DFAIT the mantle of the can-do player, rather than that of the stonewalling office worker. Why have other services not followed suit? One possibility is habit, but a more probable reason concerns identity. Within the old rules, it is a better position to be sought after rather than to be the seeker; better to answer than to ask. Being proactive means acknowledging to the competition that you are not indispensable. Therefore a prerequisite for proactiveness is recognition of other social groups as something more than passive takers. Here we have a transformation that is bound to come, but that is hampered by a lingering diplomatic self-understanding and idea of its place in society that is definitely pre-globalisation.

If there is an overall logic to the shift in political rationality under conditions of globalisation, it is to do with a change from direct to indirect rule. More is left to individuals, and control is growing more indirect, with direct control being increasingly reserved for after-the-fact situations when indirect control has turned out to be too soft to secure the desired result. This logic is working its way into diplomacy as well. Consider a move like the Danish one, where the function of information is made into everybody's concern. It hangs on indirect control being effective. By training its employees well in advance, the core of the organisation shapes the kind and styles of answers that those employees will give in most situations, including answers given when the top does not listen. The more thorough the advance training, the higher the chances are that these answers will be acceptable to the core of the organisation. Direct control will then have to kick in only when this indirect strategy does not work out. This means that the resources spent on direct control will decrease, which means that this time is available for boosting efficiency in other fields. Then consider proactiveness. It is about orchestrating social situations in advance, in the hope that the outcome will be more favourable than it would otherwise have been. By employing indirect means, one may save the use of more direct means for a later point. It is all about governing from afar. But if one wants to govern from afar, then one needs to be far-sighted. A plan for the long haul is needed in order to consider different outcomes, to listen to second opinions and to have contingency plans. All this breaks with the present *modus operandi* of diplomacy. In sum, it is not on the level of subject matter or personnel, but rather on the level of organising principles that globalisation seems to be having the keenest impact on diplomatic practice.

Notes

I should like to thank the participants of The Centre for International Governance Innovation workshop at Wilton Park, 23–25 June 2006, for comments, and Eva Fetscher for research assistance.

1. Indeed, one way of interpreting the diplomacy of the Bush era is as an overall attempt to salvage the principle of territoriality in an era of globalisation: homogenisation of

space by means of direct investment etc. in NAFTA and Europe ('the democratic peace'), attempts to make the rest of the world more compatible with the US model in most other places, use of force where this strategy is seen to have little prospect ('rogue states' like Afghanistan, Iraq, Iran), attacks on the idea of multilateral diplomacy and the institutions within which it is practiced.

2. Note that this stands in contradistinction to another tendency namely that the closer a diplomat is to the ministry leadership, the more important he or she is. Instructively, in a number of foreign ministries the key press spokesman is not even detached to the Department of Information, but is rather to be found in the Secretariat. The important information work is done not on the routinised interface with journalists, but on the more exalted level of the top politicians.

3. See, for example, Dickie (2004).

4. A recent example, which also illustrates the power of a popular culture genre, is how a series of Mohammad caricatures in a Danish newspaper spawned diplomatic activity in dozens of states.

5. See Dunn (1996).

6. We may expand Bull's point of symbolising the society of states by postulating that these people symbolise global or world society.

7. For more on DFAIT's experimentation with a proactive approach, see Bátora (2005b).

2
Global Governance: Challenges to Diplomatic Communication, Representation, and Recognition

Christer Jönsson

For decades, the decline or crisis of diplomacy has been 'a well rehearsed proposition' (Hocking, 1997: 169). Diplomacy is sometimes suggested as a candidate for the endangered species list (Cooper, 1997: 174), and Zbigniew Brzezinski's quip in 1970 to the effect that if foreign ministries and embassies 'did not already exist, they surely would not have to be invented' is frequently quoted (James, 1980: 933; Hamilton and Langhorne, 1995: 232; Hocking, 1999a: 23). Recent developments seem to have reinforced such dismal predictions. In a world of globalisation and global governance, the role of diplomacy is generally perceived to have been significantly reduced.

Globalisation and global governance

The word *globalisation* itself has come to be one of the most globalised phenomena in the contemporary world. As a catchword used by practitioners and analysts the world over to connote widely different phenomena, it runs the risk of becoming meaningless. Yet, every cliché captures the experiences and attitudes of an epoch, and today it is difficult to discuss international relations, including diplomacy, without using the word.

Globalisation obviously refers to multifaceted *processes of change*, a core aspect of which is the reconfiguration of social and political space. At stake is the notion of *territoriality*, the linking of public authority with physical space. 'Political organization is territorial when the legal reach of public authority is coterminous with certain spatial boundaries' (Caporaso, 2000: 10). Globalisation can be understood as *deterritorialisation* – 'a reconfiguration of geography, so that social space is no longer wholly mapped in terms of territorial places, territorial distances and territorial borders' (Scholte, 2000: 16). The notion of non-territorial space is alien to our traditional way of thinking about political geography. In our maps, material as well as mental, territorial states hold centre stage.

29

If globalisation, understood in terms of deterritorialisation, challenges ingrained notions of diplomacy, the concept of *global governance* underscores this challenge. Like globalisation, global governance is a rather vague and flexible concept. A common denominator of most conceptualisations of global governance is the calling into question of two traditional strands of international relations theory: (1) the state-centric perspective, and (2) the understanding of the international system in terms of anarchy.

Global governance refers to the patterns that emerge from governing efforts by a multitude of interdependent actors. It is conceived 'to include systems of rule at all levels of human activity – from the family to the international organization – in which the pursuit of goals through the exercise of control has transnational repercussions' (Rosenau, 1995: 13). The term 'governance' generally implies the formulation, implementation, monitoring, enforcement and review of rules and regulatory institutions. Global governance, in particular, is about coordinating multiple, interdependent actors, and refers to the patterns that emerge from regulatory efforts by these actors in the absence of a central authority.

Thus, global governance suggests a multi-layered rather than state-centric organisational universe. The interactions between formal institutions and global civil society as well as between public and private actors are at the core of global governance. The notion of global governance conjures up an image of a world 'comprised of spheres of authority (SOAs) that are not necessarily consistent with the division of territorial space and are subject to considerable flux' (Rosenau, 1999: 295). As states become only one of many sources of authority, the implication is that the international order is based neither on anarchy nor on hierarchy.

Diplomacy as an international institution

To the extent that diplomacy is understood as an instrument or tool of the territorial state, as in realist approaches, global governance does indeed represent a threat to diplomacy. As a variety of actors other than states enter the international arena, diplomacy is in danger of 'losing both its professional and conceptual identity' (Sharp, 1997: 630).

Using an alternative understanding, however, diplomacy constitutes a perennial international institution that 'expresses a human condition that precedes and transcends the experience of living in the sovereign, territorial states of the past few hundred years' (Sharp, 1999: 51). Diplomacy is seen as a timeless, existential phenomenon, representing a response to 'a common problem of living separately and wanting to do so, while having to conduct relations with others' (Sharp, 1999: 51). Exchange – be it of goods, people, information or services – seems to be central to the origins of diplomacy (Cohen, 2001: 25). Whenever and wherever there are political units with distinct identities, which see the need to establish exchange relations of some kind and realise their interdependence, diplomatic rules and roles are likely to emerge.

From this perspective, the nature of the relationship between diplomacy and global governance becomes a more open question. If diplomacy is a perennial institution, it seems appropriate to inquire first into its constitutive dimensions. What are the timeless parameters, within which change occurs in a long-term perspective? This, in turn, raises questions of adaptability and flexibility. How adaptable has diplomacy been throughout history to changing circumstances, and how is it adjusting to the contemporary transformations subsumed under the labels of globalisation and global governance?

In a recent book, my colleague Martin Hall and I argue that *communication*, *representation* and *reproduction of international society* are three constitutive dimensions of diplomacy (Jönsson and Hall, 2005). Diplomacy is often characterised as communication between polities. Without communication, there can be no diplomacy. Representation is another core dimension of diplomacy, insofar as diplomats are representatives of principals, who act on their behalf and stand as symbols of them and their polities. Reproduction refers to the ways in which diplomacy contributes to the creation and continuation of a particular international society by means of recognising certain political units and socia'ising them into the diplomatic community. The overall picture emerging from our broad historical overview is that diplomacy, analysed in terms of these three categories, is an institution characterised by great resilience and adaptability. To what extent, then, have the new circumstances of globalisation and global governance affected these three dimensions of diplomacy?

Communication

At the core of globalisation is the rapid development in the technology of communications in recent decades, which has compressed time and space in unprecedented ways. Geographers sometimes refer to this development as 'diminishing distance-related friction'.

While facilitating the exchange of diplomatic communication, technological innovations are often seen as challenges to ingrained diplomatic procedures. For instance, when the first telegram arrived on the desk of British Foreign Minister Lord Palmerston in the 1840s, he reputedly exclaimed: 'My God, this is the end of diplomacy!' The profound transformation of today's media and information technology has elicited similar concerns.

The most obvious effect of the information technology revolution is that diplomacy has lost its position as the main facilitator of contacts and communication across state boundaries. The gathering and transmission of information – diplomats as the 'eyes and ears' and the 'mouthpieces' of governments – have traditionally been core elements of diplomacy. Whereas diplomats during most of history had a virtual monopoly on the supply of information from foreign countries, today they face competition from the intelligence community as well as the media. While diplomats throughout history have had a reputation as 'honourable spies', intelligence has today become a separate institution, both complementing and competing with diplomacy. Several states, such as the United States and Britain, spend more on intelligence than on diplomacy (Herman, 1998: 4). Intelligence communities have bred a 'clandestine mentality' and a cult of secrecy, devaluing information obtained through open sources in foreign policy decision-making. If decision-makers in several states put a premium on intelligence reports, news media constitute other significant competitors to diplomatic reporting. Not only does most of the information reaching governments about developments throughout the world come from the media, but a large portion of diplomatic reporting consists of analyses based on the work of journalists (Davison, 1976: 391; cf. Tusa, 1996: 218). The question that is now sometimes raised is whether the importance of diplomats in information-gathering has been reduced to the verge of obsolescence. The 24-hour news reporting of today's global electronic media tends to make diplomatic reports redundant.

The common counterargument is that the information available via various media, including the Internet, will remain a significant complement to, but no substitute for, information gathered through diplomatic channels. Diplomats have always cultivated private sources as a supplement to official sources. Among such sources of information, in fact, are other diplomats. 'Communication among diplomats is a two-way street: one cannot expect to obtain information unless one is able and willing to convey information' (Gruber, 1983: 62–63).

The ease and speed of communication have affected diplomatic practices in other ways as well. For instance, direct contacts between political leaders have become more frequent. Diplomats often complain that summitry and other varieties of direct contacts between political leaders have reduced the role of diplomats; a former British ambassador wonders whether the political jet-set needs the diplomatic pedestrian any more (Jackson, 1981: 5). Moreover, the dramatic increases in the speed of communication often force decision-makers to react instantaneously to international events, bypassing traditional diplomatic channels. In the age of abundant and instant information combined with intrusive media, the moderate tempo of traditional diplomatic communication, which allowed for careful deliberations of signalling strategy and interpretation, seems irrevocably lost.

Compared to earlier periods when it took a long time to relay instructions, the actions of diplomats today are arguably much more circumscribed (Hamilton and Langhorne, 1995: 132). New communications technology has made possible ever more detailed and frequent instructions regardless of the physical remoteness of diplomats from their principals (Stearns, 1996: 75). Even before the widespread use of fax and the advent of the Internet, one ambassador complained that 'instant communications have transformed all diplomatic posts into branch offices of headquarters' (Halstead, 1983: 23). By contrast, other seasoned diplomats argue that 'because communications are now so fast, it is more feasible than it used to be for an ambassador to be part of the policy-formulating process' (Bunker, 1983: 1). 'If he is now liable to receive instructions several times a day a few minutes after they have left the minister's desk, he can give his own views with equal facility and speed and thus influence the decisions of ministers' (Trevelyan, 1973: 29).

Television and other electronic media affect the transmission of information via diplomatic signalling in various ways. The significance of nonverbal signalling and body language is enhanced. Signalling via television often implies a loss of flexibility. Signals become simplified and tend to incur commitments. Moreover, television makes the differentiation among audiences more difficult. Classic diplomacy relied on signalling to exclusive and clearly delineated audiences, with a high degree of control and the possibility to vary the message according to audience. Television, by contrast, tends to engage public opinion and does not allow for differentiated messages.

While diplomatic communication has been affected by television in uncontrollable ways, it is also true that statesmen and diplomats may exploit the new media for their purposes in communicating with the world. Diplomats have increasingly become engaged in 'media diplomacy' (Cohen, 1986; Jönsson, 1996; Gilboa, 2001). Today's media facilitate the renewed emphasis on *public diplomacy* – efforts 'to move from supplying information to capturing the imagination' (Leonard et al., 2002: 50) and influencing public or elite opinion in other states.

If the revolution in communications technology has reduced the role of diplomacy in the gathering and transmission of information, *negotiations* – 'the ultimate form of diplomatic communication' (Stearns, 1996: 132) – have increased in importance within global governance practices. Negotiations, processes of back-and-forth communication, remain key instruments to solve issues in ways acceptable to autonomous actors. Global governance entails an increased amount and variety of actors; and the more actors involved, the more negotiations.

Representation

Representation can be broadly understood as 'a relation between two persons, the representative and the represented or constituent, with the representative holding the authority to perform various actions that incorporate the agreement of the represented' (de Grazia, 1968: 461). A literature search using 'representation' as the keyword yields a plethora of works focusing on representative democracy and representative government. Principal-agent (P-A) theory is another branch of social science that has been preoccupied with relationships between representatives and represented. Principal-agent relations arise whenever one party (principal) delegates certain tasks to another party (agent). Both theoretical traditions can be applied to diplomacy. Diplomats are obviously representatives or agents who have been entrusted with certain tasks from their principals (rulers, governments).

One can make a basic distinction between representation as *behaviour* ('acting for others') and as *status* ('standing for others'). In acting for others, there are two related key questions to consider: to what extent representatives are bound by instructions from their principals, and to what extent they are free to act as they see fit in pursuit of the principals' interests? Standing for others implies the symbolic representation of principals.

The degree of restriction or leeway of diplomatic envoys has varied throughout history and it has been observed that the development of communication and transportation technology may account for some of this variation. Another factor with a more discernible effect has become whether the diplomatic agent has a single principal or receives instructions from a collective body. P-A theory pays attention to the problems of collective or multiple principals, especially the increased autonomy agents may enjoy as a result of competing preferences among principals. By analogy, the unequivocal instructions from a single sovereign leave less leeway for the diplomat than the frequently vague instructions resulting from negotiations among different actors and agencies in modern democracies. Global governance implies negotiations at several levels with a variety of actors, adding complexity to principal-agent relations. Modern diplomats thus often find themselves 'stranded between different constituencies' (Hill, 1991: 97). It is an irony of modern diplomacy, writes Paul Sharp (1996: 5), that 'the rise of democratic values which makes the extensive idea of representation necessary, simultaneously makes any idea of representation much more difficult to sustain.'

In P-A terminology, democratic polities place diplomatic agents at the end of multiple chains of principals and agents. For example, in a parliamentary democracy the electorate is the ultimate principal, delegating authority to elected parliamentarians. Parliament, in its turn, is the principal of the government. Within the government, the prime minister (or, possibly, the ruling party) can be regarded as the principal, delegating specialised authority to other ministers. Finally, the foreign minister is the immediate principal of diplomats in the field. From the perspective of diplomats, the question then arises as to which is their 'true' principal. If public opinion, parliament, the government or individual ministers do not agree, to whom should the diplomat be loyal?

The growing participation by a variety of actors in global governance has resulted in 'polylateralism' as a new mode of diplomatic dialogue in addition to bilateralism and multilateralism. Polylateralism is understood as

> the conduct of relations between official entities (such as a state, several states acting together, or a state-based international organisation) and at least one unofficial, non-state entity in which there is reasonable expectation of systematic relationships, involving some form of reporting, communication, negotiation and representation, but not involving mutual recognition as sovereign, equivalent entities. (Wiseman, 1999: 10–11)

Two prominent examples of state interaction with NGOs concern the 1997 Ottawa convention banning anti-personnel landmines and the 1998 Rome treaty establishing the International Criminal Court.

In short, the changing nature and increasing number of principals in today's world raise questions of broadened representation. Apart from state governments, other principals are increasingly taking part in international relations and thus would seem to need diplomatic agents. For instance, the lack of legitimate representatives of global currency dealers or the global NGO community curtails the state's ability to interact with crucial sets of international actors. 'This amounts to a crisis of representation and there is nothing in the existing machine that is going to help. The problem will worsen until areas of activity have also become centres of organized power and have acquired the need to deal with others like them' (Langhorne, 1998: 159).

In global conferences and multilateral fora, NGOs have increasingly been granted presence. Twenty years ago, NGOs would stage protests outside the doors of international organisations and had to gather information from the dustbins of national delegations; today many of them are involved in preparing global United Nations (UN) conferences and are routinely heard in plenary meetings. On several global issues, such as environmental protection, trade and human rights, NGOs have become key actors that cannot be bypassed in the search for viable solutions (Wiseman, 1999; Cooper and Hocking, 2000). In sum, foreign ministries and embassies have become 'co-participants' (Hocking, 2002a: 285) rather than the exclusive practitioners in the 'post-territorial diplomacy' (Keukeleire, 2000: 1) of global governance.

When it comes to symbolic representation – 'standing for others' – the diplomat is seen as a representative in the same way that a flag represents a state. Diplomatic immunity was originally justified on the grounds that diplomats embodied – and thus were to enjoy the same rights and privileges as – their sovereigns. In order for this to function, diplomats' claims to symbolic representation have to be accepted by a significant audience. One problem in our era of globalisation is that diplomats can be perceived as symbols of disliked states or '-isms'. The vulnerability of symbolic representation has been graphically demonstrated in a series of embassy occupations, hostage-taking and assassinations of diplomats in recent decades. The quality of 'standing for others' has been transformed from a rationale for diplomatic immunity to a rationale for being targets of political violence. No longer inviolable symbols, diplomatic representatives have increasingly become highly vulnerable symbols.

Reproduction of international society

Historically, diplomatic recognition has contributed to the formation and reproduction of a variety of international societies. Over the years, the principles of diplomatic recognition have varied considerably between two poles: inclusive and highly exclusive. In the Westphalian era, diplomatic recognition has been characterised by exclusiveness. Recognition has become essential to statehood, at the same time as it has delegitimised other types of political formations. Diplomatic recognition, as a 'ticket of general admission to the international arena' (Krasner, 1999: 16), has been reserved for states.

Although non-state actors participate increasingly in global governance, diplomatic recognition has not become more inclusive. If anything, recent developments have sharpened the political conditions many states require for diplomatic recognition. For instance, in response to the momentous developments after the end of the Cold War, European Community/Union member states adopted common guidelines for the recognition of new states in December 1991. Specific requirements for recognition include the presence of rule of law, democracy and human rights; guaranteed minority rights; the inviolability of frontiers; acceptance of commitments regarding disarmament and nuclear non-proliferation; and an undertaking to settle by agreement all questions concerning state succession and regional disputes. Recognition of 'entities which are the result of aggression' is expressly excluded (Doxey, 1995: 312–313). Other criteria for recognition that are used or proposed in today's world are non-dependence on foreign military support and respect for other states' rights (Peterson, 1997: 77–81).

The European Union (EU) plays a paradoxical role in contemporary practices of recognition. On the one hand, as mentioned above, it contributes to an even more restrictive or exclusive recognition pattern. On the other hand, the EU demands – and receives – diplomatic recognition as a diplomatic persona, although it does not constitute a state. Moreover, the EU seems to recognise unofficially non-state actors as participants in diplomatic processes.

The Commission's external service, consisting of delegations, permanent representations and offices in non-member states, has developed 'in the most haphazard and untidy fashion' (Hill and Wallace, 1979: 50). By 2004, the Commission was represented in 130 states, encompassing all continents, as well as at five international organisations, making it the fourth largest 'diplomatic service' in the world. In 1972, the Commission's delegation in Washington was the first to obtain full diplomatic status through legislation approved by Congress (European Commission, 2004b: 13). Today these delegations around the world enjoy full diplomatic recognition. Heads of delegation, with credentials signed by the president of the Commission, are accredited according to normal procedures and carry the rank and courtesy title of ambassador. Reciprocally, a large number of states, beginning with the newly independent African countries in the 1960s, have established diplomatic missions in Brussels (European Commission, 2004b: 15, 36, 37).

The ill-fated draft treaty on an EU constitution envisages a Union Minister for Foreign Affairs and a European External Action Service. The emergence of the EU as a diplomatic *persona* and full recognition of the EU as a diplomatic actor on par with states remains uncertain. Some would argue that several factors point in the direction of a growing diplomatic role for the EU: the increasing demand for European-level expertise, the increasing workload and financial pressures on the diplomatic services of member states (Duke, 2002: 867) and 'the emergence of a European response reflex' (Spence, 2002: 34). Others warn that the creation of a European External Action Service might trigger conflicts between national, Council and Commission staffs, which may eventually result in the renationalisation of diplomacy (Hill, 2003: 2).

At any rate, EU aspirations to become a full-fledged diplomatic actor have not replaced, but merely added new layers to, traditional diplomacy. The structure of bilateral diplomatic relations between EU member states remains intact; they all maintain embassies in other member states with the same organisation, functions and staff as in third countries, and there is no sign of this structure withering away. Nor have any other regional organisations been granted similar diplomatic status.

While initiating restrictive recognition patterns officially, the EU seems to recognise unofficially other non-state actors as participants in the diplomatic game. 'Multi-level governance' entails broad participation in EU policy processes. Thousands of special interest groups of various kinds are represented in Brussels, employing approximately the same number of persons as the European Commission. These take part in informal policy networks along with government representatives, individual specialists and members of the Commission. This means that diplomats engaged in European issues typically become engaged in 'polylateral' dialogues with NGOs, firms and subnational actors.

If the EU is a harbinger of new patterns of global governance, as many argue, its role in terms of diplomatic recognition is paradoxical. The EU appears both in a trend toward greater exclusiveness in recognition patterns and in the shaping of a more inclusive international society: first, by aspiring itself to become a recognised diplomatic actor alongside states, and second, by accepting other actors than states in diplomatic interactions.

Conclusion

Global governance draws our attention to *negotiations* as key processes and *networks* as key structures of governance. Negotiation processes at various levels are central to governance whenever the actors are not ordered hierarchically in a system of superordinates and subordinates. And diffuse formal political structures give rise to the kind of informal structures that political scientists label issue-based policy networks (cf. Jönsson, 2003). Negotiating and networking are basic diplomatic activities. In that respect, global governance does not represent any threat to diplomacy.

The real challenge seems to lie in the participation of new types of actors within global governance structures. First, the inclusion of NGOs and other actors in international interactions will in the long run raise questions of recognition. What criteria will be used to include or exclude new actors? Second, global governance also raises the more fundamental question of what kind of international community diplomacy will reflect and aid in reproducing. Will the institution of diplomacy continue to legitimise states and delegitimise other actors, or will it find ways of recognising and legitimising other actors in global governance? These are questions the international community has not yet started to address in earnest.

3

From Government to Governance: Transition to a New Diplomacy

Jan Aart Scholte

Introduction

Are diplomacy and governance indeed 'worlds apart'? Certainly, as the introduction to this book indicates, researchers on the two subjects have tended to plough separate furrows. The conference series that gave rise to the present volume forged a rare encounter between otherwise discrete academic endeavours and quickly made plain that dialogue between these two academic circles was overdue. Studies of diplomacy and investigations of governance have much to offer each other in contemporary political research. On the one hand, accounts of diplomacy can suitably be adjusted in the light of recent shifts in the contours of governance. On the other hand, accounts of governance need better to address the role of generic diplomatic processes such as representation, communication and negotiation among regulatory entities.

To set the scene for more detailed commentaries and case studies on these issues later in this volume, this chapter offers a general analysis of governance in contemporary society and identifies some implications for diplomacy in the twenty-first century. The first section below discusses the concept of 'governance' and distinguishes it from that of 'government'. Studies of diplomacy have thus far tended to rest on the more restrictive latter notion, while history has over the past half-century moved to a more complex mode of regulation. The second section of the chapter situates this recent shift from government to governance in the context of a concurrent major reconfiguration of social geography. This 'respatialisation' of society involves simultaneous and often interrelated processes of intensified globalisation, regionalisation and localisation, alongside a continued significance of country domains and their associated state apparatuses. The third section elaborates further on the multi-scalar, multi-actor, diffuse character of governance that has emerged in today's geographically more complex society. As a result one might speak of a recent historical transition from a 'statist' to a 'polycentric' mode of regulation. The fourth and final section identifies some broad changes in diplomacy that accompany this shift in the overall framework of governance.

Governance

The term 'governance' is relatively new to the English language and remains for the most part imprecisely understood. Even in French, where the word *gouvernance* has had a longer circulation, the notion is subject to widely varying understandings (Hermet et al., 2005). Other languages have recently acquired related concepts, for example, *zhili* in Chinese. Thus across the world many people have intuited a need for a new vocabulary of 'governance', a word that both resonates of and at the same time is also different from the more established concept of 'government'. Yet, when it comes to articulating an explicit rationale for the shift in language, most speakers draw a blank.

A first step in clarifying this confusion is to observe that many of the early usages (in English) of the term 'governance' related to regulatory activities undertaken by bodies other than the nation-state. For example, the word largely spread in the late 1980s with talk of 'global governance' as an alternative descriptor for what had hitherto usually been called 'international organisations' or 'multilateral institutions'. The creation of a high-profile Commission on Global Governance was particularly telling in this regard (Carlsson et al., 1995). Likewise, references to 'multi-level governance' spread in studies of emergent regional regimes, especially the European Union (EU). In respect of agencies outside the public sector, the phrase 'corporate governance' gained currency to describe the regulation of company operations. Eventually, particularly with the rise of so-called 'good governance' policies from the mid-1990s onwards, talk of governance came also to apply to national and local governments.

Common to all of these uses of the term is a concern with regulation. That is, discussions of governance always relate in one way or another to processes of formulating, implementing, adjusting and/or enforcing rules in respect of a given human collectivity. In terms of its spatial proportions, that collectivity could encompass a workplace, a village, a province, a country, a region or the planet. Once interactions and interdependences among people within a particular arena obtain a certain degree of significance, regulation is needed to bring some manner of order to that realm. Governance/regulation is therefore a primary facet of any lasting societal context. In implicit recognition of this pivotal role of governance in society, modern academic enquiry has developed a discipline of Politics (or Political Science) to concentrate on this core dimension of social relations.

Yet until recently researchers of politics tended to frame their investigations in terms of 'government' rather than 'governance'. Indeed, many universities in English-speaking countries still call their principal site of political studies a 'Department of Government'. On similar lines, Scandinavian academe names the field 'State Science' (e.g., *statsvetenskap* in Swedish). Such labels reflect an assumption – often implicit – that societal regulation is undertaken overwhelmingly if not solely through the nation-state. In other words, governance is taken to be synonymous with government.

This conflation was broadly sustainable during a particular period of history. What might be called a 'statist' mode of regulation gained considerable sway in Europe from the seventeenth century onwards and peaked across the world in the middle decades of the twentieth century. The statist methodology of conventional Political Science (including studies of International Relations within it) thus reflects the statist conditions of regulation that prevailed at the time that the discipline first consolidated. At that juncture, national governments did more or less monopolise regulatory processes in society. However, students of politics in that day tended to misread statism as a timeless human condition, when it was but a historically specific (and passing) episode.

Additional and sometimes competing sites of regulation have increasingly appeared alongside nation-states during the past half-century. 'Above' the state there has been a proliferation and growth of global as well as regional regimes. 'Below' the state widespread devolution has given many municipal and provincial authorities increased autonomy from national agencies. 'Next to' the state many regulatory tasks have come to be undertaken in whole or in part through private bodies, thereby annulling assumptions that the construction of societal rules necessarily occurs through public-sector institutions.

From the 1970s onwards, then, statist equations of regulation with government have become increasingly unsustainable. New vocabulary is required in order to discuss the wider dynamics of regulation in which government through nation-states is subsumed. Notions of 'governance' fit this bill and have therefore come into increased usage from the late 1980s. Today a substantial literature and a host of research institutes address the subject.

Initially some political researchers took the retreat from methodological statism too far. A number of writings in the early and mid-1990s spoke in this regard about the purported 'decline', 'retreat', 'demise' and 'end' of the nation-state (Guéhenno, 1995; Ohmae, 1995; Strange, 1996). A widely circulating volume of that time carried the striking title 'Governance Without Government', intimating to less discerning eyes that the state was on its way to the historical exit door (Rosenau and Czempiel, 1992).

Understandably such end-of-millennium hyperbole prompted a reaction. Counterarguments in the late 1990s stressed that states and relations among states were still very much part of contemporary politics. For these critics of 'globaloney', no other site of societal regulation came close to matching the state in terms of its range of competences, levels of resources, and degree of legitimacy (Hirst and Thompson, 1996; Weiss, 1998). Indeed, some emphasised that the state was if anything still on the rise, acquiring ever more responsibilities and ever more tools with which to execute those expanding tasks (Mann, 1997).

Today, a decade later, this polarised debate has largely passed. Both extremes are generally recognised to be unviable: the globalist position that governance is erasing government as well as the statist position that governance entails nothing more than government. Prevailing conceptions now hold that government is part of governance rather than opposed to it. Yet while states remain highly significant in contemporary regulation, they no longer hold the near-monopoly position that they did 50–60 years ago. Nor do national governments today execute regulatory operations in the same ways as in the statist past.

It therefore seems analytically most helpful to conceive of 'governance' as a generic label for societal regulation, while 'government' (in the sense of the nation-state) refers to a particular institutional apparatus through which governance can be executed. Following this usage, 'governance' is a category that can be applied transculturally and transhistorically, whereas 'government' is a culturally and historically specific way of doing governance. In certain contexts, such as the modern (often termed 'Westphalian') period, governance has been conducted more or less solely through centralised territorial governments. In other contexts, such as pre-Westphalian medievalism in Europe and pre-colonial regimes on other continents, governance has not involved national government at all. In the current post-Westphalian phase, meanwhile, states are part of governance – and an important part at that – but regulation also occurs at multiple and diverse other sites.

Thus different historical circumstances manifest different modes of governance. Much as Marx held that each society manifested a particular mode of production, and much as Foucault suggested that each society had a prevailing mode of knowledge (or in his words *episteme*), so a historical sociologist could do well to discern the underlying structure of governance that marks a given society. In world politics of the mid-twentieth century, the reigning mode of governance was statism. The contrasting circumstance half a century later is increasingly one of what can in shorthand be called 'polycentric' governance. In a polycentric mode regulation emanates from multiple kinds of sites and multiple criss-crossing links among those locales.

Respatialisation

Before elaborating on the institutional forms that polycentric governance takes in contemporary society, it can be helpful to situate the shift from statism to this new mode of governance in relation to wider current historical trends towards a more de-centred social geography. The polycentric condition in respect of regulation both reflects and reinforces a turn over the past half-century to a more multi-scalar organisation of social space. This transformation has occurred through a combination of concurrent processes of globalisation, regionalisation and localisation. These developments, together with the continued importance of country-scale spaces, provide the geographical backdrop and prompting for the emergence of polycentric governance.

Globalisation

Globalisation is probably the most discussed (and debated) of several major reconfigurations of social space that have transpired in recent history. The concept is by no means straightforward. As Christer Jönsson notes in his contribution to this volume, globalisation has been given so many meanings that it can become meaningless. However, the notion does obtain precision, distinctiveness and analytical importance when it is conceived as the growth of transplanetary – and in certain respects also supraterritorial – social connectivity (Scholte, 2005: 49–84).

What is meant by what could at first blush seem to be rather alienating jargon? In a word, 'transplanetary social connectivity' refers to the ability of persons located anywhere on earth to have direct exchanges and deep interdependencies with others located anywhere else on the planet. These links moreover have a 'supraterritorial' quality when, to some significant degree, they are not bound to and restricted by territorial places, territorial distances and territorial borders.

The large growth of global relations over the past half-century entails that social life today has obtained a much greater planetary dimension than before. Communications, travel, production, trade, money, finance, organisations, laws, conflicts, ecological developments and health problems now unfold on a global scale to overall degrees not previously witnessed in human history. In addition, people have become acutely aware of the larger role that global connections play in their lives: globality is a question of social consciousness as well as concrete connections (Robertson, 1992). For many individuals cultural identities and political solidarities have also become partly oriented to global spheres, as witnessed with phenomena like so-called 'world music' and humanitarian relief programmes. Materially and ideationally, therefore, society today operates substantially through global frames.

Intense globalisation since the middle of the twentieth century has therefore brought a key shift in the *scale* of social relations. In a more global world, society involves not just interchanges and interdependencies among people organised on the basis of localities and countries. In addition, globalisation brings an expansion of distinct transplanetary spaces that come to constitute a major site of social life in their own right. Thus, for example, today the geography of financial crises, the entertainment industry, ozone depletion, human rights and war all unfold to a significant extent on a global, planetary, world scale (Scholte, 2005: 59–75).

Many of these global social relations furthermore have a supraterritorial character that substantially loosens their bonds with the geography of longitude, latitude and altitude. For example, websites and email accounts are available at, and move between, whatever territorial locations on earth users choose to access them. Mass media broadcasts by satellite instantly cover – and to that extent transcend – any territorial distance on earth. Global ecological developments such as climate change and biodiversity loss simultaneously affect the planet as a whole, without reference to territorial borders. Likewise, global phenomena like electronic money, various infectious diseases, many commodity markets and the strategies of global organisations have supraterritorial qualities of transplanetary instantaneity (crossing any distance on earth in no time) and transplanetary simultaneity (existing anywhere on earth at the same time).

For students of diplomacy, as for others, the following key point must be emphasised: *global* relations are distinct from *international* relations. Internationality involves links between discrete territorial realms (countries). In contrast, globality entails connections within a single planetary realm. Hence it is important to distinguish between global economics (the production, exchange and consumption of resources in spaces of a planetary scale) and international economics (the links between production, exchange and consumption of resources as undertaken in nation-state-country spaces). Likewise, global culture (the construction and communication of meaning within planetary arenas) is different from international culture (the exchange of ideas, symbols and rituals between nation-state-country arenas). And global politics (the acquisition, distribution and exercise of power in transplanetary relations) encompasses much more than an international society of states.

To be sure, neither global relations in general, nor even supraterritoriality more specifically, are completely new to the past 50–60 years. For example, earlier times have known tellingly named 'world religions', an intercontinental slave trade, long-distance epidemics, and transoceanic telegraph cables, amongst other transplanetary links. Nevertheless, much data amply indicates that globalisation has unfolded at historically unprecedented rates and to historically unprecedented extents since the middle of the twentieth century (cf. Held et al., 1999; Scholte, 2005: 101–117). One wide-ranging composite measure suggests that the overall level of global links in the world rose (on a scale 0–1) from 0.23 in 1982 to 0.68 in 2004 (CSGR, 2007).

That is not to say that all human experience on the planet today is equally globalised. Data collected for the Centre for the Study of Globalisation and Regionalisation Globalisation Index just cited also shows that some regions and countries have many more global links than others. In addition, degrees of global connectivity often vary by class (e.g., professionals versus manual workers), culture (e.g., western modernity versus indigenous peoples) and other social spheres. In spite of such variations, however, all people everywhere on earth today are to one or another significant degree influenced by transplanetary connections.

Although globalisation has attracted the most academic attention, it has not been the only important transformation of social geography in contemporary history. Further trends of regionalisation and localisation have unfolded concurrently. To this extent recent decades have arguably seen as much reterritorialisation (i.e., around domains both smaller and larger than countries) as they have witnessed deterritorialisation (i.e., through some aspects of globalisation).

Regionalisation

Regionalisation refers here to the construction of social spaces that span several contiguous countries. The dimensions of regions vary considerably. For example, a region can be continental in scope, say, in relation to Africa, Australasia or North America. On other occasions a region may link the littorals of several continents, as in the Asia–Pacific, the Mediterranean Basin or the South Atlantic. Still other regions (sometimes termed 'subregions') encompass part of a continent, like Amazonia, Central Asia or Southern Africa. Meanwhile certain other regions span a borderland between several countries (in cases such as the Basque Country, Kurdistan, Lapland, or the pygmy forestlands of equatorial Africa). Whatever the proportions, however, common to all regions is a transcendence of country units without extending to a planetary reach.

Contemporary regionalisation has occurred in respect of broadly the same sorts of connections that have expanded global social spaces. For example, many companies now organise their production processes and marketing strategies on largely regional lines (Rugman, 2005). Money has taken regional forms in currencies such as the CFA franc and the euro as well as with the emergence of Asian and Latin American Monetary Funds. Civil society associations have taken regional shape through initiatives like the European Social Forum and the Inuit Circumpolar Conference. Over 270 regional trade agreements had been reported to the World Trade Organization (WTO) by 2003 (Cosbey, 2004: 2). Much travel, communications and utilities infrastructure (road and rail networks, radio frequencies, gas pipelines, etc.) has also become organised in good part on a regional basis.

Whereas several globalisation indices have been developed over the past decade, systematic comprehensive measures of regionalisation across the planet are not yet available. However, it is not necessary to await the completion of such projects (e.g., by the United Nations University Comparative Regional Integration Studies Programme) to affirm that the past 50–60 years have seen historically unprecedented extents of regionalisation. Recent history has therefore seen the concurrent unfolding of two types of respatialisation beyond countries – regionalisation and globalisation – each to previously unequalled degrees. Like globalisation, regionalisation is neither entirely new to contemporary history nor evenly spread across the world. Without a doubt, though, society today is more regionalised than ever.

The relationship between regionalisation and globalisation is complex (Hettne et al., 1999; Cooper et al., 2007). Sometimes the two trends can be in tension, for example, when regionalisation is pursued with mercantilist measures that aim to reduce or at least control global-scale connections. In this vein, some regional policies have sought to restrict global migration. Similarly, some regional trade regimes (like the Common Agricultural Policy of the EU) have restricted market access for exports from other parts of the planet. In such cases regionalisation moves world politics in the direction of competitive blocs rather than open global flows. Yet even such interregional competition is a planetary dynamic and in that sense entails a form of globalisation.

Indeed, on the whole contemporary globalisation and regionalisation are complementary and mutually reinforcing. For example, many global companies organise their production and distribution on a regional basis. Regional currencies and monetary funds often facilitate global finance and trade. Regional satellites generally form part of global communications networks. Regional-scale and global-scale governance agencies often work in tandem, as when the EU represents a group of contiguous countries in WTO negotiations, or when United Nations(UN) security operations are executed in conjunction with regional bodies such as the African Union (AU). Likewise, regional human rights regimes are part of the global human rights architecture that has developed since the 1940s. In these and other ways so-called 'open regionalism' – where regional constructions facilitate relations with the wider world – deliberately advances globalisation.

Localisation

Concurrently with respatialisation beyond country spheres, through globalisation and regionalisation, contemporary history has also witnessed considerable reorganisation of social geography within countries. This reterritorialisation of society in the direction of smaller realms might be called 'localisation'.

Like regions, local spaces come in different sizes. Some localisation has occurred around provinces, counties, federal states or 'countries within countries' such as Québec and Scotland. Other localisation has focused on a still smaller scale, for example, in respect of neighbourhoods, districts and municipalities. Common to all localisation, however, is that the spatial context of social relations falls within a section of a country.

Somewhat confusingly for the present discussion, the vocabulary of 'regions' is sometimes used to describe such substate units as well as the suprastate configurations discussed above. Thus, for example, the Network for Regional Government on Sustainable Development (set up at the 2005 Johannesburg Summit) and the EU Committee of the Regions assemble representatives of substate authorities. In everyday parlance, too, talk of regions may refer to domains such as Patagonia within Argentina or Siberia within Russia. Hence, whereas the analysis in this chapter speaks of 'regionalisation' across countries and 'localisation' within them, one could perhaps alternatively talk of 'macro-regionalisation' beyond countries and 'micro-regionalisation' inside them. Whatever terminology is employed, however, the general point remains that contemporary respatialisation has diluted the previously reigning focus of social geography on country-state-nation societies.

Contemporary localisation has had multiple cultural, demographic, economic and political manifestations. Culturally, for instance, recent decades have seen widespread revivals of indigenous peoples' and other substate ethno-national identities. Demographically, people have increasingly come to live in localised urban conurbations that, while covering only two per cent of the earth's land surface, since 2006, house over half of humanity. Economically, localisation has taken form in hundreds of export processing zones across the world as well as in translocal collaborations such as the Four Motors Agreement between Baden-Württemberg, Catalonia, Lombardy and Rhône-Alpes. Politically, localisation has been witnessed in a general worldwide trend of constitutional devolution. Recent recentralisation in Russia under President Putin runs against this grain. More indicative of the general trend are the empowerment of village committees in India and increased autonomy for the Flemish and Walloon areas of Belgium. In Malaysia, meanwhile, citizens require passports for internal travel between the federated states of the country.

At first blush localisation might seem to contradict globalisation and regionalisation. Indeed, some so-called anti-globalisation activists have advocated localist strategies that seek to delink small-scale communities from transplanetary flows (Hewison, 1999; Hines, 2000). In this vein a number of local currency schemes across the world have promoted an alternative to regionalised and globalised money flows (Community Currencies, 2006).

On the whole, however, respatialisations 'below' and 'above' the country-state-nation scale have been complementary in contemporary history. For example, localised indigenous peoples have often advanced their causes through global and regional (e.g., Pan-American) coalitions. Many local peasant groups have gained strength through the global Vía Campesina movement. The contemporary significance of so-called 'global cities' derives from their combination of local resources and transplanetary networks. Locally delimited special economic zones have offered enormous appeal to global capital with tax and regulatory concessions. Municipal and provincial governments have often pursued more ambitious initiatives in response to global ecological challenges than nation-states. In these and many other ways, the trend is sooner towards the combination of the global and the local in so-called 'glocalisation' than towards their opposition (Robertson, 2006).

Persistent nationalisation

Contrary to what some might expect, contemporary respatialisation of social life is not inimical to country domains and associated state governments and national identities. Processes of globalisation, regionalisation and localisation have certainly attenuated the near-exclusive concentration of social geography on country-state-nation units that prevailed in the period to the middle of the twentieth century. However, the national scale of social organisation (and its associated state-based diplomacy) is by no means disappearing.

On the contrary, country frameworks have arguably further consolidated at the same time that other scales of social geography have risen in importance. Countries remain highly significant contexts for the organisation of production processes, trade flows, communications infrastructure, institutional networks, citizenship, etc. Across the world, national governments are generally larger than they have been at any previous historical time. National cultures on the whole figure as prominently as ever in the construction of social identities and solidarities.

Moreover, following a pattern already observed in the relationships between other facets of contemporary geographical transformation, continued nationalisation is quite compatible with the concurrent trends of localisation, regionalisation and globalisation. For instance, most companies and currencies that operate transnationally have had a clear base country. In addition, identities affiliated to country have provided countless millions with a cherished sense of being, becoming and belonging in a more regionalised and globalised society. Indeed, the nation-state has frequently been a vital facilitator of the localisation, regionalisation and globalisation of governance, *inter alia* through relevant constitutional amendments and international treaties. Conversely, global technologies like television (with national broadcasters) and global and regional governance institutions (with state memberships) have often reinforced country-based social spaces.

Thus currently unfolding tendencies do not entail a decline in the importance of countries (nor of their associated state governments and national identities), but rather their incorporation into a more complex multi-scalar social space. History today is not witnessing the replacement of one centre of social geography (the country unit) by any other (be it the globe, the region or the locality). The different spheres of social organisation are not competing to acquire the sort of dominance previously held by country-state-nation spaces. Rather, localisation, nationalisation, regionalisation and globalisation are unfolding in tandem and involve much mutual reinforcement.

Perhaps a mindset of 'centred-ness' still captivates contemporary social thought and generates expectations that one spatial scale must overshadow all others. Hence discussions often proceed in terms of the global *or* the regional *or* the national *or* the local, when the operative conjunction should be 'and'. The structural shift in social geography is not from one 'level' to another, but from concentration and centred-ness to diffusion and decentred-ness.

A polycentric mode of governance

This co-existence and intricate interlinkage of different geographical scales of social relations is played out *inter alia* through an emergent polycentric mode of governance. In this circumstance, societal regulation occurs through complex interconnections among multiple forms of agencies. These governance bodies variously have local, national, regional and global juris-dictions. Moreover, these sites of regulation are spread across public and private sectors, including also hybrid public-private constructions. With so many institutional decision points – many of them moreover interrelated and overlapping – it can be difficult to identify the sources and trace the courses of public policy.

Instead of 'polycentrism', other theorists have referred to this condition of diffuse, multi-actor, multi-scalar regulation as 'plurilateralism', 'polylateral-ism', 'networked governance', 'empire', 'new medievalism', 'cosmocracy', 'mobius-web governance' and 'disaggregated world order (Cerny, 1993; Wiseman, 1999; Reinicke, 1999–2000; Hardt and Negri, 2000; Friedrichs, 2001; Keane, 2003; Rosenau, 2003; Slaughter, 2004). For various reasons none of these terms provides a fully adequate descriptor of the situation (Scholte, 2005: 187). Indeed, the label 'polycentrism' could itself be criticised for perpetuating a talk of 'centres' – even if multiple – when the mode of regulation in question is distinguished by its *non*-centred character. Whatever vocabulary one adopts, though, it is clear that contemporary governance differs from what might be called the 'statist' conditions of the preceding period.

Statist and polycentric modes of governance can be contrasted in five principal ways. First, under statism policy processes were relatively central-ised, whereas under polycentrism the formulation, implementation, adjust-ment and enforcement of societal rules occur in a far more dispersed fash-ion. Second, statist regulation well-nigh exclusively involved a single type of actor (namely, the state), whereas polycentric governance transpires through various kinds of actors (including local governments, national states, regional institutions, global regimes, private mechanisms and public-private combinations). Third, statist governance focused geographically on the country unit, whereas polycentric regulation reaches across several spatial scales. Fourth, statism generally worked on a basis of neatly separated territorial jurisdictions, whereas polycentrism often involves messily over-lapping jurisdictions. Fifth, and following especially from the first and fourth points, statism was steeped in concerns about sovereignty, in the sense of the assertion of absolute, supreme, comprehensive, exclusive regu-latory control by a single entity. In contrast, polycentrism entails a post-sovereign condition in which no site of governance can aspire even to approximate such a predominant position.

As already intimated, the end of stat*ism* does not entail the end – or even necessarily a contraction – of the state. States remain key governance actors in current post-statist circumstances. The difference under polycentrism is that policy processes are less concentrated on and centralised in the state. National governments share regulatory tasks with various other parties. Moreover, states in contemporary governance are themselves polycentric, in the sense that different ministries, legislative organs and judiciary bodies often pursue autonomous initiatives that are at best loosely coordinated with other parts of the state apparatus.

Thus the emergent polycentric mode of governance still involves a notable role for executive agencies of the nation-state. To understand contemporary world politics it remains important to examine the character and behaviour of the cabinets, foreign services and armed forces of national governments. Likewise, conventional international law (through interstate customs, resolutions and treaties) and international organisation (through intergovernmental institutions) continue to play significant parts within a polycentric regulatory framework. Polycentrism does not preclude the use of bilateral agreements (as witnessed in recent developments surrounding the governance of global trade), nor the possibility of unilateral action by major states (as seen in recent foreign policy of the United States Government). Hence polycentrism does not bring a demise of traditional pillars of international relations.

However, in the de-centred post-sovereign conditions of polycentrism these long-standing actors and activities do not account for the whole of a state's involvement in world politics. For example, a new multilateralism of transgovernmental networks has arisen alongside the old multilateralism of intergovernmental relations (Slaughter, 2004). Transgovernmental regulation occurs when civil servants from traditionally 'domestic' ministries in various states pursue direct contacts and collaborations with one another. Air travel, Internet, telecommunications and global conferences enable these official circles to develop their own substantial coordinations, largely autonomously from foreign ministries and other parts of the state. Perhaps the most publicly visible example of transgovernmentalism has been the Group of Eight (G8) process, in which senior officials of eight major states (especially from their economy and finance ministries) maintain regular information exchange and pursue policy coordination. Other transgovernmental networks have addressed issues of arms proliferation, competition policy, disease control, environmental protection, financial supervision, human rights promotion, migration management and trade policy. As described by researchers in the emergent field of 'global administrative law', the rules that emerge from these collaborations tend to be articulated in informal memoranda rather than official treaties (Raustiala, 2002; Kingsbury and Krisch, 2006).

Along with transgovernmental connections among national officials, other transstate networks in polycentric governance involve the legislative and judiciary branches. In respect of legislatures, the Inter-Parliamentary Union dates back to the late nineteenth century, albeit with limited consequence. Since the late 1970s other initiatives that link national representative assemblies include Parliamentarians for Global Action, the Global Legislators Organisation for a Balanced Environment, the Parliamentary Network on the World Bank, the Parliamentary Conference on the WTO, the Commonwealth Parliamentary Association, and the Latin American Parliament. Country-based political parties, too, have acquired global frames of interaction, through bodies such as the Socialist International, the Liberal International, the International Democrat Union and the Global Green Network. Judges in national courts have likewise developed a number of transgovernmental collaborations, while state-based police forces increasingly coordinate their operations against crime.

Within countries, local authorities under emergent conditions of polycentrism also have greater autonomy from national governments and their foreign ministries when it comes to relations with the wider world. Many substate governance institutions have in recent decades developed direct relationships with regulatory parties abroad. For example, scores of provinces in Canada and China, *Länder* in Germany, prefectures in Japan, and federal states in the United States have conducted a 'paradiplomacy' separately from, and sometimes counter to, national foreign policies (Hocking, 1993b; Fry, 2006). Meanwhile, municipal authorities have developed their own global collaborations through initiatives such as United Cities and Local Governments, with affiliates in 127 countries, and ICLEI – Local Governments for Sustainability, linking 500 cities, towns, counties and their associations across 67 countries on environmental issues. Hence some contemporary *global* governance takes the form of transplanetary connections among *local* governments.

As noted earlier, part of the general trend of regionalisation in contemporary social geography has been the growth of macro-regional governance frameworks (Farrell et al., 2005; Mansfield and Milner, 2005). This legal and institutional development has proceeded furthest in the case of the EU, but over recent decades most parts of the world have acquired notable degrees of regional regulation. South West Asia stands out as the striking exception that lacks a major regional governance initiative. Elsewhere the by-now dense alphabet soup includes ASEAN, AU, BSEC, CACM, CARICOM, CIS, EAC, ECOWAS, GCC, MERCOSUR, NAFTA, OAS, PIF, SADC, SAARC, UMA.[1] Although these regional institutions have been created through interstate agreement, with time they have – like any bureaucracy – acquired some life of their own. Member states and major external states continue to exert large influence over such regional governance bodies, but regional commissions, courts and parliaments have also developed varying degrees of autonomous impact. The EU has furthermore acquired several distinct regional political parties such as the European People's Party and the European Free Alliance.

Regional regulatory institutions have also begun to develop their own global networks with incipient interregionalism. So far this development has mainly involved EU relations with other regional institutions including MERCOSUR (the Southern Common Market) and ASEAN+3 (the ASEAN plus China, Japan and South Korea). This multilateralism of regions (as distinct from the traditional multilateralism of states) could well unfold further in years to come as and when regional governance apparatuses consolidate in areas outside Europe (Gilson, 2002; Hänggi et al., 2005).

Meanwhile global governance of the more traditional kind – that is, through planetary-scale intergovernmental institutions – has also experienced substantial proliferation and growth during the past half-century. These bodies include the well-known UN and WTO as well as less publicly visible agencies such as the Bank for International Settlements (BIS) and the Organisation for Economic Cooperation and Development (OECD). Not all global intergovernmental institutions have or aspire to universal state membership, as witnessed in cases like the Commonwealth, *la Francophonie* and the Organization of the Islamic Conference. The dealings of global multilateral organisations have also increasingly gone beyond intergovernmentalism alone, with the growth of involvement in their operations by nonstate actors such as firms and civil society associations alongside the traditional main relationships with states (Willetts, 1996; O'Brien et al., 2000; Scholte and Schnabel, 2002). In addition, some of these multilateral organisations have developed direct links with one another, unmediated through states: for example, as observers of each other's proceedings; and through the UN System Chief Executives Board.

To be sure, global and regional intergovernmental agencies still generally lag well behind states – particularly major states – in terms of the resources available to them (such as budget, staff, surveillance networks and armed forces) and their legitimacy. Indeed, many critics of multilateral institutions have held substantially exaggerated notions of their capacities. Certainly there is no sign of an emergent world government, in the sense of a unitary centralised public entity on a planetary scale with claims of sovereign authority and a monopoly on the legal use of armed violence. Nevertheless, bodies like the EU and the International Monetary Fund (IMF) have also become important governance players in their own right, with notable degrees of autonomy from their member states, especially weaker states in the South. National governments are therefore both policy makers and policy takers in their relations with suprastate institutions.

Thus far this elaboration of the workings of polycentrism has covered the fragmentation of the state as well as the concurrent growth of public-sector governance institutions with jurisdictions both larger and smaller than a country domain. In addition, as noted earlier, contemporary polycentrism has involved a 'lateral' growth of private regulatory mechanisms alongside state, substate and suprastate institutions (Ronit and Schneider, 2000; Hall and Biersteker, 2003). This privatisation of various areas of governance has countered widely held assumptions, inherited from statist times, that societal rules by definition emerge from and are administered through public-sector bodies. On the contrary, in contemporary politics commercial firms and civil society organisations also provide regulation for various aspects of public life.

Private governance institutions have grown with respect to all realms, from local to global. With reference to planetary fields, for example, a number of private organisations like the Global Reporting Initiative and the International Council of Toy Industries have played leading roles in developing norms of Corporate Social Responsibility (CSR). The International Accounting Standards Board has sought to improve and harmonise modes of financial reporting. Fair trade schemes have promoted alternative norms for global production and consumption of various primary commodities. Global companies today often resolve their disputes through private arbitration mechanisms rather than through litigation in state or suprastate courts (Mattli, 2001). On ecological matters, the Forestry Stewardship Council has drawn together business forums, labour unions, environmental groups and indigenous people's associations in a number of major timber producing countries to promote rules for ecologically sustainable logging. Within national realms many states have left the regulation of securities markets largely to private actors, like the Financial Services Authority in Britain. Other privatisation of governance has occurred when criminal networks and paramilitary groups have become the main regulatory force in an area, for example, in parts of Afghanistan, Colombia and Somalia.

Still further regulatory arrangements in the current polycentric mode of governance cross the public-private divide (Bull and McNeill, 2006). These hybrid constructions, which have mainly arisen since the late 1990s, involve a combination of public, commercial and/or civil society bodies. One prominent instance is the Internet Corporation for Assigned Names and Numbers (ICANN), started in 1998 as the main regulatory instrument for domain names in cyberspace. ICANN operates through collaboration between major software corporations and the United States Department of Commerce, together with several user committees that involve civil society groups. Other public-private hybrids include the Global Compact of transnational corporations through the UN (launched in 2000) and the Global Fund to Fight AIDS, Tuberculosis and Malaria (established in 2002). The governing board of the Global Fund includes representatives of government agencies, a regional governance body, firms, civil society associations and (nonvoting) global multilateral institutions.

It is as yet unclear whether the recent partial privatisation of governance is a momentary historical phenomenon soon to be reversed, or the start of a long-term trend towards a much larger regulatory role for private institutions, or something in between. On the one hand, it could be that the contemporary rise of private governance only reflects a passing neoliberalist infatuation with market forces as a panacea for society's needs. In this case, privatised regulation in areas such as corporate behaviour and financial stability would in due course be reassigned back to public-sector agencies (probably at this juncture including a larger role for suprastate bodies). On the other hand, the neoliberal and 'social market' ideas that underpin much current privatisation of governance could have greater longevity and prompt a more permanent and eventually far more encompassing turn in the character of regulation. Whatever the future direction, however, for the time being governance includes significant private aspects.

In sum, then, polycentric governance of the early twenty-first century has a complex, multifaceted character that encompasses national governments and transgovernmental networks; local authorities and translocal regimes; regional and interregional arrangements; global intergovernmental bodies and their mutual relations; private regulatory instruments that operate on and across the different geographical scales; and public-private hybrids that do the same. Additional trans-scalar governance links connect local governments with regional agencies, transgovernmental networks with global institutions and so on. Given these multifarious aspects, analysts (including students of diplomacy) who persist in wearing statist glasses miss a very large part of contemporary regulation.

For example, efforts to control the spread of HIV/AIDS have involved global, regional, national and local public agencies across the world as well as private inputs from CSR initiatives and also public-private programmes like the Global Fund. Similarly, regulatory responses to financial crises in the late 1990s drew in, among others, global institutions like the BIS and the IMF, regional forums discussing Asian and Latin American monetary funds, transgovernmental networks of state-based financial regulators, ad hoc inter-agency bodies like the Financial Stability Forum, national central banks and finance ministries acting unilaterally, local government initiatives to handle various social and economic repercussions of financial collapses and private regulatory organisations like the Group of Thirty. In the case of governing climate change, relevant actors have included global-scale bodies like the Intergovernmental Panel on Climate Change, regional frameworks like the EU, transgovernmental networks of environmental regulators, a host of national government programmes, various CSR schemes, substate authorities (like the State of California and the City of Seattle 'ratifying' the Kyoto Protocol when the Bush Administration did not) and so on.

These illustrative examples suggest that, in present times of polycentric regulation, researchers would do well to look across scales and sectors to identify the particular intricate blend of institutions that governs the given policy issue that is under examination. Each problem has its own distinctive regulatory map, one that moreover can fluctuate over time as certain actors rise to greater prominence and others recede. Unlike under statist conditions, in polycentric governance the key institutions and relations between institutions cannot be assumed in advance.

Given the many criss-crossing linkages that mark polycentric regulation, the jurisdictions of the various governance actors frequently overlap and blur. Multiple agencies claim mandates and competences over the same field of activity. As a result, different institutions can compete to take credit for policy successes, and intense finger pointing can occur in cases of failure. Consider, for instance, how national governments, multilateral institutions and private regulators assiduously blamed one another for the financial crises of the late 1990s. Likewise it is difficult to pinpoint fault for regulatory inaction on climate change. In fact the post-sovereign quality of polycentric governance entails that no party can exercise singular and ultimate decision-making authority. This dispersion of control in turn raises distinctly complicated questions regarding public accountability, as well as democracy more generally (Scholte, 2005: 348–381).

Implications for diplomacy

These wider issues of accountability and democracy are not the principal concern of the present discussion, however, which focuses instead on the consequences of the shift from statist government to polycentric governance for diplomacy. Detailed examination of various aspects of this question is the task of subsequent chapters of this book. Nevertheless, some initial general observations can help to set the context for those investigations. These comments are made below in terms of three generic functions of diplomacy: representation, communication and negotiation (cf. Jönsson and Hall, 2005).

Representation

Diplomacy has always involved the representation of one governance actor vis-à-vis others in world politics. Under statist conditions a diplomat exclusively represented one nation-state in the territorial jurisdictions of another. In medieval circumstances, the unit of governance that a diplomat represented was one or the other type of court rather than a modern centralised, bureaucratic, territorial state. In pre-colonial situations various sorts of regulatory institutions (empires, monarchies, local councils, etc.) could exchange representatives.

Under post-statist conditions of polycentrism the governance agencies that are represented in relation to each other are once again more diverse in character. To be sure, as stressed throughout this discussion, states remain highly significant in post-statist times, and hence the foreign services of states continue to figure importantly in diplomacy today. Indeed, old-style diplomats have acquired significant added responsibilities of representing national governments in a number of multilateral agencies and conferences, especially as they relate to the EU and the UN.

That said, states are today also represented abroad by other sorts of 'diplomats'. For example, national central banks and finance ministries normally supply a state's representation in multilateral financial institutions. Likewise, functional ministries tend to provide the bulk of a state's delegates to global conferences, depending on the subject at hand. Embassy staffs nowadays often include officials based in ministries other than that of foreign affairs. Moreover, the overseas development agencies of a number of OECD states (DANIDA, DFID, SIDA, USAID, etc.[2]) maintain their own permanent offices in major client countries.

Meanwhile, other governance actors besides states have also developed the functional equivalent of diplomatic services to represent them at various locations across the planet. In this vein, a number of UN agencies maintain country offices, the World Bank has Resident Missions around the world, and the IMF posts Resident Representatives in some 70 national capitals. The European Commission is represented in over 120 countries and at several global governance agencies as well (Jørgenson and Rosamond, 2002). The 'paradiplomacy' of substate authorities was noted earlier. To take one extensively developed instance, the provincial government of Québec maintains 24 offices in 17 countries and sponsors over 120 missions abroad each year (Fry, 2006). Transnational companies generally entrust the execution of CSR policies to public affairs departments that sometimes station staff at subsidiaries abroad and in any case undertake regular overseas missions. A number of civil society organisations maintain permanent representative offices at hubs of polycentric governance like Brussels, Geneva, New York and Washington, DC.

Thus actors who perform the representative function of diplomats in world politics of the twenty-first century are far more diverse than the staff of state foreign ministries working abroad. Traditional diplomats remain important, but they now work in a larger company that also includes representatives of various other kinds of governance bodies. Given the weight of inherited statist conceptions, it may prove difficult to broaden the scope of the term 'diplomat' to apply beyond national foreign services. However, the vocabulary of 'representatives' and 'missions' is more readily adaptable to wider coverage.

Communication

In addition to representing governance institutions in their relations with one another, diplomats have also had a generic function of communicating messages between regulatory actors. In statist circumstances this activity generally entailed in-person delivery of written messages from one national government to another. Under polycentric conditions diplomatic communications involve many more actors besides national foreign ministries, as detailed above. In addition, the communications often occur at distance, indirectly via third parties, and through modes other than the paper document.

Respatialisation of social relations beyond country units to regional and global spheres has occurred *inter alia* through the spread of electronic communications technologies that permit the ready transcendence of territorial distance and borders. Today's diplomats (of the multiple kinds described above) use telephone, fax and Internet far more than 'snail mail' and old-style pouches to transmit messages between head offices and field representatives. These communications operate with transplanetary instantaneity, thereby greatly quickening the pace of diplomacy. Arguably such increased speeds – coupled with the far larger volumes of communications that digital technologies enable – constrain possibilities for reflective deliberation in day-to-day decision taking.

In addition to faster and larger flows of messages among multiple kinds of regulatory actors, diplomatic communication in a polycentric mode of governance is complicated with the growth of diverse types of content. Not only are written words now transmitted in several other ways besides the post, but in addition far more communication occurs through mediated images and sounds – via telephone, radio, television and websites. Tone of voice, body language and visual backdrops all take on added significance in these communication processes. Diplomats today therefore need to have a larger toolkit of interpretive skills to decipher the messages that other parties are conveying.

With a multitude of agencies using multiple forms of communication, diplomacy under polycentric governance has become more visible to outside parties and the public at large. For one thing, it is difficult to contain information in restricted circles when many kinds of actors are involved in dense and overlapping channels of communication. Polycentric diplomacy is therefore much more prone to leaks than its statist predecessor. In addition, the spotlight of 24/7 mass media also brings many diplomatic communications into public view and makes it far harder to carry forward the confidentiality and discretion that generally characterised diplomacy in statist times. Indeed, under the currently reigning culture of 'transparency' the secrecy mode of old is widely regarded as being undesirably undemocratic. Greater openness in diplomacy in turn creates greater possibilities for third parties to intervene in and reshape the course of communications between governance actors. Aware that their messages may quickly reach third parties, diplomats tend to be more circumspect in their exchanges.

On other occasions diplomats today deliberately address their communications to public audiences in so-called 'public diplomacy'. As Bruce Gregory later details in his Chapter 14 of this volume, this mode of diplomatic communication has obtained a much-enhanced role under contemporary conditions of polycentric governance. Many states have established substantial information agencies, educational programmes, cultural exchanges and world broadcasting services as part of their diplomatic practice. Similarly, many suprastate, substate and private regulatory bodies have over recent decades acquired enlarged 'public information' and 'external relations' operations that aim through communications strategies to enhance outside perceptions of the agency in question.

Negotiation

Like representation and communication, negotiation is a third generic function of diplomacy that has become considerably more complicated with the transition from statist to polycentric governance. As negotiators, diplomats help to pilot the parties that they represent through conflicts of interests and identities. Preferably diplomats can handle these differences without the parties resorting to violence, although negotiation processes sometimes involve the threat and/or use of armed force and economic blockades, as well as the subtle violence of arbitrary social structures such as racism and gender hierarchies.

In part diplomatic negotiation has become more complex under polycentrism owing to the larger numbers and more diverse kinds of actors that are now involved in the process. The 1815 Congress of Vienna and the 1944 Bretton Woods Conference were far different affairs in this respect compared to current events like UN summits and Annual Meetings of the IMF and the World Bank. Likewise, contemporary trade governance encompasses simultaneous bilateral, regional and global negotiations that in turn each involve substate, state, suprastate, corporate and civil society actors. Many more parties with many more objectives need to be acknowledged.

Contemporary diplomatic negotiation is also substantially complicated by the cultural diversity of the parties involved. Under statist conditions, diplomats for the most part shared core assumptions, vocabularies, signals and rituals. Westphalian states often had clashes of interests and identities, but the diplomats who negotiated those differences generally drew on a common underlying knowledge framework in order to define, communicate and manage the problems. Although often highly challenging to resolve, conflicts of *national* interests and clashes of *national* identities in statist times were less difficult to the extent that the parties involved operated in broadly the same cultural mode.

In contrast, under contemporary conditions of polycentric governance diplomats (of the wider scope described before) represent not only diverse kinds of institutional actors, but also diverse kinds of collective identities. For one thing, world politics today involves several sorts of territorially identified 'peoples'. Not only are there state-nations that link national identities with the territorial jurisdiction of an existing state. In addition, many ethnonational identities are active 'below' the state (and often expressed through substate authorities), while several region-nations are emergent 'above' the state (and manifested partly through macro-regional governance bodies). On top of this multiplication of territorial identities, contemporary globalisation has also encouraged the rise of a host of non-territorial identities. Many people now associate substantial parts of their senses of being, becoming and belonging with social categories such as class, disability, gender, race and sexuality. Expression of these identities often occurs through civil society associations as well as, if not more than, through public governance agencies and associated political parties.

Clearly negotiation within a single identity frame, as marked the statist diplomacy of old, is much more straightforward than negotiating through diverse identity frames, as distinguishes diplomacy under polycentric governance. Instead of dealing solely in state-national interests, diplomacy today also involves negotiation among objectives framed in relation to various other political identities. Indeed, in contemporary politics many persons (including diplomats themselves) tend to hold far more hybrid identities, in which several conceptions of social affiliation and solidarity converge on the same individual. With hybrid identities, people may moreover shift their emphases among these different conceptions as they move between different contexts, so that much negotiation of identities occurs within the self at the same time as between various group actors.

To make diplomatic negotiation still more complex, different political identities can also involve radically different modes of knowledge. In some cases the parties in contemporary diplomatic negotiations may even bring to the table distinctly non-modern and non-rationalist life-worlds, for example, of indigenous cultures or revivalist religions. Such challenges of intercultural negotiation are not entirely new, of course, having also occurred *inter alia* when Westphalian states engaged with non-western polities in colonial encounters. However, the more reflexive modernity of the present day urges diplomats to relate to the cultural Other with post-imperialist respect, reciprocity and responsibility. The skills for such alternative negotiating practices remain on the whole underdeveloped.

In sum, the practice of successful diplomacy in contemporary polycentric governance presents a tall order. Representation must cover many more actors. Communication must handle faster speeds and larger volumes of messages delivered through multiple technologies and diverse kinds of auditory and visual signals. Negotiation must address not only a proliferation of parties, but also a diversification of political identities and life-worlds. Thus the study of diplomacy is anything but obsolete. Redefined to reflect recent historical changes, the subject has arguably never been as important.

Notes

This chapter was written while the author was Olof Palme Guest Professor at the School of Global Studies, Gothenburg University. I am grateful to the Swedish Research Council for generous support of this study leave.

1. The Association of Southeast Asian Nations (ASEAN); the African Union (AU); the Black Sea Economic Cooperation (BSEC); the Central American Common Market

(CACM); the Caribbean Community and Common Market (CARICOM); the Commonwealth of Independent States (CIS); the East African Community (EAC); the Economic Community Of West African States (ECOWAS); the Gulf Cooperation Council (GCC); the Southern Common Market (MERCOSUR); the North American Free Trade Agreement (NAFTA); the Organization of American States (OAS); the Pacific Islands Forum (PIF); the Southern Africa Development Community (SADC); the South Asian Association for Regional Cooperation (SAARC); and the Arab Maghreb Union (UMA).

2. The Danish International Development Agency (DANIDA); the UK Department for International Affairs (DFID); the Swedish International Development Cooperation Agency (SIDA); and the United States Agency for International Development (USAID).

Part II
Authority beyond the State

4
EU Governance and Global Governance: New Roles for EU Diplomats

David Spence

Introduction

The holders of international power and authority produce expectations for global governance both through their own behaviour and through the governance standards they expect and frequently require from their partners abroad. How the increasingly powerful European Union (EU) meets such expectations and imposes its requirements form a key theme of this chapter. A second theme is the innovative and mutually reinforcing interaction between EU governance and global governance, of which EU diplomats are the prime architects. Indeed, just as the evolving features of European governance have clearly resulted in new forms of diplomacy between the member states of the EU, there are new roles for Europe's diplomats outside the EU – not least at the United Nations (UN) and in relations with other multilateral and regional organisations. In fact, the practical interaction of the EU with the institutions of global governance and its self imposed role as a purveyor of norms for 'good' governance worldwide are two crucial features of a conscious process of norm-setting by European governments, their diplomats and the officials of the EU institutions.

The EU's own system of governance arguably exhibits greater transparency, higher involvement of civil society and more explicit focus on governance issues than do the majority of national systems worldwide. And diplomats operate in a more transparent system of governance at EU level than they are accustomed to at home.[1] Open government may be easier when there are no 'national' interests to defend. As a newcomer to world politics, it is not surprising that the EU's notions of 'good governance' are more explicitly and more frequently carried into the international environment by EU policy than they would be in the context of a national foreign policy, with distinct national interests to defend.[2] Yet, the global impact of EU governance is subject to two important structuring factors. First, there is a 'legitimacy' issue. The EU, and thus by definition its system of governance, seemingly lacks the full support and identification of its citizens.[3] (Though, of course, talk of its 'citizens' begs the question as to whether such a citizenry actually exists.) In fact, the EU's legitimacy issue is not about absence of legitimacy, but the absence of community, society or identity within which legitimacy might make sense (Bruter, 2005; Clark, 2005). Nonetheless, the impact of the EU on the domestic lives and international standing of its citizens is enormous.

Second, the EU's long-held view that good governance at home is comfortably exportable is increasingly questioned. As the EU shifts from being a purely civilian power to an international military and security actor, its largesse abroad is becoming more conditional and its methods of operation may be on an increasingly coercive path. The EU's political evolution thus not only raises issues of internal governance, but issues relating to evolving EU attitudes to basic norms of international society, such as respect for state sovereignty and non-interference in the domestic affairs of others. Whilst there are no foregone conclusions about the long-term repercussions of its changing role, EU activism carries implications for international governance itself (Sjursen, 2006).

Smith reminds us succinctly that 'the internal development of European Foreign Policy and the broader development of international issues and structures are co-constitutive' (Smith, 2006: 327); and this chapter exemplifies the point. It focuses on developments in European diplomatic practice against the background of general change within the international system, relating the EU's specific form of supranational governance to its efforts to influence governance in other countries. This chapter's main contribution to this book is thereby two-fold. It lies first in its articulation of the EU's specific stance on the issue of governance itself, for this stance involves taking a position on a major historical tenet of international relations – a state's normative conditions for diplomatic friendship. But it also demonstrates how the EU's interaction with other actors forms a significant contribution to the evolving institutional structure of international affairs.

Europe's changing diplomacy

European foreign policy and its impact on diplomacy

Acting together abroad has led to the establishment of closer and mutually supportive relations between diplomats at both the EU and national level in Europe, but the ontology of these relations is often contested. For example, (see Jönsson's Chapter 2 in this volume) do the new layers of bilateral diplomacy within Europe merely perform the same functions and achieve the same goals as before? And has the traditional bilateral diplomatic agenda within the EU been widened and deepened or been diluted because of the

EU?[4] Is there a distinct EU diplomacy abroad, with objectives and achievements representing more than the sum of its national parts? If any of these questions can be answered affirmatively, then EU diplomacy is something qualitatively new in diplomatic terms, rather than simply an additional layer. As Jönsson observes, much of the time national diplomats pursue specifically national objectives. However, these national objectives in so far as they relate to the world outside the EU, are largely the product of bartering in Brussels. And, through close EU coordination, some national diplomats actually come to share the objectives of their counterparts in other EU member states – even if these shared views are frequently the expression of a lowest common denominator. Importantly, the incentive, even obligation, to reach and defend agreed EU positions demonstrates that some EU diplomats have gradually come to form an epistemic community with somewhat separate personal expectations and diplomatic working procedures from those current in purely national systems.[5] Indeed, these expectations and procedures differ from the working assumptions of diplomats from member states not specifically engaged in work of crucial relevance to (and thus subject to the vicissitudes of) European policy-making. National diplomats in bilateral missions within the EU are often outflanked by international departments of domestic lead ministries. The diplomatic systems of the member states have gradually been attuned to match the fact that foreign policy *between* the member states is no longer about 'high' politics, but rather encompasses the wide gamut of policy-making traditionally falling under the category of domestic or 'low' politics. The subject matter of bilateral diplomacy in the EU is now decidedly 'domestic;' and it is certainly not the bureaucratic property of diplomats. National diplomats in the EU now only co-decide with domestic ministries. They may provide formal coordination of domestic policy inputs to EU policy, but the detailed policy process is technical, and thus escapes them. In addition, final decisions are taken in a European mould and with the cooperation of officials working for the EU institutions.

Some observers underline the weakness of the concept of European diplomacy, stressing the *de facto* dominance of two member states in Europe's Common Foreign and Security Policy (CFSP) – France and the United Kingdom. Both are former colonial powers with worldwide interests and cultural influence, both nuclear powers and both permanent members of the UN Security Council. Their power and cultural strength might be thought inimical to the view that there is an overriding specifically European interest into which national policies can and should be integrated for the benefit of all EU members. After all, if the large states make the running in CFSP policy-making, is not the whole CFSP project primarily a front for their national interests? It is certainly true that the leaders of France and the United Kingdom who pioneered the 1998 St. Malo initiative, which led to the CFSP's expansion into the European Security and Defence Policy (ESDP) and the step change for the EU from civilian to military power status, needed EU solidarity in order to both strengthen and legitimise their own national action abroad. But, the small states, too, have a distinct interest in the CFSP. Through European togetherness, their participation allows them to 'punch above their weight,' to focus on geographic and functional areas outside their national purview and practical national experience.

Overall, the EU's Member States usually make policy in concert. They coordinate closely in regular meetings of senior diplomats and foreign ministers, prepared by a welter of CFSP (second pillar) working groups, or regional or functional working groups (first, second and third pillars). It is the resulting shared objectives and policy tools, which actually constitute 'European' policy.

Challenges for EU diplomacy – national and supranational

If some form of multilevel, indeed global, governance is evolving from long assumed international anarchy, there must by definition be implications for traditional diplomacy – that is the work of foreign ministry officials representing governments.[6] EU diplomats are buffeted by the same forces which affect diplomacy everywhere, such as the impact of globalisation, finance ministry constraints, the rise of international departments in domestic ministries and the challenge posed by the media to diplomacy's key function – reporting and commenting on the news from abroad. However, if the work of European diplomats remains part of a system characterised by muddle, incapacity and bureaucratic entanglement, the CFSP and EU 'external relations,' are clearly no longer comparable to the diplomacy of a sovereign state. Moreover, if the world's diplomats believe their own diplomacy is only marginally affected by the challenges of what is termed 'multi-level governance' (Bache and Flinders, 2004), yet are daily obliged to contend with them, EU diplomats in addition contend with the diplomatic implications of the EU's internal governance, its stated supranational aspirations and its increasingly autonomous place in the new international relations. In fact, the EU's emerging roles in the system of global governance bring nuance to the much-mooted anarchy of international relations.

The EU is an actor recognised and welcomed by all. If states have historically achieved legitimacy after hard-won internal battles, the EU has had a form of legitimacy thrust upon it, since the outside world recognises it, welcomes it and places high expectations on it. There may be doubts about which EU institution represents the EU on the world scene, but there is no doubt that expectations from other international actors are that 'someone' will answer their call on Europe itself to act, as opposed to its constituent parts.[7] In a very real sense EU governance must surely epitomise the idea that the Westphalian order, in Europe at least, while not yet dead, is clearly moribund. Some of the underlying premises of this revolutionary development are transposed into the EU's normative prescriptions for the governance systems of its international partners and for global governance itself. EU norms appear in its political and financial support for similar regional arrangements elsewhere; its advocacy of privileged relations with the UN and its agencies and in the large sums of money set aside to finance good governance (i.e., governance based on the EU model) abroad. The evolution of governance in the Economic Community of West African States (ECOWAS) and the African Union (AU) are but two cases in point, as discussed below.

Not surprisingly, there are as many implications, indeed challenges, of evolving global governance for the national diplomacy of the EU Member States, as there are for EU diplomacy itself. As the current European Commissioner (EC) for external relations has put it, 'building a secure and economically strong Europe and playing a leading role in world affairs is the only sensible response to globalisation. That means building a stronger EU foreign policy. The stronger we are, the more we can achieve' (Ferrero-Waldner, 2006). In practice, the 'Ever Closer Union' long projected by the EU means ever closer collaboration between national and European officials, supervised and orchestrated by diplomats. And the rules of the new EU diplomatic game diverge singularly from those of its national counterparts. The accountability of the EU's external action to the European Parliament, for example, is frequently more extensive and complex than the accountability of national diplomats to national parliaments (Brok, 2008). The arrangements for EU Special Representatives and Commission officials, including Heads of Commission Delegations (but not, so far, national ambassadors) to provide input to the work of the European Parliament have, in a sense, demystified the diplomatic profession. There is also more public diplomacy in third countries and activism in support of EU policies and models of governance than is usual in national diplomatic systems. Finally, the combined weight of the EU in economic and financial terms as a partner for states abroad clearly surpasses that of any individual state. The size and quality of EU donorship worldwide not only increase the visibility of the EU's external action, but also underpin its ability to require conditionality for development assistance, based on acceptance of good governance precepts by the recipient. In many of the world's capitals it is the EU ambassador, the Head of the Commission Delegation, who is the most influential local European ambassador.

All these developments not only affect the lives and careers of EU officials. They also affect the character and organisation of national diplomatic systems in Europe. There are developments at two interlinked levels; on the one hand the organisation of foreign ministries and the nature of relationships of foreign ministries and national diplomats with other parts of the governmental structure and, on the other, national diplomatic contributions to patterns of EU foreign policy-making and diplomatic representation outside the EU itself. National diplomats manage and make these policies effective in a collaborative process with the EU's staff in Brussels and the Commission delegations abroad. On one reading this is a graphic illustration of how European diplomacy generally has changed. On another, analysis shows that foreign ministries and national diplomacy have adapted to the new EU diplomatic order, not perished. Indeed, far from being weakened by it, they are flourishing in a rebirth of diplomacy (Hocking, 2005a).

Yet, this rebirth has come about not only because foreign ministries in the EU have created new forms of interaction with domestic ministries and civil society. There is also an extra layer of foreign policy, namely the shift in diplomatic focus on high politics from national capitals to Brussels. The CFSP and its important security and military off-shoot, the ESDP, have also produced a significant series of changes in the diplomatic practice of EU member states abroad at times flanking, structuring or replacing national foreign policy. Both its impact on international affairs and the benefits and constraints of it for member states have been amply analysed (Hill, 2004; Holland, 2004). Equally well reported are the implications for EU diplomacy of recent endeavours to give constitutional shape to a revitalised system of European diplomacy to match the new European foreign policy – the creation of a European foreign minister with a foreign ministry and embassies worldwide, presiding over a policy mix stretching from the external representation of the domestic policies of the *acquis communautaire* to the new world of the ESDP. This is arguably a belated institutional arrival in Europe's political superstructure, mirroring changes long apparent in its economic and social infrastructure and reflecting the transition from nation-state power to a hybrid, non-state, not-quite-intergovernmental, but not yet supranationalism.[8] Despite evidence that EU foreign ministries have adapted their administrative structures and reviewed the means of achieving their international objectives (Hocking and Spence, 2005), there are few analyses of the resulting new forms of diplomatic practice, interaction and governance, which exist without the crowning achievement of formal foreign-ministry structures. They are alive and well, and living in Brussels.

In any case, the conclusion must be that the roles of foreign ministries and the diplomats of individual member states within Europe have altered substantially, creating an important and original new form of governance at the EU level, altering the relations between government departments and foreign ministries and creating new modes of interaction between governments, EU institutions and civil society (Spence, 2004). In fact, the EU institutions' dealings with civil society within the EU are a notable source of stress on systems of national governance. If key constituencies no longer look to the national governmental framework for guidance or see the necessity to influence it, because the authoritative centre of policy-making has shifted to Brussels, then governance has changed, inter-governmental relations and inter-institutional relations within the EU are evolving and new sets of relations between EU institutions and national civil societies are emerging. But, just as the term 'European civil society' is fraught with ambiguity and questionable assumptions (Outhwaite, 2000), EU governance is also a muddle desperately in need of disentanglement.[9]

The norms and values of European governance

Governance, EU governance and global governance

This chapter assumes 'governance' simply to mean the manner in which power relations are managed between governments or other state institutions (international or domestic), civil society and citizens. What 'good' governance might mean is a moot point, though a simple attempt is made below to operationalise the term. Extrapolating from this simple definition, 'global governance' refers to 'cooperative problem-solving arrangements on a global plane ... the complex of formal and informal institutions, mechanisms, relationships, and the processes between and among states, markets, citizens, and organisations – both inter-governmental and non-governmental – through which collective interests are articulated, rights and obligations are established, and differences are mediated' (Thakur and van Langenhove, 2006: 233).

With such definitions of global governance the EU is in its element, for the stuff of academic analysis of European integration and 50 years of continuous constitutional navel-gazing in Europe turn precisely around such terms and definitions. For the EU, there *should* be no exclusive claim to authoritative government at the nation state or regional level, let alone at the global level. Political authority should reside at a level appropriate to the matter at issue, according to a coordinated division of powers – the principle of subsidiarity. This is not just vague political philosophy. Nor is it necessarily naïve to postulate that optimal partnership between levels of government and categories of actor might be a sensible key to settling policy problems. After over fifty years of gradual evolution the significance of EU governance as a challenge to traditional domestic, regional and international governance cannot be doubted. The EU's legal system provides for primacy of EU law above national law. The EC can and does take EU member states to court for disrespect of their treaty obligations, and the European Court can rule against a nominally sovereign state and constrain it to change its national legislation or pay large fines for failing to comply (Tallberg, 2000). The European Parliament now possesses more influence than most national parliaments to encourage or stymie legislation and the EU's external policy worldwide (Jacobs et al., 2007). And the arrival of 'open access as organisational ideology' (Mazey and Richardson, 2006) has brought about qualitatively different relations between government and civil society in Europe.

EU policy is multilateralist, but it is nonetheless oriented by nature and design to a process of close interaction with civil society. As one former Secretary-General of the EC argued, the EU is the greatest civil power in the world (Williamson, 1993).

Governance and legitimacy

An important issue is whether the innovative form of governance described above, given its recognised democratic deficit, is legitimate. Helen Wallace (1993) has argued that legitimation in the EU may only be 'indirect legitimation via the political systems of the member states.' Yet, if the focus of power and authority has changed from the national to the European level, and if civil society with its myriad representative frameworks and NGOs has followed, the aspiration of supporters of the integration process must be that the new European system of governance is more than a new form of indirect government. Legitimate and thus good governance must surely be a form of governance accepted by electorates, recognised and supported by civil society and thus respected by the populace at home and abroad.

In fact, the EU can claim to have involved its institutions with civil society in a far further reaching manner than many of its constituent member states (Mazey and Richardson, 2006). Yet, in terms of popular democracy, the legitimacy of the EU's system of governance is more frequently declared than it is empirically established. Not only is there a 'democratic deficit,' but there are complaints from integrationists that some states opt out or in to bits of EU policy. There are also powerful calls to slow down or even reverse the process of European integration, thus stymieing the further development of this new system of governance located currently somewhere between full national sovereignty and the arrival of legitimate European government structures above state level. However, whilst the EC's White Paper on Communication (2001a) demonstrated that the public are disaffected, they are clearly highly interested in EU matters. If there is a democratic deficit, there must also be a legitimacy deficit.[10] However, the fact remains that years of governmental support for the evolving project of European integration have produced a system of binding rules and agreements, which member states may criticise, but reject at their cost and certainly show few signs of relinquishing. The process of legitimising Europe may be far from successful in terms of producing public support and identification but in terms of practical governance, all actors on the political scene now work within a set of governance parameters far removed from the parameters of national constitutional affairs and there is thus specific European governance.

But is it good governance? The answer is that it is 'good' to the extent that if democratic society is 'good' *per se*, then any extension of it must be positive, providing this does not produce waste, duplication of effort or increase public disaffection. This surely hinges on legitimacy defined as 'the foundation of such governmental power as is exercised both with a consciousness on the government's part that it has the right to govern and with some recognition by the governed that it has a right to govern' (Sternberg, 1968). Undoubtedly, there is a legitimacy conundrum in the EU, and whatever the arguments adduced on either side, it is clearly the case that the EU's potential lack of internal legitimacy stands in seeming contradiction to the EU's acquired legitimacy within the international community (Beetham and Lord, 1998).

Governance as an export commodity

The origins of the EU and its diplomats' beliefs in the virtues of supranationalism underlie the view that the nature of relations between civil society and government within a Europe freed from national conflict and characterised by its ability to resolve differences diplomatically, is a guide to which global governance might aspire. European diplomacy reflects Europe's model of governance, its open society, its professed will to promote stability, security and prosperity, as well as liberal democracy and its own model of regional integration.[11] For every country in the world there is now a basic 'common' EU policy and outside the Organisation for Economic Cooperation and Development (OECD) countries there are accepted 'country strategies,' part of which are country based 'governance profiles,' which provide a justifying basis both for EC aid and for assistance with institutional capacity building. As the EC put it in its report, 'Project for the European Union':

> The EU has a special role to play as regards globalisation. While many European operators are taking full advantage of globalisation, concerns are being voiced over what is seen as a situation in which what certain countries and certain economic entities do has an impact which no one seems to control. This perception inevitably affects the operation of democracies and the legitimacy of public authorities ... it is through the EU ... that the people can defend their model of society ... Europe is a leading international player and is better placed than others to help in the governance and stabilisation of the international system. (European Commission, 2002: 11)

The EU thereby expresses its ambition to be a catalyst in changing the governance of other countries by exporting its own model not only to prospective member states, but to the rest of the world. As a public relations brochure describes, 'the EU shows how countries can successfully pool economic and political resources in the common interest. It serves as a model for integration between countries in other regions of the world' (*A World Player*, 2004). Potential members are guided by the 'Copenhagen Criteria'; governance based on democracy, the rule of law, human rights and market economy principles (Copenhagen Criteria, 1993). Other states are on the receiving end of advocacy of the same principles through conditions attached to bilateral agreements. The EU's power and internal governance thus enhance its attraction to the outside world. Yet, to the vexation of some (from Turkey to the Balkans), as the EU makes membership and diplomatic friendship conditional on acceptance of its own rules of governance, in a distorted compromise it may currently be finding itself constrained temporarily to close its gates lest its own internal governance suffer through lack of political and administrative 'absorption capacity'.

Nevertheless, the EU's 16 neighbouring countries are currently receiving a substantial programme of economic and other aid in exchange for various reforms, following a strategy launched in 2004.[12] To help spread stability beyond its borders, the EU has raised funding for 2007–2013 by 32 per cent, to €12 billion (US$16.5 billion), including 1 billion euros (US$1.37 billion) to help trigger private lending for the most reform-minded neighbours, for more trade, increased cooperation in energy, migration and economic issues, greater financial support and more help to resolve regional conflicts. The EU offers its neighbours financial aid, expertise and easy access to EU markets in return for commitment to across-the-board reforms. The EU's 'ring of friends' programme further includes a great (and complex) variety of participants, from Israel to Ukraine to Libya, and on the EU's own insistence they tackle issues such as migration, terrorism or human rights.[13] However, while most neighbours have made progress in economic and political reforms, other areas still remain problematic, including poverty, corruption, unemployment, mixed economic performance and weak governance. The EU's determination to develop tailor-made partnerships with its neighbours and its offers to help in resolving regional conflicts, shoring up weak frontiers, increasing free trade, helping neighbours raise product norms and standards to the EU level and cutting red tape are matched by its insistence on good governance. Outside the sphere of its own enlargement and its neighbourhood policy, the EU also maintains close bilateral, contractual relations with the rest of the world. Here, to the offence of some (e.g., Australia), the EU insists on acceptance of good governance principles, requiring, for example, a human rights clause in all trade agreements, even with states unlikely to be accused of human rights abuses.

There is thus a demonstrable relationship between its internal governance and the adoption by the EU of a normative position with regard to governance elsewhere. The EU is *par excellence* an exporter of principles of good governance, and its contribution to global governance is not simply the advocacy of its model of governance and a proselytising stance on regional integration. Its emerging roles in conflict prevention and crisis management abroad, structured in terms of global governance by its special relationship with the UN and other regional organisations, both bilaterally and multilaterally, are key features of its influence. Some have argued that this is rightfully so. Ian Manners, the main reference point for this school of thought, has argued that 'the central component of 'normative power Europe' is that the EU is different from pre-existing political forms, and that this predisposes it to act in a normative way' (Manners, 2002: 242), though he is not alone in finding it increasingly difficult to separate the evolving content from the normative potential of policy (Sjursen, 2006). For, there is perhaps a parallel between colonialism's sales strategy as an enlightened policy-maker towards the poor world and the EU emphasis on good governance as an export commodity. Both arguably disguise an extension of self-interest – appearing to be doing the right thing, but maybe for the wrong reason (Bicchi, 2006). This is an accusation which can be levelled at the normative aspirations of any state, not least the United States (Sjursen, 2006). However, the EU lays claim to a role of catalyst of good global governance precisely through enlightened use of the leverage of its soft power in persuading the world to accept its norms, even if it might not always have been successful at it (Emerson et al., 2005).

The perception of the EU's neutrality, distinguished from the partisan nature of its individual member states (the United Kingdom in Sierra Leone, France in the Ivory Coast) enables it potentially to mediate where state actors might not. Its global reach enables it, in principle, to act in any region of the world with the support of its now half century presence on the ground through Commission Delegations. Its readiness to offer both short-term crisis action and long-term technical support is clearly beguiling for its less fortunate partners. And it has recently put its military strength to the service of crisis and conflict management in the Balkans and in the Democratic Republic of Congo, to name but two examples of intervention abroad, with governance packages involving not only support for efficient governance in general, but direct contributions to security sector governance through both advocacy and practical support for military or policing operations. Finally, its commitment to policy coherence, in particular where EU policies have significant impacts on developments in other countries, is allied to a broad array of instruments which facilitate its 'actorness' as an exporter of values. In short, Europe's soft power is crucial. As the external relations Commissioner has argued, 'one cannot simply export or impose ... democratic institutions. But what the EU can and must do is use its transformative power and make sure that reform can grow from within. We want to foster societal change rather than "regime change'" (Ferrero-Waldner, 2007). Indeed, the enlargement Commissioner is even more firm, arguing that

> where we can use the prospect of membership as an anchor for demo-
> cratic transformation, difficult reforms and enhancing freedoms, we
> must use it to the maximum ... In my view, the most valuable part of this

process will be the transformation of Turkey into a more open society with rich cultural diversity and a strong commitment to the values shared by all Europeans. (Rehn, 2005)

Yet, in a world rife with conflict, stress and increasing aggression, the EU may have little future merely as a soft power. States everywhere retain the formal authority and the legitimate monopoly of force at their level. The instruments to tackle global issues and thus their likely resolution need to match the scale of the problems, which reside at the regional, if not the global level. The EU's originality is that it is the only transnational forum which prescribes supranational proposals for solutions to global issues and provides a model of a supranational institutional framework for dealing with them. As a model for global governance the last 50 years of development of external policy instruments, political, economic, commercial and financial, have clearly helped the EU protect and promote European interests and values. Europe's success has placed it in a position where its Development Commissioner can argue 'Nous pouvons ensemble véritablement façonner un monde plus juste et plus équitable, et donc peser sur le destin du monde. Et parce que nous le pouvons, nous le devons' (Michel, 2006).

The creation by the Amsterdam Treaty of the post of High Representative for the CFSP has clearly enhanced the effectiveness of the EU's external action. In the past five years, military instruments have reinforced civil instruments for conflict prevention and crisis management abroad. The current discussion on fusing the mentalities and mechanisms of civil protection at home and abroad (Barnier, 2006; Boin et al., 2006) results from a separate aspect of international governance; the increasing realisation of the dialectic between internal and external security and its implications for the EU's internal policies – the environment, energy, agriculture and fisheries, transport, the fight against terrorism and illegal migration. Thus, while management of internal policy increasingly influences international relationships and plays a vital part in the EU's external influence and its contribution to global governance (e.g., Kyoto protocol), conversely, many internal policy goals depend on the effective use of external policies (e.g., counter-terrorism, the environment and climate change) (Ekengren, 2007). In all these areas Europe clearly has an independent interest in a place at 'the top table' of global governance.

In sum, the EU's relatively successful use so far of soft power may not be the end of the EU story. Over the past decade its economic and political instruments have been expanded by strengthened foreign policy, security and military instruments, so an important question is therefore whether its emerging security policies and structures will enhance its role as a contributor to global economic governance by forming an integral and influential part of emerging global security governance. And, equally important will be the rebound effects within Europe for EU governance, as the EU passes from a civil to a military power. There are 'warrant[ed] concerns about the democratic control of defence policy in Europe' (Wagner, 2006: 201), and the integrity of the EU's own internal governance is thus at risk. As Nye, again, concisely puts it, 'The absence of a warrior ethic in modern democracies means that the use of force requires an elaborate moral justification to ensure popular support' (2004a: 119). These important questions cannot be answered here[14], but it is thus evident that a moral issue lurks in the background. As political integration engenders a military component, it risks taking public opinion and civil society unawares, indeed for granted – a potential compromise of the good by the ambition of the 'better'. As time goes by, the consolidation of the ESDP may come to mean EU readiness to pursue its norms with hard power and a concomitant extension of its foreign policy into the military sphere. This may bring effects on governance not necessarily to the liking of those whose contentment with its soft power has formed part of Europe's permissive consensus for more integration. Manners (2006) argues that the horse may already be bolting, as the EU's hard power develops and its responsibilities expand to encompass military procurement, security sector reform, disarmament, demobilisation, reinsertion of former combatants and policies on small arms and weapons of mass destruction – all arguably eminently good causes – and, of course, actual military intervention. As the EU's ambitions reach further into the main crisis points around the world and it becomes militarily active in joint disarmament exercises, humanitarian and rescue missions, military advice and conflict prevention and peacekeeping, its draft Constitution, and its replacement, the 'mini-treaty', are a formal attempt to legitimise such a role. And a series of policy statements and action in the field of security sector governance (European Commission, 2006b) and disarmament, demobilisation and reintegration of former combatants (European Commission, 2006a) raise the profile and potential role of the EU in the security sector to that of the world's potential (and acceptable) democratic guide dog. Yet, as the realisation filters through to policy-making that military power may be used not only to prevent states from doing harm to their opponents abroad but also from doing harm within their own borders and to their own peoples, who can guarantee that hegemonic aspirations may not be far off?

Though the changed parameters of governance inside the EU may have had a clear impact outside, making the EU an uncontested normative or ethical civil power in international affairs, the EU's nature, and potentially therefore its governance, is fast evolving. Its relations with the rest of the world may be imbued with specific conceptions of governance, and it may increasingly see one of its most important roles worldwide as advocacy of good governance, but its newly stated intention is to use its military power to support, export and, if need be, even enforce these norms of good governance through its programmes of democracy and human rights promotion, its policies on terrorism and its advocacy of its own model of regional integration (European

Security Strategy, 2003) and its stated policy of 'effective multilateralism' (European Commission, 2003) join its new hankering for military intervention to provide a reinforced message on global governance. Good governance, EU style, may be a desirable commodity, and where failed or failing states are reluctant to identify with the associated values, provided there is a UN mandate or a clear humanitarian interest, EU diplomacy may cede its place to more robust forms of power. The danger, of course, is that 'Attraction can turn to repulsion if we act in an arrogant manner and destroy the real message of our deeper values' (Nye, 2004b). Assessing the long-term ethical impact of the EU's evolving contribution to global governance is thus far from easy (Matlary, 2006).

The EU and global governance – the institutional perspective

The EU and the UN in symbiosis

Relations between the EU and the UN are an issue of increasing academic and professional interest (Wouters et al., 2006; Ortega, 2007). In meetings between the UN and regional organisations, given its self-perception as a supranational entity, the EU sits uneasily alongside such organisations as la Francophonie or North Atlantic Treaty Organisation (NATO), which have cultural or military specificity, are not specifically 'regional' as such and have no EU-like pretensions of 'unknown destinations,' involving quasi statehood. Yet, the multiplicity of EU–UN relations puts the EU in a privileged position in terms of the institutional structures of global governance. A glance at the 'EU at the United Nations' website is enough to convince those who might doubt the claim (Europa, 2007). The EU's commitment to 'effective multilateralism' announced its ambition to play an important role in the key international institutions through representation of both member states and the Commission. As to its legitimacy, EU commitment to reinforcing the role of regional organisations for global governance was welcomed both by the UN and by other regional organisations themselves.

Compared with regional organisations the EU has a long-standing and complex *sui generis* bilateral relationship with the UN. Indeed, since the turn of the century the Commission has advocated further enhancement of these relations in its papers on 'building an effective partnership with the UN in the field of development and humanitarian affairs' (European Commission, 2001b) or 'EU–UN relations: The choice of multilateralism' (European Commission, 2003). Such statements of general purpose have been fleshed out in practice by strategic partnerships concluded between the UN and the EC with the objective of developing policy dialogue and cooperation in the fields of development and humanitarian affairs, as well as a string of other issues covered internationally by the UN family and in

Europe by the EU. These strategic partnership agreements are with various UN funds and programmes and specialised agencies – United Nations Development Programme (UNDP), World Health Organisation (WHO), Food and Agriculture Organization (FAO), International Labour Organisation (ILO), United Nations High Commission for Refugees (UNHCR) and World Food Programme – and they are made more precise by additional agreements or exchanges of letters.

Before the 2005 World Summit Outcome Document, the EC proposed that the EU consider concluding an agreement or a memorandum of understanding with the UN 'in order to provide a general institutional framework to the cooperation, building on existing cooperation modalities' (European Commission, 2005: 16). After the document's publication, the EU promised support for a 'stronger relationship between the UN and regional and subregional organisations, pursuant to chapter VIII of the UN Charter.' They added their readiness 'to expand consultation and cooperation with the UN, through a possible formalised agreement' (Council of Ministers, 2005). The resulting international relations are managed by UN and EU officials rather than diplomats *stricto sensu*. In the specific area of international political and security relations, EU–UN cooperation has been strengthened in the field of conflict prevention and crisis management on which the Commission and the UN Department of Political Affairs engage in regular desk-to-desk dialogues (Ojanen, 2006). An EU–UN Steering Committee oversees the implementation of the Joint Declaration on crisis management of 24 September 2003. There is also cooperation at field level, which extends to peacebuilding activities[15] and includes at a more mundane level, though significantly for governance, joint training for EU and UN officials. These various specific efforts at cooperation have been enhanced by the conclusion of a general EU–UN agreement on the exchange of classified information and regular separate meetings between the EU Council and the UN's Department of Peacekeeping Operations (UNDPKO). In addition to the general meetings of the UN with regional organisations, there have been regular high-level meetings twice-yearly between the EU and the UN since 2001. Enhanced cooperation between the Commission and the Council and the UN Departments of Political Affairs (UNDPA), UNDP, Department of Economic and Social Affairs (DESA) and DPKO is growing apace, and significant support is provided by EC financing or co-financing of projects and programmes administered by these UN bodies. They are regulated by the EC/UN Financial and Administrative Framework Agreement (FAFA) signed on 29 April 2003.

Thus, cooperation between the EU and the UN has long been extensive and is now fast-growing, and it would be shortsighted to affirm that this broad activity has little impact on traditional diplomacy. It may have focussed on sectoral approaches, but a new agreement of a comprehensive nature was decided in 2006 as a follow-up to the implementation of the Summit Outcome

Document. Its purpose was enhancement of the overall visibility of EU–UN cooperation in all its aspects, and the highlighting of the role of the EU as a global actor as well as a partner of the UN. By bringing under an overall umbrella existing cooperation activities and mechanisms in various fields, the comprehensive agreement was meant to foster an integrated approach to development, peace and security and human rights, thus reflecting similar concerns within the EU itself and thereby providing a fillip to greater coherence in the EU both within and between the institutions. The agreement covered new and existing sectoral areas of cooperation, including conflict prevention, crisis management, humanitarian assistance, disaster reduction and prevention, development, social issues and environmental concerns. The agreement also provided the framework for addressing horizontal issues such as planning, coherence of action, a multidimensional approach and coordination within the wider UN system.

This was, in short, a framework for overall political cooperation between the EU and the UN involving bi-annual high-level meetings in Troika format (i.e., presidency, Commission and incoming presidency) to provide political guidance in various areas of cooperation, with each meeting focussing on a specific multi-sectoral theme. In addition, where such contacts did not already exist, meetings of senior-level officials now take place both by international agreement, on the basis of the relevant legal provisions of the Treaties[16] or by a political 'agreement.' In practice the implication is a political and administrative arrangement between the UN Secretariat on the one side and the Commission and Council on the other, as the executive branches of the EU, depending on the subject area. It is thus not surprising that the diplomatic implication of this highly structured activity is permanent diplomatic representation of the EU (in fact, legally, the EC) to the UN in New York, Geneva, Vienna, Nairobi, Paris and Rome and the EC's formal status as the only non-state participant in scores of UN multilateral agreements.[17]

The UN and regional organisations – EU governance as a model

Regional organisations have proliferated and diversified since chapter eight of the UN Charter identified them as a key component of global governance (Thakur and Weiss, 2007). Not only are the UN and its agencies represented at regional level worldwide, but regionalism plays a key role in nominations to UN posts, in caucusing to coordinate policy within the UN, in the rotation of the holder of the post of Secretary-General and in the existence at the UN of an observer status for regional organisations. Moreover, despite the fact that regional integration is primarily motivated by trade concerns, with economic performance in sensibly sized market structures a main political objective, there are clear political and security interests at stake as well.[18] In addition, the watchword is now inter-regionalism, as regional organisations attempt to regulate their relations with each other.

Despite differences on what a regional organisation actually is[19] or whether a functional organisation such as the Commonwealth or 'la Francophonie' is a regional organisation at all,[20] the strengthening of cooperation between the UN and regional organisations continues. It was an uncontroversial aspect of the 2005 debate on UN reform. Indeed, such is the consensus on the issue that the Summit Outcome Document provided, in paragraph 170 (a), for expansion of 'consultation and cooperation between the UN and regional and sub-regional organisations through formalised agreements between the respective secretariats.' Relations are thus being enhanced between the officials of international organisations under the supervisory umbrella of the UN, represented by its Secretariat General, with its various component parts – DPA, DPKO, the department of disarmament affairs – and agencies, such as United Nations Educational, Scientific and Cultural Organization (UNESCO), FAO, UNHCR, Office for the Coordination of Humanitarian Affairs etc. The EC argues that 'globalisation and increasing interdependence have abolished many of the old distinctions between internal and external policy challenges'. The Commisson's Strategic Objectives for 2005–2009 emphasize the need for Europe to 'continue its commitment to effective multilateralism as the best way to engage with global partners,'[21] an aim enshrined as one of the strategic objectives of the European Security Strategy and by which the Commission means,

> more than rhetorical professions of faith. It means taking global rules seriously, whether they concern the preservation of peace or the limitation of carbon emissions; it means helping other countries to implement and abide by these rules; it means engaging actively in multilateral forums, and promoting a forward-looking agenda that is not limited to a narrow defence of national interests.[22]

So whether the 2005 'development package' or the post-2012 strategy on climate change is concerned, the Commission has offered active support. As regards global governance, the EU has prioritised the UN reform process, was instrumental in the setting up of the Human Rights Council and the Peacebuilding Commission and is working hard to strengthen environmental governance – all issues described in the 2006 report on the EC–UN partnership, launched in Strasbourg on 24 October 2007. There has thus been clear enhancement of the role of regional organisations within the UN context.

As with its general advocacy of good governance through trade and partnership agreements with individual states, the EU increasingly recommends its own model of economic and political integration as a model for its regional peers. European integration was after all a regional response to the challenge of conflict resolution between nation states, and the EU sees itself as a desirable model for regional integration elsewhere. EU policy towards the AU, for example, is not only to support it as a regional organisation but also to offer practical and financial assistance to adapt the AU's institutions of governance.

The EU's governance initiative in Africa has become an innovative way of implementing policy on governance in individual African, Caribbean and Pacific (ACP) countries and Africa in general. It provides additional funding to ACP countries according to their commitments to achieve results in democratic governance reform programmes. 2.7 billion euros from the tenth European Development Fund have been set aside for this purpose. In addition, the EU is providing political and financial support to the African Peer Review Mechanism, which provides a regional basis for comparative policy implementation, a form of participatory self-assessment for encouraging reforms at country level, mutual learning and strengthening ownership. Ghana, Mauritius, Kenya and South Africa are cited as countries 'farthest along in the process'.[23] In sum, a good deal of time and a great deal of money are invested by the EU in flanking its commitment to support other regional organisations and individual countries and providing a model for their institutional governance.[24]

Conclusion

People tend to believe the UN is a kind of world government with the ability to lay down and enforce the law as a national state government would. So, when they decry the UN's inability to send in enough troops to the world's crisis points or to impose Security Council resolutions on governments keen to assert the primacy of their domestic law and their national constitutions, they provide potential legitimacy for further UN evolution towards world government status. Yet, in a gasp of cognitive dissonance, national governments and citizens worldwide are far from content with the idea that a world government is the answer to the world's problems. One problem is that the UN is only effective when its members provide it with the means and the mandate to act. It thus lacks the legitimacy that comes with independence and elected office. Another is that national power in turn constrains the UN. There is little prospect of the UN evolving into the global government structure that simplistic extrapolation of a federal model might imply, without regional organisations, such as the EU, taking responsibility at appropriate political levels for policy and action.

Subsidiarity could be the name of the global governance game, as it is increasingly the name of the EU game. But this is a pious hope, which leaves us with the dilemma of the need for an orderly set of relations between economic and political power holders and the world's citizenry and civil society. The future might well resemble some form of global government model, but for the time being governments and society must be resigned to the ambition of good global governance, without global government, as a provisional solution to the challenge of globalisation. Significantly, the system of EU governance may be a model for such global governance. Certainly, the notion in the EU that Europe is greater than the sum of its nonetheless important parts is a strikingly apt model for the UN. That Europe is such a model, long an unspoken EU view, has become the EU's increasingly declared ambition. As the European Commissioner for Development put it in 2007 when setting out the EU's system of governance conditionality: 'Ce que l'Europe fit, l'Afrique va le faire' (Michel, 2007).

As to where diplomacy fits in, for the time being national and European diplomats have key roles to play in developing both European and global governance, but variable geometry in terms of representational networks will likely continue to prevail at national, European and international levels. Whether the future will prove a positive or negative sum game between national and EU diplomats as epistemic communities is an issue that will certainly provide pointers to the evolution of diplomacy per se. In Europe, at least, there is the real prospect of more diplomatic functions being transferred to the regional level in continuance of an already well-established process. Consular affairs, for example, or international aid may one day be managed at the European, rather than national level; they are already 'coordinated' at European level and subject to increasing 'Europeanisation'. This may encourage the EU's partners in regional organisations to reflect in their own polities the practical structures of EU governance with which they are obliged to contend. The limits to such developments will doubtless be found on the one hand in the extent to which such supranational cooperative arrangements are perceived as threats to unambiguous national presence abroad, for purposes of public and commercial diplomacy, for example. And on the other hand, developments may be limited by stresses within EU governance, brought about, for example, by the debate on the limits of political generosity to ethnic or religious minorities, or on the military component of governance at EU level, both of which are issue areas replete with implications at domestic and international levels likely to be mirrored in regional organisations elsewhere.

European governance may be a contribution to global governance by acting as an institutional role model for other regions, both in terms of its manner of coordinating and resolving issues and its capacity to provide a normative framework for others to resolve their national and regional conundrums. Evidence from ECOWAS and the AU seems to demonstrate that EU governance and government are models on which they base their own institutional modalities. They have taken on the EU's lessons for governance both because the EU's policy makes acceptance of its precepts for governance a *sine qua non* of fruitful relations, but also because of the undoubted success of the EU institutional model – even if this is questioned internally in the EU and its legitimacy is as hard to find as it is to define. Nonetheless, Europe's apparent consensus – *pace* the democratic deficit – on governance may be the basis for a similar consensus at global level. The proposal by four members of the European Parliament that the UN should itself be doted with a proper parliamentary assembly is but one element that might need consideration (Watson et al., 2007).

But painfully difficult issues lie on the horizon. Both the UN and the EU 'mask rough political reality through ostentatiously pompous rhetoric' (Ojanen, 2006), as one academic puts it. Sooner or later the EU will have to address a whole string of areas where there has been no European debate so far, but where global governance is likely to be increasingly put to the test: the use of force without a UN mandate; the doctrine of pre-emption against international terrorism; regime change and the use of force in the framework of the obligation to protect; and the idea of 'unreasonable vetoes', whether in the UN Security Council or the European Council. EU governance still needs focus, but since the destination remains unknown, perhaps for the time being, it is the journey, not the arrival that matters. But this may seem weak reasoning if, as this chapter has identified, there is a risk of civilian power Europe becoming super-power Europe, as is increasingly feared (Telò, 2006; McCormick, 2007).

In conclusion, the EU might do well to 'out' the concept of its own governance forming a basis for new forms of global governance, for these are little known concepts, despite their forming the core of EU–UN relations. Why push the idea? Because continued institutional cooperation and large leaps of faith will be needed if global governance is to contribute, in the long term, to some acceptable, even desirable, form of global government.

Notes

1. This somewhat cavalier statement requires nuance in so far as some Nordic systems are clearly more transparent than their counterparts in other European countries (Bailes et al., 2006). The Council is also not uncontestedly transparent, since it imposes strict conditions on sight of sensitive documents, arguing for example that the European Parliament has no remit for security issues. See *European Voice*, 19–25 October 2006. It is unlikely that national parliaments in general would be afforded better access, however.
2. Again, this is a broad generalisation to which there are notable exceptions; such as the UK's once declared 'ethical' foreign policy, though on the reality behind this aspiration see Pilger (2006).
3. This is recognised in the European Commission's own communication on governance. See European Commission (2001a).
4. For an insightful analysis of the state and fate of bilateralism in Europe see Bátora and Hocking (2007).

5. I differ here from the assumption of Cross that diplomats *per se* are an epistemic community, holding, rather, that there are specific epistemic communities *within* the diplomatic community (Cross, 2007). This is not the place for an exhaustive analysis of the point.

6. I avoid using the term 'diplomacy' to cover representation of anything other than states. I prefer to define diplomacy as what diplomats do professionally. Diplomats are foreign ministry-officials representing their state abroad, or usually so doing. By this I mean that these officials may sometimes return to base and are not called upon there to represent their state, but they nonetheless remain 'diplomats' in the same way as actors remain actors even when they are 'resting'.

7. This conundrum is summed up in 'Who 'ya gonna call?', *The Economist*, 1995.

8. See Bátora (2005), Robert Cooper (2003), Hocking and Spence (2005) and Spence (2006).

9. A good critical attempt at disentanglement can be found in MacMullen (2002).

10. For an insightful discussion of the issue see Barker (2003).

11. An interesting summary of the norms and values embodied in the EU's draft constitution can be found in Emerson et al. (2005) 'What Values for Europe? The Ten Commandments'. CEPS Policy Brief No. 65. Centre for European Policy Studies.

12. See European Neighbourhood Programme, available from http://ec.europa.eu/world/enp/index_en.htm

13. The 16 neighbours are Algeria, Armenia, Azerbaijan, Belarus, Egypt, Georgia, Israel, Jordan, Lebanon, Libya, Moldova, Morocco, the Palestinian Authority, Syria, Tunisia, and Ukraine. Libya, Belarus, and Syria will attend as observers

14. For more see Hänggi and Winkler (2003).

15. Examples of cooperation in the field include the hand-over of the UN Police Mission ITPF to EUPM in Bosnia–Herzegovina, the MONUC takeover from the EU military operation Artemis in the Democratic Republic of Congo, the EU pillar of the UN Mission in Kosovo, as well as peacebuilding activities such as close cooperation with UNAMA and UNDP in Afghanistan, Commission-UN cooperation on elections in Iraq, EC support and collaboration with the UN Mine Action Service (UNMAS) and UNDP.

16. In this regard, it is important to recall article 300 of the Treaty establishing the European Community which sets out the procedure to be followed for the conclusion of an agreement between the Community and international organisations, that is recommendation by the Commission to the Council for authorisation to open negotiations and a negotiating directive issued by the Council. On the other hand, article 24 of the Treaty on European Union regarding agreements between the EU and international organisations on CFSP matters, envisages authorisation by the Council to the Presidency, assisted by the Commission as appropriate, for the opening of negotiations; such agreements are then concluded by the Council. As for article 302 of the Treaty establishing the European Community, it provides that '[i]t shall be for the Commission to ensure the maintenance of all appropriate relations with the organs of the United Nations.'

17. For an analysis see Wouters et al. (2006).

18. For a recent comprehensive analysis of the economics of various regional integration endeavours see de Lombaerde, Philippe ed. (2007).

19. That is whether or not it is a regional organisation in terms of chapter 8 of the UN charter or not – the EU claims it is not.

20. They both are for the purposes of UN coordination of and relations with regional and other organisations.
21. See Commission of the European Communities, 2005b.
22. See Commission of the European Communities, 2003, 3.
23. See European Communities, 2007, 15.
24. The EU's basic document on EU–UN cooperation is peppered with references to the aspirations of the EU to be a model for other regional organisations (European Commission, 2003).

5
Business – Government – NGO Relations: Their Impact on Global Economic Governance

Raymond Saner and Lichia Yiu

Introduction

This chapter builds on previous research and exploratory studies on business diplomacy (Saner, Sondergaard and Yiu, 2000; Saner and Yiu, 2005), post-modern economic diplomacy (Saner and Yiu, 2003), development diplomacy (Saner, 2006), multistakeholder diplomacy (Hocking, 2005b) and the polylateralism of diplomacy (Wiseman, 1999). It offers new insights into the nexus between the various forms of diplomacies as they interact within the context of international business, international relations, international economic policy and multilateral trade organisations, such as the World Trade Organization (WTO).

Globalisation has transformed international economic relations around the world, affecting the economic, social and political spheres of societies and citizens. It is characterised by a complex set of interconnectivities and interdependencies with an increasing number of actors vying to influence the outcome of these economic relationships.

State and non-state actors lay competing claims to resources, markets and legitimacy and are engaged in activities traditionally defined as belonging to the domain of diplomacy. Moreover, the proliferation of state and non-state actors engaged in international economic policy-making can cause various forms of dissonances and conflicts. This 'democratisation' of the diplomatic space has also put into question whether the existing forms of discourse between these state and non-state actors hinders or furthers international economic policy-making. It has also raised the question of whether there is a need for the creation of an international governance structure that would provide a constructive policy framework within which the various actors' interactions could be embedded and channelled.

This chapter follows the following structure. As a first step, different types of contemporary diplomacy within the international economic sphere are introduced and discussed. In a subsequent section, these concepts will be illustrated by examining a multi-actor diplomacy case namely the multi-lateral negotiation of trade in Educational Services (ES)within the WTO/ GATS context.

Co-existence of divergent and convergent diplomatic roles in the international economic policy sphere

Looking more closely at the developments in the international economic sphere, one can notice a further broadening of actors involved in economic diplomacy. In addition to state actors, one can observe increasing participation in this sphere by transnational companies and transnational Non-Governmental Organisations (NGOs) who not only interact with traditional state actors but also increasingly engage each other directly on issues pertaining to international economic policy.

The new entrants to the diplomatic arena represent different groupings and organisations of local, national and international interests who pursue convergent and divergent interests. These multiple forces co-exist with each other and exercise different forms of diplomatic influence to achieve their objectives. Commenting on the increase of non-state actors, Langhorne (1998: 58) states that: 'private organisations are developing their own diplomacy both between themselves and between actors in the state system; and the way they have been doing it is remarkably reminiscent of the early days of state self representation.'

The proliferation of diplomatic roles and actors is indeed stunning. Reflecting on the role and function of non-state actors, Burt and Robinson (1999: 17, 42–43) point out that the international landscape is crowded with Multinational Corporations (MNCs) and NGOs that impact directly on the conduct of international relations, and consequently, on the conduct of diplomacy.

Focusing on the economic sphere at the international level, these newly emerged diplomatic functions and roles of the various state and non-state actors could be categorised in Table 5.1.

Table 5.1   Divergent and convergent diplomatic roles in the international economic policy sphere

	Functions	**Roles**
State actors	Economic Diplomacy	Economic Diplomats
	Commercial Diplomacy	Commercial Diplomats
Non-State actors	Corporate Diplomacy	Corporate Diplomats
	Business Diplomacy	Business Diplomats
	National NGO Diplomacy	National NGO Diplomats
	Transnational NGO Diplomacy	Transnational NGO Diplomats

Non-state actors such as national or international NGOs are adding their voices to international development policy debates by organising, campaigning and lobbying across national boundaries in order to have a greater influence on international development policy-making. This trend has gained major momentum, evidenced by the active involvement of NGOs in international cooperation for development; vocal criticism of unfettered capitalism; conflicts with multinational companies in regard to the exploitation of natural resources; and confrontations with national governments on various socio-economic development policy issues.

Faced with the growing economic and political interdependencies of markets and states, governments have to cope with the increasingly complex and at times turbulent post-modern environment, including the activities of NGOs. Governments need to find effective ways to interact with non-state 'adversaries' such as NGO pressure groups. These competent and well-networked groups monitor and evaluate the performances of governments and multinational companies and demand greater accountability and transparency of their actions. NGOs and other civil society groups have learned to galvanise public opinion to successfully forward their own agendas and effectively to demand greater social and international solidarity.

A well-documented example of successful NGO influence on development policy is Eurodad's advocacy in favour of debt relief of poor and least developed countries. Eurodad is the European Network on Debt and Development. It is a network of 52 development NGOs from 17 European countries working on international economic justice issues.

Prior to the campaigns by Eurodad, the International Monetary Fund (IMF) and the World Bank, faced with the staggering indebtedness of the Highly Indebted Poor Countries, thought that limited debt relief would make the debt of these countries 'sustainable' and allow them 'to grow out of' their debt through economic growth. In contrast, however, Eurodad emphasised that partial debt relief could not help these countries in managing their excessive debt, and that they required more substantial debt forgiveness to fight poverty. The persistent and well-coordinated influence of Eurodad led international financial institutions to adopt a poverty alleviation-based debt policy. The use of such tactics as monitoring policies of international financial institutions; sharing relevant information with other NGOs; coordinating public pressures and promoting alternative policy frameworks; and negotiating text revisions with representatives of the financial institutions and national governments constitute an excellent example of development diplomacy.[1]

Non-state actors, be they NGOs or business lobby groups, have built up formidable trans-border alliances through the effective use of web-based communication, research and publications. They exert increasing pressure on state actors at international organisations, such as the WTO, whose mandate is the setting of rules and standards in the domain of international economic governance. As depicted in Figure 5.1 below, international NGOs headquartered in developed countries, such as World Wildlife Fund (WWF), Association for the Taxation of Financial Transactions to Aid Citizens (ATTAC) and Oxfam, exert influence at times more effectively than is possible by a large number of developing country governments. For instance, transnational NGOs focusing on international economic policy create coalitions with other groups close to the Social Forum movement (also called the Porto Allegre movement). They influence the process by conducting independent policy research and writing position papers and by organising conferences for country representatives of the G77 group of developing and least developed countries. By giving advice and support, for example, they are able to aid these countries gain increased market access for their agricultural products. Most significant of all, major NGOs have gained credibility by opening up parallel policy dialogue spaces thereby directly competing with state actors.

In a similar manner, transnational companies progressively more take matters into their own hands and start their own 'diplomatic' campaigns in different arenas. The need to deal more effectively with national and

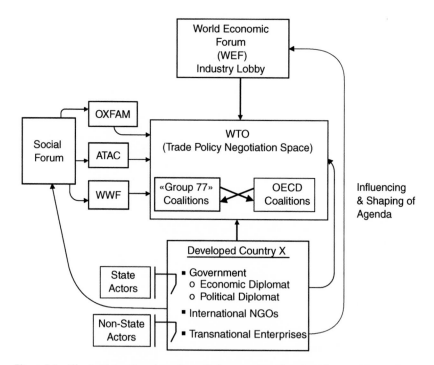

Figure 5.1 Illustration of post-modern diplomacy in a developed economy context – shaping international economic policy by state and non-state actors

international regulatory bodies focusing, for example on competition policy, labour standards, accounting standards (Basle I & II), has propelled business actors to organise their own influencing strategies rather than wait on the sidelines until the respective government representatives have completed their multilateral negotiations. Instead, they have chosen to create parallel dialogue spaces where Transnational Corporations (TNCs) formulate their own policy propositions and then try to sell these solutions to their respective governments.

Business related NGOs active in the international economic policy space such as the World Economic Forum (WEF) have ventured into the foray by organising dialogue space between governments and businesses and are now also expanding their scope of influence by inviting select groups of NGOs to these business-government conferences and meetings. Transnational enterprises attempt to influence government representatives at the annual WEF meeting in Davos or through their Brussels-based lobby groups in order to ensure that the WTO negotiations do not result in agreements that could increase their production and transaction costs. The TNC lobby groups, such as the TransAtlantic Business Dialogue, often hold parallel meetings alongside major summits (G8 Summits, EU–US Summits, etc.) where politicians meet and attempt to inject their agenda into global diplomatic processes and to safeguard their interests.

State actors of developed countries also use alternative arenas to conduct regional or multilateral diplomacy. Representatives of the Ministries of Economic Affairs or the Ministries of Foreign Affairs having to balance a larger portfolio of sovereign interests meet at the Organisation for Economic Cooperation and Development (OECD) and other fora to form coalitions and pre-negotiate common positions in anticipation of the WTO round of negotiations. At the same time, on their respective home fronts, the same state actors are often the target of the opposite influences of business and NGO actors who try to get their agenda items included in the mandate of the country's WTO negotiators.

Managing these competing and collaborative relationships requires the government officials to have the highest proficiency of diplomatic skills. Any misstep is bound to be instantaneously broadcast over the Internet creating negative political fall-out in terms of image loss.

State and non-state actors co-shaping the international economic policy sphere

Diplomatic function and roles of ministries in charge of economic and commercial policy

Faced with a myriad of multilateral standard setting organisations responsible for global economic policies such as the WTO, IMF or OECD, many governments have enlisted the participation of sector specific ministries specialised in economic and financial matters, thereby decreasing or neutralising the influence and role of Ministries of Foreign Affairs (MFAs). For instance, the US government centralised decision-making power in regard to trade negotiations at the WTO (formerly, the General Agreement on Tariffs and Trade or GATT) by creating a new executive office of the president, the Office of the United States Trade Representative, in 1962. In addition, the US government created an interagency command group based in Washington, DC to improve policy coordination during the GATT Kennedy Round thus reducing complexity, limiting inter-ministerial policy disputes and restraining external influencing by members of congress and various lobbying groups (e.g., farm and food processing industry) (Lee, 2001: 119–120).

Efforts by specialised ministries to conduct policy-related international negotiations and to influence the structure and mechanisms of global governance architecture have eclipsed the previous prominence of MFAs in economic and trade arenas. The rise of this non-traditional genre of multi-ministry international diplomacy is, for instance, apparent in Geneva where many permanent missions of industrialised countries to the WTO are staffed by a greater number of officials than is the case at their bilateral embassies in Berne. The greater amount of staff is mostly due to the ever-increasing number of non-MFA diplomats and government officials, who do not share the same foreign service traditions and who do not abide by the same mental model and the same approaches to international diplomacy. This diversity has added different, if not new, dynamism to the international relations and has resulted in greater volatility and unpredictable outcomes of a country's economic negotiations at a multilateral organisation like the WTO.

Whether conducted by traditional diplomats from the MFA or by other government ministry officials (e.g., Ministry of Economic Affairs, Ministry of Trade or Ministry of Trade & Industry) Economic Diplomacy can be defined as follows:

> Economic Diplomacy is concerned with economic policy issues, e.g. work of delegations at standard setting organisations such as WTO and BIS. Economic diplomats also monitor and report on economic policies in foreign countries and advise the home government on how to best influence them. Economic Diplomacy involves the use of economic resources, either as rewards or sanctions, in pursuit of a particular foreign policy objective. This is sometimes called 'economic statecraft' (Berridge and James, 2001: 81).[2]

Governments are also keen to use diplomacy to enhance national economic development by providing support to their own enterprises, for instance in the form of advice on how to improve their exports, e.g., through legal assistance and export incentives when needed. Such support includes helping national enterprises establish subsidiaries in other markets. At the same time, commercial diplomacy can also include functions such as the provision of support to foreign enterprises interested in investing in their respective countries. Thus, commercial diplomacy could be defined as:

> Commercial Diplomacy entails the work of diplomatic missions in support of the home country's business and finance sectors in their pursuit of economic success and the country's general objective of national development. It includes the promotion of inward and outward investment as well as trade. One important aspect of a commercial diplomat's work is the provision of information about export and investment opportunities and organising and helping to act as hosts to trade missions from home. (Burt and Robinson, 1999: 39–39)

In some cases, commercial diplomats could also promote economic ties through advising and supporting both domestic and foreign companies on investment decisions. The difference between *Economic Diplomacy (ED)* and *Commercial Diplomacy (CD)* can best be illustrated in Figure 5.2.

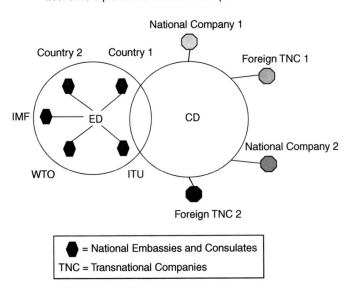

Figure 5.2 The difference between *Economic Diplomacy (ED)* and *Commercial Diplomacy (CD)*

Source: Saner & Yiu, 2003.

Recognising the importance of exports of goods and services and of foreign direct investment to national economic development, governments have increasingly stepped up their efforts in strengthening their commercial representation in major trading partner countries. Commercial diplomats both offer services in this important sphere of diplomacy and they are either civil servants or specially trained diplomats. They can also be representatives of chambers of commerce or of trading associations seconded to national embassies located in important foreign markets. In addition to the traditional function of commercial attachés, government agencies focusing for instance on strengthening internal activities of small and medium sized enterprises have also been given mandates to expand their services, coverage and presence abroad in order to support trade expansion and to conduct commercial diplomacy.

Diplomatic function and roles within multinational enterprises

In order to succeed as a business and ensure the sustainable economic viability of their investments, transnational enterprises must draw on competencies which will allow them to manage the demands of multiple stakeholders at home and abroad. Increasingly, major corporations want to be engaged in the standard setting negotiations in order to sustain their competitive advantage thereby stepping into the traditional arena of the sovereign states. These diplomatic interventions can be observed in both regional and global settings such as the European Union and UN agencies like the WTO, World Health Organization and International Telecommunication Union. Faced with these new challenges, global companies are fast to acquire greater diplomatic capacities and competencies in handling both the internal stakeholders and the external non-business stakeholders.

While companies are more familiar with influencing the governmental apparatus, traditionally known as government relations, MNCs found themselves often ill-prepared and uncomfortable in dealing with the external non-business and non-state stakeholders. Experiences have shown that the latter dealings could be highly problematic for multinational companies if badly or incompetently handled. A case in point is the lawsuit in which large western pharmaceutical companies started and lost against the South African government. The issue was whether a developing country like South Africa could provide cheaper generic drugs needed to treat the growing number of AIDS patients by suspending transnational pharmaceutical companies' patent rights (compulsory licensing option) or whether it had to comply with Intellectual Property Rights (TRIPS) of the WTO and not infringe on patent rights. The TNCs came under tremendous pressure by international NGOs and finally bowed to the mounting domestic and international pressure from activists groups and their public diplomacy machine.

The goal of the diplomatic function within a multinational company is two-fold. On the one hand, it is to ensure continuation and structural cohesion within the diverse web of headquarter and subsidiaries companies so as to reduce labour costs and business risks.[3] On the other hand, it is to deal with the company's external constituencies and stakeholder groups in terms of reputation and in regard to limiting possible pressure on the TNC exerted by various societal groups and organisations in order to maintain favourable market conditions of doing business globally. This function could be thus divided into two, namely, that of corporate diplomacy and of business diplomacy. The former, according to G. Hofstede,

> is primarily targeted at the internal cohesion within a multinational corporation. It consists of two organizational roles considered to be critical for the successful coordination of a multinational company, namely that of a country business unit manager who *should be able to function in two cultures: the culture of the business unit, and the corporate culture that is usually heavily affected by the nationality of the global 'corporation';* and that of a corporate diplomat who as a home country staff or other national is *impregnated with the corporate culture, multilingual, from various occupational backgrounds, and experienced in living and functioning in various foreign cultures. These two roles are essential to make multinational structures work, as liaison persons in the various head offices or as temporary managers for new ventures* (Hofstede, 1991: 213, emphasis original)

In contrast to corporate diplomacy, business diplomacy aims to make the external environment of its subsidiaries conducive for business activities (Figure 5.3). Demands from the local communities on corporate conduct (present, past and future) limit the range of freedom of corporate behaviour. If external constituencies and pressure groups are incompetently managed, this deficiency could quickly result in millions of dollars in costs (e.g., settling of damage claims) or lost business opportunities.

Traditionally, big enterprises hire former ambassadors or state secretaries (in the United States) to promote business contacts and in order to obtain lucrative contracts. However, business diplomacy extends beyond the domain of public relations and business contacts. It deals with on the one hand, the communities and consumer groups at the grassroots level, and on the other, with the international community. Civil society actors are far more fragmented than states or other transnational enterprises and therefore are more challenging to deal with. Nevertheless, civil society organisations can cause a multitude of challenges to transnational enterprises that cannot be ignored or swept under the carpet. Civil society actors have the possibility and capability to 'coerce' MNCs long after the wrong business practices had been corrected or proven to be unfounded. An excellent example of this is the long lasting reputational

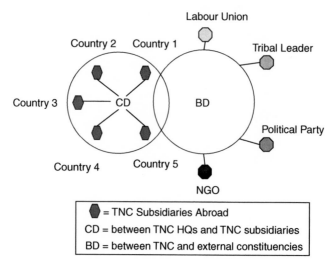

Figure 5.3   Corporate diplomat vs. business diplomat

Source: Saner & Yiu, 2003.

Note: Figure 5.3 illustrates the contrasting functions between the *Corporate Diplomat* and the *Business Diplomat* regarding their diplomatic space.

loss that Nestlé[4] had to suffer from the baby milk formula controversy. Business diplomacy against this backdrop could hence be defined as follows:

> Business Diplomacy pertains to the management of interfaces between the global company and its multiple non-business counterparts and external constituencies. For instance, global companies are expected to abide by multiple sets of national laws and multilateral agreements set down by international organizations such as the World Trade Organization (WTO) and the International Labour Organization (ILO). On account of a global company, Business Diplomats negotiate with host country authorities, interface with local and international NGOs in influencing local and global agenda. At the firm level, they will help define business strategy and policies in relation to stakeholder expectations, conduct bilateral and multilateral negotiations, coordinate international public relations campaigns, collect and analyse pertinent information emanating from host countries and international communities. (Saner et al., 2000: 80–92)

Diplomatic function and roles within non-governmental organisations

NGOs interested in economic policy focus on economic governance, international economic development and global business practice. There are also many other areas in which NGOs are active. Distinction needs to be made here between NGOs acting within national boundaries and those operating on the international level through their own foreign outlets, as well as through alliances with like-minded Transnational NGOs (T-NGOs). Economic NGOs can be categorised according to their sphere of activism as national or transnational (Figure 5.4). National NGO diplomacy refers to the diplomatic manoeuvres by civil society actors who try to bring about policy changes. Such domestic type of NGO diplomacy in the economic sphere consists of various local constituencies ranging from consumer protection, anti-corruption to shareholder groups and environmentalists. They tend to champion grassroots or national issues.

The number of national NGOs is growing in leaps and bounds partially because the public now has greater and faster access to information and yields stronger influence on corporate governance. Their voices and opinions can no longer be ignored by the holders of political and economic power. Transnational NGO diplomacy, on the other hand, is used by T-NGOs who employ statecraft in their advocacy of particular economic or trade policies in the international arena. This could range from calling for new policy initiatives (e.g., debt forgiveness for highly indebted developing countries) to calling for new international standards to reform of international economic governance structure.

T-NGOs such as the WWF, Greenpeace, ATTAC and Focus on the Global South are able to organise advocacy events and lobbying activities at cross-border levels. T-NGOs excel in creating for instance coalitions and in orchestrating mass mobilisation against international economic governance institutions such as, the WTO, WEF, IMF or transnational enterprises. T-NGOs are also capable of putting forward their own policy solutions in international arenas. Examples of arenas in which such policy solutions were promoted include, the multilateral negotiations on the Kyoto Protocol agreement, the debt rescheduling of least developed countries at the IMF, or the blocking of the negotiation of a multilateral convention on foreign investment at the OECD. In the case of the World Summit for Information Society (WSIS), representatives from the civil society at large have gotten seats on the governing body. Their inclusion at this level was unprecedented and represented the ascending power and successful diplomacy of the T-NGOs.

T-NGOs are also involved in implementing technical cooperation projects in developing and transition economies thereby complementing, at times even substituting, the effort of national governments. They also offer cutting edge research in domain areas crucial for international cooperation and crisis management.[5] True to the letter of being a 'non-partisan actor',

T-NGOs pursue their own economic agendas backed by distinctive political orientations and their own 'power bases' in terms of representation.

In contrast to national NGOs, transnational NGOs actively seek ways to influence the agenda at international governance bodies. They are doing so by putting forward their policy recommendations, by lobbying in the corridors of power and by presenting field data to confront the issue blind spots within the mainstream international community. The dialogue between major transnational NGOs and the World Bank during recent annual conferences of the Bank is one of the examples of this activity. Due to their domain expertise and their true transnational characteristics, these non-state actors have taken the lead in many international fora and narrowed the range of operational freedom of traditional diplomats.

To give an example of the complexities of post-modern diplomacy and the growing importance of NGOs, Edward Finn cites the following statement attributed to former US Deputy Secretary of State, Strobe Talbott: 'In Bosnia, nine agencies and departments of the US government are cooperating with more than a dozen other governments, seven international organisations and thirteen major NGOs...to implement the Dayton Accords' (Finn 2000: 144–145).

Seen from this perspective, it appears evident that the increasing complex arrangements of international relations lead to new challenges and opportunities for both state actors and non-state actors alike. Governmental

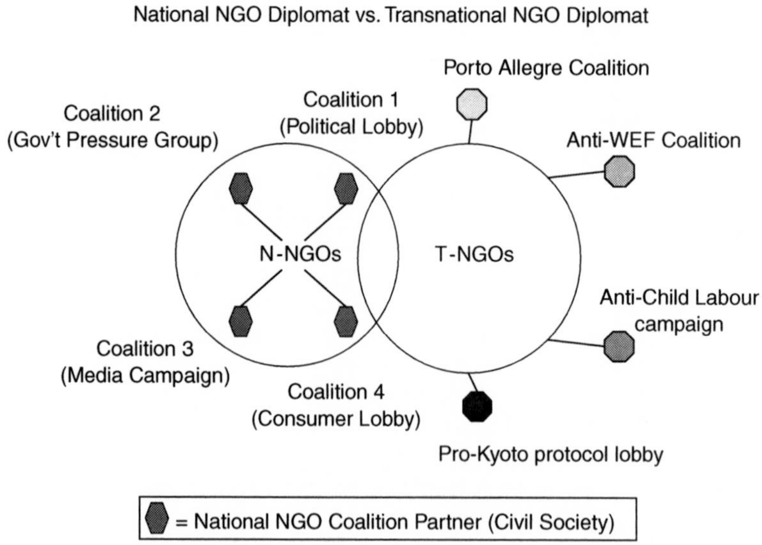

Figure 5.4 Territorial spaces of advocacy by the national NGO diplomat and transnational NGO diplomat

Source: Saner & Yiu, 2003.

diplomacy, as stated by Riordan (2003), must deal with non-state actors in order to take advantage of their knowledge, information and experiences, and to involve them in the policy and decision-making process. At the same time, if government diplomacy is able to include views by non-state actors where useful and appropriate, it might be able to reassert itself and represent legitimacy and accountability in the post-modern diplomacy context.

A case example of this post-modern diplomacy characterised by the participation of multistakeholders is presented in the section below. This case study illustrates the complex and controversial negotiations within the WTO. It also illustrates the transition from 'the club' to the 'multistakeholders' model at the WTO (Hocking, 2004a) characterised by increasing porous boundary and fuzziness in its rules of engagement.

Case example: negotiations of trade in educational services at the WTO

Education is one of 12 sectors covered by the General Agreement of Trade in Services (GATS) which together with the articles governing the global trade of goods constitute the rule making body of the WTO. Even though trade in ES has been part of the WTO since its inception in 1995, little progress has been achieved so far by the Contracting Member Parties in terms of commitments towards market access and liberalisation of their respective educational sectors.

The main reason for the slow pace of negotiations in ES is due to the often bilaterally opposed strong opinions and beliefs by various interest groups who either see education as a service sector activity, which should be open to competitive market forces, and others who consider education as being part of the public service, which governments are supposed to regulate and administrate for the benefit of equitable access of their citizens to schools and universities. The latter castigate trade in ES as being a form of 'McDonaldisation' or 'commoditisation' of education, while the first group emphasises the option to provide individuals of all countries with access to wider educational options, of higher quality and at more affordable prices than could be obtained through traditional state run and controlled schooling systems.

Vested interests, both in favour and against liberalisation of the educational sector, have been entering the debate trying to influence the negotiation process. In fact, the educational sector is becoming increasingly international and the issues debated inside and outside the WTO on trade in service more generally, have become to a large extent overtaken by the concentration on and the developments in the educational market. What follows is a short description of the state and non-state actors involved in this process and how they are attempting to influence the outcome of this multilateral economic and social negotiation process.[6]

Divergent and convergent interests around and within GATS/ES negotiations

Support and opposition towards trade in ES manifests itself across professional boundaries, international organisations, regions, and the North/South divide between developed and developing countries.

While the majority of the privately run schools in OECD countries are concerned mostly with regulations that potentially restrict the purchasing of ES, others have invested abroad and are keen on improving investment conditions, especially in regard to unhindered market access and non-discriminatory investment conditions in foreign countries. Lobbying groups representing private sector actors with Foreign Direct Investment (FDI) interests in ES have actively attempted to influence governments' negotiation positions on GATS/ES.

Some of the better-known groups like GATE (Global Alliance for Transnational Education), Sylvan Learning Systems and QA (The Centre for Quality Assurance in International Education) are closely linked to privately held schools and universities that have business interests and subsidiaries spread in multiple countries. While many of these lobby groups emanate from the United States, some are also based elsewhere as, for instance, Monash University of Australia with its many off- and on-shore campuses in East Asia. The Monash University has developed an interesting strategy as it is a public institution inside Australia but becomes a private provider as soon as it exports its ES abroad.

The large majority of publicly held schools and universities have lobbied strongly against GATS/ES. On 28 September 2001, the presidents of the European University Association, the Association of Universities and Colleges of Canada, the American Council on Education, and the Council for Higher Education Accreditation signed a joint declaration on higher education and trade in ES/GATS strongly expressing opposition to the inclusion of higher education services in the GATS negotiations. The joint declaration asks all actors in the GATS negotiations not to make commitments in ES in the context of the GATS. At the same time, the signatories expressed a willingness to reduce obstacles to international exchange in higher education using conventions and agreements located outside of a trade policy regime.

The negotiation oscillates between stakeholders pushing for liberalisations of educational markets and other stakeholders wanting to keep education out of any market access negotiations at the WTO (see Figure 5.5).

The opposition between market liberalisers and protectionists is played out within countries, between government ministries (e.g., ministry of trade versus ministry of education), between government and private sector (privately owned schools versus publicly held schools), between professional groups and public actors (teachers and student associations versus ministries of finance, education and trade).

Based on these complex interests, coalitions are being formed for or against such positions (liberalisation versus protectionism) within countries, at the WTO and outside the WTO (e.g., at United Nations Educational, Scientific and Cultural Organization (UNESCO), OECD) (see Figures 5.6 and 5.7).

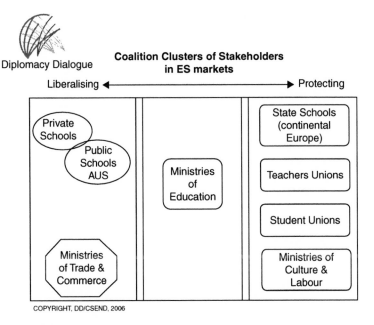

Figure 5.5 Coalition clusters of stakeholders involved in ES trade favouring liberalisation vs. protectionism (based on Saner & Fasel, 2003)

Source: Wilton Park, 2006.

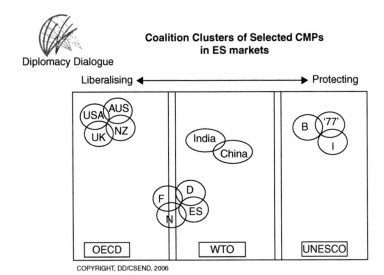

Figure 5.6 Coalition clusters of selected countries and their respective preferred institutional governance environment (based on Saner and Fasel, 2003)

Source: Wilton Park, 2006.

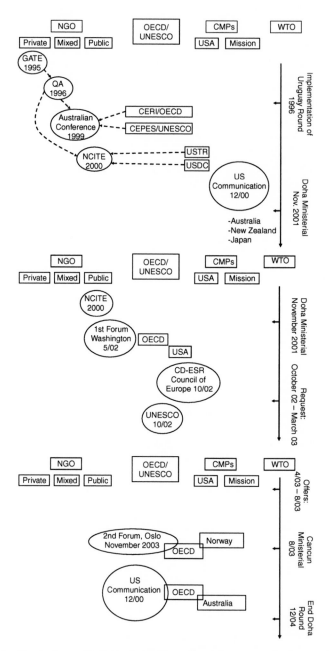

Figure 5.7   Chronology of influencing patterns by non-state actors during the GATS/ES negotiations (based on Saner and Fasel, 2003)

Conclusion

One of the unintended and unexpected developments of globalisation is the active participation of non-state actors in diplomacy. Traditionally, diplomacy has been the prerogative of ambassadors and envoys representing MFAs and central government offices and their mandates were confined to the affairs of the state. Protagonists of these new interest groups are often business executives, members of civil societies and representatives of NGOs.

Seen from this perspective, it appears necessary that different actors in the enlarged sphere of post-modern diplomacy acquire the additional competencies (domain expertise) to engage constructively in policy dialogue. Conversely, it has also become increasingly necessary that MFAs and state diplomats learn to adapt their traditional roles and functions from being more inward looking, exclusive and secretive actors to becoming more reachable, outgoing and inclusive diplomats searching for possible inclusion in economic policy-making of other actors, be they state (other ministries) or non-state actors (business diplomats and transnational NGO diplomats). Their social networks and spheres of influence need to extend beyond the confines of traditional diplomacy.

New times call for modification of traditional roles and responsibilities at the institutional level as well. The MFAs are no longer the sole guardians of diplomacy; instead they have to share the diplomatic 'space' with other ministries and learn to constructively engage non-state actors in a dialogue through proactive consultations and future oriented cooperation, to ensure the legitimacy of policy decisions and the security of policy implementation. Coalition building can consist of a mix of state and non-state actors. In a flattened world, where information and connectivity have become available to all, policy dialogue is no longer the 'birthright' of government representatives. Parameters for engagement are also not confined to state interest. Business entities and civil society bodies increasingly participate in shaping the international economic governance sphere. Without a flexible mental model and willingness to form partnerships to exploit increased information flows, new technologies, migration and the influence of non-state actors, governments will not be effective in exercising their sovereign rights in the realm of international affairs. Recognising this reality, governments of the advanced democratic countries are forming their own alliances together with NGOs in order to achieve their political aims.

Successful and sustainable international economic relations require effective dialogue and interaction between key stakeholders such as MFAs and other ministries with economic policy responsibilities, globally active enterprises and transnationally active NGOs. Since the relationship between these multiple stakeholders and constituencies can be difficult, it is of paramount importance that all six forms of diplomacies outlined in this chapter are represented in the most competent manner possible in order to ensure sustainable economic development with the highest possible equity across political and geographical boundaries.

Taking into account the increasing complexity of international relations and the participation of a growing number of state and non-state actors, the development of a more inclusive international governance structure for international economic policy is needed. But at the same time this would be very difficult to conceive and operationalise due to the proliferation of actors and the interconnectedness of economic policy issues. In order to limit trends towards fragmentation, special efforts need to be made to support the creation of an international economic governance structure that could help provide a policy framework for the interaction between state and non-state actors. Most importantly, such an enlarged global economic governance structure could help clarify the accountability and legitimacy of non-state actors while at the same time helping state actors cope with an enlarged economic governance space.

Finally, observations made in this chapter testify to the emergence of a new form of governance process in managing global interdependence and shared resources. This new form of governance is characterised by more transparent and democratic processes and its membership is based on alternative power bases which are supraterritorial in nature. The classic hierarchical governance structure is no longer agile enough in managing the existing multitude of complex relationships between state and non-state actors. In a similar vein, the traditional diplomatic structure is no longer effective in shaping and reshaping the complex, fast moving world. Further investigation of this new emerging form of global governance is called for in order to deal with the increasing turbulence of our global society.

Notes

1. For more information on NGO diplomacy as applied to Development Diplomacy, see Raymond Saner (2006) 'Development Diplomacy by Non-State-Actors: Emerging New Form of Multi-stakeholder Diplomacy', in Jovan Kurbalija and Valentin Katrandjiev, eds, *Multistakeholder Diplomacy: Challenges and Opportunities*, Malta and Geneva: Diplo Foundation.
2. For more details see G.R. Berridge and Alan James (2001) *A Dictionary of Diplomacy*, Hampshire, UK: Palgrave Publishing.
3. An example of cross-country divergence of business practice are the sources leading to labour turnover which vary considerably between countries, see for example: Raymond Saner and Lichia Yiu (1993) 'Coping with Labour Turnover in Taiwanese Companies', *The American Asian Review* 11(1): 162–195.
4. When infant formula manufacturers (Nestlé, Bristol-Myers, Abbott and American Home Products) started to sell their products to mothers in the developing world, serious health problems occurred. Mothers who opted for the baby formula needed to get supplies of clean water. This was not possible in many developing countries thereby endangering the survival of the infants. The food TNCs rejected any wrong doing but pressures by a consortium of international NGOs succeeded in

getting a new code for Marketing Breastmilk Substitutes adopted by WHO/UNICEF in 1981. As Nestlé refused to acknowledge any wrong doing, the NGOs concentrated their campaign on Nestlé even though other food TNCs practiced the same marketing approaches. The uncompromising communication policy resulted in substantial damage to Nestlé's reputational capital.

5. For an excellent example of innovative research in conflict prognosis, see Luc van de Goor and Suzanne Verstegen (1999) 'Conflict Prognosis: Bridging the Gap from Early Warning to Early Response: Part 1 & 2', The Hague: The Clingendael Institute.

6. For more information on trade in ES see Raymond Saner and Sylvie Fasel (2003: 275–308).

6

A Twilight Zone? Diplomacy and the International Committee of the Red Cross

Ivan Cook and Martine Letts

> Neither in the 1860s nor today are the causes of a war, or its legality, challenged by the International Committee. It is the way that war is conducted that matters, the way in which the men and women waging it behave towards their enemies, and the necessity of drawing up rules and codes that all those who adhere to the Conventions will respect themselves and monitor in others.
>
> (Moorehead, 1998: 29)

Introduction

The Red Cross emerged from the battlefields of Europe in 1863, at a time when information was scarce and obligations were narrow. It operated at the heart of conflict and in the shady halls of government, but rarely more widely or more publicly than that. Its objective was simple: to minimise human suffering by persuading warring parties to allow it access to zones of conflict, so that it might provide medicine and emergency relief with impunity. If the presence of the Red Cross neither helped nor hindered either side, so the argument went, its services would be to everyone's advantage – and so it has been for almost a century and a half.

The world has changed much for the better in that time. In developed countries, at least, the grim realities of war are now tempered by sophisticated codes of conduct and a greater valuation of human life. But the world is also much more open and complex, so that the simple calculus of discreet non-partisan diplomacy no longer applies as cleanly as it once did. History has conferred on the Red Cross the twin aims of upholding the corpus of International Humanitarian Law (IHL) and aiding the victims of conflict. These aims are cognate and still intimately connected, but in our globalised world they are also in tension. The successful management of that tension is perhaps the greatest challenge the Red Cross faces today.

Once the only body of its kind, the Red Cross is now surrounded by similar organisations pursuing the same goals by subtly different means.[1] Their existence is good for humanity but invites competition for attention in the public sphere, which in turn forms an intractable dilemma for the Red Cross. There have been times, since the Holocaust, when its failure to speak out publicly has reduced its moral authority and consequently its power to mitigate the humanitarian impacts of conflict. And yet, in conjunction with the evolving means and methods of warfare, public advocacy can become cripplingly political. Caught between the relative benefits of public and private advocacy, and in making unofficial but influential diplomatic representations, the Red Cross inhabits a kind of twilight zone.

The parties to conflict have changed as well. No longer are they limited to geographically bound formal states which might be persuaded by rational argument to moderate their behaviour. If terrorist organisations cannot be found, then neither can their leaders be spoken to nor their territories targeted in retribution. They have strengths, weaknesses and goals largely different from those of states and are not known to respond to the kind of representations that have been stock-in-trade for the Red Cross. In the face of asymmetrical threats such as these, neither are states so easily persuaded to play by the old rules.

Despite these difficulties, the Red Cross remains integral to humanity's efforts to moderate its grosser excesses. As the repository and guardian of international humanitarian law – and as an international player in its own right – it sets the standard by which the behaviour of states is measured. Thus, it benefits people in every corner of the world when states act to uphold the integrity and effectiveness of the Red Cross.

The movement

A plain red cross on a white background is one of the world's most widely recognised symbols. It represents a brand with unequalled strength and longevity, based not on its commercial power but on the universal spirit of compassion. The Red Cross Movement is an unusual organisation: a loose agglomeration of disparate national and international bodies connected by the spirit of their founders but separated by their different territories, structures and legal mandates. The circumstances of the Movement's origins are vital to understanding its central role in the establishment and development of IHL and its unique contemporary relationship with governments and international organisations.[2] Its origins also illuminate the challenges the Movement faces as it seeks to adapt to our changing world.

At the helm of the Movement sits the International Committee of the Red Cross (ICRC), formed in Geneva in 1863 by five private Swiss citizens.

Horrified by the scale of human suffering endured by soldiers during and after the great battles of the nineteenth century, the founders sought to encourage the establishment of volunteer relief societies for the express purpose of protecting and treating the wounded. These volunteer forces would be politically neutral in order to gain access to the battlefield, and would be established during times of peace so that they could be ready for deployment at short notice. The proposal quickly gained currency in the capitals of Europe, and the first autonomous national societies were formed within months.

Less than a year after the Committee first met, a diplomatic conference was held in Geneva at which 16 states signed a treaty codifying the Committee's principles. This was the first Geneva Convention governing the treatment of soldiers in warfare.[3] Although the ideas enshrined within the Convention were not universally new, their establishment in international law certainly was. At the core of the Convention was the principle of neutrality, a peculiarly Swiss contribution derived from that country's long and successful experience of political neutrality in Europe. Undoubtedly, neutrality has been the Movement's greatest strength, allowing its delegates unparalleled access to the victims of conflict. But neutrality is also restrictive of the Movement's ability to pursue its responsibilities assertively as the original legal and moral guardian of international humanitarian law.

The Movement now consists of three distinct parts: the ICRC; 186 national societies; and the International Federation of those societies. As a whole, the Movement's mission is:

> to prevent and alleviate human suffering wherever it may be found, to protect life and health and ensure respect for the human being, in particular in times of armed conflict and other emergencies, to work for the prevention of disease and for the promotion of health and social welfare, to encourage voluntary service and a constant readiness to give help by the members of the Movement, and a universal sense of solidarity towards all those in need of its protection and assistance. (ICRC, 1997)

This mission is to be undertaken by the Movement according to its 'fundamental principles' of humanity, impartiality, neutrality, independence, voluntary service, unity and universality. The societies' mission complements that of the ICRC, which is limited to action in favour of the victims of conflict during conflict and immediate post-conflict situations. The Federation's role is to act as the official representative of the societies in the international field and to help them coordinate their activities. Despite their different purposes and significant autonomy, these different elements of the Movement are bound not only by the Red Cross brand, but also by its International Conference, which brings together delegates from each component of the Movement and from every state party to the Geneva

Conventions, and which sets the strategic direction for the Movement as a whole (ICRC, 2006c).

The Geneva conventions and IHL

The four Geneva Conventions and their two Additional Protocols (signed in 1949 and 1977) mandate the ICRC to act in the event of international armed conflict. The Geneva Conventions have been ratified by 194 states, and the Additional Protocols I and II by 166 and 162 states respectively, making the body of international law they enshrine practically universal (ICRC, 2005a: 383–386). No other body has a standing mandate of this nature. The ICRC is neither an international organisation nor a non-government organisation, but is rather a private association formed under the Swiss Civil Code. Unlike international organisations, it does not have member governments. Unlike non-government organisations, it has a suite of rights in international law allowing it to act on behalf of the victims of conflict. As such, it has an international legal personality supported by privileges and immunities, including immunity from judicial process (Rona, 2004). With its ability to independently pursue both norm promotion and relief activities with such privileges and immunities, the ICRC occupies a unique space in the realm of international governance.

The Geneva Conventions confer the ICRC with this special status in international law, and in effect the genesis of the ICRC, the Geneva Conventions and IHL are one and the same. As a consequence, the ICRC plays a central role in the development, maintenance and protection of IHL. Alongside its humanitarian relief work, this role is the ICRC's most important function and indeed the two are closely linked. Through its constant presence in the battlefield, the ICRC identifies developments in conflict not covered by existing IHL. Since the first Geneva Convention was signed in 1864, the ICRC has made proposals resulting in revisions and extensions to IHL in 1906, 1929, 1949 and 1977 (Sandoz, 1998).

Over the years, these two interlinked functions have generated deep respect for the ICRC. The Statutes of the Movement, which have also been adopted by the states party to the Geneva Conventions, establish that the ICRC is:

> to undertake the tasks incumbent upon it by the Geneva Conventions, to work for the faithful application of international humanitarian law applicable in armed conflicts and to take cognizance of any complaints based on alleged breaches of that law [and] to work for the understanding and dissemination of knowledge of international humanitarian law applicable in armed conflicts and to prepare any development thereof. (ICRC, 1995)

It is the ICRC's responsibility to ensure that IHL is an effective and legitimate framework for the alleviation of suffering by victims of conflict. In turn, effective IHL confers both legitimacy and moral authority on the ICRC.

Neutral diplomacy

Humanitarian diplomacy describes the act of lobbying governments, authorities and other international actors to adopt and observe the principles of IHL and to accept the development of new conventions on specific aspects of warfare as they arise (ICRC, 1999). The ICRC's unique mandate to protect the casualties of war and its role as the guardian of IHL are mutually supportive, but they can also undermine each other. The source of this tension is the principle of neutrality, which is one of the Movement's seven fundamental principles and the primary source of its success in the field. Neutrality minimises the incentives for warring parties to deny the ICRC access to conflict zones but it also restricts the number of ways in which the ICRC can act to uphold IHL.

One of the most important of the ICRC's privileges as an international legal personality is its immunity from judicial process. It allows the ICRC to maintain its silence with regard to the conduct of warring parties in the event that a conflict is examined in court, which in turn increases the likelihood that the ICRC will be allowed access to the war zone by those parties. To maintain that access the ICRC prefers to lobby the parties to a conflict privately about their obligations under IHL, and to leave other methods of action to humanitarian players which do not rely so heavily on neutrality.

Working from within the ICRC, Paul Bonard (1999) identifies the key method used by the ICRC as persuasion, whereby it convinces authorities to end violations of the law by means of strictly confidential representations. This method implies a relationship of trust between the ICRC and the authorities involved, with advantages and obligations on both sides and with benefits over the long-term. Foremost of the 'persuasive organisation's' obligations is to avoid public denunciation of these authorities. The maintenance of trust often leads to more successful outcomes because it makes it politically easier for the authorities in question to take actions consistent with international law, and because the organisation has greater access both to information and the victims themselves (Ibid.: 18–22).

A disadvantage of relying exclusively on persuasion is that it can take a long time to achieve results and, in the meantime, precludes other forms of action such as public denunciation. If, in the end, persuasion fails, the consequences for the victims of the conflict – and by extension for the reputation of the ICRC itself – can be dire. The ICRC has been involved in humanitarian diplomacy in one way or another since its inception and this involvement has continually posed difficult problems for the Committee to resolve. But with the proliferation of new weapons and tactics in conflict, those problems have become ever more complex. Two distinct examples illustrate the point: the ICRC's decision to remain silent about the Holocaust; and its promotion of the Ottawa Treaty prohibiting the use of anti-personnel mines.

Hitler's Final Solution presented perhaps the most significant policy challenge in the history of the Movement. The ICRC met in June 1942 with the express purpose of deciding whether or not to make a public appeal for access to concentration camp prisoners. By then it was known that gross abuses of human rights were being committed within the camps. Nonetheless, the Committee chose to make only private representations to the Nazi Government in order to protect its neutrality and its already limited access to prisoners of war. At the time, the ICRC was the pre-eminent moral force in Europe, ideally placed to provide leadership on the issue. History has judged its decision harshly. In the words of one biographer, it has caused the ICRC 'great and lasting damage' (Moorehead, 1998: xxv–xxxi).

The ICRC's role in the establishment of the Ottawa Treaty[4] demonstrates how much the world had changed in the intervening half century. The crux of the debate for advocates of the Treaty was not so much the effect of anti-personnel mines in the course of warfare – which for the most part was seen as unexceptional – but rather that mines are injurious to civilian health thereafter (Pohling-Brown, 1997: 5). Advocates sought to position the issue as civil rather than military, and were aided in their cause by the contributions of non-governmental organisations (NGOs) and the ICRC. The process leading up to the establishment of the Treaty (the Ottawa Process) was an example of a newer form of polycentric diplomacy, as a core group of states with a clear interest in completing the Treaty cooperated with NGOs to bring more recalcitrant states to the table.

Although some commentators have credited more influence to the non-government players involved than they wielded in fact, it is true that the ICRC in particular played a significant role in publicising the issue, not least by recruiting Princess Diana to the cause. By one estimate, her advocacy on the issue brought the equivalent of US$2 million worth of public attention to the campaign. It is also clear that the ICRC's public commitment to the campaign made it easier for pro-Treaty states to position the process as non-political (Short, 1999). But for states that did not support the Treaty, the ICRC lost some of its sheen of neutrality. In effect, the ICRC lent a portion of its own credibility to the campaign, leaving the ICRC more vulnerable to political criticism.

It is questionable whether the core group's success in bringing the Ottawa Treaty into force was only due to its non-political nature. It is clear from the responses of states which did not support the Treaty, that the Ottawa Process was highly political in the sense that – whether intentionally or not – it appeared to confer competitive advantages on some states and not others. The United States argued that the Treaty benefited European arms manufacturers for technical reasons connected with the way mines are produced and ignored the (American) development of short-duration mines designed to neutralise the long-term civilian danger posed by mine fields (National Committee on American Foreign Policy, 2000). The United States also argued that the Treaty's provisions would lead directly to greater short-term military casualties in certain conflict zones, most clearly that of the demarcation line between North and South Korea (Burt, 1997: 4).

The American response to the ICRC's involvement in the Ottawa Process is worth highlighting because it indicates an erosion of one of the core benefits of neutrality – mutual trust. More recently some US senators have called for the ICRC's statutes to be changed so that non-Swiss nationals can sit on its governing bodies. It is indeed peculiar that a body with such unique international privileges should be so unrepresentative. But there is much practical value in its ability to make quick decisions free of political wrangling driven by national interests; indeed, it is said, lives depend on it. To retain that independence in the long-term, the ICRC must also retain the trust of the world's governments (ICRC, 2005b).

Michael Meyer, an international lawyer working within the Movement, has proposed a typology of humanitarian issues to guide the ICRC on how it should become involved in advocacy campaigns. The Movement, he argues, should engage in public advocacy in favour of people, not policies. As a corollary, it should take an effective, pragmatic approach rather than a purely idealistic one. It should highlight suffering without proposing specific ways of preventing it (e.g., by banning particular weapons), because such solutions are necessarily political. Ultimately it should take advantage of its unique status and differentiate itself from other humanitarian bodies in its campaigning methods rather than being drawn into competition with them. Meyer (1996) observes that within the Movement's long history of humanitarian advocacy, it has been successful precisely when it observed these principles, which preserve its neutrality and its good relationship with governments.

The ICRC has long acknowledged the importance of complementary 'advocacy first' organisations – like Amnesty International (AI) – which occupy the space created by the ICRC's reluctance to challenge governments' policies publicly. Médecins Sans Frontières (MSF) was created by a former ICRC delegate, Bernard Kouchner, specifically to fill the void left by the ICRC's refusal to publicly apportion blame in the Biafran conflict of 1967–1970. Kouchner had been appalled as much by the ICRC's intransigence as by the scale of human suffering. Consequently, MSF bears public witness to human rights abuses in addition to delivering emergency medical relief in conflict zones. But while MSF and AI provide vital operational alternatives to the ICRC, in the contemporary world they also represent competition for scarce resources.

Meyer suggests that the proliferation of specific-issue NGOs might have helped to prompt the ICRC's increased involvement in public advocacy in the 1990s, including in the Ottawa Process. In fact, this is probably truer of the Movement's national societies than of the ICRC itself, which is funded mostly by governments or government-controlled international organisations (ICRC,

2005a: 35). But the broader point is well made: Globalisation has created an information-rich environment with an expanded number of actors and a more influential role for public opinion. Governments still call the shots, but the diplomatic complexities they face often create opportunities for non-government advocacy that did not previously exist. For a century, the Movement had a virtual monopoly on independent advocacy, which it pursued in private dialogue with governments. Nowadays, it does not have the luxury of a captive audience.

Globalisation

Globalisation has complicated the ICRC's working environment no less in the field of battle than in the halls of diplomacy. The fight against terrorism is effectively a fight against a series of amorphous, transnational, non-state actors enabled by various facets of the communications revolution, most notably internet-based information exchange and easy international travel. The core humanitarian principles accepted by every legitimate state – and which have always given the ICRC its purpose – do not always apply in the case of ideological movements that lack clear territory or constituencies. Despite its avowed neutrality, it is indisputable that the Movement is a Western creation: it sprang from the battlefields of Europe; its emblem is an adaptation of a Christian symbol; its headquarters are in Geneva; and the bulk of its funding comes from Western governments, foremost among them the United States (Krähenbüehl, 2004b: 508). To Al Qaeda and others, for whom the West is the enemy, a body like the ICRC is clearly a legitimate target.

The erosion of humanitarian inviolability in conflict zones strikes at the core of the ICRC's ability to carry out its mission, as demonstrated by the October 2003 bombing of its Baghdad headquarters. The ICRC closed down its operation in Iraq as a direct result of the bombing. It would normally seek to secure its operations by maintaining neutral contact with all the parties involved in a conflict, but in Iraq that was impossible: it did not have access to the terrorist groups in question (Krähenbüehl, 2004a). Furthermore, the ICRC has found that becoming a target in one localised conflict can threaten the security of its representatives around the world.

The instant global reach of terrorist networks has added an extra layer of complexity to the challenges faced by the ICRC and other humanitarian relief agencies. In the case of radical Islamic terrorism, a *fatwa* can span the globe in a single day, prompting violence that is difficult to trace back to its source. Further, the cell structure of Al Qaeda-style terrorist organisations has the power to generate a dangerous momentum: for example, once a terrorist plot is set in motion, it might not be possible even for its instigators to prevent it from being carried out. Under these conditions it is very difficult for the ICRC to identify worthwhile interlocutors, let alone engage with them in critical dialogue.

Writing in the *Harvard Human Rights Journal*, Kenneth Anderson (2004) identifies two proximate causes of the breakdown in humanitarian inviolability: the ideological inspiration of globalised terrorist groups and a blurring of the boundaries between emergency relief and post-conflict reconstruction. The second of these is addressed below.

The ICRC was conceived as an emergency relief organisation in an age long before the notion of post-conflict reconstruction gained currency in international relations. Even today, the ICRC's narrow mandate and its reliance on the principle of neutrality suggest that it should confine its operations to emergency relief. Anderson believes that in the context of both Iraq and Afghanistan, the ICRC, the United Nations and other humanitarian agencies were pursuing contradictory goals: they sought to combine politically neutral humanitarian relief with the kind of institutional reconstruction that requires serious political commitment to the values of democracy, pluralism and human rights. With agencies' neutrality thus compromised, it is no wonder that the opponents of these values saw fit to attack them (Ibid.: 42–43).

A related threat to the ICRC's neutrality is presented by the risk of 'instrumentalisation', whereby states appropriate the good name of humanitarian action to help generate support for their campaign against terrorist activities. In Iraq, some governments have stated that their presence in the field is 'mostly humanitarian', while the provincial reconstruction teams in Afghanistan effectively institutionalise the conflation of military and humanitarian operations (Krähenbüehl, 2004b: 508).

The ICRC takes considerable steps to resist the pressures of instrumentalisation. It will not accept delegates from countries involved in a conflict or occupation when working alongside their military. It did not accept Australian delegates in the initial phase of its operation in East Timor, nor in the Solomon Islands once the Australian-led Regional Assistance Mission had been deployed. Despite accusations of an overly exclusive approach, the ICRC remains convinced that maintaining its independence is still the best way to meet the interlinked objectives of protecting both victims of conflict and its delegates in the field.

Anderson's clear distinction between political and non-political action is attractive because it offers an operational framework for the ICRC that reflects its core principles. But in practice it might not always be possible for the ICRC to draw that distinction and remain effective. As an international lawyer working within the Movement points out, the provision of emergency, rehabilitation and development aid do not follow neatly one after the other, but inevitably overlap. 'A blood transfusion programme, for example, can meet an urgent need for blood to operate on the wounded, comprise the rehabilitation of a building destroyed during the conflict, and help build the capacities of medical personnel via targeted training' (Harroff-Tavel, 2003: 469). Viewed in isolation these actions may not be overtly political in nature, but they take place in the wider – and inevitably political – context of rehabilitation and reconstruction.

If the ICRC is to continue to have an impact, therefore, it might be necessary to enshrine a more sophisticated interpretation of its basic principles. Neutrality has never been more than a means to an end, and when the protection of basic human welfare conflicts with the strict avoidance of political alignment, the two imperatives may be carefully weighed and a bespoke course of action pursued. The ICRC's President, Jakob Kellenberger, has articulated four conditions which must be met before such a decision is made:

> Serious, repeated breaches of international humanitarian law must be occurring. We must be witnesses of these breaches ourselves, or we must know about them from absolutely reliable sources. Repeated approaches on our part must have had no effect and we must be convinced that going public is in the interests of the victims. (ICRC, 2005b)

Kellenberger's rules of public engagement have been tested no more strenuously than over the detention of prisoners at Guantanamo Bay and in Afghanistan. ICRC delegates have been permitted access to these prisons by the US authorities, as is required under international law, and with some exceptions the daily treatment of the prisoners has fallen within the guidelines set out by the Geneva Conventions. But the ICRC is deeply concerned that many of these prisoners are being detained outside any legal framework – a condition directly contrary to IHL. Apparently unable to convince the US authorities to rectify that condition, the ICRC has chosen to speak publicly on the issue in the hope that the pressure of international opinion will have more effect (ICRC, 2006e).

Kellenberger also felt compelled to respond to critics who claimed that the ICRC had not done enough on behalf of the prisoners by revealing that its private representations had, in fact, met with some success (ICRC, 2005b). Ironically, perhaps, Kellenberger was damned both ways: the ICRC's reputation was bound to suffer to some degree – with either the public or the authorities – whether he spoke out or not.

The ICRC has also spoken out about the treatment of inmates at the Abu Ghraib prison in Iraq. Its terse statement clearly projects a sense of the difficulties involved in taking a public position on the issue when both doctrine and experience suggest that it should remain silent. Referring to reports presented privately to the US authorities, the statement reads in part: 'In these reports – which are confidential so as to prevent humanitarian issues from becoming politicised – the ICRC requests that appropriate action be taken, where necessary, to stop the mistreatment of prisoners or to improve their conditions' (ICRC, 2004). The world is now well aware of the nature of that mistreatment following the emergence of photographs depicting the systematic degradation of prisoners at Abu Ghraib. It is likely that the ICRC would have been criticised had it failed to highlight the abuses publicly, but also that it lost a degree of trust with the US government because it did.

The ICRC's public response to the July 2006 conflict between Israel and Hezbollah's forces in southern Lebanon consisted of a general rendition of the responsibilities of parties to a conflict under IHL, as well as carefully balanced criticism of both sides for specific acts (the detention of Israeli soldiers and the use of rockets by Hezbollah, and the use of bombs and a ports blockade by Israel). The tone of the piece is that of an impartial umpire before a big game warning known offenders not to act up, and asking that the rules of a fair fight be respected (ICRC, 2006d). A press release from November 2006 calls for an international response to the use of cluster munitions, which continued to cause civilian injuries throughout southern Lebanon four months after hostilities ceased (ICRC, 2006a). Though Israel is clearly the responsible party, it is never named as the culprit.

The circumstances of the war against terrorism have led some, especially in the United States, to question the relevance of IHL to the modern conduct of hostilities. The US Attorney-General, Alberto Gonzales, once described the Geneva Conventions as 'quaint and outdated'. This sent shockwaves through the ICRC, as did the review of IHL's applicability in the context of contemporary asymmetrical warfare, which was initiated by the Swiss Government in collaboration with Harvard University. The ICRC has stoutly defended the currency and applicability of IHL, and its critics have since conceded that it covers most contingencies even though its application may vary according to context. The ICRC continues to participate in reviews of the effectiveness of IHL alongside interested parties including the Australian Government.

Funding and the private sector

The need for a subtle balance of principles and practical exigencies extends to the ICRC's relations with an expanded range of actors, including those from the private sector. The ICRC believes that it is well within its interests to engage with the business community, particularly where companies are stakeholders in conflict-prone areas. It applies the same principles of confidentiality in those dealings as it does in its relations with governments and parties to conflict. Its primary aims are to promote the corporate understanding of IHL and to share information about situations of humanitarian concern, but it will also consider active logistical cooperation with companies in conflict zones when necessary. Companies can benefit from the relationship because it helps to secure a stable business environment and bolster their public image. But the potential for mismanagement is evident: the ICRC must take the greatest care that it does not give the appearance of bending to private interests (ICRC, 2006b).

A related risk attends the establishment of corporate relationships as part of the fundraising activities of many of the Movement's national societies (Carbonnier and Desjonquères, 2002). Currently these relationships have little bearing on the ICRC itself because its own funding is largely free of corporate connections; however, where actors unfamiliar with the structure of the Movement conflate its separate parts, it can lead to misunderstandings and poor public perception. In 2004, the ICRC derived 80 per cent of its income from governments. The vast majority of that portion came from Western countries led by the United States, which contributed 22 per cent of the total income. Half of the remaining 20 per cent came from the European Commission, while national societies and other sources contributed approximately 5 per cent each (ICRC, 2005a: 35).

Nonetheless, the ICRC is actively looking for untied corporate funding from the business sector on the same basis as it receives funding from governments. The actions of multinational companies have considerable international and in-country impact, especially in states that have poor governance. Properly managed, there is no reason why corporate funding cannot contribute to the ICRC's mission by providing it with a more diverse and stable funding base.

Conclusion

The ICRC has always dwelt in a twilight zone in its relationships with states and other international players. Its twin aims are to provide direct relief to the victims of conflict and to protect and uphold the body of international humanitarian law. Both aims serve its *raison d'être*, which is to prevent human suffering wherever and whenever possible. To ensure the best access to victims of conflict the ICRC must remain politically neutral, but to protect and develop IHL and to safeguard victims of war it must also engage in international diplomacy. For this reason, the ICRC usually prefers to engage in private diplomacy, relying on its unique legal mandate and its deep empirical understanding of the consequences of conflict to lend its private voice weight with the community of states. But there are also issues that require the pursuit of public diplomacy, especially where a failure to declare support for humanitarian principles can harm both the victims of conflict and the ICRC's own public image. It is the ICRC's difficult task to make the right choice of when to speak out and when to stay silent.

Globalisation has complicated the operating environment in a number of ways. In modern zones of conflict the boundary between emergency and reconstructive action has become blurred, and the ICRC must be careful to pick its way through the minefield of competing imperatives. As Marion Harroff-Tavel (2003: 491) writes, 'the construction of peace is not the primary objective of humanitarian practitioners, but to lose all interest in the matter, on the pretext that this responsibility lies first and foremost with others, is tantamount to an abdication.' Public expectation and those of the international organisations with which the ICRC shares its fields of operation both complicate the humanitarian terrain.

In relation to any given conflict or humanitarian issue the number of interested actors has ballooned, from stateless international terrorist organisations that do not respond to the ICRC's traditional methods of engagement to issue-based NGOs which promote and rely on the increasing strength of public opinion to further their aims. The ICRC must judge whether to compete for public attention in this evolving environment or to rely on its traditional private diplomacy, with an eye to its sources of funding, its good favour with states and the effectiveness of this method in the face of stateless organisations.

Still, the ICRC's international legal personality affords it the status of an important diplomatic player. It has adapted to the changing international landscape just as the Geneva Conventions have been updated in response to the changing nature of warfare and other theatres of conflict. While the ICRC can never replace the role of states in the maintenance of peace and security, it is a critical governance actor in helping to establish the conditions for peace and development. Whether as a provider of lifesaving services, protector of the victims and prisoners of war, deliverer of messages or reuniter of families separated by conflict, the ICRC has acted in a quasi-diplomatic role that to this day has not been fundamentally contested by states or civil society.

In a number of cases it remains to be seen whether the difficult decisions in recent years were rightly or wrongly made. Has the ICRC's public advocacy of arms control measures significantly devalued its neutrality in the view of states? If so, was the moral weight and technical expertise it lent to the establishment of new international law worth that price? Has its record of success in pursuing private diplomacy in the context of the 'war on terror' been damaged by the increase in its public advocacy on the legal status of prisoners of war?

As the primary sponsors of the ICRC and as the ultimate representatives of humanity, states should be as concerned with these questions as is the ICRC itself. At its inception in 1864 states were quick to recognise the value of an organisation dedicated to the pursuit of humanitarian aims, and their citizens have been reaping the very considerable benefits ever since. If they are to continue to do so, it is in the clear interest of states to support the work of the ICRC and to make its negotiation of the complex contemporary environment as easy and as fruitful as possible.

Notes

1. Amnesty International, Médecins Sans Frontières and CARE to name but three.
2. IHL should not be confused with the body of human rights enshrined in the Universal Declaration of Human Rights, which is not contingent on or driven by the ICRC.

3. The second, third and fourth Geneva Conventions, signed in 1949, extend the protections of the first convention to the conduct of warfare at sea and cover the treatment of prisoners of war and the protection of civilian persons in times of war, respectively.

4. The treaty's correct title is the Convention on the Prohibition of the Use, Stockpiling, Production and Transfer of Anti-Personnel Mines and their Destruction. It has been acceded to by 155 countries since 1997. It came into effect in March 1999, and completely bans all anti-personnel mines. Notably, neither the United States nor China has signed the treaty.

7
Research Institutes as Diplomatic Actors

Shankari Sundararaman

Introduction

Inter-state relations, today, are not limited to the government or the state alone. As a result of growing challenges, several participants have emerged who influence and act within their respective boundaries to impact upon the way states, both individually and collectively relate to one another. The multiplicity of actors within the state and the transnational character that they have begun to represent are critical to the analysis of this volume's theme. In this chapter, I intend to look at the manner in which research institutes function as diplomatic actors. The relevance of this particular topic lies in the fact that an existing space within the domains of governance and diplomacy can accommodate the views of several different groups that have a relevant impact on the formulation of policy. Policy is closely related to governance: that is, where there is good governance the policy initiatives must take into account the 'greatest good for the greatest numbers'. Within this scope therefore, it becomes significant to have a larger representation of voices that push forward policy initiatives and play a crucial role in determining the behaviour of the state itself, acting as internal custodians of state policy. It is within this space that the role of research institutes as diplomatic actors begins to be defined and articulated.

As diplomatic actors, research institutes have been confined to what is often referred to as the track II position, which is significantly different from a track I position that is more focused on government and state-level actors alone. However, today with the growing emphasis on the roles played by non-state actors, there is a tendency to move away from the traditional parameters that determine state policy and to look at the manner in which non-state actors have been able to play an effective role. The role of these non-state actors typically fits into the descriptions offered by the liberal and the constructivist schools of international relations. Both these schools look at the use of institutionalism as a mechanism of inter-state relations. The constructivist context also looks at the realm of ideas and how non-state actors can act as 'agents' of ideas that can institute a shift in policy-relevant matters (Caballero-Anthony, 2005: 158). Through the use of the constructivist prism, it becomes possible to perceive the changes taking place on a larger scale as a result of the players that constitute the track II processes. There is a generation of 'new ideas, shapes, attitudes and approaches within and among states that may be taking place as ideas find their way into concrete policies' (Ibid.). The significance of focusing on these non-state actors as agents of ideas and change lies in their ability to disperse – through their engagement – inter-subjective ideas on how inter-state relations can be furthered. This offers a kind of building block on which states can establish channels of conduct for inter-state and even inter-regional mechanisms that push policies ahead (Ibid.).

Track II is defined clearly as those groups that do not occupy what is termed as the 'official space', in the diplomatic process. In many ways, the term remains somewhat ambiguous because in several cases track II also includes members from the official process when acting in their private or personal capacities. In fact, this inclusion of track I actors with track II processes has even led many analysts to coin the term track 1.5, which is a mixture of state and non-state level actors. The term 'track II diplomacy', often shortened to simply 'track II', was coined by a former American diplomat, Joseph Montville, to refer to negotiations by non-state actors on issues that normally fell into the official diplomatic sphere. Within the literature that relates to conflict resolution, track II has a broader connotation: it encompasses the role of non-governmental groups involved in the resolution of conflict, even at the grassroots level (Ball et al., 2005: 8). In the early 1980s, the term was used to refer to a group more broadly associated with people-to-people contact in attempts to resolve disputes. This was a different approach and it was believed that the process was distinct because it was not at the state-to-state level, where suspicions tend to limit the scope of negotiations between groups. In particular, issues relating to national interest and security often have the effect of restricting the ability of state-level players in achieving real breakthroughs in conflict resolution (Ibid.).

According to Montville, the effectiveness of track II lies in its capacity to appeal to a sense of common goodwill among actors at a level that is separate from the state and may be guided by a sense of reasonableness (Davidson and Montville, 1981: 155). In fact, works have contributed to developing the idea of track II diplomacy both in the field of conflict resolution itself and in approaches to multilateralism. Indeed, within the realm of promoting multilateral security approaches, several government officials have been known to participate in their private capacities to promote regionalism within track II dialogues, which reflects clearly the debate between the terminologies of track II and track 1.5 (Job, 2002: 241–279). Track II has also acted as an effective tool in addressing economic security issues through the use of non-state-level actors within multilateral groupings (Morrison, 2002: 547–565). While the actual boundaries of the processes discussed here are often blurred and fail to fit into clearly distinct and defined limits, what is specific to this particular analysis is the way they shape the processes that include a role for them. Within this dimension, track II, therefore, refers to a broad network of academics, experts, members of civil society and government officials, often acting in their private capacities (Kerr, 1994: 400). Referring specifically to track II diplomacy, there is a greater focus on the use of 'unofficial contact and interaction aimed at the resolution of conflict, both internationally and within states' (Caballero-Anthony, 2005: 158). The processes of track II diplomacy consist of several players that are outside the official parameters of the diplomatic sphere and include academics, research scholars, think tanks and, more broadly, members of civil society groups.

Track II process as epistemic communities

To determine the manner in which track II processes have evolved and restructured the nature of diplomatic behaviour, I draw upon the role assigned to epistemic communities as analysed in the works of Peter Haas. In his analysis of the study of policy, Haas states that the core of the issue lies in the debate that emanates between 'determinism and free will' (Haas, 1992: 1). Haas also remarks that the policy process itself is comprised of three critical issues – the system-level factors that shape national behaviour, the unit-level factors that influence national behaviour from within and the complex tensions that arise from the interplay between these two factors (Ibid.). Within the policy-making processes, these tensions arise from two factors. First, whether or not policy-makers within the state can sufficiently identify national interests, is itself an issue. Second, if they are able to do so, can they make these choices independently of the groups that they claim to represent or would the views of these groups be accommodated into the policy-making apparatus? (Ibid.).

Another critical factor is whether policy-makers can consistently move towards the choices that not only affect the state in a positive manner, but that also take into consideration the benefits to different groups involved. This becomes particularly relevant in the context of the tensions between the foreign policy concerns of the state and the domestic compulsions that may conflict with it.[1] Adding to the existing complexity of the relations between foreign policy and domestic compulsions is whether actors within the state have the capacity to understand the anarchic nature of the international system. This understanding would ultimately lead state-level actors to adopt policies that are consistent with this dynamic. In this context, Robert Keohane asserts that the capacity of the state-level players to comprehend the international system would lead to the application of policies based on two approaches – either through theories of rational choice and deductive methods or through interpretive-type choices (Keohane, 1988: 379–396; Haas, 1992: 2).

There is a basic understanding that both the systemic changes and the domestic compulsions within the state can either inhibit or enhance state behaviour (Haas, 1992: 2). But within this spectrum, states have a greater latitude to choose the optimum policy options based on their own formulations or on the influence from those groups within the state that drive policy choices. What is significant to this particular analysis is that there is a critical juncture at which the systemic conditions, knowledge on specific issues and national policy choices do not merely interact with one another but also overlap with each other. At this juncture, the control over knowledge is an essential factor bringing with it the development of 'new ideas and information' from which 'new patterns of behaviour can emerge and prove to be important determinants in international policy coordination' (Ibid.: 3). Within this context, an epistemic community is described as a 'network of professionals with an authoritative claim to policy-relevant knowledge within that domain or issue area' (Ibid.). In the description given by Haas, an epistemic community might consist of professionals from different disciplines; however, within the community these professionals would be united by a set of shared values. Haas describes these four values as follows:

1. A shared set of normative and principled beliefs, which provide a value-based rationale for the social action of community members;
2. Shared causal beliefs, derived from their analysis of practices leading or contributing to a central set of problems in their domain and which then serve as the basis for elucidating the multiple linkages between possible policy action and desired outcomes;
3. Shared notions of validity – that is, inter-subjective, internally-defined criteria for weighing and validating knowledge in the domain of their expertise, and;
4. A common policy enterprise – that is, a set of common practices associated with a set of problems to which their professional competence is directed, presumably out of the conviction that human welfare will be enhanced as a consequence (Ibid.).

This wide and encompassing definition also includes in it the notion that epistemic communities share an understanding of their domain in an inter-subjective manner. Among the community, there is often a commonality of interests that define the way a subject is analysed, understood in terms of its causes, beliefs, validity and the option of the courses that may be followed (Ibid.).

Research institutes as diplomatic actors

Earlier reference was made to critical junctures that involve interplay between the three factors governing policy decisions, and it is within this critical juncture that a role emerges for research institutes or think tanks in the arena of international diplomacy. In this chapter, the terms 'research institutes' and 'think tanks' are used interchangeably. The aim is to see how they fit into the analysis of identifying epistemic communities within states and have within their domain the capacity to be influential in the transnational sense.

Definition

The term 'think tank' emerges into academic parlance in the aftermath of the Second World War, when American strategic thinking began to identify key components to the policy-making process in terms of the provision of information for the structuring of security policy. The RAND Corporation was in fact one of the first to emerge in this capacity and provided a team of experts who could look into the domain of American security concerns and identify the manner in which policy could be shaped (Stone, 2005: 2). The term began to acquire popularity in the 1960s to refer to a team of specialists undertaking intensive study of important policy issues (Ibid.). In many ways there is no single definition of a think tank. It is generally accepted, however, that the term reflects a particular policy enterprise where knowledge and policy interact.[2] For the sake of this current analysis, think tanks are defined according to a United Nations Development Programme (UNDP) Report (2003: 6) as those, 'organizations engaged on a regular basis in research and advocacy on any matter related to public policy. They are the bridge between knowledge and power in modern democracies.'[3]

Function

It is this particular aspect of the think tank or research institute that defines the scope of its function – that is, its relevance lies in its ability to act as a bridge between the production of knowledge and the formulation of policy. This link between these two parts is understood to be tenuous and each part is often seen as contradicting the other. In fact, the usual assessment of this relationship between research and policy is that it is an uneasy one, where unrealistic expectations are held on both sides. Despite this awkward relationship, there is a widely held view that research can positively contribute to the decision-making process as it is a field of 'knowledge accumulation through experience and scientific process' (Stone et al., 2001).

While research adds to the quality of decision-making, there is often a feeling among the research community that there is no political audience for the work that they produce. Similarly, there is a view among the policymakers that research is seeking answers to theoretical, rather than pragmatic questions, thereby remaining too esoteric from the realities that drive policy decision-making (Stone, 2002: 5). Particularly in the context of states, where policy-related issues tend to be addressed behind closed doors, there is little interaction between the research community and the corridors of policy-making.

What needs to be taken into consideration is the capacity of the research community to provide a new set of ideas based on the groups they seek to represent in their study. Recently, there has been increasing agreement that different disciplines have the ability to provide new ideas and knowledge within their respective fields that challenge the old ways of thinking. Even within disciplines such as political science and international relations there have been significant ideational shifts that have impacted the nature of research; as a result, research has begun to focus more on issues relating to the development of ideas and political influences that determine the way inter-state relations are carried out. It is significant then, to understand how research communities and policy-making processes interact with one another. As a field where new ideas and thoughts are constantly generated, research has the capacity to qualify the policy-making arena by introducing a more focused approach. It allows bringing into the policy framework a larger dimension in terms of intellectual output from various specialised groups. In the current context of international relations, this is increasing in importance as policy-making becomes more and more specific, and related issues are being critically studied for minute details. For this reason, there is greater focus on rigorous research among professionals to assist in the policy-making process (Ibid.). Within this context, Wallace (1998: 26) best describes the function of think tanks as one that carries out 'research relevant to policy, there by promoting public debate and questioning conventional wisdom, leading to formulation and dissemination of alternative concepts'. This increased function of research has led to the development of research institutes or think tanks that foster the interplay between more academic research and input in policy analysis. In the following two sections of this chapter, I look at the development of research institutes and also focus on the case that best defines the role of research institutes in international diplomacy: the Association of Southeast Asian Nations (ASEAN) Institutes of Strategic and International Studies (ASEAN-ISIS) in the Asia–Pacific region.

Development of think tank traditions

The entire logic of think tank development is closely tied to the period after the Second World War. In the period prior to this, research institutes and think tanks were 'primarily an Anglo-American phenomenon' (Stone, 2005: 3). Since the end of the Second World War, however, the think tank tradition has developed around the world with institutes emerging both in Europe as well as in Asia. While overall there has been a sizeable increase in the number of think tanks and research institutes in most countries, it is within liberal democracies that they have been most significant in terms of their emergence and functioning.[4] While in many cases research institutes have followed the Anglo-American notions of independence from the state or government, thereby remaining largely autonomous, in many other countries particularly within Asia, the traditions of research institutes have been such that they are often semi-independent and closely linked to government and/or to individual political figures (Ibid.).[5] The development of traditions, such as independent systems and institutions, is often clearly seen in the more liberal, western democracies rather than in the Asian context, where the state structures tend to influence the way institutions develop, including research institutes. The western view that think tanks or research institutes should be free from political biases is critical to the role they play within each state. In contrast, most research institutes that developed in the Asian context often operated inside corporations that were heavily reliant on the state. Furthermore in the case of Asia, the political system itself is one that is based on patronage. As such, the right of the political élite to bestow favours upon different groups characterises the manner in which these systems undermine the capacity of research institutes to grow independently. One strong example of this is the case of East Asia and particularly China, where think tanks were government-sponsored and there was often a strong patron-client relationship between the scholars and the political leaders themselves.[6] In India, several think tanks have evolved and some have strong linkages to the government – especially those that receive total or partial government funding. Others have a strong dependence on foreign donors, which may at times inhibit critical and independent thinking.

In their leading work on the traditions of think tanks, Stone and Denham look at the emergence of these research institutes over a period of time and trace four significant waves in the growth of think tanks the world over. First, in the period prior to the Second World War, the emergence of think tanks began to take place as a response to the practical problems resulting from urbanisation, industrialisation and the economic growth of the early twentieth century (Ibid.). These are referred to as the first generation think tanks and among them the Brookings Institution and the Russell Sage Foundation were well known. The Chatham House and Fabian Society were also among those of this first generation category (Ibid.).

Second, the ideational factors that drove the world into two camps immediately following the end of the Second World War provided the *raison d'être* for the flourishing of several other think tanks across Europe, especially those that looked at issues relating to foreign policy as well as security and development. The emergence of several independent states following the decolonisation process also contributed to the development of interest in the study of the third world; indeed, this too had an impact on the emergence of a category of institutes that focused on specific areas of study relating to the broader disciplines of history, politics, economics and social issues among these countries (Ibid.).

The third phase of think tank proliferation began in the 1970s and was characterised by the height of the Cold War and the fundamental changes taking place – especially those changes in the shaping of inter-state relations within the bipolar environment of the time. It was also distinguished by the political instability of states in Asia, Latin America and Africa (Ibid.). There was a heightened awareness of security issues relating to the proliferation of weapons and the Cold War conflict itself. On the economic side the questions that concerned research institutes focussed on development issues and related indicators.

There is an emerging view among analysts that a fourth wave is now in progress. This new wave does not necessarily relate to the kind of organisations being established and/or subject matter being studied, but rather to the nature in which inter-state relations are changing. The growing impact of civil society in many countries, coupled with the transnational character that ideational factors have acquired, is pushing forward the growth of research interaction across borders, which is being seen as the influence of both globalisation and regionalisation (Stone, 2005: 4). In fact, this aspect of the fourth wave of development is covered in the last section of this chapter and looks at how Asian–Pacific diplomacy has been impacted by both globalisation and regionalisation (Soesastro, 2003: 1–34). The efforts at institution building in Asia–Pacific are significant in terms of the roles played by track II groups like the ASEAN-ISIS. The ASEAN-ISIS is an amalgamation of research institutes in Southeast Asia and has been effective to a moderate degree in helping to push forward certain agendas that were difficult to achieve through the functioning of the track I process alone (Wanandi, 1995: 56–66).

What is significant about this last stage of think tank development is that within this period one sees the impact of research institutes and think tanks as 'epistemic communities' that have the capacity to go beyond domestic limits and play a role in the transnationalisation of ideas and opinions. Since the process of globalisation is one that transcends national and state boundaries, it has the capacity to transmit ideas beyond the geographic limits of state structures and territoriality. Not only does the growth of ideas become relevant within the policy-making structures of the state, but the spreading of ideas beyond borders also allows for their impact on group policies within regions. However, while this remains theoretically true, in actual reality the issues are far more complex and are driven to a large extent by the reactions of the political élite as well as by the politics between nation-states. This is important to keep in mind, particularly in view of the claim that research institutes function on the basis of a scientific approach rooted in non-partisan and non-ideological foundations. Again the point can be made, that while this remains true in theory, in many cases their development can be hampered by narrow political agendas and also by the dictates of funding groups.

This manner, in which institutes themselves are impacted by narrow political ideologies and funding sources which hamper their functioning, is relevant to the nature of the think tank or research institute itself. In the process of think tank development, five categories have been identified:

1. Independent, civil society think tanks established as non-profit organisations;
2. Policy research institutes located in or affiliated with a university;
3. Government-created or state-sponsored think tanks;
4. Corporate-created or business-affiliated think tanks, and;
5. Political party (or candidate) think tanks (Stone, 2005: 4–5).

Interplay between research and policy

The significance of the identification of think tanks along these lines is indicative of how capable they are in affecting policy changes. In most countries, the policy-makers aim to keep tight control of the process by delegating limited authority to the groups from whom they may seek ideas and information. In this sense, the research institutes remain within the control of the policy-makers, who allocate authority to them. Deterring research institutes from achieving their full potential as 'epistemic communities' – and frustrating the furthering of interests of the experts involved – is the process where policies made are often interpreted on narrow political terms (Haas, 1992: 12–17).

The reliance on research institutes to assist in the framing of policy at the inter-state level is crucial, particularly given that the range and complexity of issues critical to diplomacy today are greater than they ever have been. The contemporary international system is far more multifaceted – with complex political systems, increased number of actors (who may or may not share commonality of views on certain issues and overlapping of views on others), expanding global economic networks and coping with the challenges to state administration from within (Ibid.). Such factors tend to support greater dependence on research institutes to assist in policy-making. This is a very significant factor as it offers an important space for the emergence of newer avenues for representation and the exchange of ideas. This is where the role of research institutes becomes effective in influencing policy-making. Policy-makers may not always have a clear and in-depth understanding of issues; in fact, there have been cases where the interplay between research and policy-making emerged as an outcome of crisis. This is because in a crisis situation there is a period of time during which power is absent and this provides the space for the research community to enter into the arena of policy discourse (Ibid.).

Under conditions of stress, research institutes can be effective in two ways. First, they can seek out the cause-and-effect relationship and provide advice for the kinds of action that need to be taken. As a community that looks at issues in an objective manner, research institutes can use their expertise to identify winners and losers within a given a situation. Second, they can provide valuable information on the inter-linkages and might be able to understand how events may unfold (Ibid.). Therefore, one of the significant aspects of research – that is, prediction – could contribute to the planning of policy initiatives based on the identification of trends that are likely to emerge.

Research institutes can also assist in defining what is in the self-interest of the state as well as the groups represented in it, which can help in the initiation of policies that address the concerns of all, whereas a state-centric approach to policy may focus too narrowly on what the state itself requires. The significance of these objectives can be better fulfilled in circumstances where the policy-making options are less politically motivated. In the case of states that have the capacity to include the views of groups in their policy-making initiatives, the research community has the ability to provide critical alternatives for the issues that drive the concerns of policy-makers. According to E.E. Schattschneider, the fact that the groups are able to provide alternatives is itself 'a supreme instrument of power' (Schattschneider, 1975: 66; Haas, 1992: 16). Where policy-making is narrowly defined by the elite power plays of politics, the role for alternative views becomes the instrument through which change can be instituted. By the use of causal rationale, the capacity to influence the decision-making process is considerable – both in terms of eliciting greater support from groups outside the policy-making process as well as impacting the decision-making (Schattschneider, 1975: 66; Haas, 1992: 16–17).

The case of ASEAN-ISIS/CSCAP

Growing interdependence, globalisation and the emergence of a multitude of players in international relations has seen the emergence of think tanks as transnational actors and an independent variable (Rugland, 2002: 84). Having dealt at length with the issue of research institutes as diplomatic actors in the policy-making process, the final section of this chapter looks at one of the leading case studies specific to the Asia–Pacific region.

In the context of Southeast/East Asia, the economic boom in the region led to the unprecedented growth of research institutes. In many ways, this growth replicated the views of the states themselves that sought legitimacy of rule by fostering rapid economic growth. The authoritarian structures actually pushed forward the modernisation programme and the think tanks were essentially 'a small group of people whose technical and scientific know-how was limited to a narrowly defined policy sector'(Ibid.). Think tanks in this period proliferated in two basic sectors – economics and security. According to Simon Tay, both these sectors were closely interlinked (Soesastro, 2003). It was believed that economic growth would lead to regime consolidation and this would be dependent on an international environment where the tension of conflict was minimised, if not altogether eradicated. Economic development was also a crucial indicator of how the state could cope with internal threats to security that emerged from communist insurgency (Ibid.).

Therefore, as a result of two factors, cooperative and comprehensive security emerged as the major components of the national and regional development policies of the states in Southeast Asia.[7] The first of these involved the manner in which regime consolidation and economic development are interlinked, and the second, the need to include communist insurgency into the comprehensive security approach. The view that cooperative security would provide an environment within the region that would allow the states to focus upon their own economic development without the diversion of having to contend with conflict in the region, was a significant step in the realisation of the goal of national and regional development. Similarly, the comprehensive security strategy was conceived to address the threats posed by internal dynamics of the states, which comprised of communist insurgency, the threat of economic disparity within the state and cultural and environmental issues. (Soesastro, 2003: 21–34).

The aim of addressing these issues led to the development of the track II initiative in the region under the auspices of the ASEAN-ISIS. The initiative brought together think tank experts, diplomats, military officials and politicians – the latter three in an unofficial capacity. According to one of the founding members of the ASEAN-ISIS initiative, Jusuf Wanandi, the process was entrusted with the task of focusing on issues that were considered sensitive in official negotiations. As a result, the advantage of the track II process emerged from the fact that participants could freely discuss issues that had deterred progress in crucial areas of interest in an environment that was confidential (Wanandi, 1995: 56–66).

The track II initiative developed in two key areas. First, the field of economic cooperation was enhanced under the patronage of the Pacific Economic Cooperation Council. This grouping of academics, officials and members of corporate/business groups was a widely acclaimed network that formed the blueprint for the establishment of the Asia–Pacific Economic Cooperation (APEC) (Notter and MacDonald, 1996). Second, on the security aspect of regional cooperation, the track II move was spearheaded by the ASEAN Institutes of Strategic and International Studies. Registered in 1988, its basic objective was to promote regional cooperation within the Asia–Pacific region with the hope of strengthening cooperation and research on issues relating to strategic and security matters. Originally, the group consisted of only members from research institutes or think tanks within the Southeast Asia region. The founding members were:

1. Centre for Strategic and International Studies, Jakarta;
2. Institute of Strategic and International Studies, Malaysia;
3. Singapore Institute for International Affairs, Singapore, and;
4. Institute for Security and International Studies, Thailand (Caballero-Anthony, 2005: 161).[8]

Added to this list was a single member from the Philippines, Professor Carolina Hernandez, who forged the way for other members of the academic community to join and who later brought into the group, the Institute of Security and Development Studies in the Philippines. With the expansion of ASEAN itself to include newer members, the Institute for International Relations in Vietnam and the Cambodian Institute for Cooperation and Peace also joined the ASEAN-ISIS (Notter and MacDonald, 1996). In many ways, the group has been successful in acting as a catalyst for the functioning of the track I diplomacy through the establishment of mechanisms and institutional frameworks. However, its success in terms of actual efforts to push forward regional security issues is a critical factor and that has been seen by the manner in which two treaties were initiated: the Treaty of Amity and Cooperation (TAC) and the Treaty on the Southeast Asian Nuclear Weapon-Free Zone (SEANWFZ).

One of the key initiatives that the ASEAN-ISIS furthered was lobbying for the widening of the TAC in the region. Established in the early 1970s, the TAC initially included only the original five members of the ASEAN but was later opened to the newer members. With an increase in ASEAN activities to cover the newer members and the establishment of institutionalised inter-action with both China and India, ASEAN has expanded the scope of the TAC to cover these countries. While some analysts may claim that the TAC is not worth the paper on which it is written, there is no doubt that some degree of importance can be attributed to it as it is regarded as a Magna Carta for the peaceful settlement of disputes in the region. As new states have acceded to the TAC, there has been a further expansion to cover new countries that have been brought into the dispute settlement mechanism. This is a critical factor that has been pushed forward by the ASEAN-ISIS (Ruland, 2002: 88).[9]

The SEANWFZ initiative started in the 1980s as a track I proposal, but only began to take shape much later as the move to push for the realisation of the case came through the ASEAN-ISIS. In 1995, at the behest of the group, the 5th ASEAN Summit finally launched the SEANWFZ – to which all the members have acceded. However, this attempt by the ASEAN-ISIS has been met with limited success, as it has been unable to convince the nuclear weapons states to endorse it. In fact, the United States has refused to endorse the treaty on the grounds that its security interests in Northeast Asia are vital and will not therefore fit into the requirements of ASEAN's expectations (Moller, 2001: 154). India's willingness to endorse the SEANWFZ has been welcomed by the region and has proved to be a significant move in the furtherance of important diplomatic ties.

In the early 1990s, in response to calls for the formation of a multilateral security mechanism for the region, ASEAN took on a leadership role. Following the model of the Organization for Security and Cooperation in Europe, both Canada and Australia sought to establish a similar pattern for security cooperation in the Asia–Pacific region and this led to the creation of the ASEAN Regional Forum (ARF).[10] With the establishment of the ARF, the ASEAN-ISIS became the central pivot for the foundation of the Council for Security Cooperation in the Asia–Pacific (CSCAP), which was the track II process of the ARF. Established in 1993, this was to 'provide a structured process for regional confidence building and security cooperation among countries and territories in the Asia–Pacific region' (CSCAP, 1993). Apart from the ASEAN-ISIS members, the CSCAP had other member institutes from the Asia–Pacific region including the Strategic and Defence Studies Centre at the Australian National University, in Canberra; the Japan Institute of International Affairs, in Tokyo; Joint Centre for Asia–Pacific Studies at both the University of Toronto and York University, in Toronto; the Seoul Forum for International Affairs; and the Pacific Forum at The Center for Strategic and International Studies (CSIS), in Honolulu. These institutional affiliations across the region widened the scope for cooperation on matters relating to maritime security, comprehensive and cooperative security building efforts and also increased the scope of confidence building measures. In many respects, despite the effectiveness of the group with regards to certain issues, the responses of the multilateral institutions in the region leave a sense of failure in addressing events that have critically challenged the region – like the Asian Financial Crisis, the security threats relating to terrorism and non-traditional security problems such as the environmental haze crisis. Within the context of the changing realities of the regional environment, the approach of these multilateral institutions – of which the ASEAN-ISIS is a part – leaves much to be desired. Among the key drawbacks has been the inability to progress on issues relating to preventive diplomacy, which is a key pillar of the ARF process, making any forward movement very difficult.[11]

Conclusion

There is no doubt that with the increase in the number of players that determine the functioning of inter-state relations today, there is a wider scope for the role of the track II initiatives in both regional economic and security cooperation. Undoubtedly, as the complexity and diversity of inter-state relations expands, there is likely to be an increasing space for actors at non-state levels. While the state will most likely remain a referent for much of these debates, there is room for the expansion and exchange of ideas through the participation of knowledgeable groups acting at the sub-state level. The capacity of these groups to carry on a dialogue without the formal structures of state practice liberates them from the tedious task of official or prescribed approaches. This is particularly true in situations where the state may not be able to function in the dialogue process. Here, the role of track II as a community and mediator can transcend state and national boundaries, effectively furthering diplomatic ties.

One of the issues that may hamper the development process will be whether or not academic communities themselves are tightly restricted by ideological mindsets. Clearly, any development towards a greater role for research institutes and academic interaction in the policy-making arena will need to include a de-politicisation of academic communities, especially within the scope of the negotiations concerned. The second challenge will involve the manner in which states react to one another. The international system is dominated by a sharp inequality of power distribution. Any attempt to evolve a role for research groups will require a level playing field, allowing for the transmission of ideas. There needs to be a greater resolve among the decision-makers to understand the benefits of the track II process – not purely in a rhetorical sense, but also to actualise the content and vision that it brings to inter-state relations.

Notes

1. For a detailed analysis of the way in which the policy-making and the domestic lobbies within the state interact in the decision-making process, see Robert Putnam (1988) 'Diplomacy and Domestic Politics: The Logic of Two-Level Games', *International Organization* 42: 427–460.
2. For the debate over the definitional aspects of the think tanks please see the chapter by Diane Stone and Mark Garnett (1988) 'Think Tanks, Policy Advice and Governance', in Diane Stone, Andrew Denham, and Mark Garnett, eds, *Think Tanks Across Nations: A Comparative Approach*, Manchester: Manchester University Press, 1–20.
3. See Diane Stone (2006) 'Think Tanks and Policy Advice in Countries in Transition', in Toru Hashimoto, Stefan Hell, and Sang-Woo Nam, eds, *Public Policy Research and Training in Vietnam*, Tokyo: Asian Development Bank Institute, 38–109, cited in the UNDP Report (2003) *Thinking the Unthinkable: From Thought to Policy. The Role of Think Tanks in Shaping Government Strategy: Experiences from Central and Eastern Europe*, Bratislava, New York, NY: UNDP Regional Bureau for Europe and the Commonwealth of Independent States.
4. For a detailed analysis of the development of think tank traditions in Europe please see, Philippa Sherrington (2000) 'Shaping the Policy Agenda: Think Tank Activity in the European Union', *Global Society* 14(2): 173–189.

5. See also Diane Stone and Andrew Denham, eds (2004) *Think-Tank Traditions: Policy Research and the Politics of Ideas*, Manchester: Manchester University Press.
6. For a detailed analysis of the development of think tanks within China please see, Shai Chen-Ming (2004) 'The Chinese Tradition of Policy Research Institutes', in Diane Stone and Andrew Denham, eds *Think-Tank Traditions: Policy Research and the Politics of Ideas*, Manchester: Manchester University Press, 141–162.
7. The view that cooperative security would provide an environment within the region that would allow the states to focus upon their own economic development without the diversion of having to contend with conflict in the region was a significant step in the realisation of that goal. Similarly the comprehensive security strategy was conceived of as an answer to address the internal dynamics of the states: communist insurgency, the threat of economic disparity within the state and the cultural and environmental issues that dictated the internal threats had to be addressed only through these two options. For a detailed analysis see, Muthiah Alagappa, ed. (2002) *Asian Security Order: Instrumental and Normative Features*, Stanford: Stanford University Press.
8. See also, Desmond Ball (1994) 'A New Era in Confidence Building: The Second Track Process in the Asia-Pacific Region', *Security Dialogue* 25(2): 157–176.
9. Also see, Shankari Sundararaman (2004) 'Politics and Security in Southeast Asia: Prospects for India-ASEAN Cooperation', *International Studies* 41(4): 371–386.
10. For an assessment of how ASEAN and ASEAN-ISIS plays a pivotal role within the Asia-Pacific region see, Shankari Sundararaman (1998) 'The ASEAN Regional Forum: Reassessing Multilateral Security in the Asia-Pacific', *Strategic Analysis* 22(4): 655–665.
11. For a detailed analysis of the regional security architecture in the Asia–Pacific region see, Vinod K. Aggarwal and Min Gyo Koo (2006) 'Asia's New Institutional Architecture: Managing Trade and Security Relations in a Post-September 11 World', BASC Working Paper Series 2006–01, 1–41. See also, Ralf Emmers (2006) 'Security Relations and Institutionalism in Southeast Asia', BASC Working Paper Series 2006–07, 1–33.

Part III

Targeting the Policy Arenas of Interaction

8
The New International Security Agenda and the Practice of Diplomacy

Shaun Riordan

Both the scope and nature of the international security agenda have evolved significantly in recent years (Riordan, 2003). This reflects changes in the geo-strategic environment and in the way we think about security. These changes have serious implications for global governance issues and how diplomatic services should be reconfigured to tackle them.

The new international security agenda

Traditionally, international security was thought of in terms of the security of states within the international system. An international security threat implied a threat to the stability or integrity of a state or group of states. Thus, the international security agenda focused on issues such as the strategic balance of power, regional conflicts, civil wars or weapons proliferation. However, in a post-Cold War world this definition of international security in terms of the security of the state became problematic. For instance, it did not include international terrorism. International terrorism, for example of the Al Qaeda variety, can kill horrific numbers of citizens, but it does not threaten the stability or integrity of any Western state (and few other states). Nevertheless analysts could hardly have excluded terrorism from the international security agenda, especially after 9/11. Even before then, some analysts in the United States began to redefine international security in terms of the economic and physical welfare of the citizen within the state (Brower and Chalk, 2003). This redefinition, by focusing on the individual within the state rather than the state, allowed terrorism to be included within the international security agenda. However, it also inevitably, and radically, expanded that agenda to include a range of new issues such as organised crime, epidemic illnesses, environmental degradation, mass migrations, poverty, competition for natural resources and international financial stability. Ironically, many of these new issues have a significantly better claim to inclusion under the old definition of international security than terrorism. Mass migration, poverty, environmental degradation and international financial instability can (and have) threatened the stability or integrity of states or groups of states (there are numerous historical examples of collapse of states or state systems that can be attributed to one or all of these factors[1]). Of course so too has epidemic disease threatened the stability of states – a topic that will be discussed later in this chapter.

The multiple challenges of the new international security agenda have several features in common:

1. They are all interconnected and interdependent. They can often reinforce each other creating spirals of ever more serious and ever broader consequences (sometimes referred to as positive feedback loops). For example, the poverty and ignorance that drive farmers to overuse land does not only lead to environmental degradation in the form of soil erosion, but yet more poverty. This vicious circle is reinforced by increasing the risk of disease and migratory pressures. Migrations both spread disease and increase poverty and environmental pressures in neighbouring communities. The pressures of migration, poverty, environmental degradation and disease call into question the governmental and other institutional structures of a region or country, opening up opportunities for organised crime and international terrorist groups, quite aside from the increased risk of civil or other conflict. And so it goes on. The key point is that these issues must be tackled as a whole, not individually;
2. There are no ready-made solutions or 'right answers'. Nor is it always clear what policy objectives should be. Expert opinion can disagree radically, with even the broad road to follow in dispute. Solutions (if they exist) or responses must be developed through dialogue and discussion;
3. No single country, or even regional group of countries, can tackle any one of these issues alone, let alone all of them. The new international security agenda demands a new level of global collaboration;
4. Collaboration must extend beyond governments and political élite to the extensive set of civil society actors if it is to be effective;
5. These issues involve high levels of expert knowledge – the old style gentleman diplomat no longer has a role in tackling the challenges of the new international security agenda.

Epidemic disease – an international security threat

The example of epidemic diseases helps to illustrate the issues. The security threat posed by epidemic disease should be clear from the experience of 1918, when the outbreak of Spanish influenza killed more people in one year than the four years of carnage in the First World War, and contributed to the collapse of the German army on the Western Front that same year. A more recent example has been the economic and social devastation wrought in Sub-Saharan Africa by HIV/AIDS. While some observers may be tempted to dismiss the impact of HIV/AIDS in these countries as a consequence of poverty – and corrupt tyrannical government – the example of the Republic of South Africa shows the impact and security implications of this disease even for a modern and relatively wealthy parliamentary democracy. According to one recent report (Brower and Chalk, 2003), the levels of HIV already in the South African Army are such that it cannot effectively be deployed abroad for African peacekeeping operations, with severe implications for that continent's security. Given the levels of HIV in relevant sectors of future generations, the report warns that South Africa could be left without any reliable security or policing organisations within 15–20 years. Such a reality would question the viability of governance not only in South Africa, but throughout the African continent.

Epidemic diseases also have severe economic consequences that fall within the new definition of international security. HIV/AIDS has wrought economic as well as human devastation in Sub-Saharan Africa. But even less severe diseases, with lower rates of mortality, can have serious consequences in a globalised economy. Severe Acute Respiratory Syndrome (SARS), for example, killed relatively few and disappeared quickly. It nevertheless caused serious short-term damage to the Asian tourist industry and the airlines that service it. The overall effects of Avian Flu are yet to be seen, but even if it remains contained as at present, its impact on the agricultural and tourist sectors of the countries where it has occurred is nevertheless quite substantial.

Nor are epidemic diseases primarily a problem for developing countries, with few if any implications in the West. Westerners are in many ways more vulnerable than ever before. The interdependence of a globalised world and the mass movements of people and goods across borders offer ample opportunity for disease transmission. Modern means of transport exacerbate the risk. Whereas even 60 years ago, a journey from India to Europe took weeks by boat, ample time for a disease to emerge and the ship be quarantined upon arrival, the same journey now by plane takes hours – well within the incubation period of most diseases. A passenger can board and disembark from a plane visibly healthy, with a disease emerging much later once the individual has been reintegrated into society. By the time the disease has been diagnosed, it may already have spread, and be established within the community. The vulnerability is reinforced by the abuse of antibiotics for minor ailments in Western societies (not to mention the mass use of antibiotics in animal feeds), which has radically reduced their effectiveness by allowing viruses to develop antibiotic immune strains. This is compounded by the devotion of resources by drug companies to research treatments for profitable 'diseases of the rich'[2] rather than epidemic disease. Taken together, these factors imply that if, or when, a major epidemic disease does reach Western shores, the West's armoury to combat it will be much reduced.

A security strategy for epidemic disease

Tackling the security threat from epidemic diseases requires a proactive strategy of engagement involving those countries in which these diseases are likely to emerge. This should include the enhancement of public health systems to ensure prompt diagnosis, effective response and the global, early warning of new disease strains, as well as effective public health education to reduce unnecessary health risks. Although the broad lines of such a strategy may be clear, it will still require a genuine dialogue, both to understand the local cultural and social realities that will affect implementation, and to secure the full, willing collaboration of those countries with weaker public health systems and at most risk of primary outbreaks of epidemic diseases. The dialogue and collaboration will have to extend beyond governments and political élite to medical professionals and others involved in public health at all levels. Furthermore, the dialogue must extend beyond governments in the West, to medical professionals, drug companies and relevant NGOs, to name but three.

More to the point, governments and diplomats may not be the most effective agents for the implementation of such a strategy. Firstly, foreign governments may not be reliable interlocutors. It is, for example, now clear that the Chinese government initially sought to conceal outbreaks of Avian Flu from the international community. Even if a foreign government is well-intentioned, it may not have the internal structures required to monitor health developments within its own borders. Without engaging with a broad range of health professionals, Western governments may have little hope of discovering what is happening in much of the world. However, such an engagement may prove difficult as diplomats often do not have the necessary expert knowledge; attempts to engage may be misinterpreted by host governments as interference in their internal affairs (or even espionage); and such attempts equally may be treated with suspicion by foreign health professionals themselves.

The recent scare with the Avian Flu outbreak demonstrated that these health issues are at last being taken seriously, at least while they remain in the headlines. Nevertheless, it is questionable whether the techniques being deployed at the diplomatic level are ready for the challenge. The reaction to the discovery of Avian Flu in Turkey both illustrates the problems and indicates some of the solutions. Western governments and their diplomats provided Turkey with ready-made solutions, and then criticised the country, often in public, for not following the advice adequately or quickly enough. The diplomatic activity concerning this outbreak was limited to government and political élite circles. Little thought appears to have been given to whether this patronising and top-down approach improved Turkey's response to Avian Flu: it is unclear whether it really garnered the collaboration sought by Turkey's health care professionals, or whether in fact it alienated both the political élite and health care professionals (not to mention broader Turkish society). Even if it can be argued that, in the short-term, the outbreak was contained without loss of human life, it ignores the longer term costs. The threat of epidemic diseases requires a continuous vigilance that only willing collaboration can provide.

An alternative bottom-up, or dialogue-based approach, might have implicitly admitted that Western countries had no ready-made solution. Furthermore, it might have focused on working with medical professionals in the field rather than government officials in Ankara (perhaps through Western health-oriented NGOs). It even could have emphasised the value of, for example, Britain as a partner based on its recent exposure and experience with both Bovine Spongiform Encephalopathy (BSE) and Foot-And-Mouth Disease (FME), and thus the valuable knowledge this partner could have shared. It is suggested that such an approach would have secured a far fuller and more genuine collaboration at all levels of Turkish society; discouraged the Turkish bureaucracy from hiding uncomfortable evidence that they might otherwise have found embarrassing; and built a solid base for long-term collaboration in the future.[3]

Implications for the practice of diplomacy

The new international security agenda has serious implications for how diplomacy is done, and who are the players. While diplomats retain an important role in engaging in debate with other governments and political élite, they are often not the ideal (and can even be counterproductive) agents for engaging with foreign civil societies. As government representatives, they can lack credibility and detailed expert knowledge of the crucial issues. Their key role of maintaining relations with government officials can conflict with engaging with broader civil society, especially if the government concerned is corrupt or repressive and is hostile to the possible implications of the engagement. Diplomats may not have established ways of engaging with key elements of civil society – they may not encounter them in the course of their normal diplomatic duties or social life: creating artificial channels of approach can provoke suspicions that they have hidden agendas or ulterior motives, both within the civil societies with which they are trying to engage and with the governments to which they are accredited. In many countries, the appearance of being too close to foreign diplomats can be dangerous, both professionally and/or in terms of one's own safety.

Engaging with foreign civil societies may often best be done by the non-governmental agents of our own civil societies (Riordan, 2004). More often than diplomats, these agents have credibility – at times to the extent that they are seen as critical of their own governments. Many do have specialist knowledge of the key areas. They often already have relationships through the global NGO networks that allow access to civil societies, or can draw on shared interests or areas of expertise to establish them. They are deniable in a way that diplomats are not, so that their engagement with civil society can be pursued in parallel to maintaining normal diplomatic relations with existing governments. The role of government, and diplomats, in relation to these non-governmental agents is primarily as a catalyst, coordinating their activities within a broader strategy, encouraging those not already engaged in such activities, and on occasion providing discreet technical and financial support. But government officials must bear in mind that many potential agents will be reluctant to be seen as too close to, or acting at the behest of, government. Indeed, such an appearance could undermine the very credibility that otherwise represents much of their added value. Actors within government will therefore need tact, openness and understanding.

NGOs are not entirely unproblematic interlocutors for foreign civil societies. They have their own agendas, which may on occasion provoke as much conflict as collaboration (e.g., the insistence of human rights NGOs on gay rights can provoke problems in more conservative societies). Nor are they necessarily particularly representative of their own societies – they have no formal democratic legitimacy and frequently leave much to be desired in terms of internal democracy. Many of the larger NGOs have professionalised themselves to the extent that their 'executives' differ little from government diplomats (or even corporate executives). The key is not that NGOs are better interlocutors for foreign civil societies than diplomats because they are in some sense more moral, but that often their existing networks mean that they are already better plugged in to those societies than government representatives. Nevertheless, they should never be more than part of a richer mix of less formal networks, such as academics, journalists or local chambers of commerce. The criteria should be practical: above all, access and credibility in any given civil society.

While effective (and discreet) public diplomacy at home with NGOs and other civil society groups may be an essential precursor to their engagement in successful public diplomacy abroad, equally important may be 'semi-detached' governmental bodies, which retain a certain independence and cultural/intellectual prestige. These bodies are able to engage with civil societies at home and abroad, acting both as a catalyst and entrepreneur in promoting exchanges across a range of cultural, social and political topics. In the United Kingdom, the British Council is increasingly playing this role, to some extent giving it priority over its traditional English teaching or narrower cultural promotion roles (or even subsuming these latter roles in its broader engagement of overseas civil societies). Within the British Council there had been an attempt to redefine this broadening of its activities to promote dialogue between different civil societies and different cultures, using the term 'Mutuality' to distinguish it both from public diplomacy and traditional cultural relation (Rose and Wadham-Smith, 2004). The Council is seen as a leader in this field, with both the Goethe

Institute and Alliance Française keen to follow (and there is debate in the United States about establishing an analogue to the Council).

Re-thinking the structure and culture of foreign services

Managing the new international security agenda also has significant implications for the structure and culture of foreign ministries. Dialogue-based or collaborative diplomacy needs time to work: it does not produce instant results. Foreign ministries therefore need to be able to anticipate better which will be the key issues in the medium- to long-term and the international climate in which they will operate. This in turn implies the need to develop a capacity for long-term policy thinking and geo-political analysis. Western foreign ministries are notably weak in both. Overly hier-archical decision-making processes, and their consequent administrative burdens and emphasis on conformism rather than innovation or creativity, condemn officials to short-termism, both of policy-making and analysis.

The gathering of good intelligence or information and its effective and timely analysis are as essential to the new international security agenda as to its Cold War equivalent. But just as the agenda itself has broadened, so has the type of information needed and the most effective ways of gathering it. If the traditional diplomat has lost his monopoly on the management of international relations, so has the traditional intelligence officer lost his monopoly on the gathering of intelligence. Rather than depending on the secret services of the nation state, whether human spies (Humint) or intercep-tion of electronic and other communications (Sigint), much of the informa-tion on the new international security agenda is to be found in the dense networks of interaction between NGOs, academics and other non-state actors. Accessing this information will be less a question of covert operations than developing effective collaborative relations, whether directly or indirectly, with the actors in these networks. Some may argue that non-democratic governments cannot be trusted even on the less traditional aspects of the new security agenda (e.g., the initial reaction of the Chinese government to the outbreaks of both SARS and Avian Flu), and that thus even in these areas covert operations will still be necessary. While both Humint and Sigint will indeed continue to be necessary to deal with issues such as terrorism and organised crime, they are likely to be counterproductive in other areas. The point of a collaborative paradigm of diplomacy is precisely that it releases flows of information that might otherwise be concealed within xenophobic and defensive government structures. Indeed, the issue in most areas of the new international security agenda may not be the lack of informa-tion so much as an excess. The key then will be to develop analytical tools that enable governments to navigate successfully in a highly complex and interconnected world.

In fact, historically the problem with foreign policy-making may always have been poor analytical techniques rather than lack of information (the latter is a convenient excuse for both analysts and policy-makers). Foreign ministries should learn from the experience of the private sector, which makes extensive use of the scenario planning techniques developed by Shell in the 1960s and 1970s, as well as newer modelling techniques derived from network and complexity theory (Ormerod and Riordan, 2004; Riordan, 2006). Traditional 'predict and control' models, in which analysts predict a single 'most probable' future and decision-makers then design a maximising strategy for that single future, no longer function in an ever more complex world. The private sector increasingly uses the newer techniques to generate multiple scenarios or possible futures. Possible strategies are then tested and refined across the possible futures for robustness and adaptability. In other words, the chosen strategy is one that does acceptably well in all the scenarios, not just exceptionally well in only one. Drawing on these techniques, foreign policy machines should be restructured to allow the development of medium- to long-term objectives against various future possible scenarios which can provide the framework in which a foreign policy strategy to secure these objectives can in turn be developed.

It is for debate where the analysis and planning operations should be located. One suggested possibility is linked to the extent to which European governments have moved coordination of European policy, and indeed European strategy, out of foreign ministries and into the equivalent of the prime minister's office. Thus European policy in Britain is now decided by the European Secretariat of the Cabinet Office, in France by the Secrétariat general du Comité interministirériel pour les questions de cooperation économique européenne (SGCI) and in Germany in the Federal Chancellor's Office. In the United Kingdom, the Assessment Staff responsible for analysis and assessment is in the Cabinet Office. This suggests the creation of strategic overseas planning and analysis departments 'above' foreign ministries in prime ministerial or presidential offices, along the lines of the National Security Council.

There needs to be a change of culture as well as structure. Western foreign ministries remain tied to a 'closed' paradigm of decision-making, in which policy is decided and then 'sold' to other governments. Policies once decided may indeed be changed, but only as a result of 'defeat' by foreign governments. This paradigm largely holds true even between close allies. But it is inadequate, and even counterproductive, if the aim is to secure the collaboration of a broad range of partners and their civil societies. Dialogue-based diplomacy requires a more open decision-making process, in which broad policy objectives are set, but in which detailed policies emerge as part of the dialogue process. Dialogue involves listening as well as talking, and accepting that one does not have all the answers and that others might have alternative valid solutions.

Although a major part of the new diplomacy will fall to non-governmental agents, embassies and diplomats abroad will continue to play an important role. They too will need radical changes of culture and structure. Diplomats will continue to have an important role in engaging members of the political élite, and in many cases, key journalists and commentators as well. To do so they will need to be more open and willing to go 'off-message' and to engage in genuine dialogue and debate. Their knowledge of the countries in which they are posted, which will remain of enormous importance, will need to be augmented by greater expert knowledge of key national and international issues to give them credibility. To perform this role successfully, embassies and diplomats need to be encouraged to, and rewarded for, taking risks. In the engagement with broader civil society, their primary role will be as 'diplomatic entrepreneurs', looking for and identifying opportunities for engagement; communicating these opportunities to the relevant non-governmental agents; and, where necessary, facilitating the first steps in engagement. They will only be able to do this effectively if they are part of the informal network established with the non-governmental agents at home. These diplomats will also need to get out into the action, and not only in capital cities. The current departmentalised embassies, and the increasing micro-management from foreign ministries, pose serious obstacles to these public diplomacy roles.

Larger Western embassies tend to spend too much time in self-administration, managing both personnel and large embassy estates, and interacting with other diplomats. A premium is placed on the ability to handle the paperwork sent from headquarters, rather than local networking. Future embassies need to be slimmer and more flexible; less tied to prestigious buildings and more structured around functional networks. In the future five or six well-prepared and well-motivated diplomats with clear objectives, travelling constantly and linked to the foreign ministry network through their mobiles and laptops will be far more effective than the current 30 to 40 diplomats bound to their desks.

Other newer management techniques derived from network theory may also need to be introduced to deal with the complexity and multi-faceted nature of the new international security agenda. The British Diplomatic Service has already introduced, albeit on a modest scale, crisis teams ready to be deployed at short notice to respond to an emergency. This could be further developed with databases of diplomats deployed in routine positions at home or abroad, with details of specialist skills and abilities, who can be brought together rapidly into a unit for a specific purpose or crisis, and then disperse again afterwards. The concept is similar to that of swarming (Arquilla and Rondfeldt, 2000), developed in the military context in recent years at RAND. If technology has produced a much vaunted 'Revolution in Military Affairs', it is quite possible that the new international security agenda may demand a similar 'Revolution in Diplomatic Affairs'.

Notes

1. See Jared Diamond (2006) *Collapse: How Societies Choose to Fail or Survive*, New York, NY: Penguin Books Ltd.; Joseph Tainter (1988) *The Collapse of Complex Societies*, Cambridge: Cambridge University Press.
2. Investment in R&D by pharmaceutical companies continues to focus on diseases such as cancer and heart disease, which by being prominent mainly in wealthy countries offer better prospects of financial gain (as well as such 'vanity' drugs as Viagra).
3. See Jan Melissen, ed. (2005) *The New Public Diplomacy: Soft Power in International Relations*, Basingstoke: Palgrave Macmillan; see also Mark Leonard and Vidhya Alakeson (2000) *Going Public*, London: Foreign Policy Centre.

9
Towards a New Architecture of Global Governance for Responding to the HIV/AIDS Epidemic

Franklyn Lisk

HIV/AIDS: a global epidemic and development challenge

The Human Immunodeficiency Virus/ Acquired Immuno Deficiency Syndrome (HIV/AIDS) affects millions of people in all regions of the world. According to the latest estimates by the Joint United Nations Programme on HIV/AIDS (UNAIDS) and the World Health Organization (WHO), over 40 million people worldwide are currently living with HIV and AIDS, and about 25 million people have died of AIDS-related illnesses since the disease was first diagnosed a quarter of a century ago (UNAIDS/WHO, 2005). In 2005 alone, about 5 million people were newly infected with HIV and, despite improved access to treatment and care, AIDS claimed over 3 million lives in that year. The vast majority of HIV/AIDS infections and deaths have been in sub-Saharan Africa (SSA), where some of the worst-affected countries with national adult HIV prevalence rates as high as 30–40 per cent are to be found, but HIV/AIDS is now a global phenomenon.

The global nature of the HIV/AIDS epidemic is reflected in the latest update on the epidemic by the UNAIDS/WHO, which reported with respect to other regions that: growing epidemics are underway in Eastern Europe and Central Asia; there is the real danger of the virus spreading rapidly in the large and populous countries of South and South-east Asia, such as China, India and Indonesia where the reported low national HIV prevalence rates mask a potentially explosive situation; the total number of people living with HIV in East Asia increased sharply by one-fifth (to nearly 900,000) in 2005, compared with previous years; national infection rates remain high in the Caribbean, making the region still the second most affected after SSA (UNAIDS/WHO, 2005). Although the number of people living with HIV in

145

developed countries is comparatively low – due to a combination of effective prevention methods, the widespread availability of Antiretroviral (ARV) therapy and good healthcare facilities – there are concerns that increased risky behaviour among certain vulnerable groups and the migration of people originating from regions and countries with serious epidemics could increase substantially the number of new diagnoses (Commission of the European Communities, 2005a; UNAIDS/WHO, 2005).

Without doubt, the HIV/AIDS epidemic is now one of the worst public health disasters in human history and a humanitarian crisis of extraordinary scale. Apart from being a human tragedy, HIV/AIDS also has particularly profound economic and social development implications. First, AIDS is concentrated in the working-age population and, hence, affects mainly those who are in the prime of their productive lives. The International Labour Organization (ILO) estimated that about two-thirds of the total number of people living with HIV and AIDS in 2004 were either formally or informally employed (ILO, 2004b). The fact that the epidemic disproportionately affects those with critical economic and social roles in society is a major drawback vis-à-vis development.

Second, AIDS is a fatal disease for which there is no known cure, and its immediate development impact is on mortality, life expectancy and population growth rates. Through its demographic effects and its manifold social and economic consequences, HIV/AIDS has evolved into a serious threat to sustainable development in many developing countries. There is evidence from highly-affected countries that AIDS is a factor in slowing the pace of economic growth and undermining efforts to reduce poverty.[1] It is now widely believed by the United Nations (UN) and the international community that HIV/AIDS is a major obstacle to the achievement of the Millennium Development Goals (MDGs), which were established by the UN at the Millennium Summit in September 2000.[2] Furthermore, the Summit also recognised that the socio-economic impact of the AIDS epidemic in developing countries was affecting international economic equality through the widening of the gap between the rich and the poor countries. The economic and social consequences of the epidemic constitute a strong case for responding to HIV/AIDS at both national and international levels as a major development challenge, rather than merely as a public health issue.[3]

From a development perspective, implicit in AIDS responses, are key issues of governance at global and national levels, which affect capacities to intervene and, hence, the effectiveness of such responses. The importance of governance in the context of AIDS responses was most evident in the discussions at the UN General Assembly High Level Meeting on HIV/AIDS at the beginning of June 2006, which reviewed progress in the global response since the adoption of the *Declaration of Commitment on HIV/AIDS* by the UN General Assembly Special Session on HIV/AIDS (UNGASS) in June 2001 (UN, 2001a). A progress report prepared by UNAIDS for the June 2006 UN meeting noted that the lack of progress in responding to HIV/AIDS and containing new infections in certain regions and countries, as well as the failure of governments to deliver on their UNGASS commitments, were linked to weaknesses in governance-related factors. Such factors included the lack of political leadership and commitment; the low priority accorded to AIDS in development agendas; the insufficient spending on HIV prevention and AIDS treatment; and the failure to address human rights abuses which affect access to HIV/AIDS services (UNAIDS, 2006). Similarly, a report on the implementation of UNGASS commitments prepared by the International Council of AIDS Service Organizations (ICASO) and released to coincide with the June 2006 UN meeting concluded that, apart from capacity constraints, many governments are falling behind on efforts to contain and reverse the spread of the epidemic as pledged in 2001, because of their failure or unwillingness to use the governance tools at their disposal (International Council of AIDS Service Organizations, 2006).

Domestic and international demands of global governance to support effective HIV/AIDS responses have highlighted the important role of diplomacy in influencing initiatives for managing the epidemic at various levels. The interface between governance and traditional diplomacy has been particularly pronounced in the context of initial efforts by the international community to put HIV/AIDS on the international development agenda. As outlined later, this involved essentially dialogue between governments conducted within the UN system and the G8 group of wealthy nations, regarding issues such as resource transfers, access to drugs and the protection of the human rights of HIV and AIDS sufferers, based on notions of a common approach and collective responsibility for fighting AIDS. This type of traditional state-based 'summit' diplomacy was soon complemented by a new form of 'multi-stakeholder' diplomacy, which recognised the important role of key non-state actors – civil society, private sector businesses, NGOs, AIDS activists – in emergent structures of global governance responding to the HIV/AIDS epidemic within the context of an increasingly globalised world, which itself gives rise to changing concepts of diplomacy. New and relevant norms and standards for global governance of health are emerging from the multi-stakeholder process of managing HIV/AIDS at national and global levels: governments will have to work with other forces in society, and no longer have the final say, in the design of HIV/AIDS policy and programmes and their implementation.

Against the background of the new model of diplomacy, the issue of global governance in the context of the management of the HIV/AIDS epidemic should be examined in light of three significant developments in contemporary international political economy: (1) the negative impact of globalisation on economic growth and livelihood in some of the worst-affected, and also some of the poorest countries in the world; (2) the enormous challenge that these countries face in trying to respond effectively to the impact of HIV/AIDS on their economies and populations, while at the same time being subjected to the limitations imposed by existing rules, norms and practices of global governance; and (3) the intensification of global interdependence in respect to economic and other interests, brought about by rapid globalisation of the world economy, which carries not only risks which are health-related but that also pose a threat to global and national and security.[4]

The above developments are underlined by the paradoxical situation wherein the resources required for fighting the global HIV/AIDS epidemic globally are controlled by the rich countries of the Global North that are the least affected, while the scale of the problem is enormous in the developing countries of the global South. Furthermore, serious doubts are raised about the efficacy of existing governance structures and the mechanisms of relevant global institutions for promoting and facilitating effective AIDS responses at both the global and domestic level. Weaknesses in global governance for AIDS responses are manifested in terms of the constraints on mobilising additional financial resources and improving access to life-saving AIDS drugs. Then there is also the need at the level of global institutions for a public policy approach, based on the economic concept of 'public goods', emphasising that controlling the spread of the global HIV/AIDS epidemic serves the common interest of both rich and poor countries. This is also related to the changing concepts of diplomacy, as mentioned above, and the need to bring together this world of diplomacy and that of contemporary global governance agenda.

This chapter analyses how the ability of the state to address the threat posed by HIV/AIDS to sustainable development is affected by existing governance structures and the mechanisms of global institutions. First, it reviews the challenges of putting HIV/AIDS on the international development agenda. Then it highlights existing weaknesses in global governance with respect to the outcomes of international economic, financial and trade arrangements, arguing for the need to modify and adapt existing rules and norms to improve the effectiveness and the substantive importance of AIDS responses at national and global levels. Finally, the foundation of a new architecture of global governance for AIDS responses is presented, including institutional structures and policy requirements to meet the present and future governance needs for effective AIDS responses at global, regional and national levels. Throughout this chapter, it is argued that it is essential to ensure transparency, accountability, stable economic, social and political environments, and sound management of resources, regardless of whether governance is at global, regional or national levels.

Putting HIV/AIDS on the global development agenda: progress and challenges

Initially, the main concern of the rich industrialised countries about the global AIDS crisis was how to control the spread of HIV infection to their populations, with the increased movement of people across national borders facilitated by globalisation. It was not until the beginning of this millennium that the rich countries began to show genuine concern about the development impact of the epidemic in poor countries. In June 2000. when Japan hosted the G8 Summit, the meeting adopted the *Okinawa Infectious Diseases Initiative* which reaffirmed that infectious diseases such as HIV/AIDS and malaria are not only a health issue but also a formidable challenge for global development in the new millennium. The G8 leaders backed the Okinawa Initiative with commitment of financial resources toward global efforts to control the spread of HIV/AIDS and other predominantly third world infectious and parasitic diseases. In December 2000, the Okinawa Initiative was followed up by the Okinawa International Conference on Infectious Diseases, which adopted an action plan to give concrete form to the notion of a 'partnership' between the G8 and the developing countries to fight HIV/AIDS. This move resulted in agreement on a new financial mechanism, which ultimately led to the establishment of the 'Global Fund to Fight AIDS, Tuberculosis and Malaria' (hereafter referred to as the Global Fund) in 2002.

The main function of the Global Fund is to rapidly raise and disburse funding for programmes that reduce the impact of HIV/AIDS, tuberculosis and malaria in low- and middle-income countries. This institution was deliberately designed by its 'founders' and principal backers, the rich industrialised countries, to stand apart from and operate outside the UN system. It was to incorporate significant civil society participation in decision-making both in its own governance structure and in country level operations. For example, civil society constituents from the Global North and South are represented with full voting rights on the Fund's board. At the national level, it is required that representatives of civil society and other non-state actors should be an integral part of the Country Coordinating Mechanism (CCM), which is responsible for preparing and submitting project proposals to the Global Fund as well as overseeing and monitoring progress during implementation. The CCM is considered an essential structure of the Global Fund's architecture and was designed to reflect commitment to local ownership and broad-based participation.

After nearly five years in operation, the performance of the Global Fund has been mixed and the results so far do not suggest that this model – which excludes the UN system from having control over substantial additional AIDS resources – has been as successful as envisaged. While there have been definite achievements in mobilising significantly large financial resources for highly-affected low-income countries, the spending of money at the country level has been beset by bureaucratic inefficiencies surrounding disbursement and implementation, poor project management, and even in some cases, corruption. Furthermore, the Global Fund's limited outreach structures have impeded the ability of national administrators to ensure that resources are getting to those who can use them most effectively and lack of resources has led to insufficient monitoring and evaluation. In addition, some believe that keeping the Global Fund apart from the UN system is contributing to further fragmentation of the global response to HIV/AIDS and, possibly, even resulting in the spending of yet more resources on overhead costs (Lisk and Cohen, 2005).[5]

At the Gleneagles G8 Summit in July 2005, the United Kingdom as host government unveiled a comprehensive plan for Africa recovery (Commission for Africa, 2005), which among other things identified HIV/AIDS as the greatest development challenge of the time. The highlight of the Gleneagles Summit was a commitment to achieve near-universal HIV/AIDS treatment by 2010 and, to this end, the leaders agreed to increase substantially global resources for the fight against HIV/AIDS, including replenishment of the Global Fund and debt cancellation, which should leave poor countries with more fiscal space for responding to the impact of AIDS on their economies and populations. However, as will be argued later, debt relief initiatives have not led to substantial benefits for most of the heavily indebted and worst-affected countries in terms of their capacities to mobilise additional resources for AIDS response. The major International Financial Institutions (IFIs) that are charged with implementing these initiatives are still operating mainly on the basis of concerns for macroeconomic and financial stability, which may not be consistent with desirable and practical efforts to respond urgently and effectively to HIV/AIDS as a national emergency. Hence, despite the G8 commitments on HIV/AIDS, financial support for controlling the epidemic is still far from secured: the Global Fund has been recently experiencing difficulties with its replenishments; and UNAIDS had a projected funding gap in excess of US$7 billion per year for HIV/AIDS services in developing countries between 2005 and 2007.

In the United States, President Bush made use of his 2003 State of the Union Address to announce the President's Emergency Plan for AIDS Relief (PEPFAR) initiative, and later at the Monterrey UN Summit on Financing for Development, earmarked within this initiative up to US$15 billion over five years to support national efforts in the fight against AIDS in a number of developing countries. Later in the same year, the European Commission launched its own comprehensive HIV/AIDS strategy, which committed increased financial and technical resources and proposed partnerships with developing regions to confront the global epidemic in the new millennium (European Commission, 2004a). In May 2005, the 25 members of the European Union (EU) committed a minimum of 0.51 per cent of their gross national income to foreign aid by 2010, with a substantial amount of that earmarked for the fight against HIV/AIDS. In the same year, Japan also announced aid increases of US$10 billion, with a sizeable proportion going to the Global Fund. Such bilateral and multilateral commitments, however, tend to reflect donor preferences that may not directly correspond to national priorities, strategies and objectives in AIDS responses; this, to some extent, seems to have been the case with the

PEPFAR, which initially excluded certain types of prevention interventions and the use of cheaper but effective generic AIDS drugs from its programme activities.

It was obvious that the rich countries were now seeing AIDS as an obstacle to sustainable development in many countries and, thereby, to the growth of the world economy. The enormous increase in global economic activity in the past two decades has generated increasing interdependence of countries and led to the progressive 'disappearance' of national boundaries with respect to trade and financial flows between countries, and the accompanying movement of goods and people. Furthermore, the impact of globalisation on international travel, with the advent of budget airlines, has resulted in the greater mobility of people between countries. The intensification of economic and social interaction and increased population mobility created conditions ideal for the rapid transmission of epidemics such as HIV/AIDS. This has led to increasing recognition in the rich countries that it is in the common interest of everyone, in both poor and rich countries, to take action to control the spread of a major global epidemic.

The shift in development thinking, from viewing AIDS as purely a health issue to the acknowledgement that it must be tackled as part of a broader global development agenda, was further evidenced by actions taken at the highest level of the multilateral system and in the context of international development policy and assistance. The establishment of the Millennium Development Goals as part of the UN Millennium Declaration highlighted the significance of tackling HIV/AIDS as an international development concern. One of the eight MDGs is specifically about controlling and reversing the spread of HIV/AIDS (MDG 6); it was acknowledged that failure to meet this particular goal will also seriously endanger progress towards the other MDGs that focus on reducing poverty, hunger, childhood mortality, etc. HIV/AIDS was most visibly recognised as a mainstream issue on the international development agenda with the convening of the UNGASS in 2001, when global leaders signed on to a Declaration of Commitment to fight the epidemic as a major development challenge.

The meeting of the ministerial-level Development Committee of the World Bank and the International Monetary Fund (IMF) in April 2001 discussed HIV/AIDS as a development policy issue and recognised the need for increased assistance by the IFIs to seriously-affected countries. The World Bank by then had launched the Multi-Country AIDS Programme in Africa with about US$500 million available in loans and credits to support national AIDS programmes, although disbursement has been rather slow. It has been alleged that programmes of the IMF unduly constrain health spending in poor countries, even when external financing is potentially available. While countries can theoretically set up their own spending priorities, the IMF through its monitoring function can impose spending limits in the health sector, such as wage bill ceilings and freezes on recruitment, on the ground of fiscal sustainability. The issue could become more serious for AIDS responses as countries seek to utilise large amounts of aid (e.g., Global Fund grants) specifically earmarked for scaling up prevention and treatment of HIV and AIDS. The prevailing situation needs to be redressed through practical recommendations pertaining to the implementation of macroeconomic and health sector policies.

The 2001 Doha Declaration of the World Trade Organization (WTO) on the relationship between the organisation's agreement on intellectual property rights pertaining to drugs under patent and public health, was precipitated mainly by the need to improve the access of developing countries to essential drugs to treat AIDS and related diseases. The Declaration established the rights of countries to take action to secure drugs at affordable prices as a means of protecting public health, including compulsory licensing and the manufacturing of generic AIDS drugs. However, many affected countries are unable to make use of compulsory licensing exceptions due to insufficient or absent manufacturing capacity. Part of the challenge at country level concerns the lack of knowledge or capacity regarding the extent to which flexibilities associated with the Trade-Related Aspects of Intellectual Property Rights (TRIPS) Agreement can be employed in the context of ARV, or what mechanisms are available in the WHO or elsewhere for tracking drug cost in resource limited settings and ensuring that the latest available products are available for national programmes. The situation is further compounded by bilateral trade agreements which may undermine TRIPS provisions.

Notwithstanding the inclusion of HIV/AIDS on the international development agenda, at the country level, governments are still treating HIV/AIDS as essentially a public health issue rather than a broader development challenge and, hence, failing to address the need for improved governance in AIDS responses. For example, the ability of some of the worst-affected countries to 'pay' for effective AIDS responses is seriously compromised by the pressure on them to make repayments on external debts to multilateral and bilateral creditors. Similarly, having laws that guarantee access to ARV therapy matters little, if there are no facilities nearby that provide the service. Such laws matter even less when most people living with HIV and AIDS are allowed to die, while life-saving drugs are kept out of their reach because of the rules of international trade pertaining to the production and sale of pharmaceutical products.

At the international level, the inclusion of HIV/AIDS on the global development agenda has not been pursued mainly on account of concern about impact on *global inequality* – and the need to narrow the gap between rich and poor countries – but because of increasing global *interdependence* which necessitates collective action by both the rich and poor countries to control the spread of a global epidemic. Consequently, sufficient attention has still not been given at the international level to the system of global governance needed for addressing the AIDS epidemic effectively. Hence, although the fight against HIV/AIDS is recognised at the global level as a major development challenge, the question of the governance of relevant global institutions in relation to AIDS responses was hardly addressed in the Millennium Declaration or other global commitments by the international community and its multilateral organisations. Even when cognisance was taken of the need for good governance as a requirement of development at both national and international level, there was little clarity and specificity about structures and mechanisms and which governance functions should be national and which should be global.

Global governance and AIDS response: opportunities and deficits

Global governance as used here refers to the structure of international institutions and related mechanisms and practices, as well as rules (laws, norms, codes), which affect the capacity of countries to formulate, plan, implement and monitor HIV/AIDS strategies, policies and programmes. The organising principle of global governance is multilateralism, but the global response to HIV/AIDS also involves the participation of other actors including bilateral development agencies, transnational private sector enterprises and international non-governmental and civil society organisations.

Global economic governance: managing globalisation

Global economic governance is about the management of the world's economic activity, which today is to a large extent characterised by globalisation – a process spearheaded by the liberalisation and expansion of flows of trade, investment and technology across frontiers, and resulting in the growing interdependence of national economies. Economic globalisation has redrawn the boundaries of economic activity and made it difficult to separate national and multilateral interests. The combination of the spread of HIV/AIDS globally and the rapid globalisation of the world economy in the past two decades is believed to have undermined the capacity of some of the worst-affected countries to respond effectively to AIDS.

Present arrangements for the governance of international economic relations make it difficult for countries on the fringe of the world economy to benefit from the opportunities created by globalisation. Because they are structurally underdeveloped and have weak links with the global economy, these marginalised economies are more vulnerable to external shocks and the negative impact of globalisation. Without appropriate and timely action at the international level to facilitate integration and beneficial economic links with the world economy for this group of countries, they are likely to remain poor and disadvantaged and with little prospects to resist the threat posed by AIDS to their development.

There are many countries in SSA for whom globalisation has resulted in anxieties rather than challenges and global risks rather than global opportunities (Cohen, 1998a; Stiglitz, 2002). AIDS has increased these anxieties and risks and, in turn, made it difficult for these countries to be integrated into the global economy. Hence, although globalisation may have created opportunities for the accelerated development of life-extending drugs and technologies to tackle AIDS, poor and marginalised countries are less likely to benefit significantly from these breakthroughs under existing governance structures and arrangements for managing the world economy.

Insofar as globalisation has contributed to economic slowdown in some developing countries, it can be argued that this leads indirectly to increases in poverty at the household level through, for example, loss of jobs and income-earning opportunities. It is now known that poverty and AIDS are strongly correlated in a bi-directional relationship: AIDS causes poverty and poverty is driven by AIDS. AIDS is thus a manifestation of poverty conditions that exist as well as the outcome of unsustainable social and economic livelihoods brought about by the epidemic. Already, there is evidence that poor households in those countries are becoming poorer because of the impact of AIDS, and that the poor are extremely vulnerable to becoming infected with HIV (Bonel, 2000; Sachs, 2005b).

As already noted, the global AIDS epidemic is affecting global economic growth and the distribution of the benefits from this growth between rich and poor countries. Increases in global economic inequality exist not only in terms of differences in per capita income between countries, but also with respect to significant differences in key indicators of socio-economic and human development such as life expectancy, infant mortality, health, education and nutrition. This is a situation that could be worsened by the inability to control the spread of HIV and treat those who are suffering from AIDS.

The prevailing disadvantaged situation of poor countries in the global economy clearly affects their governance responsibilities, including the capacity of governments to respond effectively to the epidemic and its impact on their populations. The inability of poor countries to benefit from globalisation under present global governance arrangements has given rise to demands for a new architecture of global governance that would enable these countries to respond more effectively to the threat posed by HIV/AIDS to their development. While it is widely accepted that the process of globalisation is irreversible, adjustments to the governance of relevant international institutions could lead to fairer and more equitable outcomes of globalisation. This was strongly advocated by the ILO in its World Commission on the Social Dimensions of Globalization report, which called for a more equitable pattern of international development in terms of the distribution of benefits of global growth between rich and poor countries (ILO, 2004a).

Changes in the rules of global economic governance, so as to recognise and take account of the social dimensions of globalisation in policy-making, are needed to create flexible conditions that could facilitate the full participation of marginalised countries in the global economy. This would enable them to take advantage of the opportunities afforded by globalisation and, thereby, enhance capacities to respond effectively to HIV/AIDS and address the reversal of development gains in areas such as education, health, life expectancy of working-age adults, infant mortality and child deaths, and decline in living standards.

Global financial governance

This concerns the rules and procedures by which the IFIs are regulated and how they do business. It is argued below that the present architecture of international financial governance is still not sufficiently flexible and adaptable to the needs of poor and least developed countries which hinders their ability to respond effectively to HIV/AIDS.

Some of the countries worst-affected by HIV/AIDS are also incurring heavy and unsustainable debt burden, which represents a huge barrier to progress in the fight against the epidemic. Repayment of debts to multilateral institutions and rich countries by some of the poorest countries in the world has in some cases amounted to diverting resources needed to respond effectively to current losses and sufferings due to AIDS. Until recently, global institutional arrangements for debt management operated on the basis of rules that suggested that, even while the AIDS epidemic is destroying lives and livelihoods, debt repayment should take precedence over human needs. Some would argue that even with recent adjustments, exiting institutional arrangements still do not go far enough to support the poor countries' mobilisation of the additional resources needed to protect current and future generations from the threat of HIV/AIDS.

Let us consider the case of the 'Heavily Indebted Poor Countries' (HIPC) initiative, which was launched in 1996 by the two major IFIs (the World Bank and the IMF) as a way of helping poor countries manage debt repayments without jeopardising their development prospects. At present, some of the developing countries most seriously affected by HIV/AIDS do not even qualify for HIPC assistance even though they are 'poor and heavily indebted'. In general, qualifying for debt relief under the HIPC initiative often entails the adoption of austere externally-imposed macroeconomic reforms over a period of at least three years as an indication of debt sustainability. This stems from one of the norms of the IFIs: that debt relief should not be seen as a reward for poor economic performance – which, in their view, constitutes a potential 'moral hazard'.

In the light of the threat posed to sustainable human development by AIDS in many poor and least developed countries and the need for additional financial resources to avert this threat, a good case can be made to re-examine the eligibility criteria for HIPC qualification including revising downwards key debt sustainability ratios. Certainly a strong moral case exists for not allowing debt repayment obligations and concerns for macroeconomic stability to stand in the way of desirable efforts to control the spread of HIV, treat AIDS sufferers and reduce poverty at the country level.

Indications are that even some of the HIV/AIDS-affected countries that are receiving assistance with debt repayment under the HIPC initiative may not have benefited much in terms of enhancing capacity to mobilise additional resources for AIDS responses. About one in three of all persons infected with HIV – that is, around 13 million people – live in countries classified by the World Bank and IMF as HIPC countries. These countries have some of the highest adult HIV prevalence rates in the world, and AIDS-related illnesses claim more than a million lives each year in the HIPC countries. Several of the HIV/AIDS-affected HIPC countries are reported still to be spending a sizeable part of government revenues on debt repayments. Half of the 26 HIPC countries in mid-2005 were still spending at least 15 per cent or more of their total revenues on paying off debts, and some were spending more on debt servicing than on health or education (Oxfam, 2002a; Todorova, 2003). Converting debt repayments into public investments in health and education could make a real difference in AIDS responses. The IFIs should confront the fundamental challenge of integrating debt relief into a coherent resource mobilisation strategy for fighting AIDS.

Another governance issue that is linked to the HIPC initiative concerns the willingness of governments of HIV/AIDS-affected countries to transfer HIPC dividends to AIDS responses: just how much of the savings arising from debt relief is going towards financing HIV/AIDS services at country level. Data for ten low-income African countries benefiting from debt relief under HIPC suggest that together only about 5 per cent of their HIPC savings were budgeted for AIDS activities in 2001 (Hecht et al., 2002).

The World Bank later launched the 'Poverty Reduction Strategy Paper' (PRSP) as a complementary initiative to the HIPC: all eligible HIPC countries were required to prepare PRSPs to ensure that savings on debt relief go toward poverty reduction. The PRSP was also designed to help low-income countries mainstream poverty reduction into national development planning. Given the obvious link between poverty and HIV/AIDS at country level, the PRSP is also viewed as a mechanism that could contribute to more effective AIDS responses. It was envisaged that the PRSP could become a means of mobilising additional resources from both multilateral and bilateral sources for financing poverty reduction and AIDS response programmes simultaneously.

On the basis of evidence, the PRSP initiative has so far not in reality been particularly successful in helping low-income countries mobilise additional resources for AIDS response. The UNAIDS Secretariat reviewed the first generation of 25 full and interim PRSPs prepared by sub-Saharan countries and found that while most of the countries concerned included HIV/AIDS in their PRSPs, the majority of PRSP documents hardly included any analysis of the relationship between AIDS and poverty. As planning tools, the PRSPs have often not included clear estimates of resource implications for responding to HIV/AIDS or set goals and targets for prevention and treatment, nor have they always included or reflected the main components of the corresponding national AIDS strategies. This could be because of strong external influence in the development of these PRSP documents, as distinct from taking into account national priorities and objectives associated with AIDS responses at the country level. PRSPs, as such, have not provided a sound basis for making decisions about AIDS funding in the context of national strategies and action plans. More should be done to integrate HIV/AIDS concerns into PRSPs, and to encourage donors and the international community to make use of this mechanism to increase financial support to poor countries to fight AIDS.

Governance of trade liberalisation

Trade liberalisation in the context of globalisation has not benefited many low-income primary producing countries that are on the margins of the global economy. Consequently, there are calls for the opening up of markets to poor countries and greater market access opportunities for their products, through the removal of restrictive trade practices and export subsidies in the developed countries (Stiglitz and Charlton, 2005). This would constitute the core of desirable reforms in the governance of trade liberalisation, which could provide better opportunities for developing countries to expand and diversify their exports and, hence, help to increase capacities to respond effectively to HIV/AIDS.

Specific to the governance of trade liberalisation in the context of AIDS response is the TRIPS Agreement of the WTO, which has been at the centre of controversy when applied to the production of essential drugs needed to treat AIDS and related diseases. The Doha Declaration on the relationship between TRIPS and public health, adopted at the fourth WTO Ministerial Meeting in 2001, gives poor countries the right to postpone the implementation of patent protection until 2016. Implicit in this are both opportunities and challenges of implementing new flexible arrangements within TRIPS to address compulsory licensing and generic manufacture of AIDS drugs under patent. South Africa and Brazil have both successfully claimed the right to manufacture and use cheap, generic drugs for the treatment of AIDS.

Although the Doha Declaration on the TRIPS Agreement established the rights of countries to take action to secure drugs at affordable prices as a means of protecting public health as a national concern, there are still provisions in the agreement that allowed for more stringent patent protection which can artificially raise prices for vital life-extending medicines and technologies needed to fight AIDS in the future. Furthermore, while progress has been made in driving down prices of certain ARV drugs, as already noted, the availability of new and more effective medicines for the treatment of

AIDS and other opportunistic diseases at affordable prices is still a challenge for developing countries which lack the resources and technology to carry out the necessary R&D.

A new architecture of global governance for AIDS response: requirements and prospects

Action at the international level

We have argued that existing governance structures and mechanisms of global economic institutions do not provide favourable conditions for poor countries to respond effectively to HIV/AIDS. Hence, there is an urgent need for a new architecture of global governance for AIDS responses. In this regard, there are a number of important requirements that will need to be met. First, the new architecture should address the fact that global public policy has so far paid little attention to the implication of the impact and policy outcomes of globalisation on the governance of AIDS, which, in turn, affects the capacity of poor countries to respond adequately to the threat of the epidemic. Second, the new architecture should include elements that are responsive to the economic needs of poor countries, as well as reflect the scale of the global AIDS epidemic as an international development issue. Third, it is important to link the new architecture of global governance for AIDS responses with the ability of developing countries to implement strategies and policies that address both AIDS and poverty simultaneously. Fourth, the new architecture of global governance for AIDS responses should be made more socially responsible by recognising the need for a balance between economic gains and social progress, and the need to avoid policies that exacerbate social tensions. It is necessary to put in place new governance structures and mechanisms that could bring about fairer outcomes of the liberalisation of international trade and financial flows, as well as more socially responsible patterns of globalisation.

A new global governance architecture for managing HIV/AIDS will undoubtedly bring into focus the relationship between the 'hard' issues (e.g., financial governance based on the Bretton Woods institutions and WTO models) and the 'soft' issues (e.g., standard-setting based on UNGASS targets, WHO's 3 × 5 initiative,[6] ILO's Code of Practice) of the global AIDS response. In addition to the need for an appropriate division of labour between the 'hard law' and the 'soft law' institutions, the global governance of AIDS response should also focus on the relationship between poor countries and their development partners who provide financial and technical assistance. This will cover such key development policy and planning issues as ownership, convergence between partners, consensus on short-term needs and long-term goals, and policy guidelines and coherence.

Recognition that the AIDS epidemic is global and that it threatens everyone, and that the consequences are much greater than those in public health alone, have to be understood in the context of the new architecture. The need to control HIV transmission globally underlines the importance of the mobilisation of resources for a global response to AIDS. Governments of the rich industrialised states, in consultation with the international community and the multilateral system, have a vital role to play in assuring the provision of health as a global public good that serves the common interest of both poor and rich countries by controlling the spread of the global HIV epidemic. This will require innovative mechanisms based on the principle that put people at the centre of development, and the recognition of HIV/AIDS as an important international public policy issue from several perspectives: public health, human rights, sustainable development, social justice and equity.

There are strong arguments for controlling the spread of HIV and AIDS as a matter of global public policy and in the common interest of both rich and poor countries. These arguments underlie the funding and otherwise supporting responses by the rich countries and the international community, since there are negative 'spillovers' or benefits for all from either doing nothing or doing something. A good case can thus be made for external transfers and subsidies from richer countries, so as to ensure that effective policies are put in place and implemented by resource-poor countries. The alternative is for richer countries to face the probability of much higher economic and social costs, as a consequence of the spread of the HIV infection to their own populations. Self-interest, as such, would lead richer nations to seek support through international cooperation, and material and other types of contribution to the global efforts to combat HIV/AIDS. This will be a cost-effective investment on their part and at the same time yield benefits to those countries facing deep and intractable development challenges due to HIV/AIDS. Appropriate global and multilateral governance structures need to be put in place as 'intermediate' and 'final' global public goods.

Finally, bold initiatives need to be undertaken in a number of key areas of the governance of globalisation, including the enhanced participation of developing countries in multilateral governance: greater transparency and accountability at all levels of governance; the formulation of guidelines with regard to governance responsibilities; and the development of open and innovative partnerships, for example, between rich and poor countries, between donor and recipient governments, between the public and the private sector, among governments of developing countries, and among governments, social partners and civil society. The institutional capabilities to undertake comprehensive and complex economic and social policies in many developing countries should be enhanced by more egalitarian international public policy to enable these countries to participate fully in the global economy.

Action at the national level

At the national level, changes in governance should be aimed at making governments more responsible and accountable to their populations for effective action to protect them against AIDS. Some governments in highly-affected regions and countries have become masters of the rhetoric of rights, but made very little efforts in translating them into action. For example, providing legal protection against the discrimination of people living with HIV, as many countries do, matters little if governments fail to enforce it. This brings into focus the notion of democratic governance in relation to the capacity of the machinery and institutions of government to respond effectively to AIDS and its impact on society. Democratic governance has its foundation in the concept of nation-building and evokes the idea of 'shared understanding' between those who govern and those who give their consent to be governed, effectively a 'deal' between the state and its citizens.

In relation to the management of HIV/AIDS as a development challenge, the key issues are: (1) the accountability relationship between governments and their populations including civil society and People Living with HIV/ AIDS (PLWHA), and between governments and their external partners and donors; (2) the responsibility of government to provide health as a 'public good'; and (3) recognition of the human rights of PLWHA and their families. The practice of governance in relation to integrating HIV/AIDS responses into the national development planning framework should address possible trade-offs between emergency and developmental action, centralised and decentralised planning, control and participation, and public good and individual rights.

In some highly-affected countries, political instability and armed conflict have posed additional burden to the development challenge of coping with HIV/AIDS. Barring the resolution of existing conflicts and the smooth implementation of political succession, efforts to fight AIDS will remain thwarted due to weak governance and weak governments. Governments should be empowered to own and play a vital role in the development process through capacity-building and a participatory development strategy. Improvement of governance at both the domestic and multilateral levels and the development of innovative and dynamic partnerships between governments and donors could bring about sustainable growth and development that would facilitate effective AIDS responses.

Action at the regional level

As in the case of national action against AIDS, it would appear that the threat posed by the HIV/AIDS epidemic for regional economic integration and development is still not fully appreciated by key regional organisations. In SSA, for example, the African Union and sub-regional groups such as the Southern Africa Development Community (SADC) and the Economic Community of West African States (ECOWAS) have passed resolutions and even engaged in the design of multi-sectoral programmes, yet there continues to be far too little commitment to comprehensive regional approaches. Part of the explanation for this situation lies again in the failure of institutions, irrespective of the level, to respond to HIV/AIDS as a wider development problem. The HIV/AIDS crisis has continued to be seen as primarily one of health and, as such, has not received much political support as a development challenge.

Regional integration for enhancing economic and social development could play an important role in AIDS response. It would assist the mobilisation of resources and attract donor support for certain initiatives that transcend national boundaries (e.g., EU support to SADC); strengthen negotiating positions of groups of developing countries vis-à-vis developed countries and international institutions in procurement of AIDS drugs and universal access to treatment; facilitate knowledge and skill development and transfer that could support effective response at the country level; and enhance accountability through the framing of regional codes and standards and a common approach to the implementation of multilateral monitoring mechanisms (e.g., UNGASS review, African Union/The New Partnership for Africa's Development (AU/NEPAD) peer review). Regional HIV/AIDS networks and centres/institutions can also facilitate local human resource development and promote effective partnerships in multilateral and global HIV/AIDS projects and initiatives.

Public policy responses at the regional level need to be based on a more general understanding of causes and effects, including linkages between regional conflicts and AIDS. Furthermore, policies need to be located in a space that is simply not national, but recognises the mutual benefits to be derived through regional coordination and regional action. Regional AIDS response institutions and networks could play an important catalytic role in generating a sustained and informed commitment by national policy-makers and stakeholders to a set of policies and programmes that represent well-funded comprehensive responses to HIV/AIDS. Attention needs to be paid also to regional partnerships between developed and developing countries (e.g., EU-NEPAD), as well as between developing countries themselves, South-South cooperation (e.g., Latin America–Africa), as a way of improving the effectiveness of AIDS response at country level.

Conclusion

This chapter has argued that the present system of global governance stands in the way of effective response to HIV/AIDS and other development challenges. The need for improved governance of global institutions to support effective AIDS response at all levels has become more obvious with the growing recognition by the international community and other stakeholders that the global HIV/AIDS epidemic threatens everyone and that the consequences are greater than public health alone. The urgency of this need is underlined by the realisation that in a world of unequal partners, globalisation does not seem to be benefiting poor countries with marginalised economies – many of which are also seriously affected by HIV/AIDS.

Attention has therefore been focused on the conditions and requirements for managing globalisation better and arriving at fairer outcomes of the process, in terms of greater economic well-being and social justice for all. This is complementary to an improved system of global governance system for effective AIDS response. The market-driven process of globalisation should be made conducive to a more egalitarian style of economic development and a more broad-based pattern of social development. Action is needed to invigorate equity concerns in the governance of globalisation in combination with mechanisms that incorporate social dimensions into the outcomes of the process. This, in turn, should provide developing countries with opportunities to benefit from globalisation and improve their prospects for responding to the development challenge of the HIV/AIDS epidemic.

The chapter has also stressed the need to explore alternatives to existing rules, policies and governance structures and mechanisms. International economic and financial rules must incorporate flexible arrangements and 'exit clauses' to allow disadvantaged countries to reassert their priorities as a national concern when these priorities clash with obligations to international institutions and unnecessary market discipline. These alternatives should be seen as an integral part of sustainable international economic and financial arrangements, characterised by stable and egalitarian global growth and based on policies built around the achievement of the MDGs.

In conclusion, it was noted that capacities of developing countries to respond effectively to HIV/AIDS also require adequate space for sound democratic governance. This is to ensure that the economic gains resulting from globalisation are accompanied by improvements in social indicators of progress, such as health and education. Recognition of common interests at the regional (supra-national) level and the need for harmonisation of policies and coordination of actions is necessary in planning AIDS response at the country level, as this could also lead to more cost-effective responses.

Notes

1. See, for example, Cuddington and Hancock (1994) as well as Greener et al. (2000).
2. The Millennium Development Goals (MDGs) are targets for eradicating global poverty by 2015 and promoting sustainable development, which were established within the framework of the Millennium Declaration adopted by the UN Millennium Summit in September 2000. See Sachs (2005a); UN (2006); and ILO (2006).
3. See Cohen (1998b); World Bank (2000); Barnet and Whiteside (2002); Lisk (2002); McPherson (2002), among others, for evidence to support the case for addressing HIV/AIDS as a development issue.
4. The security threat posed by HIV/ AIDS was explicitly recognised at the United Nations on 10 January 2000 when the UN Security Council had a full discussion on the global HIV epidemic; this was the first time that the Security Council had discussed a non-political or military issue in the context of its mandate.

5. See also, Secklinelgin (2005); UNICEF (2006); and Sidibe et al. (2006).
6. The '3 × 5' initiative was launched by the WHO in 2003 as a global target to provide 3 million people living with HIV and AIDS in low and middle-income countries with life-prolonging Antiretroviral (ARV) treatment by the end of 2005. This was regarded as a step towards the internationally established goal of universal access to HIV/AIDS prevention and treatment by 2010.

10
Family Dramas: Politics, Diplomacy, and Governance in the WTO

Rorden Wilkinson

In his account of the impact of family relations on personal development popular psychologist Oliver James offers a scenario of inter-family relations that provides a useful metaphor which helps us think about the kinds of trade politics, the diplomatic styles and behavioural patterns, and system of governance that the World Trade Organization (WTO), and the General Agreement on Tariffs and Trade (GATT) before it, has given rise to. James argues that,

> Families are similar to a theatrical drama. Like fictional characters, we are each assigned a scripted role, tightly directed in its performance, clothed in psychological costumes and required to sing and dance to our family tune. This is proven whenever there is a family gathering – at Christmas, for example. From the moment we gather on Christmas Eve or the day itself, our parents and siblings demand that we enact our appointed role. Never mind that we may have long since ceased to be the clever one ... the attention seeker or the moaner, our family treats us just as they always did and within minutes of walking through the door we are back in the nursery. The achievements and independence of adulthood are swept away and we find ourselves performing a role that we thought was long obsolete. (James, 2002: 32)

Much of what James describes is pertinent to WTO ministerial meetings and underlines a point about the WTO generally. We would merely substitute the family for the WTO, Christmas for the ministerial meeting, the parents for the United States and the European Union (EU) (as the institution's architects and most powerful members), and the siblings as a sample of WTO members ranging in size and shape but which would nevertheless include India, Brazil, Trinidad and Tobago, Zambia, Bangladesh and Korea to reflect what happens during the WTO's biennial road-show.

To elaborate, during each meeting a series of behavioural patterns unfold that are common to all ministerial meetings and the script ascribed to each character appears remarkably familiar. Like all family Christmases, differences exist in the way in which the meeting is played out; they, nevertheless, produce strikingly similar patterns of behaviour – a proclivity to crisis and collapse; domineering by the United States and EU; a 'plot' to load the text of a ministerial document by the Chair of the General Council/WTO Director-General/negotiating group facilitator causing a squabble among the family members; India and Brazil overcome their economic differences to forge a united front; Korea (and most of the rest of the Group of 10)[1] push hard for an extension of WTO rules into new areas; and coalition formation begins among the leading developing countries with the least developed members quickly following suit. We could also add to this list: an opening few days that comprise political grandstanding, speculation among the press and NGOs as to the outcome of the meeting, a period of not-much-negotiating before pressure builds and round-the-clock meetings take place eventually resulting in an agreement or the meeting's collapse; a fall out between the press and NGOs over demonstrations in the conference centre by one or two of the latter; protests on the streets; heavy-handed tactics by the local police; and a preparatory period that fails to adequately prepare the ground for a successful conclusion to the meeting, among others.

While the family drama metaphor should not be stretched too far, it does provide a useful way of illustrating the extent to which, despite changes over time, the manner in which the WTO was created and the roles assumed by member states therein strongly influences the kind of politics that takes place, the diplomatic styles and behavioural patterns of members, and the system of governance that this has produced. This is irrespective, to return to (and paraphrase) James, of the achievements of each participant and the institutional adjustments that have been made since the Organization was first created.

This chapter uses James' metaphor as a way of exploring why political interaction in the WTO is the way it is, the reasons underpinning the diplomatic styles assumed by key states and the kind of system of governance this has produced. In other words, it explains why something akin to a family drama exists and appears to repeat itself, why states assume the roles they do and why this kind of interaction leads to a particular set of 'familial' relations. The chapter begins by setting out a measure of what we know about the peculiarities of international institutions as a framework for understanding politics, diplomacy and governance in the WTO. The chapter then uses this as the basis for a discussion about the antecedence of the WTO because – as James encourages us to believe – institutional (or, in his terms, 'childhood') development matters. The chapter then explores why the WTO gives rise to the kind of politics, diplomacy and governance that it does before offering concluding comments.

The aims of the chapter are two-fold. First, the chapter aims to show that much of what occurs in the WTO today is the product of a particular process of institutional development. This is not to say that the manner in which multilateral trade regulation has evolved in the post-war era has *determined* the kind of political interaction, diplomatic styles and system of governance associated with the GATT and WTO. Rather, the chapter shows how the institution's creation, the way it has evolved, the political and economic context in which that evolution has taken place, the characteristics of each member state and the manner in which members have interacted have combined to forge a particular arena that gives rise to the WTO's unique brand of politics, diplomacy and governance. Second, the chapter aims – much like James' suggestion that to modify the influence of what happens in the early years there needs to be a major change (James, 2002: 274) – to illustrate that despite compelling reasons for reform of the WTO, the task of correcting the anomalous way the institution structures the behaviour of its participants is far from easy. In the absence of a radical departure from the existing way the institution operates, or the onset of a wider systemic event (such as a change in the overall distribution of world power), attempts to alter the kind of politics, diplomacy and governance to which the WTO gives rise are unlikely to bear fruit. In pursuit of these aims as well as to develop the argument further, the chapter first fleshes out a modicum of what we know about international institutions as a way of giving substance to the family metaphor.

What we know about institutions

The literature on international institutions tells us that the kind of politics, styles of diplomacy and system of governance generated by an institution is shaped (but not strictly determined) by the manner in which it was created and developed through time. International institutions tend to be products of, and reflect the distribution of power within particular historical moments and their purpose is to assist in securing, stabilising and perpetuating that particular order.[2] The United Nations (UN) was, for instance, created to promote peace (as well as to ensure as far as was possible cooperation between the United States and the Soviet Union) by locking into place the Allied victory at the end of the Second World War; and the composition of the UN Security Council reflected the distribution of power at that time (the United States, United Soviet Social Republic, China, France and the United Kingdom). Likewise, the economic institutions created after the Second World War sought to lock in place a particular kind of social and economic system favoured by the Allied powers (for the most part welfare state capitalism); and the way in which the institutions were constructed reflected western preponderance (a preponderance amplified by the Soviet Union's decision not to be involved in the International Monetary Fund

(IMF), World Bank, International Trade Organization (ITO) and, once the ITO projected had become moribund, the General Agreement on Tariffs and Trade) – of which the weighted system of voting in the IMF is perhaps the starkest example.

Existing wisdom tells us that once created, international institutions tend to shape the behaviour of participating states in ways that produce particular outcomes. Moreover, we know that these behavioural patterns tend to be reflections of the original purposes for which the institution was created – that is, institutions tend to embody rules and procedures designed to produce (or at least generate a general tendency towards the production of) outcomes consistent with the purposes for which the institution was established. We know that institutional innovators – that is, those states that establish institutions in the first place – tend to construct them in a manner that best serves their interests and preserves any advantages that may accrue from the institution vis-à-vis later entrants. Robert Wade characterises this process as 'kick[ing] away the ladder' (2003: 632, 621–630); Robert Keohane suggests more mildly that is because 'significant advantages must accrue to institutional innovators, such as conferring on them control over future rules or creating barriers to entry to potential competitors…Otherwise, latecomers could free ride on the accomplishments of their predecessors, and anticipation of such free riding would discourage institutional innovation' (Keohane, 2002: 253).

We also know that international institutions are important devices for facilitating wider social and economic change; and they are one means by which the tensions and conflicts that may arise from such changes can be mitigated. As Craig Murphy has shown, international institutions have, since the middle of the nineteenth century, assisted in the periodic replacement of lead industries by helping make it profitable for firms to invest in new technologies. As he puts it, international institutions 'have helped create international markets for industrial goods by linking *communication and transportation infrastructure*, protecting *intellectual property*, and reducing legal and economic barriers to *trade*' (Murphy, 1994: 2, emphasis original). He continues,

> At the same time the world organizations, and the other systems of governance to which they point, have helped mitigate conflicts that go along with the expansion of the industrial system: they privileged some workers in the industrialized nations, insured investment in previously less developed countries (LDCs), and strengthened the states of the less industrialized world. (Murphy, 1994: 2)[3]

Existing wisdom also tell us that institutions are arenas in which conflicts tend to be played out. This is an inevitable consequence of the clashes produced by the pursuit of differing national interests. This conflictual dimension is exacerbated by the tendency for institutions to reflect the interests of dominant states and institutional innovators. Nevertheless, we also know that these conflicts tend to be resolved in accordance with the existing distribution of power: that is, the resolution of conflicts tends to produce outcomes that offer only modest concessions to non-dominant states and certainly none that threaten the prevailing distribution of power.[4] The decision to create a permanent organisation designed to explore the relationship between trade and development – in the form of the United Nations Conference on Trade and Development (UNCTAD) – following heated debate in the GATT and the UN General Assembly, but to remove from the original proposals any substantive means of addressing the poor trade performance of developing countries, provides one compelling example; the decision to adopt an addendum to the GATT in the form of Part IV in 1965 (dealing with the relationship between trade and development) but to do so without requiring (merely encouraging) the industrial states to act in a manner beneficial to their developing counterparts provides another.

Finally, we know that fundamental changes to the way international institutions operate, the behavioural patterns they generate and the kind of governance they produce are seldom observed. Very few of the international institutions established since the middle of the nineteenth century have ceased to exist; even fewer have changed what they do to the extent that it is *dramatically* different from their original purpose. The League of Nations is the most obvious example of an international institution that has ceased to exist. It was, however, an institution that failed to reflect the prevailing distribution of power at the end of the First World War and was, as a result, inherently unstable – though many of the practices and procedures developed in the League live on (and shape state behaviour in comparable ways) in the United Nations. The International Labour Organisation (ILO) is perhaps the most dynamic of institutions in that it has, through necessity, had to undergo a process of continual reinvention to maintain its relevance.[5] The ILO, nevertheless, still exists to provide a forum for the discussion and promotion of international labour standards. In this way, the institution does not differ markedly in purpose from that for which it was established in 1919, albeit that the manner in which it goes about that purpose has itself changed.[6]

That said, we know that (in rare cases) fundamental change does have the capacity to take place. We know that change can result from a single or a combination of multiple external and internal factors, such as changes in the global distribution of power, through alterations in existing rules, to changes in personnel within a particular office or division; or it can result from pressure brought to bear as a critical mass developed from a long process of incremental adjustment. So, while it might be the case that change is rare among international institutions (particularly because most global institutions were created in the post-Second World War era and as such they reflect a balance of power which, in large measure, remains intact), it is, nevertheless, useful to identify moments wherein change has the capacity to take place. These instances are called 'critical moments' (Bulmer and Burch, 1998: 605) because they contain the potential (albeit one that is not necessarily realised) to bring about a fundamental departure from existing practice.

Taken together the various facets of what we know about international institutions helps us understand why things happen in the way that they do in the WTO. We know that institutional development matters. It matters who created an institution, why it was created, how it was created, what rules and practices were put in place to give rise to particular kinds of behaviour and outcomes, what accommodations were reached with non-dominant actors to ensure their participation, and how the institution has developed through time. Each of these factors matters because they play a role in shaping the kinds of politics, diplomacy and governance that an institution produces. To put it in terms of the family metaphor, to comprehend why relations unfold in the manner that they do it is first necessary to understand how the family was forged; the context of its creation and subsequent development; the relations of power between the establishing parents, between them and their offspring, as well as those among the siblings; the rules, practices, norms and decision-making procedures that have been put into place; as well as the manner in which the family has developed over time. So, to better understand why the kinds of trade politics, the diplomatic styles and behavioural patterns, and system of governance are produced by the WTO, we need to establish the organisation's antecedence.

The emergence and development of multilateral trade governance

The WTO's general purpose, core principles, legal framework and operating procedures are all continuations, adaptations, variations or developments of elements of a trade institution designed to work in tandem with the IMF and World Bank for the purposes of reconstructing a war-ravaged and depression weary world economy – what was to have been the ITO but which became, as we see below, the GATT – in the wake of the Second World War. To cut a long, detailed (and important) story very short,[7] the GATT was originally designed to kick-start a process of liberalisation that would enable the United States to take advantage of the unique economic circumstances in which it found itself at the end of the war (including overcoming the post-war depression) as well as to assist the European powers with a measure of reconstruction. Importantly, this liberalisation was targeted at reducing barriers to trade in those goods in which the United States had a comparative and competitive advantage, and that Western Europe needed to assist with reconstruction – largely manufactured, semi-manufactured, industrial and capital goods. The GATT was not deployed to liberalise trade in agriculture, as this was politically sensitive to both the United States and the European powers; nor was it designed as a vehicle to facilitate trade-led growth for states outside of the Western Alliance. What existed among the Allied powers, then, was a shared interest in the creation of an institution designed to liberalise trade in *some* but not all goods. In this way, the GATT sought to govern trade in a highly selective fashion – a feature of its system of governance that was to have a marked impact upon the way the institution would shape the behaviour of its contracting parties further down the line.

However, despite agreement between the United States and United Kingdom (the principal architects of the post-war economic institutions) on the general shape and purpose of a trade institution, marked differences existed about its precise content. These differences ranged from the rules and procedures governing trade to the commercial sectors covered by, first, the ITO, and, once that project had become moribund, the GATT. Disagreements persisted on, for instance, balance-of-payments rules (particularly relating to the point that states were able to suspend Most-Favoured-Nation (MFN) vis-à-vis a trading partner in times of worsening balances-of-payments situations), Britain's imperial preference system (which effectively locked the United States out of markets in the Empire) and the extent tariffs would be cut.[8] Moreover, when taken in combination with the manner in which tariff reductions were pursued – through a process of exchange between *the most significant trading nations* (via the principal-supplier rule) in rounds of negotiations – these disagreements often resulted in tense and protracted political interaction wherein the collapse of a round, the threat of a collapse and political grandstanding became normal and indeed expected patterns of behaviour. Moreover, as the institution developed, the number of signatories to the GATT increased and further rounds of negotiations were conducted, this pattern of politics became entrenched. The result was the construction not only of a selective system of governance but also one wherein the mechanisms producing that governance – that is, the negotiations – were inherently conflictual.

Early developments in the way the GATT was deployed as a mechanism of liberalisation compounded the manner in which the behaviour of the General Agreement's contracting parties was structured. First, slower-than-expected European recovery in the immediate post-war years reinforced an almost exclusive concentration on the liberalisation of industrial, manufactured and some semi-manufactured goods. Second, additional efforts were made to exclude agriculture from the GATT's remit in the form of waivers and other restrictions. Third, in response to acute competition from East, South and Southeast Asia measures were put into place to formally exclude textiles and clothing from the liberalisation process. These measures ranged, in the first instance, from voluntary quotas limiting exports from Japan, Hong Kong, Pakistan and India to, later, the short-term and long-term agreements on cotton textiles and the notorious Multi-Fibre Agreement.

These three developments combined to infuse the GATT with an asymmetry of opportunity. The GATT was increasingly deployed in a manner that served the trade interests of the leading industrial states while the interests of their developing counterparts were increasingly crowded out by measures that further protected agriculture, and textile and clothing producers in the North. In other words, the early development of the GATT accentuated the already selective manner in which it governed international trade. Two of the consequences of this asymmetry are noteworthy. First, the asymmetrical fashion in which the GATT was deployed served to fuel developing country hostility towards the General Agreement. Second, this hostility added to the adversarial nature of trade negotiations. Not only were negotiations fraught affairs precisely because they were based on a notion of reciprocity that failed to determine what constituted rough equivalence in the exchange of concessions[9] (which most interpreted as offering as little as possible in the expectation that more would be forthcoming) they were compounded by the growing perception of injustice harboured by developing countries. The result was to make trade negotiations evermore fraught affairs.

This kind of political interaction had a marked impact on the way existing and new entrants were socialised in the GATT. For the existing members, a culture of expectation around the inflammatory and protracted nature of trade rounds developed. Moreover, an expectation developed that the United States and, first, the United Kingdom and, later, the EU would be at loggerheads (and that they would be the bad guys in future scripts) but that they would nevertheless be pitched against the developing states. As the EU grew to rival the United States in economic terms[10] this became an established pattern. For new entrants, the round-the-clock meetings, political grandstanding and proclivity to crisis (a feature of GATT politics since the General Agreement was first negotiated) appeared to be normal and socialised these states to expect (as well as act out roles consistent with) this kind of politics. As the number of entrants increased, and pressure developed to extend the commercial remit of the GATT across successive rounds of liberalisation, trade politics became ever more inflammatory.

The practices and procedures that developed to govern negotiations did not help either. Because of the unique nature of the GATT (as a provisional agreement, rather than a formal organisation that sought merely to coordinate market opening opportunities among a group of signatories) firm rules governing the contract of trade negotiations were not established. Indeed, the preference among the original contracting parties was for an absence of formal procedures so that the institution would not appear to be a formal organisation and thus trouble national legislatures (the ITO had been felled in part because of perceptions in the US Congress that the Organisation would infringe upon US sovereignty in the areas of economic and labour policy). As a consequence, procedures for conducting negotiations were developed on-the-hoof with reference only to the broadest guidelines.

The absence of formal procedures, in turn, generated a proclivity for informality in the way in which negotiations were conducted. One outcome of this was the emergence of the infamous 'green room' meetings wherein an elite group of contracting parties would meet to hammer out agreement on the shape and direction of the trade agenda.[11] A second outcome was the wider use of caucusing among groups of states to work out coherent positions in an attempt to shape the negotiating agenda. This has, in part, resulted in the hosting of mini-ministerials (Jawara and Kwa, 2003: 230–231) – gatherings of small groups of states ahead of a ministerial meeting that have acquired a status nearly as infamous as green rooms – during the WTO years and, in part, formed the basis of the coalition formation that has come to characterise contemporary trade politics.[12]

A third outcome was the pursuit of consensus as the way decisions are reached in negotiations. Early experiences with voting in the GATT proved ineffective in pushing forward an agenda that largely suited the leading states. This, in turn, generated a preference for consensus-based decision-making wherein all parties would negotiate until dissent had been eradicated. However, this threw up a further problem. During the early GATT years a number of negotiations occurred wherein only a proportion of the contracting parties actually actively participated (the fourth round of GATT negotiations is the most notable in this regard where, although the launch of the negotiations had been widely supported, in the end only 25 of the 39 contracting parties agreed to participate). This proved to be a less than satisfactory outcome, particularly for the leading industrial states, (1) because a perception emerged that those states not participating were nevertheless benefiting from the concessions negotiated under the GATT's MFN rule (so-called free riding); and (2) because it limited the potential value of concessions exchanged to the sub-set of states that were negotiating (rather than including all, or nearly all, of the contracting parties). The result was that a preference emerged for negotiations to be conducted on the basis of a single undertaking (a requirement that all participants accept and are bound by the results of the negotiation, albeit with lengthier implementation schedules and other minor modifications for developing countries).

These developments, in turn, led to a fourth outcome. To ensure that a consensus would be forged around an often contentious trade agenda, pressure was increasingly brought to bear on 'problem' states through a mix of 'forum plus' tactics (such as linking WTO negotiations to the passage of other trade and non-trade agreements, and circumscribing trade negotiators in situ by telephoning capitals) and arm-twisting in meetings. The use of arm-twisting and forum plus tactics, in turn, compounded developing countries hostility (as the most frequent recipients of such actions) towards the leading industrial states (particular the United States and EU).

A fifth outcome that emerged was the use of texts as the basis upon which negotiations would proceed. While the use of a text as the basis upon which negotiations would proceed was not in itself problematic (and is established practice in parts of the UN system) the role of negotiating chairs and/or negotiating group facilitators in the crafting of texts at various stages during negotiations has been the cause of some consternation. Notably, the perceived basis towards the interests of the United States and the EU in the crafting of texts was a contributing factor in the collapse of the WTO's Cancun ministerial meeting in September 2003.[13] Inevitably these developments have led to a lack of transparency in negotiations that has compounded matters further.

Given the manner in which the GATT/WTO system has developed, it is unsurprising that trade politics has taken the form it has. The GATT was first negotiated as a means of liberalising trade in areas of particular interest to its founding contracting parties (and even then really only the United States, United Kingdom and, later, the EU). Yet, because the mechanism for achieving this goal was negotiation based on reciprocal exchange, disagreement became a normal feature of trade politics. Moreover, the adversarial nature of trade politics was exacerbated over the course of the GATT's formative years by the selective fashion in which the General Agreement was deployed. The result was to produce a situation wherein two major conflictual fault-lines have come to underpin trade politics – the first between the United States and the EU as the major players, and the second between these two states and the developing countries. That said, these two fault lines are themselves the product more of perception than reality. While it is certainly the case that discord along these axes are important aspects of trade politics, tensions among member states are played out in myriad ways across numerous issues. Nevertheless, the perception of US/EU and North/South hostilities, prevalent not only in scholarly and journalistic commentary on trade negotiations but also among negotiators, acts to cloak the full extent of WTO politics.

The WTO's family scripts

Unsurprisingly, this kind of political interaction has given rise to a number of scripts – that is, roles assumed by key players – in their interaction in the WTO. For the United States and the EU, their role, rightly or wrongly, is deemed to be both villains in the piece – principal protagonists, dominant parties and bullies – as well as gatekeepers of possibility. At key times, both have acted in this way; but they have also displayed behaviour which does not confirm to these roles. They are nevertheless cast in this way, and this in turn affects the behaviour of other member states.

India and Brazil have long since been a tag-team. Though they have quite different economic interests, they have, since the days of the Group of 77 (G77) and the Non-Aligned Movement (NAM), cooperated as self-identified leaders of their respective spheres of influence. They have, as self-proclaimed anti-imperial states, also taken on the role as counter-weight to the United States and the EU lending them the role of naysayers. The scripts they play out have been enhanced by their prominent role in the Group of 20 (G20) and in orchestrating bouts of mass alliance formation (such as the Group of 110 at Hong Kong, albeit that this was more for the benefit of the assembled media than for the actual negotiations). It has also recently seen India and Brazil ushered into the core decision-making group (the Five Interested Parties – FIP – and, with the inclusion of Japan, the Group of 6 – G6) replacing the quad.[14] Yet, while India and Brazil have often been cast in this light, they have been far from the disrupters many have portrayed them as in the roles they have recently adopted.[15] Indeed, more than any other leading developing countries they have a strategic interest in the current round's conclusion and, more generally, progress in the WTO.

Japan is an interesting case. Publicly quiet in trade diplomacy, but nevertheless significant because of its economic weight and its membership of the quad (along with the United States, the EU and Canada), Japan's process of socialisation has been quite different. On joining the GATT in 1955, 40 per cent of the contracting parties implemented article XXXV empowering them to withhold MFN in their trading relations with Japan. Justified on the basis that Japanese goods would create significant market disruption to producers in Europe and North America (though the United States was not part of the initial action, two years later it negotiated a bilateral agreement with Japan restricting Japanese imports), this action had the effect of nullifying a significant proportion of the benefits of membership. The result is that Japan spent most of its time in the GATT trying to overcome this discrimination. One consequence of this is that Japan became an 'aggressive legalist',[16] a role assumed in response to the need to be seen to be clear and precise in overcoming discrimination through the proper application of GATT/WTO law. Hence, Japan is among the most technically adept of all WTO members, participates with great frequency in all WTO dispute settlement matters, and bases its interaction on a well worked out understanding of the rules. Moreover, while it is the case that Japan has deviated from this role – notably in discussions surrounding multifunctionality in agriculture and in its role in the G10 – the broad perception of Japan as an aggressive legalist has stuck.

Similarly, the manner in which Malaysia, Singapore, Indonesia, Bangladesh, the Caribbean states, Mexico, the Eastern European states, West and East Africa, Central and Southern Africa and others have been socialised, has had a marked impact on the diplomatic styles each has assumed as well as the proclivity some groups of states have for forming coalitions (it is, for instance, unsurprising that when faced with an institutional environment clearly dominated by the leading industrial states that developing states would combine in an effort to increase their negotiating leverage. This has been the case since the 1948 Havana conference, though a Nigerian led coalition of 21 states in the early 1960s is probably the forerunner of this behavioural pattern) – though, importantly each has deviated notably from these roles at key moments in time.

The point here is not that the diplomatic style assumed by each of these states is predetermined by their socialisation into the GATT and WTO; rather their experience of the institution has helped shape their diplomatic behaviour. Moreover, because these roles are well-known, when a family gathering occurs (such as a WTO ministerial), it is almost inevitable that each of these states will, in some measure, be perceived to be assuming the script that has been written for them and others will act in accordance with that perception.

How the multilateral trading system keeps moving forward

However, one final part of this family history needs to be put into place if trade politics are to be properly understood. In combination, the asymmetrical manner in which the GATT and the WTO regulates trade (the Uruguay round establishing the WTO was as asymmetrical as the preceding rounds despite the conclusion of agreements on agriculture, and textiles and clothing[17]), the adversarial and contested nature of trade politics, and the manner in which these factors influence the behaviour of member states produced a propensity for crises to occur and, on occasion, for negotiations to collapse. This propensity to crisis and collapse has been an endemic feature of trade politics since the ITO negotiations and has been exacerbated over time as the asymmetry of opportunity given rise to by the deployment of the GATT and, since it was formed, the other agreements administered by the WTO (of which the GATT is one) has been extended, the number of participating states has increased, and the arena of trade regulations has deepened and widened.[18] Curiously, however, this propensity *has not* rendered the system of trade governance inert either temporarily or for longer periods of time. Moreover, at no point has a crisis or the collapse of negotiations either significantly disrupted the further development of trade governance or damaged the institution. This is because crisis has a peculiar procedural function in the GATT/WTO.

Since the United States first attempted to launch a new round of negotiations in the wake of the Tokyo round a clear pattern of crisis, near collapse/collapse, post-crisis politics, and movement forward can be observed. In this pattern, crisis is brought about by growing pressure over attempts to move the trade agenda forward and in ways that prove unpopular with the wider membership. Once this pressure has built to such an extent that movement forward proves impossible, the negotiations 'collapse' (or, in GATT/WTO speak, they are declared 'suspended'). Such moments are followed by periods of reflection (what I have called post-crisis politics) wherein member states take stock of events before gradually engaging in a process of returning to the negotiating table. In each case when GATT/WTO negotiations have collapsed (or when significant moments of deadlock have been reached), a period of post-crisis politics has followed. This, in turn, has been followed by a return to the negotiating table and a commencement with the negotiations notably with agreements being concluded that are more far reaching than the negotiations had originally intended.

At least three factors have ensured that a return to the negotiating table is possible following a collapse. First, each collapse has taken place during periods wherein a widespread consensus has existed over the role trade liberalisation plays in promoting economic growth. Collapses have not, for instance, resulted from fundamental objections to liberalisation *per se*. As such, collapses have been about the substance of the negotiations or the manner in which they have been conducted rather than their innate value. Second, the alternatives to liberalisation outside of the confines of the GATT/WTO have held little attraction for all involved. For the leading industrial states, pursuing market openings though bilateral and regional agreements alone promises relatively smaller gains for relatively greater cost (in terms of diplomatic effort and so on). For developing countries, pursing liberalisation outside of the GATT/WTO can be a particularly thorny exercise. Without the protection afforded to them by a multilateral forum, developing countries are susceptible to bilateral arm-twisting and, potentially, concluding trade agreements that are even more asymmetrical than those concluded under GATT/WTO auspices. Third, and perhaps most importantly, trade negotiations have historically been framed in such a way that they encourage a return to the table following periods of crisis. In every moment wherein a crisis or collapse has looked possible, key trade officials – normally leading negotiators from the industrial states as well as the Director-General of the GATT/WTO and the UN Secretary General, among others – have warned that a breakdown in the negotiations could usher in a return to the economic fragmentation of the 1930s. The truth of course is that such a return has, in the post-war era, looked far from likely. Nevertheless, framing the negotiations in such a way is a useful rhetorical device for encouraging a quick resumption.

Conclusion: breaking the cycle of family drama

What the preceding analysis tells us is that the way in which the GATT/WTO was forged as an institution and the manner in which it developed thereafter matters. It was designed to serve a particular and quite specific purpose from which is has yet to deviate – that is, to provide the institution's leading states with market opening opportunities in areas wherein they have a competitive and comparative advantage while at the same time forestalling liberalisation in those sectors that are both politically sensitive and susceptible to decline (principally agriculture but also textiles and clothing). A reading of the history of the GATT/WTO also tells us that to ensure the continued participation of (as well as an increase in numbers of) non-core states, a series of sweetners has been agreed. Early in the chapter we noted the negotiation of Part IV as an addendum to the GATT in 1965 as one example; the inclusion of agreements on textiles and clothing, and agriculture provides a second. We have also seen how the system of governance produced by GATT/WTO rules in combination with the adversarial nature of trade negotiations has lent trade politics a contested quality, and that the degree of contestation has grown as the trade agenda has expanded, as the number of participants has increased, and as successive rounds of negotiations have cut the tariffs (and other barriers to trade) in some sectors to a point where squabbling over what remains has become inevitable. These developments, in turn, have encouraged states to behave in particular ways and for these behavioural patterns to become entrenched (though not set in stone). Finally, we have seen how the asymmetry of the GATT/WTO's deployment, the manner in which the institution has developed, the contested nature of trade politics and the behavioural patterns of member states have imbued the system with a propensity to crisis and collapse; but, importantly, we have also seen that crisis and collapse has come to have a procedural function taking the trade agenda forward. To put it in terms of James' metaphor, the WTO has become a deeply dysfunctional family wherein the peculiarities of its development have entrenched squabbling between parents and siblings alike and where patterns of behaviour appear to occur and reoccur without end but the family nevertheless moves forward.

The problem confronting us then is how do we break out of this family drama, particularly as its perpetual replaying is producing a system of governance that does not equitably reflect the interests of all of its members and it increasingly encourages members to engage in modes of behaviour that are not necessarily consistent with the realisation of their trade objectives? Again, without wanting to stretch the metaphor too far, it is useful to return one last time to James' work on childhood development and the impact of the family thereon.

For James, the way to break out of the behavioural patterns crafted by developmental socialisation is through a form of self-knowledge known as 'insight' by which he means self-recognition that a pattern of behaviour exists, that it has a particular cause and that to change behaviour requires recognising that the behaviour exists in the first place, identifying the cause and actively setting out a plan to bring about an alternative behavioural pattern. In many ways, this is precisely what needs to happen with the WTO. By simply identifying symptoms – such as the dominance of industrial states in trade negotiations, the inequity of green room meetings, the problems of using texts as the basis for negotiations and the like – and developing solutions to these symptoms, the problems of the WTO will be perpetuated.

So, for instance, while a better decision-making structure could be put in place involving the whole membership, in isolation this would not solve the problem of perpetuating asymmetries. Indeed, by opening up decision-making to the whole membership on a meaningful basis, negotiations may actually become more prone to crisis and collapse with the possibility that very little might actually be achieved. In turn, this could run the risk of the institution becoming moribund.

What is needed instead is a process of self-recognition that identifies not only the manner in which trade negotiations are conducted and the behavioural scripts that members adopt but the process of negotiating itself as part of the problem; it also requires that serious consideration be given to the role of trade liberalisation in promoting economic growth (and, more importantly, development of the poorest); it requires that serious attention be given to piecing together an institution that serves the interests of all; and it requires that the solution arrived at is done so in a consensual, equitable and transparent fashion. The problem, of course, is that the GATT/WTO was established for a particular purpose. And despite the moans and groans expressed about the institution's ability to deliver, it has played a role in facilitating economic growth in the industrial states since it was created, though it has done relatively less for the global South. Much like the problem of UN Security Council reform, wherein abolishing the veto or adding to the number of permanent representatives requires that those with privilege effectively vote themselves out of office, the interests vested in the current system are unlikely to agree to such a root and branch exercise. Without it, however, the WTO's family drama will continue to persist, with the caveat that Christmases are likely to become ever more terse affairs.

Notes

1. The Group of 10 comprises Bulgaria, Chinese Taipei, Korea, Iceland, Israel, Japan, Liechtenstein, Mauritius, Norway, and Switzerland.
2. See Cox (1996: 99).
3. Also see Cox (1996: 138).
4. See Cox (1996: 99, 137–140).
5. See Hughes (2002).
6. See Haworth et al. (2005).
7. See Wilkinson (2006) for a more extensive treatment.
8. A particularly noteworthy incident involved the United States and the 'low tariff' countries (Austria, the Netherlands, Belgium, Luxembourg, Canada, Denmark, France, Germany, Italy, Norway, and Sweden). The problem here was that in order for meaningful concessions to be extracted from their trading partners, concessions of roughly equivalent value had to be offered to the low tariff countries. However, with relatively low tariff levels to start with, these countries were unable to gain meaningfully because they had very little to offer in return. This advantaged those contracting parties with relatively high general tariff levels or those with considerable tariff peaks in key products (which included the United States).

9. For more on the basis of the principle of reciprocity, see Wilkinson (2000: 100–114).
10. On near equal terms from the Kennedy round (1964–1967) onwards, see Lee (2001).
11. As John Odell describes

    During the Uruguay Round Director-General Arthur Dunkel invited chief negotiators from the states representing three-fourths of world trade to meet off the record, first in a small conference room in the DG's office suit. Other members were not notified that a meeting would occur, no written summary of remarks was prepared... After complaints from the excluded, Dunkel shifted to hosting private dinners at his home. The table accommodated up to 24 chairs and no deputies – only chief negotiators as he called them – were welcome (Odell, 2005: 433).

12. But which also was a feature of the GATT, see Narlikar (2003).
13. See Narlikar and Wilkinson (2004).
14. The Five Interested Parties are Australia, Brazil, the European Union, India and the United States. The quad is Canada, the European Union, Japan, and the United States.
15. See Narlikar (2007).
16. See Araki (2007).
17. See Wilkinson (2007).
18. The role of crisis in the functioning of the multilateral trading system is explored in greater detail in Wilkinson (2006).

11

The World Summit on Information Society and the Development of Internet Diplomacy

Jovan Kurbalija

The World Summit on Information Society (WSIS), ending in 2005, was the most recent in the series of global United Nations (UN) summits that started with the 1992 Rio Earth Summit.[1] The main objective of the WSIS was to discuss the effects of Information and Communication Technologies (ICT) on modern society.[2] The unique feature of the WSIS was its two-phase organisation, including two main summit events: one at Geneva in 2003 and the other in Tunis in 2005. The Geneva summit aimed at identifying main issues, principles and lines of action. The Tunis summit, often described as a 'Summit of Solutions', focused on implementing the broad framework agreed upon at the Geneva summit.[3] The Tunis summit also finalised the WSIS negotiations on internet governance and financial mechanisms, two issues that had remained unresolved after the Geneva phase. The overall WSIS process lasted between May 2002 (the first African Regional WSIS Conference) and November 2005 (the Tunis summit).

Internet governance emerged as the chief issue at the WSIS agenda. Given its specificity, internet governance required the introduction of a new policy structure in the WSIS process. Participants in the Geneva WSIS Summit in 2003 decided to establish the Working Group on Internet Governance (WGIG) as a specific diplomatic mechanism, based on the equal participation of governments, civil society and the business sector. After producing the Report on Internet Governance, the WGIG ceased to exist in June 2005. The WGIG was an innovation in the existing, mainly inter-governmental, diplomatic system (Table 11.1).

The purpose of this chapter is to identify new developments and innovations in diplomatic practice resultant from the WSIS and WGIG. First, I describe the overall WSIS framework and specific aspects of the WGIG. Second, I identify the new developments and innovation in diplomatic practice that I think are likely of lasting importance. I will do so through comparing WSIS diplomatic practice to the practices developed during other major UN summits

Table 11.1 Major WSIS and WGIG official events

	Date	Event
Geneva phase	May 2002	African Regional WSIS Ministerial Conference in Bamako
	June 2002	Prepcomm 1 in Geneva
	January 2003	Asian Regional WSIS Ministerial Conference in Tokyo
	January 2003	Latin American and Caribbean WSIS Ministerial Conference in Bavaro
	February 2003	Western Asia Regional WSIS Ministerial Conference in Beirut
	February 2003	4th Meeting of the UNICTTF in Geneva
	February 2003	Prepcomm 2 in Geneva
	July 2003	WSIS Intercessional in Paris
	September 2003	Prepcomm 3 in Geneva
	November 2003	Prepcomm3bis in Geneva
	December 2003	Prepcomm3bis in Geneva
	December 2003	Geneva WSIS Summit
Tunis phase	June 2004	Prepcomm 1 in Hammamet
	November 2004	Establishment of the WGIG
	November 2004	1st WGIG meeting in Geneva
	November 2004	West Asia Regional WSIS meeting in Damascus
	January 2005	African Regional WSIS conference in Accra
	February 2005	2nd WGIG meeting in Geneva
	February 2005	Prepcomm 2 in Geneva
	April 2005	3rd WGIG meeting in Geneva
	May 2005	Arab Regional WSIS conference in Cairo
	May 2005	Asian Regional WSIS conference in Tokyo
	June 2005	Asian Pacific Regional WSIS conference in Teheran
	June 2005	Latin American Regional WSIS meeting in Rio de Janeiro
	June 2005	4th WGIG meeting in Geneva
	July 2005	Final Report of the WGIG
	September 2005	Prepcomm 3 in Geneva
	November 2005	Tunis WSIS summit

held since the Rio Earth Summit in 1992. Finally, I discuss if a new type of diplomacy dealing with ICT/internet issues, usually described as internet diplomacy, has emerged from the WSIS and WGIG processes.

Context and evolution of the WSIS/WGIG process

The WSIS originated in the 1990s, a period of optimism initiated by the end of the Cold War. The 1990s was also a time of rapid development of the ICT and the internet. In 1998, in their Resolution 73, participants of the Minnesota Conference of the International Telecommunications Union (ITU) decided to start preparations for the WSIS. Only two years later, however, the global scene for the organisation of the WSIS had changed substantially, due to two major developments.

The first important development was the burst of the so-called dot-com bubble in 2000. The dot-com bubble developed in the period 1995–2000 with the rapid growth of the value of stock in the ICT/internet field. However, the sudden deflation of the value of much of this stock in 2000 led many internet companies into bankruptcy. By 2001, the rhetoric of unlimited possibilities in the development of the internet that had dominated the 1990s was replaced with techno-scepticism and the level of investment in the ICT/internet area sharply decreased.

The second significant development influencing the organisation of the WSIS was the terrorist attacks of 9/11, which affected the WSIS process just as it did many other aspects of global policy. The post-Cold War era of the 1990s, characterised by an attempt to introduce new forms of diplomatic cooperation, was replaced by the post–9/11 period. The centrality of security concerns re-established the position of states in international relations and substantially reduced enthusiasm for novelty in managing global affairs.

Only a few months after the 9/11 attacks, through its Resolution 56/183 of 21 December 2001, the UN General Assembly made an official decision to hold the WSIS. Although the optimism of the late 1990s shaped the language of the UN resolution, the policy reality – influenced by the dot-com crash and the events of 9/11 – had changed dramatically. Both the agenda setting process and the participation in the WSIS reflected the new policy reality.

The agenda

The setting of a diplomatic agenda is a highly important part of any multilateral diplomatic process that can substantially influence the outcome of negotiations.[4] By setting the agenda, negotiators decide on the scope of negotiations and priority of issues to be negotiated. In the WSIS process, four main challenges characterised the agenda setting process: the agenda delimitation, the multi-disciplinary nature of WSIS issues, uncertainty and prioritisation.

The agenda delimitation

With the pervasive use of ICT and the internet in modern society, it is difficult to find any aspect of human existence outside its influence. Such pervasiveness led toward the risk that almost any issue might be included in the WSIS agenda.[5] To accommodate this possibility, the WSIS chose a very broad approach by including a long list of issues in the Geneva summit documents, the Documentation of Principles and the Action Plan. One of the main purposes of the Geneva phase was to map the field, so most issues were merely mentioned and described. The Tunis phase streamlined the agenda in main action lines dealing with: internet governance, e-government; e-business; e-learning; e-health; e-employment; e-environment; e-agriculture; e-science; public governance; and ICT for development, information and communication infrastructure; access to information and knowledge; capacity building; the enabling environment; building confidence and security in the use of ICT; cultural diversity and identity; linguistic diversity and local content; media; and ethical dimensions of the Information Society.[6]

The multi-disciplinary nature
of WSIS issues

The multi-disciplinary nature of the WSIS-related issues added to the complexity of agenda setting. Most issues had a variety of technical, socio-economic, developmental, legal and political aspects. One of the underlying dilemmas in setting the agenda was whether the WSIS concerned technology itself or the effects of technology on society. This confusion of technical and social approaches was noticeable in all aspects of the WSIS process, not only in setting the agenda but also playing a determining role in the composition of delegations and the focus of discussions.

Uncertainty

The WSIS operated in the context of much uncertainty regarding the future development of the internet, and this uncertainty affected the agenda of the WSIS. For example, in 2002 when the WSIS process started, Google was just one of many search engines. At the end of the process in November 2005, Google was established as the primary internet company shaping the use of the internet. In 2002, the use of blogs was in its infancy. Presently, bloggers sway governments, push the limits of freedom of expression and have considerable influence on social and economic life. The list could continue with mentions of Skype, YouTube and iPod.

Due to a lack of consensus and understanding of some technical developments, the WSIS followed the least common denominator approach, resulting in vague provisions. The real problem will emerge in the future when some important issues will require policy choices and operative decisions (e.g., spam and internet security). One possible approach, increasingly used in the European Union (EU), is that of technology neutral regulations, which contain provisions that could be applied to various technologies. For example, some provisions should be applicable to the internet, broadcasting and telephony. With the increasing convergence of digital technologies (TV over the internet, internet telephone) technology neutral regulations are the only possible solution for preserving a coherent policy framework.

Prioritisation of agenda issues

Although it did not figure initially in the WSIS agenda, internet governance emerged as the priority issue taken up by the WSIS. Its importance was reflected in the time spent on negotiating internet governance issues, both in the main WSIS process and in the specially designed WGIG. In fact, one of the main criticisms of the WSIS is that the internet governance debate 'hijacked' overall WSIS negotiations and took the focus away from developmental issues, which were supposed to be the main issues on the WSIS agenda. As indicated in the main preparatory documents, the WSIS was designed to provide some solutions for narrowing the digital divide that separates rich countries from poor ones by increasing the use of the internet and ICT in the developing world. The WSIS was also supposed to provide a stronger link with the Millennium Development Goals. It is widely perceived that the WSIS did not provide a major breakthrough on closing the digital divide.

Participation

It is not surprising that multistakeholder participation was one of the catch phrases of the WSIS process. Prior to the WSIS, the UN had expended considerable effort to involve business and civil society in its activities.[7] In addition to this general policy trend of the UN Summits, multistakeholder participation was natural in discussions of the information society and the internet, since non-state actors had taken predominant roles in the development and the maintenance of the internet. The business community had developed the technological infrastructure, including computers, networks and software. Civil society, academia and the internet community had been vital players in the internet field, including the development of internet protocols, creating content and developing online communities. On the other side, governments were latecomers in the field. Many expected that the specific positions of stakeholders in the development of the internet would result in the creation of new forms of global multistakeholder diplomacy. These expectations were partially met, especially through the establishment of the WGIG and the Internet Governance Forum.

The UN General Assembly Resolution 56/183, the formal basis for conveying the WSIS, invited 'intergovernmental organisations, including international and regional institutions, non-governmental organisations, civil society and the private sector to contribute to, and actively participate in the intergovernmental preparatory process of the Summit and the Summit itself.'

Although it invited other stakeholders to participate, the resolution clearly emphasised the inter-governmental nature of the WSIS.

The expectations that non-state actors would participate equally and the formal stipulation about the inter-governmental nature of the WSIS collided at the first WSIS preparatory meeting (Geneva, June 2002), which drafted rules of procedures. The conflict was unavoidable. Governments refused to grant non-governmental actors equal footing in the WSIS process. Civil society and the business sector received the status of observer that they had held during previous major UN conferences.

After a difficult start, a multistakeholder perspective gradually developed during the WSIS process. While the WSIS remained formally an inter-governmental process, governments informally opened many channels for the participation of non-state actors. The most successful multistakeholder participation occurred in the WGIG process with equal and full participation of all stakeholders.

The multistakeholder work of the WGIG was expected given the specifics of the internet governance field. In internet governance, a regime already functioned around the Internet Corporation for Assigned Names and Numbers (ICANN), the Internet Engineering Task Force (IETF), and other organisations. With the exception of the US government, participation of governments in this regime had been low. The major difference between negotiations regarding internet governance and other global negotiations – such as environmental negotiations – is that, while in other negotiations, inter-governmental regimes gradually opened to non-governmental players, in internet governance, governments had to enter an already existing non-governmental, ICANN-based regime.

Governments

With the exception of a few developed countries, most countries were newcomers to the field of internet policy and governance. Even for advanced ICT/internet countries, the WSIS posed numerous challenges. The main challenge was to deal with the multi-disciplinary nature of WSIS issues that involved technological, social, economic and legal aspects.

National coordination

Governments had to organise national participation in the WSIS. They had to make decisions regarding the ministry in charge, and how to engage the technical community, the business sector, civil society and the many other actors who were often more involved in internet policy than the governments themselves. Most countries started planning their participation in the WSIS through 'technical' ministries, usually those that had been responsible for relations with the ITU. Gradually, by realising that the Information Society is 'more than wires and cables', governments involved officials from other, mainly non-technical ministries, such as those of culture, media and defence. The principal challenge was to harness support from non-state actors such as local universities, private companies and NGOs that had the necessary expertise to deal with the issues on the WSIS agenda. Canada and Switzerland, for example, involved non-state actors in national delegations for the WSIS summit.

The whole process of setting national WSIS structures and deciding on national positions on various WSIS issues was a learning experience for most governments. A clear evolution of levels of expertise and quality of contributions occurred during the WSIS process. A feedback process also took place in which many governments shaped their national policy on the internet under the influence of the global WSIS negotiations.

'Diplomatisation' of internet policy issues

Also relevant to the positions of governments at the WSIS was that the WSIS put the internet on the global diplomatic agenda. Prior to the WSIS, the internet had been discussed primarily in non-governmental circles or at the national level. 'Diplomatisation' of internet policy issues stimulated different reactions. As Kenneth Neil Cukier, technology correspondent for *The Economist*, stressed:

> by elevating the issue to a formal United Nations summit, this by nature escalates the importance of the topic inside governments. As a result, issues about the Information Society, that were treated by less political and less visible parts of the government – as science and technology and policy or as a media and cultural matter – were shifted to foreign ministries and long-standing diplomats, who are more accustomed to power politics and less knowledgeable of technology issues and the Internet's inherent requirement for cooperation and interdependence. (Cukier, 2005b: 176)

The diplomatisation process had certain positive effects on the discussions at the WSIS. For example, diplomats provided non-partisan contributions to long-standing debates on ICANN-related issues (domain names, internet numbers and root servers). They had the advantage of being latecomers in an arena of already deeply entrenched positions in the internet governance debate (e.g., the ICANN vs. ITU debate discussed below). The contributions of diplomats were particularly noticeable in the WGIG debate. The diplomatic leadership of the WGIG (Chairperson Nitin Desai and Executive Director Markus Kummer) created an inclusive atmosphere where differences among representatives, including those of the technical community, did not block the process. The WGIG resulted in the WGIG Final Report[8] that voiced differences but also provided process-related solutions to the future discussion by establishing Internet Governance Forum.

Importance of Geneva-based permanent missions

For many governments, their permanent missions in Geneva were important – if not vital – players in the WSIS process. Most WSIS activities occurred in Geneva, the base of the ITU, which played the main role in the WSIS process. The first WSIS summit in 2003 took place in Geneva and all but one of the preparatory meetings were held in Geneva, which made permanent missions based in Geneva directly involved in the WSIS process.

For large and developed countries, the permanent missions were part of the broad network of institutions and individuals that dealt with the WSIS. For small and developing countries, permanent missions were primary and, in some cases, the only players in the WSIS process. The WSIS portfolio added to the agenda of usually small and over-stretched missions of developing countries. In many cases, the same diplomat had to undertake the tasks associated with the WSIS along with other issues such as human rights, health, trade and labour. Additional pressure on small missions arose because the WSIS process usually involved parallel meetings and workshops. The complexity of the WSIS issues and the dynamics of activities made it almost impossible for many small, and in particular small developing countries, to follow developments, let alone have any substantive effect. As a result, some small states supported a 'one stop' structure for internet governance issues.[9] The sheer size of the WSIS agenda and the limited policy capacity of developing countries in both capitals and diplomatic missions remained one of the main obstacles for their full participation in the WSIS process. The need for capacity building in the field of internet governance and policy was recognised as one of the priorities of the WSIS Tunis Agenda for the Information Society.[10]

Business sector

The business sector had a low profile in the WSIS process. As one of the representatives of the sector indicated, business was involved in 'damage control'. At the WSIS, the main concern of the business sector was the possibility of opening discussions on intellectual property rights on the internet. After the WSIS decided to leave the internet intellectual property issues for the World Intellectual Property Organisation (WIPO) and the World Trade Organization (WTO), the business sector's interest in participating in the WSIS process further diminished.

The biggest ICT/internet companies such as Microsoft, Adobe, Oracle, Google and Yahoo did not follow actively the WSIS process. No powerful software lobbying associations attended; even the Business Software Association (representing software companies in dealing with international policy issues) had no active representation. Instead, the International Chamber of Commerce (ICC), well known as the main association representing small- and medium-sized enterprises, represented the business sector. The ICC rarely represents the software industry in dealing with delicate policy issues in the context of the WIPO or the WTO. Although the ICC made active, professional input to the WSIS and WGIG, many thought that the representation of the global business sector by the ICC was a signal of the lack of interest on the part of the business sector in the WSIS.

Civil society

Civil society was the most vocal and active promoter of a multistakeholder perspective at the WSIS. The usual criticism of civil society participation in other multilateral fora had been a lack of proper coordination and the presence of too many, often dissonant voices. In the WSIS, however, civil society representation managed to harness the inherent complexity and diversity through a few organisational forms, including a Civil Society Bureau, the Civil Society Plenary and the Content and Themes Group. Faced with limited possibilities to influence the WSIS through the formal process, civil society groups developed a two-track approach. They continued their presence in the formal process by using available opportunities to intervene and to lobby governments. In parallel, they prepared a Civil Society Declaration as an alternative vision to the main WSIS declaration adopted at the Geneva summit.

At the WGIG, due to its multistakeholder nature, civil society attained a high level of involvement. Civil society groups proposed eight candidates for the WGIG meetings, all of whom were subsequently appointed by the UN Secretary General. In the Tunis phase, the main policy thrust of civil society organisations shifted to the WGIG, where they influenced many conclusions as well as the decision to establish the Internet Governance Forum (IGF) as a multistakeholder space for discussing internet governance issues.

International organisations

The ITU was the central international organisation in the WSIS process. The ITU hosted the WSIS Secretariat and provided policy input on the main issues. For the ITU, the WSIS was important for a number of reasons. The ITU was not the main protagonist of internet policy developments, and it was losing its traditional policy domain due to the WTO-led liberalisation of the global telecommunications market. The latest trend of moving telephone traffic from traditional telecommunications to the internet (through Voice over Internet Protocol (IP)) added to the erosion of the traditional telecommunication policy domain regulated by the ITU. Many observers viewed the leading role of the ITU in the WSIS as an attempt to re-establish itself as the most important player in global telecommunication policy, now increasingly influenced by the internet. The possibility that the ITU might emerge from the WSIS process as the most important global internet organisation caused concern in the United States and other developed countries – while creating support in many developing countries. Throughout the WSIS process, this possibility created underlying policy tensions. It was particularly clear in the field of internet governance, where tension between ICANN and ITU had existed – even before the WSIS – since the establishment of ICANN in 1998.

Another issue concerned the problem of how to anchor the multi-disciplinary WSIS agenda within the family of UN specialised agencies. It was felt that a predominant role of the ITU was risky, as it could lead towards a techno-centred approach to the WSIS agenda. Non-technical aspects of the ICT/internet, such as social, economic and cultural features, are part of the mandate of other UN organisations. The most prominent player in this context is United Nations Educational, Scientific and Cultural Organization (UNESCO), which addresses issues such as multilingualism, cultural diversity, knowledge societies and information sharing. The balance between the ITU and other UN organisations was carefully managed. This balance is also reflected in the WSIS follow-up process, with the main players including ITU, UNESCO and United Nations Development Programme.

Other participants

Beside the formal stakeholders recognised by the WSIS, other players who were not officially recognised as stakeholders, such as internet communities, had considerable influence on both the way the internet runs and how it was developed. They participated in the WSIS process through the presence of the four main stakeholders, primarily through civil society and the business sector.

Internet communities

Internet communities consisted of institutions and individuals who had developed and promoted the internet since its inception. Many were based in US universities where they primarily functioned to set up technical standards and to establish the basic functionality of the internet. Internet communities also created the initial spirit of the internet, based on the principles of sharing resources, open access and opposition to government involvement in internet regulation. From the beginning, they protected the initial concept of the internet from intensive commercialisation and extensive government influence. The early management of the internet by online communities was challenged in the mid 1990s after the internet became part of global social and economic life. Internet growth introduced a group of new stakeholders, such as the business sector, that came with different professional cultures and understandings of the internet and its governance, which led to increasing tension. For example, in the 1990s, internet communities and Network Solution were involved in a so-called Domain Name System (DNS) war, a conflict over the control of the root server and the DNS.

Today, the main organisational forms that accommodate internet communities are the Internet Society and IETF. In times of increasing commercialisation of the internet, it is difficult to preserve the early spirit of internet communities and the consideration of these communities as a special policy group has been criticised.[11] For example, in the WSIS/WGIG process, criticism was expressed that the internet communities could no longer have a leading role in internet governance. According to this view, with more than one billion users the internet has grown out of its initial policy framework. Any internet governance regime must reflect this growing internet population and the Internet's influence on social and economic life. In this line of argument, as the boundary between citizens and internet users blurs, more involvement of parliaments and other structures representing citizens is required, rather than those representing internet users, such as internet communities. In the WSIS, this criticism came particularly from those who argued for more involvement of government in internet governance.

Internet corporation for assigned names and numbers (ICANN)

ICANN is the 1998 compromise solution for the DNS war. Formally speaking, ICANN is a private entity established under California law. It received functional authority to manage internet names and numbers from the US Department of Commerce via a special contract. In the WSIS process, ICANN was frequently criticised for its position in the existing internet governance regime, and for having special ties with the US government. Through an almost continuous process of reform, ICANN had become increasingly international. It had an international board of directors, meetings held in different regions, and an international staff. However, the 'umbilical cord' linking ICANN with the US government remained the main source of concern. In the WGIG debate, various options regarding the reorganisation of ICANN were discussed, including that of developing ICANN as a *sui generis* international organisation that should both accommodate a multistakeholder approach and become anchored in the international legal framework. Formally speaking, the WGIG Report only presented the various options without opting for any in particular.

Procedures and processes of negotiations

Procedures are essential for the smooth running of negotiations. Although some perceive them as an unnecessary formality, they have an essential function in any negotiation. The rules of procedure provide an anchor for potentially chaotic developments in negotiations. They also ensure equity and transparency in the process. To ensure equity and transparency, many small and developing countries favour 'formalisms', which involve a strict adherence to procedural rules. Alternative forms of participation very often require additional human resources, which could lead to *de facto* inequality in negotiations.

The WSIS followed typical UN summit rules of procedure established during previous UN Summits.[12] The UN summit rules of procedure are close to the UN General Assembly rules of procedure. The WSIS also developed informal practices in conducting negotiations, often referred to at the WSIS, as a 'WSIS practice.'

Informal practice

Many elements shape an informal practice, including participant readiness to interpret rules of procedure in a flexible way, the need to reduce the process transaction cost and specific professional cultures of communities involved in negotiations. At the very beginning of the WSIS process, in an effort to avoid establishing a precedent that could be used in other multilateral negotiations, many countries refused to allow the full participation of non-state actors.

However, these countries were aware of the specificities of WSIS and WGIG processes and allowed participation of other stakeholders far beyond the formal framework. Most informal practices related to the opening up of the negotiation process to other stakeholders, primarily to civil society and business sector groups. Informal practices were particularly noticeable in observer participation in the meetings, making interventions, and effecting the negotiations.

Observer participation

No restrictions were placed on the participation of observers in meetings. Observers participated in plenary and subcommittee meetings. In the phase leading towards the Tunis summit, observers also attended meetings of the Group of Friends of the Chair, which played a vital role in drafting the basic negotiating document. Observers intervened in the WSIS by delivering statements in official meetings. During PrepComm meetings prior to the Geneva summit, the observers had 45 minutes every day reserved for interventions. Each main stakeholder – including, international organisations, business groups and civil society representatives – had 15 minutes for interventions. The minimum 45-minute intervention time was established as a WSIS practice. In many cases, observers were granted additional time for their interventions. Observers were also involved in preparing and running round tables and panels at both Geneva and Tunis.

Observer participation in negotiations

Although observers did not have decision-making rights, WSIS informal practices helped them to influence negotiations through various techniques. First, observers' written contributions were included in the compilations of the inputs alongside those of governments. Accordingly, observer proposals became visible to negotiators and, thus, more likely to be integrated in the negotiating text. Second, observers intervened in negotiating sessions by using a 'stop-and-go' approach (Kleinwächter, 2004). The chairperson periodically stopped official negotiations, allowing observers to make an intervention. Although it was a discretionary right of the chairperson, the stop-and-go approach gradually became part of WSIS informal practice.

The WSIS leadership clearly intended to increase the inclusiveness and transparency of the process. However, in some cases, inclusiveness and transparency were not impeded by political decisions, but by organisational requirements. First, many actors in attendance had various professional and cultural commitments. An already complex group of over 180 governments had to make room for additional non-state entities that, very often, had a limited experience in multilateral diplomacy. Organisational forms established by civil society[13] and the business sector[14] reduced the complexity, but they did not solve the problem of managing the large number of contributions to the negotiating process. Second, in critical junctures, the negotiations required deal brokerage with a limited number of participants. It was simply impossible to negotiate deal brokerage with more than 10 or 20 key players. For example, the brokerage of the final deal on internet governance

Table 11.2   Excerpt from the reading guide

Par	Convergent views	Divergent views	New items
	General comments		
12	The Information Society must serve the interests of all nations.	Different proposals concerning the list of countries and groups to be specifically addressed (e.g., LDC, Africa, SIDS, Landlocked etc.)	Government – Empowerment of developing countries – Pay attention to groups that are socially exploited Observers – ICT to support sustainable development – Mention human rights, gender equity, and freedom of expression – ICT to be used across the economy – Knowledge as heritage of humanity and basis for citizen choice – Traditional media are still major providers of information – Media have a central role in the Information Society

Source: 'Reading Guide WSIS03/PCIP/DT/6', 2 July 2003, available from http://www.itu.int/dms_pub/itu-s/md/03/wsispcip/td/030721/S03-WSISPCIP-030721-TD-GEN-0006!!PDF-E.pdf.

Table 11.3   Excerpt from WSIS compilation of comments

Existing text	Sources of proposed text	Proposed text
1. We recognise that it is now time to move from principles to action, by encouraging stakeholders to take the Plan of Action one step further, identifying those areas in which progress has been made in implementing the commitments undertaken in Geneva, and by defining those areas where further effort and resources are required.	Informal Coalition on Financing and Gender Caucus (joint submission)	[replace with] 1. We recognise that it is now time to move from principles to action, while considering the work already being done for implementing the Plan of Action and identifying the areas of such progress, all stakeholders must define those areas where further effort and resources are required, and jointly develop appropriate strategies and implementation mechanisms at global, national and local levels. In particular, we need to identify peoples and groups that are still marginalised in their access to and utilization of ICT.
	Togo	1.those areas in which progress has been made, or is being made, in implementing

Source: 'Compilation of Comments on Chapter One (Implementation Mechanism) and Chapter Four (The Way Ahead) of the Operational Part WSIS-II/PC-2/DT-6 (Rev. 2)', available from http://www.itu.int/wsis/docs2/pc2/working/dt6rev2.doc.

at the Tunis summit involved primarily the EU, the United States, China, Brazil, Russia, Canada, and Australia. The WSIS leadership had constantly to keep a balance between transparency and efficiency. Keeping the right balance was often more an organisational than a policy issue (Tables 11.2 and 11.3).

The WGIG process

In understanding the way the WGIG operated, it is important to emphasise that the WGIG was not, in a formal sense, a negotiating body. The main function of the WGIG was to exchange information and to provide expert input on internet governance to the main WSIS negotiating process. This specific mandate helped in developing a full multistakeholder practice. The WGIG did not have written and official rules of procedure; rather, business was conducted according to certain rules that were either articulated explicitly or accepted tacitly by participants. The important element in developing this practice was the considerable experience that Chairperson Nitin Desai had gained in organising previous UN Summits.[15] His in-depth knowledge of the UN rules of procedure helped him to distil the best and avoid those that could have led to controversy. The main developments in the WGIG process included changes in rules regarding: multistakeholder participation and representation; inclusiveness and legitimacy; time-management; and inductive and deductive approaches.

Full multistakeholder participation and representation

The WGIG included representatives from the main WSIS stakeholders: governments, the business sector, civil society and international organisations. Other experts and technologists participated, particularly those who attended as part of the civil society contingency, but also as part of government and business sector representation. All participants had equal rights to participate and intervene in WGIG activities.

Inclusiveness and legitimacy

Although the WGIG included a wide range of representation, in order to expand it even further the WGIG leadership introduced the practice of open meetings before the WGIG regular meetings held at the UN in Geneva. Open meetings attracted many actors who were thus able to intervene directly. The WGIG also facilitated online participation through an internet broadcast of real-time transcripts, audio-casts and video-casts of meetings. In this way the WGIG increased its legitimacy in the internet community, which was very cautious about the overall WSIS process.

Time-management

The WGIG operated under considerable time constraints. In only nine months (between October 2004 and June 2005), it had to provide an authoritative Report on Internet Governance for the final negotiations prior to the Tunis summit. In this short time-span, the WGIG also had to develop trust among participants who came from different and sometimes opposite positions regarding internet governance. The WGIG leadership used a blend of various traditional and online approaches in order to complete its task in the limited period.

Online phases harnessed various views. Prior to each session, the Secretariat summarised the main developments in the online phase and proposed a list of a limited number of issues for face-to-face meetings. For highly controversial issues, the Secretariat proposed that a few members who represented different views prepare background material. The WGIG was also ready to alter any approaches that would lead to an impasse (e.g., premature discussion on the definition of internet governance).

Inductive and deductive approaches

In early meetings, the issue of a definition of internet governance took precedence. At the meeting in February 2005, the group entertained a prolonged discussion regarding normative vs. descriptive definitions of internet governance. The WGIG leadership decided to change this top-down approach requiring a definition first and a subsequent discussion of concrete issues. The group selected an inductive approach to matters by analysing concrete issues and gradually building a broader framework, including a definition of internet governance. For highly controversial issues, such as control of the root server, the WGIG leadership decided to go into 'issue dissection' to identify sub-aspects. This helped to move from rhetoric to a substantive discussion. Ultimately, issue dissection reduced suspicion, identified common points, and substantially improved the level of discussion.

Texts and drafting

A text is the backbone of diplomatic negotiations. Ultimately, any negotiating activity, from formal to informal, results in the adoption of a final text. The WSIS was a text-intensive exercise. The number of contributions grew due to the submission of contributions through the web. This option led to greater expectations regarding the inclusion of ideas and concepts in the final text. In the Geneva phase, the Secretariat and Chair had to analyse almost 3000 pages of participants' contributions to produce the nine pages of the Declaration of Principles and the 13 pages of the Plan of Action. It made the drafting process both a considerable policy and technical challenge.

Types and forms of WSIS documents

The selection of the type and form of a diplomatic document is part of the negotiation itself. [16] For example, the most frequent use of a Chair's text was to propose the next version of the text after tidying up various amendments and inputs. Sometimes a Chair's text serves to provide face-saving for parties who have to make potentially embarrassing concessions.

As well, 'non-papers' have specific functions in multilateral negotiations. Non-papers are usually 'trial balloons' aimed to explore new ideas and options: they are informal and unofficial documents, often produced on paper without logo or any other official sign. In the WSIS, the 'anonymity' of non-papers disappeared. There was clear indication as to the country that proposed the non-paper. For example, Switzerland used non-papers to introduce new ideas for the Tunis phase. Although having higher official relevance in the WSIS process, the document's description as a non-paper indicated its informal character.[17] The WSIS extended the traditional use of non-papers by using them as Chair-texts. In November 2003, the WSIS Chairperson, Adama Samassékou, used a non-paper to introduce a new version of the negotiating text (Samassékou, 2003). The text was the result of consultations and negotiations and was produced on summit letterhead. Essentially, it was a Chair-text, but the indication that it was a non-paper strengthened the exploratory and informal nature of the proposed text.

The final documents of the WSIS were legally non-binding documents, similar to general UN declarations. They have different names, distinguishing them and reflecting their content. The Geneva Summit adopted the titles, Geneva Declaration of Principles and Geneva Plan of Action. The Tunis Summit adopted, Tunis Commitment and Tunis Agenda for the Information Society.

Reference framework: language and cognition

The WSIS and WGIG were important steps in the development of a global internet policy and an internet governance regime. Experience from other international regimes (e.g., environment, air transport and arms control) has shown that such regimes tend to develop a common reference framework, including values, perception of cause-and-effect relationships, modes of reasoning, terminology, vocabulary and jargon. The reference framework is highly relevant in the international political arena as it shapes how actors see particular issues and what actions they take.

In the WSIS and WGIG processes, the involvement of diverse professional cultures, including that of diplomats, technologists, media specialists and human rights activists complicated the development of a common reference framework. These groups entered the WSIS/WGIG processes with specific languages and different understandings of important concepts. Negotiating parties tried to affect the WSIS by influencing the development of the reference framework. In particular, three elements contributed to the shaping of the WSIS/WGIG reference framework: (1) the use and interpretation of important terms and concepts; (2) approaches and patterns; and (3) use of analogy.

Use and interpretation of important terms and concepts

Different professional and national cultures assign different interpretations to different terms. Reducing interpretational differences was a significant challenge to normal communication at the WSIS/WGIG. Considerable progress was made between the first preparatory meetings in 2002 and the Tunis summit in 2005.

Internet

One of the underlying issues of the WSIS process was internet governance. The ITU and many developing countries wanted this issue on the WSIS agenda. Others, such as the United States and other developed countries, did not want internet governance on the agenda. Consequently, in the early meetings of the WSIS the internet did not figure in the WSIS documents and discussion; for example, the 2002 Pan-European Bucharest Declaration does not refer to the internet at all.[18] The Internet emerged as a topic for discussion at the WSIS regional West Asia meeting in February 2003 and internet governance appeared on the WSIS agenda only after that meeting. At the next WSIS PrepComm, held in February 2003, the question of internet governance was introduced. Subsequently, internet governance gradually became the central issue on the WSIS agenda.

Diplomatic signalling using the term 'Internet' continued after the WSIS. In November 2006, at the ITU conference, the term appeared in the ITU resolution on internet governance with lower-case 'i' instead of the usual, upper case 'I'. The US ambassador in charge of internet governance expressed concern that the ITU spelling of the word without a capital letter might signal an intention to treat the internet like other telecommunication systems internationally governed by the ITU (Shannon, 2006).

Prefixes: 'e-' – 'virtual' – 'cyber' – 'digital'

The prefixes 'e-', 'cyber', 'virtual' and 'digital' are used to describe various ICT/internet developments. Their use originated in the 1990s and implied different social, economic and political influences on the development of the internet. For example, academics and internet pioneers used both 'cyber-' and 'virtual' to highlight the novelty of the internet and the emergence of a 'brave, new world'. The prefix 'e-' is usually associated with e-commerce and the commercialisation of the internet in the late 1990s. 'Digital' came into use primarily in technical fields and also received prominence in the context of the 'digital divide' discussion.

In the international arena, the prefix 'cyber-' is rarely used, with the exception of cyber-crime found in the title of the Council of Europe's *Convention on Cyber-Crime* (Council of Europe, 2001). The word 'virtual' also rarely appears in international documents.

The prefix 'e-' has garnered particular favour in the EU, where it describes various policies related to e-science and e-health. In the WSIS, 'e-' was introduced at the Pan-EU Bucharest Regional Meeting and became predominant in all WSIS texts, including the final documents.

Governance

In the 2003 WSIS debate on internet governance, a controversy arose over the term 'governance'[19] and its various meanings. According to one meaning, governance is synonymous with government. Many national delegations had this initial understanding, leading to the interpretation that internet governance should be the business of governments. This interpretation clashed immediately with a broader meaning that includes governance of affairs of any institution, including non-governmental institutions. This was the meaning accepted by internet communities, since it describes the way in which the internet was initially governed.

An additional source of confusion was the translation of the term governance into other languages. In Spanish, the term refers primarily to public activities or the functions of government (*gestión pública, gestión del sector público*, and *función de gobierno*). The reference to public activities or government also appears in French (*gestion des affaires publiques, efficacité de l'administration, qualité de l'administration*, and *mode de gouvernement*). Portuguese follows a similar pattern by referring to the public sector and government (*gestão pública* and *administração pública*).

The early confusion about the term was clarified through the work of the WGIG. The broader definition was adopted, which includes management functions in governments, the business sector, civil society and international organisations. The broader understanding of the term 'governance' also inspired the creation of the IGF, which became the main WSIS follow-up body in the field of internet governance. The IGF includes equal participation of all main stakeholders.

Approaches and patterns

Other elements that contributed to the shaping of the WSIS/WGIG reference framework were the approaches and patterns of negotiations. During the WSIS and WGIG, some clear approaches and patterns in negotiations emerged. They shaped discussions and aided in the alignment of different interests and perceptions in debate. Different attitudes could be found in regard to approaches to technical and policy aspects, to 'old-real' vs. 'new-cyber' understanding of the internet policy, and regarding an 'if it ain't broke, don't fix it!' attitude.

Technical vs. policy aspects

The relation between technology and policy was one of the significant and underlying challenges of the WSIS process and one frequently mentioned in policy statements. At the Opening Session of the WSIS-Geneva in December 2003, then UN Secretary General, Kofi Annan, stressed that in the WSIS 'we are embarked on an endeavour that transcends technology. Building an open, empowering Information Society is a social, economic and ultimately, political challenge.' (United Nations, 2003) The question of the relation between technical and policy aspects of the internet turned out to be highly complex and it became difficult to draw a clear distinction between them. Technical solutions are not neutral. Ultimately, each technical solution or option promotes certain interests, empowers certain groups and, to a certain extent, affects social, political, and economic life.

With the internet, the early online community was the original arbiter of technical and policy issues. With the growth of the internet and the emergence of new stakeholders in the 1990s – mainly the business sector and government – the unity between technology and policy was broken. The internet community no longer had predominant policy control and control devolved to business entities such as Network Solutions. The reform of internet governance, including the creation of ICANN in 1998, was an attempt to re-establish the lost balance between technical and policy aspects.

'Old-real' vs. 'new-cyber' approaches

Two distinct approaches to many WSIS and WGIG issues became apparent: 'old-real' and 'new-cyber'. Groups using the 'old-real' approach argued that the internet had not introduced anything new to the field of governance. In this perspective, the internet is just another new device, no different than its predecessors – the telegraph, the telephone or the radio. For example, in legal discussions, proponents with this approach argued that existing laws could apply to the internet with only minor adjustments. As long as it involves communication between people, the internet is subject to the same regulation as other telecommunication devices (Goldsmith, 1998: 1199).[20] In the economic field, those with this approach argued that no difference exists between regular and 'e-commerce'. Consequently, society needs no special legal treatment of 'e-commerce'. Proponents of the 'old-real' approach were also against e-tax moratoriums. In the WSIS negotiations, those with an 'old-real' approach influenced the decisions to exclude a discussion of intellectual property issues in the context of the WSIS. According to this approach, no reasons sufficed to treat intellectual property rights on the internet differently than their treatment in the WTO and WIPO.

Proponents of the 'new-cyber' approach argued that the internet was a fundamentally different device from all previous ones. Thus, it requires fundamentally different governance. This perspective was particularly popular during the early days of the internet and individuals even hoped that the innovative, early method of governing the internet, utilising a 'rough consensus and running code', might become the model for regulating other areas of human activities. The main premise of the 'cyber' approach was that the internet managed to de-link our social and political reality from the world of sovereign states. Cyberspace is different from real space and it requires a different form of governance. However, despite its early popularity, the 'new-cyber' approach did not have a decisive influence in WSIS debates.

'If it ain't broke, don't fix it!'

As soon as the internet governance debate started in the WSIS, supporters of the ICANN-based system launched the slogan, 'if it ain't broke, don't fix it!'. The slogan represented the opinion that the current, ICANN-run internet infrastructure was robust and highly functional. It also reflected the professional concern of many technologists about the alteration of a system that worked well. During a WGIG discussion, the debate became more sophisticated. While consensus existed regarding the achievements of ICANN in running the internet infrastructure, many governments pointed to the problem of the link between ICANN and the US Department of

Commerce. They argued that the 'if it ain't broke, don't fix it!' approach could provide blanket immunity from any changes to current internet governance, including changes not necessarily related to technical issues. One approach that the WGIG adopted was to dissect problems and analyse specific aspects of the internet governance system. Detailed analysis of problems and issues anchored discussion in real advantages and disadvantages of possible solutions and avoided simplification and potential tension.

Use of analogy

Since the WSIS was a new field, it stimulated an intensive use of analogy. Analogy helped participants to understand a new concept by comparing it to what they already knew. In the initial phase of the WSIS, the internet community used analogy primarily to explain basic concepts to diplomats and other newcomers to the field. With increasingly informed discussion, all main stakeholders involved in the process used analogy as rhetorical tools.

Internet – telephony

During the early days of the internet, the use of the telephone for dial-up access strengthened an analogy between the internet and the telephone. In addition, a functional analogy holds between the telephone and the internet, since both facilitate direct and personal communication. At the WSIS, those who opposed the regulation of internet content used this analogy to support their position. If the internet were analogous to the telephone, the content of internet communication would not be subject to control, since the telephone is not subject to content regulation. A more recent analogy between the telephone and the internet appeared in discussions on managing internet numbers and names. Volker Kitz argued that internet names and numbers could be managed in the way that telephone numbers are managed internationally (by national operators and the ITU as international coordinator).[21]

Internet – mail/post

The analogy between the internet and the mail is an analogy in function – namely, the delivery of messages. The name itself, 'email', highlights this similarity. In the WSIS process, Paul Twomey, the Chairperson of ICANN, used an analogy between the postal system and the function of ICANN:

> If you think of the Internet as a post office or a postal system, domain name and IP addressing are essentially ensuring that the addresses on the front of an envelope work. They are not about what you put inside the envelope, who sends the envelope, who's allowed to read the envelope, how long it takes for the envelope to get there, what is the price of the envelope. None of those issues are important for ICANN's functions. The function is focussing on just ensuring that the address works. (BBC News, 2005)

In this analogy, Twomey highlights the limited technical role that ICANN plays in overall internet governance. This analogy also answers frequent misinterpretations of the role of the ICANN as 'global internet government' in charge of all aspects of the internet, including the content.

Other analogies appeared in the internet-related discussions, but were not particularly apparent in the WSIS debate. These include analogies between the internet and television, the internet and libraries, the internet and VCRs or photocopiers, and the internet and a highway.

Use of internet-based diplomatic tools

Use of notebooks and the internet in conference rooms

An important innovation occurred with the introduction of wireless technology (Wi-Fi).[22] At the beginning of the WSIS process in 2002, Wi-Fi was a relatively new technological innovation used by participants from technically advanced countries, and even then only in specially designated areas. At the end of the WSIS process, in 2005, Wi-Fi had become a mainstream tool for many participants.

Wi-Fi access introduced many developments to traditional conference diplomacy. It facilitated the participation of an increased number of civil society and business sector representatives at the WSIS meetings. For most of them, the WSIS activities ran parallel to their day-to-day work. However, participation in WSIS meetings required prolonged absence from work. Through Wi-Fi, they managed to be present at WSIS meetings and continue their regular work through the internet. This facility allowed more people to participate in WSIS meetings.

For diplomats, a Wi-Fi connection provided constant contact with their ministries of foreign affairs and other government departments dealing with WSIS issues. In some cases, a Wi-Fi network of notebooks enabled the coordination of initiatives among representatives physically present in the conference room. Computer exchange complemented and sometimes replaced the traditional ambiance of diplomatic meetings involving short chats, *tête-à-tête* exchanges and corridor diplomacy. In person, physical movements can reveal the dynamics of negotiations or even be part of diplomatic signalling. This aspect of *in situ* diplomatic negotiations will change with the use of Wi-Fi.

Some small states created virtual Wi-Fi based networks in the conference room and were able to react quickly to proposals, amendments and other interventions proposed at meetings, all without leaving their seats or computers. It was an effective way of coordinating national positions in multilateral negotiations. Wi-Fi connections also provided real-time reporting from diplomatic meetings. Participants, especially those from civil society, commented on developments in the conference room via blog, chat and other internet-based facilities. Wi-Fi facilitated real-time consultation via the internet.

e-Drafting of diplomatic documents

The WSIS was an exercise in complex text management as the final text was the result of many inputs, amendments and comments. ICT/internet provided numerous tools for group drafting, starting from the simple use of the 'track changes' tool in Word for Windows and WIKI-based tools, to more sophisticated drafting platforms.

Most WSIS text drafting utilised an LCD projector displaying the negotiated text on a large screen, with an assisting operator inputting changes in the main text as proposed by delegates. The room could immediately see the amended version of the text. This tool was particularly effective with the track changes option, which showed deletions and insertions in the text. The WSIS frequently relied on such e-drafting. It subsequently became a methodology adopted by all stakeholders involved in the WSIS deliberations introducing: a faster negotiation process; a simpler control of changes and avoidance of mistakes in the text; and the preservation of a log of proposals and amendments.

Mailing lists

Mailing lists are often used for communication in international circles. They can be helpful in testing new ideas and in diplomatic signalling. They were particularly important during the WSIS process. Some mailing lists, such as the internet governance list, became focal points for shaping views on internet governance issues.[23] Although civil society made the majority of postings, all stakeholders, including diplomats and governments, followed the public lists.

A mailing list was also the official exchange tool of the WGIG. During and between the four meetings of the WGIG, the 40 members relied on a mailing list for ongoing discussions. Thousands of messages were exchanged between regular meetings. The multistakeholder composition of the Working Group (diplomats, business people, NGO representatives, academics) was also reflected in the utilisation of the mailing list. Non-governmental representatives (civil society, academics and business) posted the majority of messages. Diplomats, by contrast, were very reluctant to use the mailing list as a medium of communication, confirming the in-built professional caution to put matters in writing that might eventually create an official commitment.

e-Transcripts and diplomatic reporting

The role of diplomatic reporting, at least in multilateral diplomacy, may change with the introduction of real-time e-transcripts. This innovation was introduced in public meetings of the WGIG in April 2005. All interventions were transcribed simultaneously by special stenographers and displayed on the big screen in the conference room. While delegates were speaking, transcriptions of their speeches appeared on the screen. Given the centrality of text in diplomatic activities, the e-transcription innovation had an important effect on the diplomatic *modus operandi*. A verbatim, written record made many delegates choose carefully the level and length of their verbal interventions.[24] This development considerably increases the transparency of diplomatic meetings and will inevitably have an effect on diplomatic reporting summarising the findings of the event.

Websites

Both the WSIS and WGIG made use of websites as official communication tools.[25] The WSIS website was particularly important in providing an overall map of the highly complex negotiation process. Websites provided announcements and updates about the process and had an important management function in planning WSIS activities.

In three distinct ways, websites were an important tool in the management of documents in the WSIS/WGIG processes. First, they served as a repository for all documents and materials, including all official documents, lists of participants and contributions by various stakeholders. Second, through the websites, all stakeholders were in a position to submit their contributions in preparations for meetings. Even those stakeholders who could not physically attend meetings could provide input. Third, the possibility of posting contributions online helped in bypassing organisational controversies about the rights of stakeholders to distribute documents at the official negotiation venues. For example, while at the first WSIS preparatory meetings, complaints arose concerning non-governmental organisations distributing documents at the official WSIS venue, postings to websites circumvented this issue at later meetings.

Conclusion

In general, the WSIS/WGIG did not create substantive or, as some have argued, revolutionary changes in diplomatic processes, at least in a short-term perspective. However, in a long-term perspective, some WSIS/WGIG innovations, especially in the field of internet governance, could lead towards more substantive changes in diplomatic practice.

The main yardstick to use in this assessment is the practice developed during previous UN summits. In many respects, no major differences from previous summits are notable: the formal process of the WSIS was inter-governmental and states were not willing to alter the formal rules of procedure. As in previous summits, innovation happened in informal practice. States were more open to innovative diplomatic practice through flexible interpretation and implementation of rules of procedure. The innovations introduced through informal practice aimed, for the most part, at increasing the participation of non-state actors in the WSIS proceedings.

Straying from the UN model, however, the WGIG introduced a few unique changes in diplomatic practice, with the potential to be further developed in the future. The WGIG was more than an expert, advisory group, but less than a decision-making body. It did not produce official UN documents but it substantially influenced WSIS conclusions on internet governance. The WGIG was a compromise in which pro-ICANN governments let internet governance issues officially emerge and be placed on the multi-lateral agenda and in which other governments, mainly from developing countries, accepted multistakeholder participation. This compromise resulted in the success of the WGIG. Internet governance will remain on the global agenda through the Internet Governance Forum, established as a follow-up to the WSIS. In this context, the WGIG will be a useful example for the future development of multistakeholder partnerships on the international level.

Use of ICT/internet-based tools in multilateral diplomacy

Due to two factors, the WSIS and WGIG made a major advance in the use of ICT and the internet in multilateral diplomacy. First, during the WSIS process wireless technology matured and became both functional and affordable. It enabled participants to access the internet using their computers in the conference room. Parallel to the development of wireless technology, a boom in internet applications, including blogs and WIKI (usually known as 'Web 2.0'), substantially increased the participation of internet users in the development of the content and interaction of the WGIG. The second factor affecting the WSIS/WGIG was that many summit participants were Information & Communications Technology (ICT)-informed people and technologists. They introduced a new diplomatic playing field by intensive use of online tools. Others had to follow.

Perhaps the most important impact of WSIS/WGIG on diplomatic practice was the novel use of online tools, which also influenced various aspects of diplomatic practice including higher transparency, broader participation via the internet, e-reporting and higher efficiency of the drafting process.

Emergence of internet diplomacy

It remains to be seen if the WSIS/WGIG contributed to the development of a new internet diplomacy for dealing with ICT/internet issues. The WSIS/WGIG clearly showed that it is very difficult to develop one international regime that will deal with all ICT/internet issues. Numerous regimes already focus on specific areas such as internet governance (ICANN), intellectual property, standardisation and privacy protection. Each of these regimes has its specific forms of practice.

Given the focus of the WSIS/WGIG discussion, the most relevant is the ICANN-led regime for internet governance. ICANN was developed by non-state actors with limited governmental participation (with the exception of the role of the US government). Some attempts at the WSIS to create a new global internet governance regime were questioned by those who pointed out the existing, fully functional and robust internet governance regime found in ICANN. The prevailing view was that instead of creating a new internet governance regime, it would be better to fix the deficiencies of the current ICANN-based system.

The WSIS/WGIG dynamics that pushed the internationalisation process of ICANN could as well lead to the creation of a new type of international mechanism combining the best elements of ICANN practice (a multistakeholder perspective, transparency, flexibility) and those of international organisations (legitimacy, accountability, due process). These developments could lead to some qualitative changes in diplomatic practice, including the development of a new type of diplomacy – internet diplomacy.

Notes

1. Kremenyuk and Lang stated the following criteria for classifying a UN event as a summit: (1) the event is global in nature and open to all governments; (2) it covers global issues with multi-disciplinary aspects; and (3) new actors, in addition to national states, are involved in various capacities. The WSIS fulfilled all of these criteria. See Victor A. Kremenyuk and Winfried Lang (1993) 'The Political, Diplomatic and Legal Background', in G. Sjostedt, ed., *International Environmental Negotiation*, London: Sage, 1–16.
2. The WSIS was the first comprehensive (in issues) and global (in participation) attempt to address an effect of the ICT/internet on society. Previous attempts to address some international aspects of the ICT have occurred. One of the first was the G7 Ministerial Conference on Global Information Society held in 1995 in Brussels, followed by other meetings held in the framework of the G7 (later G8). In the UN framework, besides the 'ritual' UN General Assembly Resolution on Information Society, more concrete action was stimulated by the Y2K or Millennium bug. At that time, the UN General Assembly adopted Resolution 52/233, 'Global Implications of the Year 2000 Data Conversion Problems', suggesting numerous concrete actions and promoting a multi-stakeholder approach.
3. The reference to a 'Summit of Solutions' was frequently made by Yosio Utsumi, Secretary General of the ITU and Secretary General of the WSIS. See Daniel Stauffacher and Wolfgang Kleinwächter, eds (2005) *The World Summit on the Information Society: Moving from the Past into the Future*, New York: UN ICT Task Force Series 8, xviii.
4. For empirical research on the importance of agenda setting for negotiations, consult Charles R. Plott and Michael E. Levine (1978) 'A Model of Agenda Influence on Committee Decisions', *American Economic Review* 68: 14–160; Michael E. Levine and Charles R. Plott (1977) 'Agenda Influence and Its Implications', *Virginia Law Review* 63: 561–604.
5. For more information about internet governance issues and the WGIG agenda consult Jovan Kurbalija and Eduardo Gelbstein (2005) *Internet Governance: Issues, Actors and Divides*, Malta: DiploFoundation, available from http://textus.diplomacy.edu/textusbin/env/scripts/Pool/GetBin.asp?IDPool=641.

6. For a list of the issues, consult WSIS implementation by action line, available from http://www.itu.int/wsis/implementation/index.html.

7. In relations between the United Nations and the business sector, the main initiative is the UN Global Compac, launched in 2000 to involve the business sector in global affairs. In relations with civil society, the main development was the *Cardoso Report on the UN-Civil Society Relations*. The report proposes numerous measures for more intensive involvement of civil society in UN activities.

8. The WGIG report is available from http://www.wgig.org.

9. The convenience of 'one stop shopping' was one of the arguments for establishing the ITU as the central internet governance player.

10. Capacity building for internet governance and policy is mentioned in paragraphs 23, 51 and 71(h) of the Tunis Agenda for the Information Society (2005) World Summit of Information Society, 18 November, WSIS-05/TUNIS/DOC/6(Rev. 1)-E, available from http://www.itu.int/wsis/docs2/tunis/off/6rev1.pdf.

11. For a comprehensive review of criticism of the current positions of internet communities consult Willy Jansen (2005) 'Internet Governance: Striking the Appropriate Balance Between all Stakeholders', in William J. Drake, ed., *Reforming Internet Governance: Perspectives from the Working Group on Internet Governance (WGIG)*, New York: UN ICT Task Force Series 12, 35–40.

12. According to the WSIS Secretariat, the WSIS Rules of procedure followed the template of the World Summit on Sustainable Development (Johannesburg 2002) and the Finance for Development Summit (Monterrey 2002). For more information, consult http://www.itu.int/wsis/basic/multistakeholder.html.

13. Civil society organisational infrastructure included a Civil Society Bureau, the Civil Society Plenary, and the Content and Themes Group.

14. The business sector established the Coordinating Committee of Business Interlocutors (CCBI).

15. Nitin Desai was the organiser of the Johannesburg Summit on Sustainable Development (2002), the Monterrey Conference on Finance for Development (2002), the Copenhagen Summit on Social Development (1995), and the Rio Conference on Environment and Development (1992).

16. Sometimes, the choice of a particular type of document is a diplomatic signal, particularly in bilateral relations. For more details on the use of types of documents in diplomatic negotiations consult, G.R. Berridge (1995) *Diplomacy: Theory and Practice*, London: Prentice Hall, 161.

17. The Dutch government used a non-paper in a similar way in the UN Security Council discussion on a professional, rapidly-deployable UN force. For more on this consult Johan Kaufmann (1996) *Conference Diplomacy: An Introductory Analysis*, 3rd edn, London: Macmillan, 151.

18. For the evolution of the use of the word 'Internet' in the preparation for the Geneva summit consult, DiploFoundation (2003) *The Emerging Language of ICT Diplomacy – Key Words*, available from http://www.diplomacy.edu/IS/Language/html/words.htm.

19. Governance is from the Latin *gubernaere* meaning to steer a ship.

20. Here, Goldsmith argues that the internet is not functionally different from other communication media (e.g., telephone, mail). Hence, existing legal rules and procedures based on the conflict of law can be applied to the internet-related cases. New cyberspace law is not required.

21. Volker Kitz provides an argument for the analogy between administration of telephony systems and internet names and numbers. See Volker Kitz (2004) *ICANN May Be the Only Game in Town, But Marina del Rey Isn't the Only Town on*

Earth: Some Thoughts on the So-Called 'Uniqueness' of the Internet, available from http://www.smu.edu/csr/articles/2004/Winter/Kitz.pdf.

22. 'Wi-Fi' is the underlying standard which is used for wireless communication by computers, cameras, TV sets and other digital devices.

23. The governance mailing list was hosted by Computer Professionals for Social Responsibility. It is available from https://ssl.cpsr.org/mailman/listinfo/governance.

24. One can find an example of a transcript from the WGIG meeting at http://www. wgig.org/June-scriptmorning.html.

25. Institutional affiliation appeared in the addresses of the WSIS and WGIG website. The WSIS website had the address http://www.itu.int/wsis/, which indicated an ITU ownership of the WSIS process. The hosting of the WGIG was controversial at the negotiations. After the refusal to have the ITU host it, the UN Secretary General conveyed it and, consequently, the WGIG had an 'independent' address, http://www.wgig.org.

Part IV

Restrictive Dichotomies and Open-Ended Trajectories

12
'A Home at the United Nations': Indigenous Peoples and International Advocacy

Megan Davis

Introduction

Over the past three decades, Indigenous peoples have successfully forged a presence within the United Nations (UN) and international law as a result of their organised international advocacy, raising awareness of the distinct nature of Indigenous peoples' rights and the unique human rights challenges that contemporary Indigenous communities face (Anaya, 2004: 56–58). In 2001, Indigenous peoples celebrated the first session of the Permanent Forum on Indigenous Issues (Permanent Forum/PFII) – a forum established for permanent coordination of Indigenous peoples' issues within the UN system. When the then Secretary General Kofi Annan opened the UN Permanent Forum, he declared to the Indigenous peoples present: 'you now have a home at the United Nations'. While many Indigenous representatives delighted in this effusive welcome, many have reserved judgment upon the Permanent Forum and questioned the effectiveness of entrenching indigenous diplomacy within the UN's bureaucracy (Havemann, 2001: 24–25; Stewart-Harawira, 2005: 18).

The establishment of the Permanent Forum was the result of a decade of successful diplomacy to create a permanent Indigenous presence within the UN system. Indeed Indigenous peoples have been one of the great beneficiaries of the UN human rights system – Australia being a good case in point as manifested in the *Racial Discrimination Act 1975* (Cth) and the High Court decision in *Mabo vs. Queensland*.[1]

It is also true that the UN has been transformative in the way that many Indigenous groups are able to bypass the state – whether they be Indigenous peoples in post-conflict states or those groups avoiding the utilitarian realities of liberal democracies with limited electoral cycles – to raise awareness of human rights violations (Morgan, 2004: 481–500). Even so, there are some serious challenges facing Indigenous people's international advocacy efforts. In 2006, the inability of the UN to pass the Draft Declaration on the Rights of

Indigenous Peoples (WGDD) reflects years of hostilities between Indigenous peoples and state members at the Commission on Human Rights (CHR) Working Group centred on elaborating the declaration, and perhaps better reflects the true position of Indigenous peoples within the UN system. The likely closure in the near future of the Working Group on Indigenous Populations (WGIP) the only Indigenous working group with a standard-setting mandate is worrying for Indigenous peoples, particularly given that the Permanent Forum was not granted a standard-setting mandate. The PFII is proving to be a case of form trumping substance and it is clear that caution requires renewed emphasis when it comes to evaluating the success of Indigenous peoples' diplomatic practices at the UN today (Davis, 2005: 4–7).

Part I of this paper is an overview of the framework of Indigenous mechanisms at the UN: the WGIP; the Working Group elaborating a WGDD; and the Permanent Forum on Indigenous Issues. Part II considers the successes and challenges of Indigenous peoples' advocacy within the UN system examining in detail the Permanent Forum on Indigenous Issues. Indigenous successes and failures are similar to those experienced by other Non-Governmental Organisations (NGOs) advocating human rights issues within the UN. However, the difference is that the presence of the Indigenous voice is especially important, in that the issues raised by Indigenous peoples consistently call into question the very legitimacy of the notion of state sovereignty and the Westphalian construct, and provide an enduring conscience for member states, particularly the most anti-Indigenous rights states, the United States, Canada, New Zealand and Australia. It is a constant reminder that much of their power and wealth is predicated upon an unjust system and the theft of Indigenous lands, territories and resources and the continuing piracy of their cultures. Furthermore, it is a reminder that the UNs' proven inability to adequately negotiate a compromise between these binary positions is a failure of diplomacy and calls into question the universality of human rights that is at the core of its mission.

Part I: indigenous peoples advocacy at the United Nations

In 2003, an editorial in *Foreign Policy* magazine declared that globalisation has delivered Indigenous peoples 'newly acquired political clout' having 'transformed intolerance for human rights violations, for ecological abuses and for discrimination of any kind into increasingly universal standards among governments, multilateral bodies, NGOs, and the international media' (Naim, 2003: 96). In particular, the *Foreign Policy* editorial linked the increased influence of Indigenous peoples politically with the work that is being conducted at the UN on Indigenous peoples' rights:

> the United Nations spurred the internationalization of the Indigenous-rights movement by launching an initiative to establish a universal

declaration of Indigenous rights. A working group representing governments and Indigenous organizations has met annually in Geneva and, although the declaration remains bogged down, the process has helped create an active and relatively well-funded global network of Indigenous groups and other organizations interested in the subject. (Naim, 2003: 95)

This is all true – the genesis of the global network of Indigenous people began in the 1970s with what Anaya describes as, 'a new generation of men and women educated in the ways of societies that had encroached upon them' who 'began drawing increased attention to demands for their continued survival as distinct communities with historically based cultures, political institutions and entitlements to land' (Anaya, 2004: 56). It became what Falk has described as the 'first truly intercivilizational critique of the prevailing human rights discourse' (Falk, 2000: 151).

The growing awareness of the plight of Indigenous peoples as a serious human rights issue compelled the UN Sub-Commission on the Prevention of Discrimination and Protection of Minorities to engage UN diplomat Jose R. Martinez Cobo to conduct a comprehensive study on the 'Problem of Discrimination against Indigenous Populations' in 1971 (United Nations, 1986). The Cobo study was a key development for Indigenous peoples issues within the UN human rights system. It provided an unofficial working definition for the UN of 'Indigenous peoples':

[Indigenous peoples] are those people having an historical continuity with pre-invasion and pre-colonial societies who consider themselves distinct from other sectors of the societies now prevailing in those territories or parts of them. They form at present non-dominant sectors of society and are determined to preserve, develop and transmit to future generations, their ancestral territories, and their ethnic identity, as the basis of their continued existence as peoples in accordance with their own cultural patterns, social institutions, and legal systems.

It was during the time in which the Cobo report was compiled that the first NGO conference was held in Geneva in 1977 on discrimination against Indigenous populations in the Americas (Anaya, 2004: 57). It was organised as a project by the NGO sub-committee on racism, racial discrimination, apartheid and colonisation. It was the combination of Indigenous lobbying, the NGO conference and the Cobo study that led to the establishment of the first WGIP by the Economic and Social Council (ECOSOC) and the CHR in 1982.

Working group on indigenous populations

The WGIP membership is constituted by five independent experts from the Sub-Commission on the Promotion and Protection of Human Rights. The Working Group meets annually in Geneva and attracts the highest number of participants than any other working group meeting in the UN system. The Working Group meets for one week, and until the Permanent Forum was established, was regularly attended by between 700–1000 Indigenous peoples (United Nations, 2006: 6). Its agenda covers a wide range of Indigenous issues from review of developments within states to annual thematic consideration of particular challenges to Indigenous communities such as the right to: development; traditional knowledge; health and education. The agenda is flexible and speakers are often allowed to speak for up to ten minutes (Pritchard, 1998: 44). When compared to the PFII, the WGIP holds the lowest possible position on the UN hierarchy as a working group of the Sub-Commission on the Promotion and Protection of Human Rights. However the WGIP has a comparatively strong mandate (United Nations, 1982). The mandate includes standard-setting, which led to the drafting of a UN Declaration on the Rights of Indigenous peoples (United Nations, 1994). This was the WGIP's most significant achievement – the drafting of a declaration on Indigenous rights in which Indigenous peoples fully participated and were consulted (Burger, 1996: 209). The WGIP has also conducted numerous expert seminars and studies such as: a study on the relationship between Indigenous peoples and their lands; a study on treaties, agreements and other constructive arrangements between states and Indigenous populations; and a study on the protection of the heritage of Indigenous peoples.

The next major development in indigenous diplomacy at the international level was the proclamation by the General Assembly of the International Year for the World's Indigenous Peoples, and in 1994, the International Decade of the World's Indigenous Peoples (1995–2004). The first decade, was coordinated by the High Commissioner for Human Rights based in Geneva. In 2004, the General Assembly declared a second International Decade of the World's Indigenous Peoples and this was to be overseen by ECOSOC and its administration falls to the PFII in New York.

The draft declaration on the rights of indigenous peoples

In 1995, the UNCHR Working Group commenced with elaborating a WGDD. The original draft was written by the Working Group members in consultation with Indigenous peoples who had participated in the development of the text since 1985 (Ibid.).

The draft declaration when passed will not create any binding obligations under international law. It is possible that the declaration would have effect in law if the rights contained within were elevated to the level of a convention in which those signatories become legally bound by the instrument or by virtue of customary international law. While not legally binding, draft declarations, 'are evidence of evolving standards and form, a crucial part of the process by which guiding statements of principles become binding law' (Triggs, 1999: 2).

The United Nations special rapporteur for indigenous issues

The Special Rapporteur on the situation of human rights and fundamental freedoms of Indigenous peoples was established by the CHR in 2001 (United Nations, 2001b). The current Special Rapporteur, Rodolfo Stavenhagen from Mexico has presented two reports to the General Assembly and his mandate was renewed in 2004 by the CHR.

His mandate as defined by the CHR is to gather, request, receive and exchange information and communications on violations of Indigenous people's human rights and fundamental freedoms from all relevant sources, including governments, Indigenous peoples themselves and their communities and organisations. The Special Rapporteur is also charged with formulating recommendations and proposals on appropriate measures and activities to prevent and remedy violations of the human rights and fundamental freedoms of Indigenous people. His mandate is also to work in close relation with other special rapporteurs, special representatives, working groups and independent experts of the CHR and the Sub-Commission on the Promotion and Protection of Human Rights. The Special Rapporteur also undertakes country visits. He has visited and presented reports upon the situation of Indigenous peoples in Guatemala, Philippines, Mexico, Chile, Colombia and Canada. He has also recently visited New Zealand and South Africa.

Part II: indigenous diplomatic practice: success and challenges

Indigenous diplomatic success: establishment of a permanent forum on indigenous issues

Advocacy for a permanent body within the UN began early on in WGIP history because of a realisation that the WGIP could not effectively deal with the many issues facing Indigenous peoples. In fact, the WGIP as a working group of the Sub-Commission on the Promotion and Protection of Human Rights was at the lowest rung on the UN hierarchy and was only temporary. Indigenous representatives argued that a permanent forum could better respond to Indigenous peoples' issues, particularly if that forum had an Indigenous membership alongside that of the member states. This would reflect the right to self-determination by allowing Indigenous peoples control in the decisions that affect them. In 1991, the prospect of a permanent forum dealing with Indigenous issues was discussed at the UN Conference on Indigenous Self-Government that was held in Nuuk, Greenland. The final recommendations of the meeting included the proposal for an Indigenous presence within the UN on a permanent basis.

Again in 1993 at the Vienna World Conference on Human Rights, Indigenous peoples took the opportunity to promote the idea of a permanent forum and this led to a recommendation in the Vienna Declaration and Programme of Action for a permanent forum as the key outcome of the International Decade of the World's Indigenous Peoples. In 1993, the General Assembly requested the CHR to consider establishing a permanent forum. The Commission requested the WGIP to consider a forum in 1994 and the WGIP recommended that consultations begin and in 1994, the General Assembly endorsed the recommendations made by the WGIP. Therefore, following the Vienna Conference two working groups were conducted to elaborate on the minutiae of a permanent forum. The first working group was held in Copenhagen, Denmark (26–28 June 1995) and the second was held in Santiago, Chile (June 1997). And the important boost to Indigenous advocacy for a forum came in 1995 when the Secretary General conducted a review of existing mechanisms relating to Indigenous peoples. He noted that there was no regular system for the exchange of information on Indigenous peoples issues between states, UN agencies and Indigenous peoples (United Nations, 1995):

> What emerges from the review is both encouraging and troubling... there are apparent lacunae and inconsistencies within the United Nations system on this issue... there are virtually no mechanisms in the United Nations organizations which give the nominated representative of Indigenous organizations or peoples an opportunity to provide expert advice or take part in decision-making... the fact that there are now a number Indigenous related programmes and projects being implemented and planned by United Nations agencies only underlines the striking absence of a mechanism to ensure regular exchange of information among the concerned and interested parties – Governments, the United Nations system and Indigenous people – on an ongoing basis.

It is important to note that during this time of formal UN discussions regarding the establishment of a forum, there were also a number of Indigenous peoples' own conferences that were held during this period. There was the First International Indigenous Peoples Conference for the establishment of a permanent forum within the UN in Chile in May 1997 and a Second International Indigenous Peoples Conference in March 1998 in Panama. In 1998, there was also an Asian Indigenous Peoples workshop on the Permanent Forum expressing concerns that forum membership should reflect an equality of membership between states and Indigenous peoples. In 1998, the Arctic Indigenous Peoples also had a meeting on the Permanent Forum. During this year, the CHR decided to establish an ad hoc working group for the creation of a permanent forum that met in 1999 and again in 2000. In 2000, the Commission adopted a resolution establishing the Permanent Forum (United Nations, 2000). The mandate included six specific areas of interest: economic and social development, culture, the environment, education, health and human rights and the Permanent Forum was empowered to:

1. Provide expert advice and recommendations on Indigenous issues to the Council, as well as to programmes, funds and agencies of the UN;
2. Through the Council raise awareness and promote the integration and coordination of activities related to Indigenous issues within the UN system;
3. Prepare and disseminate information on Indigenous issues.

The Permanent Forum was established under Article 68 of the Charter of the UN, which states that 'ECOSOC shall set up commissions in economic and social fields and for the promotion of human rights and any other commissions as may be required for the performance of its functions'. The Permanent Forum was to be held annually with the first meeting in May 2002 in New York and the following meetings to be held in either New York or Geneva. The membership would consist of 16 state and non-state experts. The state members were to be based on the five UN regional groups and the three additional seats were to be rotated among the five regions. For the first term, the regional groups of Latin America and the Caribbean, Western Europe and Asia had the additional seats. The Indigenous representatives were nominated on the basis of seven geo-cultural regions with one seat to be rotated. This was a great success for Indigenous diplomacy and it is the only permanent forum in the UN system where member states formally share membership with civil society representatives.

The Commission on human rights, working group elaborating a draft declaration on the rights of indigenous peoples: conflict over working methods

Since the establishment of this working group only two articles have been provisionally adopted. And in 2006, the UN General Assembly's Social, Humanitarian and Cultural committee, also known as the Third Committee, voted to delay consideration of the text for one year. The seemingly intractable problems that have beset the Working Group since its inception have been the subject of great controversy among Indigenous peoples. Originally, the Indigenous strategy from the beginning was a policy of 'no change'. This meant that Indigenous peoples would not support any changes to the text whatsoever and was a strategy that was developed in the Indigenous caucus. It was in the WGIP that the idea of an Indigenous caucus developed and eventually took charge in formulating responses to government interventions and crafting caucus positions that would be made on the floor. The working method was that caucus positions would be collective, reflecting decisions taken on matters related to the Draft Declaration or the PFII. The caucus always had a Spanish speaking leader and an English speaking leader. For both the WGIP and the WGDD, it was the World Council of Churches that would annually host Indigenous caucus meetings providing translation, along with the Swiss based Indigenous Peoples' Center for Documentation, Research and Information (DOCIP) hosting Indigenous caucus strategy meetings.

Since the inaugural Working Group while some states have expressed an unwillingness to accept the text in its original form – mainly the Canada, Australia, New Zealand and United States Alliance ('CANZUS') and the United Kingdom – most states, particularly those Latin American states with large Indigenous populations, such as Mexico, Guatemala, Costa Rica, Venezuela, Ecuador and also Denmark, have stated consistently that they can accept it in its current form. For many years the Working Group was at an impasse on the text of the declaration with self-determination being the key sticking point:

> Indigenous peoples have the right to self-determination. By virtue of that right they freely determine their political status and freely pursue their economic, social and cultural development. (United Nations, 1994)

Indigenous people argue that this right is the cornerstone upon which the entire Declaration of Indigenous Peoples Rights is predicated. Without acceptance of the right to self-determination, the catalogue of other rights protected in the body of the Draft Declaration cannot be effective. The official reports of debates at the working groups on the Draft Declaration clearly show, however, that some states, mainly the 'CANZUS' alliance, are heavily influenced by traditional concepts of territorial integrity and non-interference as well as concern for the financial implications of many social-economic protections rights in the text (Iorns, 1996: 199). This has meant that in combination with the 'no change' strategy the Working Group failed to provisionally adopt any articles in almost a decade of work.

From the outset states began drafting an alternative text reflecting the various political objections of some of the more powerful states like the United States, Canada and the United Kingdom to land rights, self-determination and cultural protection articles. These redrafted articles were then annexed to the official UN Working Group reports. Indigenous peoples began to fear a situation where the majority of the articles in the text would be redrafted and reinterpreted without Indigenous input because of the 'no change' policy held by the Indigenous caucus.

One of the major concerns for Indigenous participants was that the actual drafting was conducted by states, in private sessions called 'informal consultations', during the two weeks allocated by the UN for the meeting time (Davis, 2002: 6). Transparency issues became the subject of heated debate in those particular working groups in 2001 and 2002 for which the Chairperson was severely criticised. While state consultations in private and informal meetings are not uncommon in the UN, it is expensive for Indigenous people to attend these meetings for two weeks. Indigenous peoples travel to Geneva to work and debate the original text of the Draft Declaration as adopted by the Sub-Commission on the Promotion and Protection of Human Rights, not to spend the duration of each day waiting as states participate in the drafting of an alternative text in a private room. The drafting of this alternative declaration is aimed at reaching a states' consensus with a considerably modified and effectively watered-down version of the original text. At the February 2002 Working Group (the 2001 meeting was postponed), Indigenous people were invited to attend the private government meetings, without speaking privileges but were offered 15 minutes of question time at the end of each session. Procedural controversy over the Draft Declaration continues. Indigenous peoples were continually informed by state representatives and UN representatives that this was not unusual in multilateral draftings, yet it created hostility between Indigenous peoples and the chairperson.

The universal position of the Indigenous caucus since the commencement of the Working Group to reject any amendment was predicated upon a belief that any amendment would corrupt the original text and would mean that all aspects of the declaration are negotiable. Indigenous peoples argued that there was a significant risk of Indigenous rights being formally derogated in international law through a weaker and diluted text. For example, states like Australia insisted on using domestic laws to hijack consensus on different provisions in the text.

During the 1998 and 1999 Working Group meetings, there were attempts by some Indigenous leaders to create momentum and consensus in terms of negotiation with states on the text (Pritchard, 2001). Mick Dodson of Australia, who was a member of the Aboriginal and Torres Strait Islander Commission (ATSIC) delegation many times and is now the South Pacific representative on the PFII, formulated the most serious attempt at reforming the official Indigenous policy toward the textual debate at the Working Group. Dodson drafted a list of principles establishing standards by which the text could be amended (these became known to states and Indigenous peoples as 'the Dodson principles'). The Dodson principles stated that the textual amendment of the Draft Declaration must be founded 'on the basis of a very high presumption of the integrity of the existing text'(Ibid.). Dodson argued in his proposal that:

In order to rebut this presumption, any proposal must satisfy the following criteria:

1. It must be reasonable,
2. It must be necessary,
3. It must improve and strengthen the existing text.

In addition, any proposal must be consistent with the fundamental principles of:

1. Equality,
2. Non-discrimination,
3. The prohibition of racial discrimination.

The Dodson principles were rejected by most Indigenous participants and this ended any momentum toward serious contemplation of amendments to the text. Many Indigenous leaders including S. James Anaya and Mick Dodson ceased attending the working groups. The Indigenous position of 'no change' effectively became untenable because states continued to draft an alternative text. Gradually individual Indigenous representatives began to break ranks with the Indigenous caucus. In 2003, 2004 and 2005, there had been ongoing negotiations between states and Indigenous peoples to broker a compromise. In 2004, an Australian representative suggested that the Chairperson 'get out the butchers paper and we all sit around the billy'[2] and work out a solution. Whether related to that suggestion or not, the Chairperson arranged for an overhead projector and worked on amendments with transparencies and a pen. This allowed all present in the room to follow visually the discussions on amendments. Significant advances were made in that week simply by changing the working procedures. The Chairperson then broke Indigenous leaders into groups with different state representations and each group worked on re-drafting various controversial articles. The active participation of Indigenous peoples in the re-drafting exercises created a sense of ownership over the text and the process.

Teething problems at the permanent forum on indigenous issues

In advocating for a permanent UN body focused solely on Indigenous issues, the emphasis has been upon hierarchy within the UN system and upon Indigenous control. The Permanent Forum is frequently exhorted as being successful because it is situated at the highest possible level for a forum – at the same level as the CHR. However the high level may not automatically equate to a similar level of priority given by the UN and states to Indigenous issues. Nor does it mean the Permanent Forum will have the capacity to achieve what most Indigenous peoples fundamentally want – reform within member states. This reflects a weakness in Indigenous strategy with an over reliance on the UN human rights systems as well as unrealistic expectations of the UN.

The conundrum of Indigenous peoples' claims and the UN as a states body is particularly highlighted by the ongoing debate regarding Indigenous peoples' right to self-determination. The right to self-determination as it applies to Indigenous peoples remains controversial within the UN system particularly with members of the 'CANZUS' group, as evidenced by the deadlock at the UN Working Group on the Draft Declaration. It is, as many Indigenous leaders still reiterate, a states body.

Initially, there were problems with the operation of the two-week meetings in New York that highlighted the limited capacity of the Permanent Forum to embody what Indigenous peoples had envisaged in the working groups conducted to establish a forum. The agenda of the two-week meeting deals with only three of the mandated areas intensively each year and the other three mandated areas are dealt with in a cursory fashion. They are rotated each year. It is impossible to know this prior to the meeting as there is little information available on how the meetings are actually conducted. This information is increasing as the Permanent Forum is entering into its fifth year and processes are improving as the forum changes and staff become more skilled at running these meetings.

Another challenge for Indigenous participants is that the central purpose of the forum is to make recommendations to ECOSOC to undertake research or work in the area of Indigenous peoples. For this reason, the only substantive aspect of an intervention on the floor is the recommendation to ECOSOC made by the Indigenous representative. Of course this is integral to the Permanent Forum because the role of ECOSOC is to consider ways in which UN agencies and programmes can better integrate Indigenous issues into their programmes. However, for Indigenous participants from Australia for example who have a long way to travel to simply provide recommendations, the Permanent Forum is limited in what can be achieved; indeed recommendations could be easily faxed to the Secretariat. The 'review of developments' agenda item at the WGIP permitted a serious review and analysis of legal and political developments within the home state and so was a powerful agenda item. Such frank discussion of domestic developments is neither integral to the Permanent Forum's work nor tolerated by states. For example in 2004, Indigenous peoples' microphones were turned off if they excessively criticised states on the floor and the final report was remitted back to the PFII for amendment because of excessive criticism of Indonesia's repressive measures in Aceh. Many Indigenous peoples have also argued that the mandate could be changed in the future to include standard-setting. This would be an unlikely future development. In particular, at the 2004 WGDD there was an overwhelming disapproval on the part of Indigenous peoples that the Permanent Forum could provide a role overseeing the implementation of the Draft Declaration when passed by the General Assembly. Despite such a provision being in the original text of the Draft Declaration, it is difficult to see how the uneven nature of expertise of the members on the Permanent Forum and indeed its restrictive mandate would allow the Permanent Forum to be an adequate arbiter of the complex and intricate legal issues that may arise with regard to the implementation of the Draft Declaration.

There are other ongoing simmering tensions such as the location of the Permanent Forum. New York is where the ECOSOC secretariat is based and Indigenous peoples felt the Permanent Forum would be closer to the power base of the UN in New York; however, much of the human rights system is based in Geneva. Moreover, it is expensive for most Indigenous representatives to fly to New York and stay in accommodation for two weeks in midtown Manhattan, particularly if the purpose is to write recommendations which one could as effectively devise and fax from one's home country. This comment does not intend to diminish the importance of networking between other Indigenous groups and UN agencies. The Permanent Forum also has an excellent timetable of side events.

One notable problem is that the Permanent Forum meetings rarely commence on time. During the first three years, the meetings were always bookended with numerous prayers by Indigenous representations that frequently expended up to 20–30 minutes of time. The time wastage during this period was also due to members being late and drafting the report as the meeting progresses. The time is generally made up by cutting time limits of papers and/or cutting speakers altogether. These kinds of teething problems have changed since the first years of the PFII's existence. There also appears to be an uneven nature in the experience, authority and expertise of Indigenous members of the Permanent Forum. There are concerns with individuals' degrees of 'expertise' or indeed 'community' or 'grassroots' authority – though these things are always difficult to measure. Interestingly, in the first round of membership of the Permanent Forum, the female representative of the South Pacific region, Mililani Trask from Hawaii, was extremely effective in her role, particularly during the two-week meeting, yet she was the only Indigenous representative not to have her term extended.

Conclusion: the future of indigenous peoples

With the commencement of the second International Decade of the World's Indigenous Peoples, there was increasing support from states for the WGIP to be dissolved. The argument in favour of dissolution of the WGIP is that its work duplicates much of that of the Permanent Forum. However the WGIP mandate is significantly different to the mandate of the Permanent Forum, not least of all because the WGIP has a standard-setting mandate. With the possible cessation of the WGIP and the failure of the Draft Declaration to pass the General Assembly in December 2006, the PFII has no mandate to continue standard-setting and therefore, would have muted substantive impact upon Indigenous peoples rights in international law.

The international legal regime for Indigenous peoples, although cause for optimism, is merely a means to an end rather than an end in itself. Indigenous peoples need to remind themselves that while they may have a home at the UN, what Indigenous peoples are advocating for is real and substantive change within state borders. It would be a sad day to realise that successful Indigenous diplomacy led to the establishment of a Permanent Forum in which Indigenous peoples can network, make the odd recommendation and visit the Guggenheim, but results in no substantive change in domestic law and similarly no agreed Indigenous human rights standards in international law. And this informs growing agitation in Indigenous circles to divert time and resources from the PFII to the international human rights committees and put some real pressure back on governments. Nevertheless, the achievements Indigenous peoples have made since the beginning of their organised international movement cannot be underestimated. The UN and its discourse on universal human rights has been transformative for Indigenous peoples and the ability to network with other Indigenous groups whether in New York or Geneva means that they have access to ideas and the development of standards and policies that are gradually being implemented in Indigenous communities and in domestic legal systems around the world. In this respect, Indigenous diplomatic practices have been successful.

Notes

1. Mabo v Queensland [No 2] (1992) 175 CLR 1 (3 June 1992).
2. From author's personal notes taken at meeting as an academic observer.

13

Interfaith Dialogue, Diplomacy, and the Cartoon Controversy

Samina Yasmeen

Islam has acquired a significant place in international politics since the terrorist attacks on the United States in September 2001. It is both demonised and engaged by those who acknowledge the role played by religion, particularly Islam, in partially determining the course of global and regional developments. For some, Muslims subscribe to an outdated form of allegiance to religious symbols and ideals of Islam with a propensity to engage in violence. Such analysts and practitioners of world politics emphasise the need to contain and curtail militancy linked to religious views by exploring and accepting the inherently violent and anti-democratic nature of Islam and Muslims. Others are reluctant to adopt a categorically negative view of Islam and opt for a more nuanced understanding of the diversity of views and practices among Muslims. Often acknowledging the role played by economic and political factors in creating militancy, they favour policies designed to engage 'moderate' Muslims in the agenda of bridge-building between Islam and the West. Interfaith dialogue has entered the lexicon of world politics: the analytical space traditionally reserved for secular understandings of global politics is gradually opening up to discourses centred round the salience of religion. At the same time, practitioners of world politics have focused on the need to build bridges across religious and civilisational divides. Governmental leaders and agencies are entering an arena where they have to deal with faith and its manifestations in today's world. Such a change raises a number of questions about the relationship between institutions and practices of traditional diplomacy and the demands of interfaith dialogue. Can the established institutions of diplomacy perform the role of bridge-builders across religious divides? Do our conceptions of diplomatic agents need to be revisited and broadened to include those who can adequately engage in such dialogues? What considerations and principles need to guide the course of such engagements to ensure their sustainability?

This chapter addresses these questions with reference to the developments surrounding the 'cartoon controversy' of 2005–2006. It places the discussion of the controversy within the context of the emerging emphasis on inter-faith dialogue. It argues that, despite the relatively greater emphasis in the post 9/11 era on the need for dialogue, the controversy initially exhibited two divergent views on the notion of sacred. Diplomatic institutions, symbols and practices emerged both as communicators of these differences as well as the targets of the resulting anger within the Muslim world. At the same time, the controversy manifested the relevance of alternative agents who played a role in creating and/or containing the divergent discourses on sacred spaces. The list of these agents included, among others, business interests who wanted to contain the fallout from the controversy for economic reasons. The experience suggests that increasingly efforts need to be coordinated among traditional and alternative agents of diplomacy in the religio-civilisational arena. Such efforts, the chapter argues, need to be guided by rules of engagement which reflect respect, equality and fairness to all parties involved if the project of building bridges across faiths is to be successful.

Diplomacy and interfaith dialogue: an emerging trend

Diplomacy can be defined as the process and art of communication and negotiations with the ultimate purpose of containing, managing and/or resolving disputes. The process continues during conflicts as well, with parties involved seeking ways to either end the confrontation or to reduce the ultimate costs incurred by those involved in the dispute. The history of such interactions and processes is not new: tribal structures as well as Greek city-states engaged in what can be safely identified as diplomatic engagements. The modern understandings of diplomacy, however, date back to the Italian traditions of diplomatists who communicated the views and opinions of their respective sovereigns to others. Building on these traditions, diplomatic institutions and traditions have emerged in parallel to the rise of state as the main unit of global politics. Diplomacy has been accepted and acknowledged as the domain in which a state operates and communicates its views to other states. The process occurs against the backdrop of the balance of power: the relative equilibrium or the absence of it determines the tenor of diplomatic exchanges as well as the issue areas covered by states.

Interfaith dialogue, in contrast, operates in the realm of beliefs and ideas of sacredness. The aim of the dialogue is essentially not to eliminate or reduce conflict between followers of different religious traditions but rather to promote an acceptance of difference. This is essentially due to the fact that religion invokes and evokes a belief and a *fundamental commitment* to notions of truth and sacred. Followers of different religious traditions view human place and its relationship to the sacred differently. Instead of establishing the primacy of one fundamental commitment over another, therefore, interfaith dialogue focuses on finding spaces where mutual coexistence is possible.

Traditionally the established religious institutions of different faiths had dominated the process. Religious clergy engaged in intellectual debates to establish the validity of religious views held by each other. Sovereigns representing different religious traditions often supported them in these processes. Sometimes these sovereigns also co-opted followers of other religions into their state structures as advisors and ministers. This enlarged the space in which ideas and practices of coexistence were developed. The Abbasids, for instance, employed and promoted Jewish and Christian scientists and artists. Similarly, Emperor Akbar actively engaged Hindu advisors as a mechanism of building interfaith links with the ultimate aim of strengthening the Mughal Empire. Gradually, however, the interfaith dialogue shifted primarily to the non-state sphere. Societal groups (including those from religious denominations) engaged in discussions and activities to build understanding across faith boundaries. During the post-Second World War era, therefore, the agency of interfaith dialogue rested with non-state actors who primarily engaged groups in their local areas. In the Nuba mountains of Sudan, for example, Christians and Muslims lived together peacefully with their respective leaders showing tolerance and active cooperation with each other. A Christian built both the mosque and church in the region (Julie Flint 'Hidden Holy War in the Hills', *The Guardian*, 22 July 1995). Similarly, in Indonesia the syncretic traditions continued to provide the basis on which Muslim, Christian and Hindu communities coexisted in the largest Muslim state.

The relegation of interfaith dialogue to the societal sphere reflected the nature of the Cold War system with its emphasis on rationality coupled with balance of power calculations. Religion and culture were considered to reside outside the domain in which states conducted their relationships. The trend did not change despite the emergence of transnationalism in the 1970s and the increased migration of Muslims into a number of Western states. The Gulf Crisis and War of 1990–1991 followed by the end of the Cold War heralded an end to such attitudes: as Saddam Hussein used the Islamic card to muster support for his ill-conceived invasion of Kuwait, Islam attracted attention as a new factor in international politics. Partly such attention stemmed from the views held by some Muslims that the West had substituted the 'red menace' with the 'green menace' as the main target of its attention. The discourse of civilisational clash in 1993 reinforced such views. As analysts debated the validity of Huntington's ideas of an inherent clash between Islam and the West, some came to accord this thesis the status of an established reality. Against the background of such views, some societal groups (particularly in Western liberal democracies) opted to 'learn' more about Islam. This search for knowledge and understanding invigorated the process of interfaith dialogue. Mostly guided by Christian churches of all denominations, it took the form of localised meetings among Muslims and members of other religious denominations. At the same time, interfaith organisations were either created or strengthened in countries with a relatively longer history of Muslim immigration.

The increased frequency of interfaith initiatives in the societal sector also contributed to some governmental leaders to begin to focus on the need to build bridges across civilisational lines. Prince Hasan bin Talal of Jordan took the lead in this process. Apart from emphasising the need to build understanding across religious divides, he established an Institute which encourages the exchange of information between different groups (ArabicNews.com, 1998). Prince Charles in Britain adopted a similar approach by supporting the Oxford Centre for Islamic Studies. President Khatami of Iran also floated the idea of a Dialogue of Civilisations with an emphasis on cross-cultural understandings.

The process gained momentum after the 9/11 terrorist attacks on the United States. The US-led war on terror and the increased focus on Muslim militancy created fear and a discourse of the West targeting Islam. The necessity to counter such discourse as a necessary corollary to engaging Muslim states and societies in countering terrorism contributed to a new found preference for interfaith dialogue among state actors. Keen to highlight the appreciation that the United States was aware of the diversity among Muslims and was only targeting militants, Washington took the lead in engaging Muslim leadership. In addition to meeting leaders from the American Muslim community, the Bush administration also set the tradition of diplomats promoting themselves as agents of interfaith understanding. Ambassadors posted to Muslim countries like Pakistan, for example, joined other Muslims in fasting during the month of Ramadan. They also began sending greetings to Muslims during the festivals celebrating the end of Ramadan (Eid-ul-Fitr) and Hajj (Eid al-Adha). Even in some Western liberal democracies, American diplomats engaged local Muslim populations and extended felicitations during the Islamic festive seasons.

This new blurring of the boundaries between the traditional roles of diplomats and interfaith organisations occurred in other countries as well. The process was aided by two parallel trends: Western liberal democracies (including Australia) also wanted to reinforce their understanding of the nuanced differences among Muslims. At the same time, governments in Muslim majority states sought to legitimise their participation in the war on terror and counter allegations that they had become partners in a Western agenda of subjugating Muslims. Keen to alter the domestic balance between radicalised and moderate populations, they opted for a role as bridge-builders across religious divides. This complementarity of interests resulted in some low-key interaction among members of Muslim majority states with those from Western liberal societies. In some cases, countries like Australia engaged some Muslim representatives to participate in interfaith dialogue at the regional level. The process invariably involved diplomatic institutions that had previously not specifically acknowledged the role of religion.

The relative quiet diplomacy was combined with more overt and symbolically significant references to the need for interfaith understanding. After the terrorist attacks on the United States, Pakistan's President Musharraf promoted the idea of enlightened moderation with an emphasis on building links with the West. Such unilateral declarations were soon complemented by joint calls for cooperation among followers of different religions. In September 2004, the newly elected Spanish Prime Minister José Luis Zapatero mooted the idea (later co-sponsored by Turkey) of creating a UN-sponsored 'alliance of civilisation between the Western world and the Arab and Muslim world' (BBC, 2004; Fraerman, 2004). The Alliance was to serve as a mechanism for 'deepening political, economic, cultural and educational ties' between the two civilisations. Then UN Secretary General, Kofi Annan, formally endorsed the project in September 2005 with the setting up of a high-level group for the 'Alliance of Civilisations'. The composition of the group, which held its first meeting in November 2005, manifested the realisation among decision-makers that state and civil society structures needed to cooperate in the agenda of interfaith dialogue. The nominated members of the Alliance were drawn from government institutions, international organisations, academia and eminent leaders from across the globe. In addition to former Iranian President Khatami, Bishop Desmond Tutu and former Indonesian Foreign Minister Ali Alatas, it also included renowned analysts like Karen Anderson and John Esposito who have made their mark in broadening understandings of Islam and other religious traditions (United Nations, 2005). The high-level group was charged with the task of assessing the nature of, and response to, the threat to peace and security from religious extremism at both the institutional and societal level. Importantly, it identified governments, international organisations and societies as the stakeholders in the process of combating religious extremism and building understanding. Those engaged in the art of diplomacy in the new millennium were clearly indicating their acceptance and support for multidimensional interaction and cooperation in an era of increased emphasis on religious identities.

The cartoon controversy: differing interpretations

The controversy surrounding the publication of cartoons of Prophet Mohammad occurred against the backdrop of these efforts to build bridges across religious divides. Commonly dubbed as the 'cartoon controversy', it started with the printing of 12 caricatures of the Prophet in a Danish newspaper, *Jyllands-Posten*, on 30 September 2005. Drawn by a number of cartoonists, these ranged from the Prophet depicted as a wanderer accompanied by a donkey to one of him with a halo, which resembled horns. The most controversial cartoons showed Prophet Mohammad wearing a turban carrying the *shahadah*[1] in front and with a lit fuse, and one of him holding a dagger while flanked by two *niqab*-clad women.[2] In the first phase of the controversy, which could be identified as the silent protest, Danish Muslims complained about the publication of the cartoons and demanded an apology from *Jyllands-Posten*. They also tried to engage the Danish government in securing an apology and controlling what they perceived to be growing Islamophobia in Denmark. The failure to secure the apology or governmental support led a group of Danish Muslims to tour the Middle East with information about the cartoons and other perceived indications of anti-Muslim trends in Denmark. In early January 2006, the second and violent phase of the controversy started: when a Norwegian newspaper *Magazinet* reprinted the cartoons, Muslim frustration and anger grew. That newspapers from other states, including Bulgaria, France, Germany, Italy, Spain, Switzerland, New Zealand and Ukraine reprinted these cartoons further aggravated the situation. An action-reaction phenomenon ensued. Instead of remaining confined to a debate within Denmark, it emerged as an issue involving heated debates on the place of Islam in today's world and the inherent incompatibility between Western and Muslim civilisations. The negative reactions also took the form of violent demonstrations across a number of Muslim majority states costing loss of lives and property. It invariably involved governments of the Muslim and non-Muslim world.

Both the phases of the controversy were marked by two diametrically opposed views on the logic and appropriateness of publishing these cartoons. Although there were some slight variations, these views could broadly be categorised as representing those held by Western societies on the one hand and the Muslim communities on the other. The predominant view among the Western societies assigned priority to the right to freedom of speech and expression. In fact, such views had formed the basis for the process which led to the original publication of the cartoons. In 2004, a Dutch film-maker, Theo Van Gogh, was unfortunately murdered after producing the movie, *Submission*. The movie depicted the plight of Muslim women who are abused and tortured by men using Islamic injunctions. While the message resembled the criticism voiced by a number of Muslim feminists, the medium adopted reflected a lack of understanding of the place accorded to religious scriptures. That Qur'anic verses were inscribed on the nearly naked body of a woman recounting the abuses perpetrated in the name of Islam infuriated some Muslims. Although the movie did not attract the same attention among Muslims as the cartoons, the violent response to its production had regional repercussions. Subsequently, a Danish writer, Kare Bluitgen, could not find artists willing to draw illustrations for his book for children on Prophet Mohammad. The atmosphere of fear caused the cultural editor of *Jyllands-Posten*, Flemming Rose, to invite 40 cartoonists to draw caricatures of the Prophet.[3]

Once the cartoons were published, the dominant argument remained one of supporting freedom of speech in Western secular societies without fear of retribution. In Denmark specifically, it was argued, democratisation and the introduction of the parliamentary system had allowed Danes the freedom to publish their ideas 'in print, in writing, and in speech' subject to them being held responsible in a court of law. But more broadly, it was argued that the European Convention on Human Rights and the International Covenant on Civil and Political Rights also endorsed these rights. Coupled with the focus on secularism, it was claimed, 'the West' had moved to a stage where making fun of religious views and sensitivities was considered acceptable. Newspapers in Western societies referred to this view as justification of their decision to reprint the cartoons as the controversy entered the second phase.

Such views on the admissibility of publishing cartoons of Prophet Mohammed stood in marked contrast to the dominant opinion among Muslims.[4] For them, the cartoons had violated the sacred space allocated to Prophet Mohammad in Islam as the messenger of God's message. Drawing upon the interpretation that prohibits pictorial depiction of all human beings, Muslims have developed a relative consensus in favour of not drawing illustrations of Prophet Mohammad. Some exceptions to this consensus do exist, but even those accepting the practice of pictorially representing the Prophet clearly articulate that it must be done with the respect and veneration due to him by virtue of his religious status. While the debate on his infallibility as a human being is an ever-present feature of Muslim society, he is respected and revered as God's chosen messenger who communicated the message of Islam to humanity (and not just Muslims). Specifically for Muslims, he is seen as the teacher, the guide and the spiritual leader who gave life to the Qur'anic injunctions by demonstrating and interpreting their relevance in daily life. To put it simply, along with the Qur'anic injunctions (which are believed by Muslims to be God's message), Prophet Mohammad is believed to occupy the sacred space that must not be violated. The cartoons published by *Jyllands-Posten* were seen by Muslims as blatantly ignoring such limits in the name of freedom of speech. Given that they were published as the perceived Islamophobia increased in Europe, the cartoons also acquired a symbolic value in political terms: they were seen as evidence of a concerted effort/conspiracy to marginalise and violate the rights of Muslims and Islam globally.

The relevance of traditional diplomacy?

Against the background of these different views on the meaning and appropriateness of the cartoons, and the violence related to the controversy, the question arises as to what lessons can be drawn about the interface between traditional diplomacy and interfaith dialogue?

From the outset, the controversy demonstrated the continued but limited relevance of traditional diplomatic channels of communication in dealing with interfaith issues. The first signs of such limits emerged during the 'silent protest phase' of the controversy. Within a fortnight of the cartoons' publication in Denmark, ambassadors and diplomatic representatives from Turkey, Saudi Arabia, Iran, Pakistan, Egypt, Indonesia, Algeria, Bosnia and Herzegovina, Libya, Morocco and Palestine wrote a letter on 12 October 2005 to Denmark's Prime Minister Anders Fogh Rasmussen. They complained about the 'on-going smearing campaign in Danish public circles and media against Islam and Muslims', and included the publication of the 'demeaning caricatures of Holy Prophet Mohammad (PBUH)' as one of the examples. They argued that 'Danish press and public representatives should not be allowed to abuse Islam in the name of democracy, freedom of expression and human rights, the values that we all share'. The letter hinted that if continued, the smear campaign could 'cause reactions in Muslim countries and among Muslim communities in Europe'. The letter also asked the prime minister to 'take all those responsible to task under law of the land in the interest of inter-faith harmony' and requested an urgent meeting with him (Letter by the Muslim Representatives, 2005).

It appears that the Danish prime minister did not fully appreciate the sentiments that had prompted the ambassadors to use diplomatic channels to express their anguish and concern. Instead, approaching the issues from a different standpoint, not only did he refuse to meet the ambassadors but also declined to get involved in the issue of the cartoons' publication. This response rested on the premise that the Danish government did not control the news media and could not contravene the state's laws on the freedom of speech. But he did mention the right of those offended to bring expressions and acts of blasphemous or discriminatory nature to the courts. Despite such a response, the Egyptian ambassador continued to communicate his government's displeasure over the publication of the cartoons through diplomatic channels. He even sent letters to the UN Secretary General expressing regret at the publication of cartoons and requesting categorical 'statements from the Danish Government on the need to respect all religions and desisting from offending their devotees' (cited in Wikipedia, 2006). As a group of Danish Muslims toured the Middle East with a dossier including the 'offending cartoons, governmental representatives of Muslim states further got involved in the episode. The dossier was presented to the meeting of the Organisation of Islamic Conference (OIC) in December 2005.

The second phase of the cartoon controversy reaffirmed the continued but limited relevance of traditional diplomatic institutions. As the information about the cartoons was publicised in the Muslim world, demonstrations were held in a number of Muslim countries to express their anger. The demonstrators targeted Danish, Norwegian, German and British embassies in Indonesia, Pakistan, Syria, Iran, Lebanon and other Middle Eastern states to vent their anger at the perceived insults to Prophet Mohammad. So strong was the reaction that the Denmark government was propelled to withdraw its diplomatic staff from some countries at a short notice. Meanwhile Saudi Arabia had already recalled its ambassador to Denmark, while other Muslim states issued strong statements directly and through their respective embassies expressing their anger at the publication of the cartoons. At one level, these developments suggested the inability of traditional diplomatic institutions to deal with religious issues. However, that some Muslim states chose the symbolism of recalling ambassadors, and others targeted the embassies of 'offending countries' paradoxically also reflected the continued relevance of these institutions. Furthermore, it is interesting to observe how the interface of governance and diplomacy appeared quite clearly in this case with diplomats launching appeals both through and to international institutions of governance, such as the OIC and the United Nations (UN), when their attempts at bilateral diplomacy did not prove as successful as hoped.

The second phase was also marked by active use of diplomacy to contain the damage done by the publication of the cartoons. The Danish foreign minister issued statements that initially expressed an acceptance that the cartoons had hurt Muslims. In a letter to the Secretary General of the Arab League and the Secretary General of the OIC on 6 January 2006, for instance, the Danish foreign minister, Dr Per Stig Møller stated that 'the Danish Government understood that Muslim circles had felt hurt and offended by the Danish newspaper's drawings'. He also stressed that his government 'respects Islam as one of the world's major religions and that it has no wish and no agenda to insult, mock or in any other way behave disrespectfully towards Muslims' (Ministry of Foreign Affairs of Denmark, 2006a). As the violent demonstrations increased, the Danish prime minister and foreign minister also distanced themselves from the decision to publish the cartoons. On 31 January 2006, for instance, the Danish prime minister categorically stated that he would not have 'chosen to depict religious symbols' in the way adopted by *Jyllands-Posten* (Ministry of Foreign Affairs of Denmark, 2006c). Three days later, both the prime minister and the foreign minister called a meeting of ambassadors to highlight their commitment to respecting Islam as a religion, and refuting some of the rumours that were circulating about the mistreatment of Islam and Muslims in Denmark. The emphasis was on the country's unqualified respect for Islam and its commitment to cooperation with Muslim states (Ibid.).[5]

The Danish government made active use of cyberspace to communicate these conciliatory messages. The statements by Danish leaders were given prominence on the website of the Ministry of Foreign Affairs of Denmark. Specifically, they were publicised through the diplomatic posts in a number of Muslim states. The websites included a series of statements aimed at dispelling the misconception that the publication of the cartoons was reflective of Danish lack of respect for and discrimination against Muslims and Islam. One Question and Answer section, for example, stressed that there had been no cases of the Qur'an being burnt in Denmark, that Muslims are not persecuted in Denmark and do have the right to demonstrate. Refuting some other rumours that emerged among sections of Muslims across the world in the wake of the controversy, the same section clarified that the Danish government did not intend rewriting the Qur'an or making a film about Prophet Mohammad. It also highlighted that the Danish prime minister and the foreign minister had expressed regret at the publication of the cartoons and that it was possible to prosecute *Jyllands-Posten* for publishing the cartoons. Equally important, the website identified the Danish government's commitment to invigorating interfaith dialogue as a means of preventing such events in future. These and other similar statements remained easily accessible months after the cartoon controversy died down. The websites of Danish embassies in Saudi Arabia and Pakistan, for instance, carried links to statements by the prime minister and foreign minister as late as December 2006.

Given that the cartoon controversy had spilled across the borders into other European states and engulfed a number of Muslim countries, traditional diplomatic institutions also became active in other states and in institutions of international governance. A number of Muslim leaders made strong statements condemning the publication of the cartoons. Their diplomatic representatives communicated such messages to the host states in the West.[6] The response from Western states reflected a growing understanding of the role played by religious sensitivities: while referring to the freedom of speech, these representatives increasingly acknowledged the hurt caused by the publication of the caricatures. Significantly, they placed the controversy within the broader context of inter-civilisational relations. A growing emphasis was placed on the need to build understanding between Muslims and Western societies. The European Union's High Representative for the Common Foreign and Security Policy, Javier Solana, visited Muslim states including Egypt and talked of his 'profound desire to recuperate relations between the European Union and the Muslim world' (Turkish Press, 2006). Other European leaders also articulated such views. Spain, which had played a pivotal role in the creation of the UN Alliance of civilisation, urged the Vatican to support an initiative promoting understanding between Arabs and the West. The European Union also signed a joint statement with the Organization of Islamic Conference and the UN in February 2006 on protecting religious symbols.[7]

Despite the flurry of these diplomatic activities and statements by governmental leaders, the violent phase of the cartoon controversy did not end quickly. This, in turn, highlighted the increasing role of non-state actors in undermining or sidestepping the traditional diplomatic channels of communication on interfaith issues. To begin with, non-state actors had created the crisis: *Jyllands-Posten* had published the cartoons and had refused to apologise for the offence caused to Danish Muslims. The group of Danish imams, in turn, prepared a dossier detailing instances of persecution of and discrimination against Islam and Muslims in Denmark. Not all the information contained in the dossier was factually correct. But by publicising it to the wider Muslim community, they sought to strengthen their position vis-à-vis other local Danish groups in a religious-based dispute. Given the special status accorded to Prophet Mohammad among Muslims, such support was almost guaranteed. This is not to suggest that differences did not exist among Muslims on the appropriate response to the offence caused by the publication. While some suggested a measured and effective response, others favoured the strongest possible expression of anger at the disrespect showed to a religious icon in Islam. Irrespective of the lack of clarity on what such responses entailed, a relative consensus existed among Muslims around the world at the need to address the hurt caused by the publication of the cartoons. Instead of being restricted to debates on the pros and cons of freedom of speech in Denmark, the controversy shifted into a new space where the cartoons emerged as the symbol of Western hostility towards Islam and Muslims. The response took the form of violent protests in some cases. Effectively, therefore, the cartoon controversy clearly demonstrated the ability of non-state actors to become initiators of interfaith dialogue embroiling governmental representatives as well.

Paradoxically, the controversy also established the limits to the ability of non-state actors to control the direction of events related to interfaith issues. Having circulated the cartoons and the coverage of discriminatory acts and speeches by Danish civil society groups, the imams lost control of the response in the second phase. As the demonstrations turned violent and Western newspapers continued to either reprint the cartoons or express an intention to do so, the group of Danish imams who had publicised the caricatures softened their demands. The call for an apology was replaced with demands that respect for Prophet Mohammad be restored and that he be described, 'as the man he really was in history, and that he gets the respect he deserves' (Gudmundsson, 2006). But the ferocity of the demonstrations prompted *Jyllands-Posten* to soften its stand as well. After initially refusing to apologise for publishing the cartoons, the editor-in-chief, Carsten Juste (2006), issued an apology on 30 January 2006 arguing that 'the drawings were not intended to be offensive, nor were they at variance with Danish law'. But he admitted that the cartoons had 'indisputably offended many Muslims' and apologised for it without any qualification. He went on record that the cartoons did not constitute part of a campaign against Muslims in Denmark and the rest of the world:

> Because of the very fact that we are strong proponents of the freedom of religion and because we respect the right of any human being to practice his or her religion, offending anybody on the grounds of their religious beliefs in unthinkable to us. That this happened was, consequently, unintentional.

The apology was accepted by Muslims in Denmark indicating that they were prepared to move into a new stage of reconciliation and building bridges between Muslims and the wider Danish society. But, despite these exchanges and announcements, the demonstrations did not subside. If anything, they continued unabated with the death toll mounting. It was obvious that an interfaith issue, once raised by societal groups, could become hostage to emotions. Political groups, as was the case in Pakistan, could also exploit these emotions as part of their own machinations (Khan, 2006). Ultimately it was only when the anger subsided that the situation came under control.

Business interests and interfaith dialogue

The cartoon controversy also brought into focus the role of business interests as alternative agents of diplomacy. The phenomenon is not new: the transnationalism that emerged at the turn of the 1970s had already established the relevance of 'new diplomats' in world politics. The pro-Arab attitude adopted by Aramco in the 1973 Arab-Israeli war was a vivid example of this role. Instead of following the trend set by the United States, the oil company sided with the Arab hosts and participated in the oil-embargo. Clearly, its economic interests had dictated its stance in a regional conflict with long-term implications for developments in the area. But the events surrounding the publication of the caricatures of the Prophet suggested that the environment in which these new diplomats have to perform is more complex than before. At the same time, it also emerged that business interests do have the space for and ability to play a role, albeit limited in nature, in issues of religious nature. In this particular situation, the case of Danish and Norwegian exports to the Middle East amplified this role.

As the opinions diverged along essentially religious/civilisational lines with Western states reaffirming the right to freedom of speech against the Muslim demands for an apology, an action-reaction phenomenon was set in motion at the societal level as well. Angered by the predominant view among Danish people that *Jyllands-Posten* need not apologise for the caricatures and the Norwegian paper *Magazinet's* decision to reprint them, civil society groups in the Middle East pressed for a boycott of Danish and Norwegian imports. SMS messages were sent around the region urging all Muslims to not buy products from the offending states. Email messages also circulated within and beyond the Middle East. With attachments of the caricatures and the offence they had caused, the messages urged all Muslims to take action. One message, for instance, informed the recipients of the contents of the cartoons, attached their copies, and asked: 'You have a father, mother, and sister. What will you do if someone humiliate [sic] them.' Then it called for a boycott of 'Danish products such as Nido, Anchor, Laurpack or any Danish product'. Religious leaders also urged worshippers to support the boycott. Within days, dairy products from Denmark and Norway were withdrawn from supermarkets in Saudi Arabia, Kuwait, Qatar, Bahrain and the United Arab Emirates. In some cases, the shelves containing dairy products from these countries were cordoned off with a sign 'Danish Products'. In others, the products were removed with signage 'Danish products were here' (Arla Foods, 2006a).

The boycott seriously affected the exports from Denmark and Norway. Arla Foods, for instance, estimated that the suspension of orders and sales of their food products through some 50,000 outlets in the region would cost DKK 400 million to its shareholders. Concerned at the prospect, it actively engaged the Muslim communities in the region. On 26 January 2006, the Executive Director of the company, Finn Hansen stated:

> Arla Foods regrets the effect which the cartoons have had on many Muslims. For many years, Arla has traded, and enjoyed good relations with consumers in the Middle East. In fact, *we have more Muslim than Danish consumers*. We respect all religions and wish to *express our sympathy and understanding for those who feel wronged* by this incident. Obviously, Arla Foods does not support anything that offends people's religion or ethnic background. (Ibid.)

In addition to placing this statement on the company's website, Arla Foods also actively drew attention of Muslims to the regret expressed by Danish government. The Danish ambassador to Saudi Arabia, Hans Klingenberg, for instance, had issued a statement that Denmark respects all religions. While posted on the Danish Embassy website, the media in Saudi Arabia ignored the statement. At the height of the controversy, Arla Foods decided to pay for its publication in Saudi Arabian newspapers as a sponsored advertisement (Arla Foods, 2006b). It also publicised the statements by Danish Muslims thanking the prime minister for his contribution in resolving the conflict and the suggestion for a joint mission of Danish Islamic organisations, the Ministry for Foreign Affairs and the Confederation of Danish Industries to Saudi Arabia and the Saudi Grand Mufti as a means to ending the boycott that had 'harmed Danish businesses' (Arla Foods, 2006c). The company, however, was also keen to indicate that it was guided by more than mere business interests. It actively supported the agenda of promoting and supporting interfaith dialogue. Indications to this effect were present during the height of the controversy.

The emergence of alternative diplomatic agents and the continued (even if limited) relevance of traditional diplomats was also reflected in the last days of the cartoon controversy. A constellation of agents worked together appealing for calm and the need to communicate feelings and ideas to avoid future conflicts (BBC News, 2006). Moderate Muslim groups in Denmark and elsewhere in Europe stressed that members of the Islamic community would serve the cause of Islam better by peaceful communications instead of resorting to violence. The Catholic Church also expressed regret at the disrespect shown to the Prophet. Governmental leaders (e.g., in Pakistan) also urged calm and asked for an end to violent demonstrations as a means of expressing hurt feelings. Governments and civil society groups in Western liberal states also actively promoted the cause of interfaith dialogue (Ministry of Foreign Affairs of Denmark, 2006b). Together, these efforts finally took the controversy away from the centre-stage of world politics.

The pro-negotiation agents have not stopped their efforts in the post-controversy days. Danish Muslims are increasingly engaged by the government (Buch-Andersen, 2006). They, in turn, are increasing their efforts to 'teach' others about Islam. Even Arla Foods has remained an active diplomatic agent. While relying heavily upon cyberspace and print-media, the company has continued to reaffirm its commitment to interfaith dialogue. Parallel to an advertising campaign to recover the lost economic grounds, it has actively supported humanitarian initiatives in the Middle East. Importantly, it has expressed its intentions 'to support activities aimed at creating greater understanding between the world's religions and cultures' (Arla Foods, 2006d). Such a shift in emphasis from purely business interests to acceptance of the significance of interfaith dialogue indicates that the agenda of new diplomats is also expanding. In an era of technological advances and increased globalisation, these agents are emerging as non-traditional agents of diplomacy in areas of religious understanding.

Diplomacy and interfaith: whither now?

The cartoon controversy has established that interfaith dialogue is not the sole domain of either civil society groups or diplomats. Increasing globalisation and the linkages between societal groups across states have created a condition where ideas freely flow and can trans-mutate into something other than their intended meanings. Under such circumstances, misunderstandings can arise and sensibilities can be hurt. Societal groups have acquired an ability to communicate and interpret these messages without necessarily any reference to the established state structures that dealt with the art of negotiations in the past. Given the increased prominence of religion in political discourse, this creates a condition where both governmental and societal groups can create, sustain or resolve conflicts. The chances of their success, even if measured in relative terms, increases if they cooperate in identifying the causes of ideological conflicts and misunderstandings. Civil society groups and diplomatic institutions, in other words, need to cooperate if the agenda of interfaith dialogue is to be successfully implemented.

The notion of interfaith dialogue, however, needs to be broadened beyond involving those from the established religious traditions. The cartoon controversy has amply demonstrated the importance of such a rethinking of the definition of interfaith. Given that a large majority of those living in Western liberal democracies either identify themselves as secular or are averse to formally participating in organised religious traditions, a narrow and rigid definition of interfaith runs the risk of excluding a large number of those who shape ideas. It also runs the risk of creating an artificial notion of centre and periphery with those from established religious traditions occupying the centre space in interfaith dialogue. The fact that those at the assumed periphery can disrupt the rhythm of any dialogue by questioning the very principles on which it is being conducted suggests that including them will serve the purpose of establishing and sustaining real dialogue across civilisational and religious divides.

The broadening of the notion of interfaith needs to be accompanied by expanding the membership of those engaged in the project. Until recently, clergy representing different traditions has predominantly conducted the religious dialogues. Such restrictive participatory arrangements are essentially governed by assumptions that religious clergy play a special role in shaping the views of the masses. While this view may be correct for a minority, the cartoon controversy demonstrated that agents other than the clergy were equally able to contribute to the misunderstandings. While Muslims circulated messages urging other co-religionists to protest the publication of cartoons, those from the Western tradition also vented their anger at Islam's perceived intolerance and denial of the right to freedom of speech. That not all of them were from the clergy on both sides suggests that interfaith dialogue needs to draw support from the wider public and give them a sense of ownership of the process as well.

Equally importantly, the question of diversity in religious traditions and gender balance needs to be addressed with reference to interfaith dialogues. The growing emphasis on building bridges across civilisational divides has unfortunately become hostage to two tendencies: first, its emphasis on religious representation has generally excluded those perceived to be 'less religious'. Even when the scope of representation is broadened, it still remains limited to those who look religious. This problem is particularly significant in terms of representation of Muslims in such dialogues: those subscribing to traditional Islamic dress code receive more attention as worthy participants of interfaith dialogue than the majority of Muslims who opt for less orthodox interpretation of their religion. Second, generally the process of engaging people from diverse religious traditions tends to be biased in favour of men. Women tend to remain under-represented despite the fact that they often occupy centre-stage as symbols of religious differences.

Most importantly, the cartoon controversy has highlighted the relevance of perceptions and imagery in creating and sustaining conflicts around religious identities. It has also drawn attention to the need for accepting that all understandings of one's relationship to spatial and spiritual realm can be equally valid. Any attempt to privilege one understanding over another can create conflict or lengthen the time taken to resolve differences. During the cartoon controversy, Western societies generally privileged freedom of speech over the Muslim focus on the perceived insensitivity to *their* notion of sacred spaces. Against the background of Western colonisation and a more recent negative focus on Islam, it contributed to ideas of Western hostility towards Islam. An expression of understanding of the hurt caused may have avoided a lot of problems that emerged once the issue got out of the control of those who publicised it. Muslims also needed to understand that accurate communication of what is considered sacred and why, might have contributed to some resolution earlier than was the case. Essentially, the controversy has highlighted the need to revisit the logic underlying the dialogues: instead of appropriating 'the truth', all those engaged in interfaith dialogue need to accept that our 'Truths' are mere truths for those who view the reality and the world differently. Developing such an approach requires exposure to other religious and cultural traditions. Such a change, in turn, depends upon developing long-term strategies that enable people of all religions to interact and learn from each other. It also depends upon accepting that such knowledge is not the route to establishing superiority of one faith/belief system over another.

In the short term, the growing relevance of religion in world politics, magnified through the cartoon controversy, suggests that both diplomatic and governance institutions will increasingly have to deal with future controversy centring around different notions of sacred as well as debates on secularism vs religious beliefs. Diplomats need to be trained in religious and cultural diversity, as well as the nuanced differences within religious traditions. This does not supersede the traditional emphasis on issues of 'high politics'. Instead, diplomatic training programmes could help those who engage in the art of communication, resolution and management of conflicts, to appreciate the blurring of lines between state and non-state spheres. Such understanding would attune them to emerging fault lines linked to religious or cultural beliefs *before* they result in conflicts. Without such training, we may continue to witness cycles of religion-related conflicts and crises that we cannot afford.

Notes

1. *Shahadah* is the primary declaration of faith by Muslims which states that 'There is no God but Allah, and Prophet Mohammad is God's messenger'.
2. *Niqab* refers to a particular form of veiling that completely covers a woman's face except for her eyes.
3. Later, Flemming Rose provided a detailed account for his decision to commission these cartoons in terms of a preference for cultural inclusivity of Muslims. See Flemming Rose (2006) 'Why I Published the Muhammad Cartoons', *SPIEGEL ONLINE*, available from http://www.spiegel.de/international/spiegel/0,1518,418930,00.html.

4. See, for example, Tariq Ali (2006) 'This is the Real Outrage', *Khaleej Times*, 15 February.
5. See also, Ministry of Foreign Affairs of Denmark (2006) 'Danish Prime Minister's Interview in Al-Arabiya', Danish Embassy, 3 February, Madrid, available from http://www.ambmadrid.um.dk/da/menu/OmOs/Nyheder/PrimeMinisters InterviewInAlArabiya.htm.
6. Based on personal communication with a senior Pakistani diplomat on his role during the cartoon controversy, December 2006.
7. The statement built upon the UN General Assembly resolution of 16 December 2005 on the need to combat defamation of religious with specific references to Islam. United Nations, Resolution adopted by the General Assembly, A/Res/60/150, 20 January 2006.

14
Public Diplomacy and Governance: Challenges for Scholars and Practitioners

Bruce Gregory

Public diplomacy, a term once known only to a handful of practitioners and scholars, is now part of a global conversation. Foreign ministries from London to New Delhi to Beijing use public diplomacy as an instrument of statecraft. Rare is the government today that does not require its diplomats and other professionals to understand, engage and influence global publics. Significantly, public diplomacy is no longer confined to the realm of statecraft. International and regional organisations employ public diplomacy to advance multilateral objectives. Non-state and sub-state actors engage in public diplomacy while pursuing governance activities that were once the domain of states. Concerns about what publics think and do are central to the way political actors compete, collaborate, communicate and govern.

This chapter will look first at public diplomacy as a concept. Although political actors seek to shape ideas and influence opinions for many different reasons, public diplomacy is an instrument with a set of widely shared defining characteristics. These characteristics distinguish public diplomacy from other instruments of governance and from non-governance related discourse within societies. Second, it will suggest that non-government groups and individuals increasingly engage in public diplomacy, not just when partnering with governments, but also when they independently engage in governance. Third, it will encourage scholars to contribute more to a systematic understanding of public diplomacy, its principles and practices, as well as its strengths and limitations. The chapter will conclude with several suggestions for collaborative inquiry between scholars and practitioners: connecting hierarchies and networks, leveraging technologies and trust and increasing knowledge about public diplomacy as an instrument of governance.

What is public diplomacy?

The term 'public diplomacy' was not used throughout much of the twentieth century. The usual terms were information, cultural relations, educational exchanges, public affairs, international broadcasting and propaganda. In the 1970s, public diplomacy gained currency in the United States through Congressional hearings (United States, 1977) and reports of the US Advisory Commission on Public Diplomacy (a bipartisan Presidential panel given this name in 1979 as a successor to separate advisory panels on information and educational exchanges created in 1948). The term was increasingly accepted by practitioners in the US Information Agency, who found 'public diplomacy' a useful umbrella label for government information, cultural and international broadcasting activities and a way to avoid the invidious connotations of the word 'propaganda'.

In the 1990s, a few practitioners began to look at changes in diplomacy as part of a broader inquiry into accelerating globalisation, creation of new information technologies and the increased power of non-state actors. Canada's former Ambassador to the United States, Allan Gotlieb (1991: vii), led the way. 'The new diplomacy', he wrote, 'is to a large extent public diplomacy and requires different skills, techniques, and attitudes than those found in traditional diplomacy.' Subsequent projects on public diplomacy included: the US Institute of Peace's *Virtual Diplomacy Initiative* (1997); Barry Fulton's *Reinventing Diplomacy* (1998); the online *Net Diplomacy* studies (2001); Mark Leonard's multi-country study of public diplomacy practices supported by the UK's Foreign Policy Centre (Leonard, 2002); and a study conducted by a Defense Science Board (2001) task force at the request of the US State and Defense Departments. Changes in power and global politics, these studies concluded, would require a transformation in diplomatic practice in which public diplomacy would be in ascendance.

Government structures and labels began to change. The British government appointed a Foreign Office Minister of State for Public Diplomacy and implemented a Public Diplomacy Strategy Board to coordinate activities of the Foreign & Commonwealth Office, the British Council and the BBC World Service. The United States created an Under Secretary of State for Public Diplomacy and Public Affairs. Most European Union countries, Canada, India, Japan and several other countries have public diplomacy departments in their foreign ministries. China has embarked on a soft power strategy that includes public diplomacy activities long common in Europe and North America (Kurlantzick, 2007). The United Nations (UN), North Atlantic Treaty Organisation (NATO) and other associations of states engage in public diplomacy.

Sub-state actors, including mayors and governors, also conduct public diplomacy. When Chinese President Hu Jintao visited the United States in April 2006, his welcome in Seattle, Washington by political leaders and Microsoft CEO Bill Gates was seen to be more successful than his welcome in Washington, DC. The governor of Washington engaged in public diplomacy when she publicly welcomed a Confucius Institute in Seattle and proposed establishing a state cultural centre in China.

Widespread use of a phrase does not mean agreement on its purposes and analytical frames. Jan Melissen (2006) observes that there is 'no one-size-fits-all' model when it comes to public diplomacy. Countries use public diplomacy to strengthen economic performance, support long-term foreign policy goals, enhance visibility, project identity, prevent and manage crises as well as counter adverse stereotypical images. Small and middle powers are challenged with employing public diplomacy to achieve their desire to be noticed – and to be noticed for the right reasons – in the face of limited resources for such strategies. Discussions of 'the new public diplomacy' need no longer give central importance to debates about US public diplomacy, Melissen maintains, although he suggests that others can learn from its strengths and limitations and from the many reports produced by think tanks and advisory bodies in America's non-governmental sector after 9/11. The clearest lesson from the American experience is that public diplomacy cannot succeed if it is inconsistent with foreign policies and military actions (Melissen, 2005: 6–10). To this it should be added that US public diplomacy is limited also by structural and cultural factors. In American political culture, military spending vastly exceeds all other foreign affairs budgets combined, and American commitment to public diplomacy has been episodic. Except in wartime, Americans have long been averse to government 'propaganda ministries', whatever they may be called.

Despite variety in the way political actors view public diplomacy's ends, ways and means, it can be instrumentally defined through the identification of a few widely shared conceptual elements. Public diplomacy is an instrument used by states, associations of states, non-governmental organisations, and individuals to:

Understand attitudes, cultures, ideas and media frames of events and issues;

Engage in dialogue between people and institutions;

Advise political leaders, policy-makers and practitioners on public opinion and communication implications of policy choices;

Influence opinions, behaviour and social practices through communication strategies, actions, narratives with message authority; and

Evaluate the impact of activities over time and adapt.

These elements describe an instrument that is broadly political and analytically distinct. It is one among a range of persuasive and coercive instruments used to serve interests and values. Public diplomacy is a tool available to political actors when establishing goals and priorities, and it is a strategic consideration when they analyse trade offs among costs, risks and benefits. It is used to set agendas, explain threats and opportunities, influence discourse in civil society, advocate policies and build political consent. Public diplomacy is also critical to the use and success of other political, economic and military instruments. Whether it is called public diplomacy or something else, it is an essential instrument of governance.

However, naming this instrument is not a trivial matter. Names shape understandings positively and negatively. In naming, we judge as well as describe. There are other candidate terms: strategic communication, political communication, cultural diplomacy, branding, propaganda, perception management and information operations. Some have undesirable connotations, while others are less rewarding conceptually. For now, public diplomacy is a consensus choice for a bite-sized label that is more conceptually relevant than alternatives, although 'strategic communication' is gaining ground in the United States.

Public diplomacy differs from education, journalism, advertising, public relations and other ways that people communicate for non-governance related reasons in societies. Educators discover and share knowledge. Journalists gather, frame and report news. Commercial enterprises market and advertise to produce profits. By contrast, public diplomacy imports methods and discourse norms from these elements in society and depends heavily on private sector partnerships. Education norms matter in academic exchanges. Peer review ensures that scholars funded by government grants are chosen on the basis of academic merit, and not for partisan reasons or their policy views. International broadcasters import journalism norms and build institutional shields to protect them from interference by policymakers in news gathering and reporting. Political leaders, diplomats and military commanders engaged in public diplomacy adopt public relations methods and political campaign strategies.

Public diplomacy professionals value the practical benefits of truth and credibility. They seek to achieve these norms through their words and actions, and they usually pay a political price when they fail to do so. Many prefer institutional arrangements that separate them from the work of foreign ministries (e.g., the UK's British Council and the US Broadcasting Board of Governors). They also value structural firewalls between open and covert information operations. In addition to diplomats and government broadcasters, public diplomacy actors include public and private sector professionals engaged in educational and cultural exchanges, communication consultants to political leaders, democracy activists and military officers engaged in open information operations. They collaborate and compete in organisations and tribal cultures where their identity and behaviour are associated with particular norms, rules and skills (Gregory, 2005).

Three time frames are essential to defining public diplomacy. One is driven by the relentless demands of around-the-clock news and media relations. If political leaders and diplomats do not get inside news streams, others will, often with perspectives disadvantageous to their work. A second time frame relates to communication campaigns on high value policies that may last months or years. Choices matter because not all policies require public diplomacy campaigns, nor are resources available to conduct them effectively on all policies. A third time frame involves long-term engagement – relationships between people and institutions – in the realms of ideas, culture, shared knowledge, reasoned dialogue and vigorous debate on issues. Investments in this time frame are made for decades and generations.

Public diplomacy has limits. It does not trump flawed policies or weak political leadership. Governments are constrained because much of what their citizens and societies project, and much of what global publics perceive, is beyond government control. Results can take years to achieve or may never be achieved at all. Success is difficult to measure, although not impossible with appropriate methods and sufficient resources. Shared understandings may not overcome deep disagreements or conflicts of interest.

Public diplomacy as an instrument of governance

The use of public diplomacy as an instrument by governments is generally accepted. But is it also an instrument used by non-governmental groups and individuals when they engage in governance activities independently, not just in association with governments? Here James Rosenau's (1992: 4) definition of governance is helpful.

> Governance is not synonymous with government. Both refer to purposive behavior, to goal oriented activities, to systems of rule; but government suggests activities that are backed by formal authority, by police powers, to insure the implementation of duly constituted policies, whereas governance refers to activities backed by shared goals that may or may not derive from legal and formally prescribed responsibilities and that do not necessarily rely on police power to overcome defiance and attain compliance. Governance, in other words, is a more encompassing phenomenon than government. It embraces governmental institutions, but it also subsumes informal, non-governmental institutions whereby those persons and organizations within its purview move ahead to satisfy their needs, and fulfill their wants.

Rosenau (1997: 146) also suggests that in place of a government's command mechanisms, governance relies on '*control* or *steering* mechanisms, terms that highlight the purposeful nature of governance without presuming the presence of hierarchy'.

Adapting from Rosenau's definition, we can make a case that many non-state actors conduct activities intended to understand, engage and influence global publics in support of goals that satisfy needs and fulfil wants. They may act in ways that are less accountable, and their actions may or may not be backed by the power and legitimacy of government authority. Nevertheless, should a different name be used for what non-state actors do when they employ the methods and time frames of public diplomacy in support of governance interests and values? Is what they do political communication, or outreach, or discourse, or advocacy or something else? Should public diplomacy be limited to state actors who advance interests and values backed by formal government authority? Changes in global governance suggest it is increasingly difficult to make categorical distinctions between state and non-state public diplomacy.

Consider three examples. When Bernard Kouchner went to Nigeria in 1968 to deal with humanitarian calamities in Biafra, he led what Paul Berman (2005: 230) calls a 'one man insurrection against the Red Cross', its principles of neutrality and silence, and its emphasis on discretion in return for access. Kouchner wanted an emergency medical organisation 'capable of reacting to crises around the world quickly and flexibly, and yet capable also of reporting on whatever volunteer workers might happen to see'. It would be a 'more political Red Cross', an organisation that could act and speak, 'devoted to health, and also to truth'.

Today, the Nobel Prize winning Doctors Without Borders is a global organisation devoted to providing emergency medical care in more than 70 countries and 'to speaking out'. Its staff and volunteers conduct campaigns for access to essential medicines, speak at national and international conferences, arrange informational events and travelling exhibitions and manage public education projects. The organisation's 2004 budget was $568 million – 89 per cent from private donations, 11 per cent from 'international agencies and governments' (Médecins Sans Frontières, 2007). 'Advocacy is an integral part of our work', its US director Nicholas de Torrente (2002) said in a speech on the organisation's activities in Afghanistan. At the same time, and in effect building a firewall to protect credibility, he rejected then-Secretary of State Colin Powell's call for NGOs to be part of a US-led "'combat team" forming a military, political, economic, and humanitarian response against terrorism'.

The National Endowment for Democracy (NED) was established in the United States in the 1980s as a 'quasi-autonomous non-governmental organisation' to fund labour, business and political party organisations engaged in promoting democratic institutions and values in other countries. Modelled on Germany's political party foundations, NED is a government-funded private corporation with an independent board and staff. Counterpart institutions include Canada's International Centre for Human Rights and Democratic Development, the UK's Westminster Foundation and foundations in many other countries (Lowe, 2003).

NED's mission is to help build civil societies and strengthen democratic institutions (National Endowment for Democracy, 2005). Government funds provide most of the capital and non-government groups do most of the work. NED's supporters view the private sector, rather than government, as more appropriate to the work of democratisation. Standing apart from short-term government policies, they value bipartisan, long-term approaches. Their goals are to foster values and institutions essential to democratic governance; their means are networks, and networks of networks.

The Internet Corporation for Assigned Names and Numbers (ICANN) is a non-profit California corporation established in 1998 to regulate the Internet's domain names and technical elements. ICANN replaced a single individual, Jonathan Postal, who worked at the University of Southern California under contract to the US Defense Department's Advanced Research Projects Agency. Seen as a way to bypass bureaucratic inefficiencies in the International Telecommunications Union, ICANN has been described as 'an experiment, a bottom-up, multi-stakeholder approach toward managing a global resource on a nongovernmental basis' (Cukier, 2005a: 10). ICANN's critics concede its efficiency and flexibility, but question its transparency, accountability and legitimacy. Some view it as another example of American unilateralism. The United States frames ICANN as a liberal alternative to state regulation, a way to manage the Internet as a 'highly robust and geographically diverse medium' (United States, 2005a) through government consultation with the private sector and civil society.

ICANN maintains an informational website but does little policy advocacy. In effect, ICANN subcontracts its public diplomacy to the US government and likeminded constituents. Speeches by US officials express American views on Internet governance. Former UN Secretary General Kofi Annan supported Internet management as an 'effective collaboration among private businesses, civil society, and the academic and technical communities' and urged change that would make 'governance arrangements more international', meaning more intergovernmental, and more responsive to Internet growth in developing countries (Annan, 2005). ICANN remains a private corporation that provides a public good. These examples suggest several considerations in thinking about whether non-state actors who engage in governance also engage in public diplomacy by virtue of using its methods and time frames. First, Doctors Without Borders, NED and ICANN provide public goods to society as non-state actors. They do so independent of the command authority and taxing powers of states, although in varying degrees each receives government funds.

Second, each undertakes activities intended to understand, engage and influence global publics. There are operational differences, but each does so in ways and time frames analogous to government public diplomacy. Doctors Without Borders acts independently. NED conducts its own advocacy activities and occasionally provides a forum for US government officials on policy issues (Bush, 2005). ICANN relies on the US Government for its public diplomacy.

Third, governments and non-state actors face similar challenges. Both must find ways to gain attention in a world of media saturation and information abundance. To communicate effectively both must have deep comprehension of cultures and influence networks. In order to build political will for governance activities, they must be credible in words and symbolic actions as well as in the quality of the public goods they provide. For Doctors Without Borders, credibility means disassociation from governments, whether it is distance from Colin Powell's counter terrorism government/ NGO 'combat teams' or speaking out against government actions that lead to humanitarian tragedies. NED depends on government funds, but argues that 'such support cannot be governed by the short-term policy preferences of a particular US administration' (National Endowment for Democracy, 2005). For ICANN, credibility means matching actions with words and messages framed by its constituents in ways that appeal to its sceptics. Commenting on the decision of the World Summit on the Information Society to leave management of the Internet to ICANN, US officials were quick to observe that the task now is to expand Internet technologies to the developing world to create jobs and improve economic opportunities (United States, 2005b).

Despite many similarities between governments and non-state actors in global governance, critics point out crucial differences. Jessica Mathews (1997) argues that while NGOs have great strengths – focus, credibility, expertise, energy, passion – they have significant limitations as well. NGOs judge public acts by how they affect particular interests. As they expand, they often make choices driven by the need for larger budgets and make compromises that limit their flexibility and independence. In Clifford Bob's analysis (2005: 37), NGOs set goals and make 'cost/benefit calculations' based less on altruism and principles than on maintenance and survival. Other differences relate to public priorities and accountability. Donna Oglesby (2006) observes that, however benevolent their agendas, 'NGOs are most often advocates for a single issue and never have to face the trade-offs required of governing'. Anne-Marie Slaughter (2004: 9–10) makes the accountability point. There are 'many ways in which private actors now can and do perform government functions ... The problem, however, is ensuring that these private actors uphold the public trust.' Government's role in governance is 'distinct and different'. Governments, at least in a democracy, must represent all their different constituencies.

These are strong arguments. Nevertheless, governments also regularly demonstrate preferences for particular interests rather than consensus. Although governments have been better than non-state actors at providing the hard power needed for security, they frequently are less able and willing than non-state actors to provide services that can mitigate threats to security. Private military actors, on the other hand, increasingly provide hard power services to non-state actors, including such humanitarian organisations as CARE, Oxfam, Save the Children and the International Committee of the Red Cross (Singer, 2006). Formal government agreements enhance legitimacy, but they are not the only source of legitimacy (Fukuyama, 2006: 155–178). Non-state actors can act in ways that build trust and legitimacy based on pragmatic understandings and long-term public approval of their actions. Globalisation's impact on sovereignty and the growth in legitimate governance activities outside the domain of states have consequences for how we think about all the instruments of power, including public diplomacy.

Implications for scholars and practitioners

Much of the analytical work on public diplomacy has been done by think tanks, advisory panels and retired practitioners. Their reports focus attention and many offer good advice, but most of their recommendations look broadly at desired goals rather than at the means and political will needed to achieve them. Many emphasise past accomplishments enabling advocates to justify priorities and budgets advantageous to the tribal cultures in which they are comfortable. Largely missing in this literature, is scholarship that bears directly on public diplomacy (Lord, 2005). The work of two European scholars and two Americans suggests academics have much to contribute to a more comprehensive understanding of public diplomacy.

Jurgen Habermas

Habermas' thinking about the public sphere as space between the state and private institutions and his theories of language, networks and communicative action inform elements of public diplomacy that emphasise engagement and discourse (Habermas, 1991, 2006). Cultural diplomacy, people-to-people exchanges and even advocacy activities to the extent they entail shared knowledge and common ground, benefit from a reading of Habermas (and the American philosopher John Dewey). Cultural diplomats value his concepts of listening, dialogue, reasoned argument, openness to the opinions of others, learning through questions, not talking at cross purposes and working out common meanings.

Scholars such as Michael Walzer (2004: 90–109) appreciate Habermas' discourse logic and contributions to deliberative democracy. Walzer contends, however, that politics has other important values that are both non-deliberative and necessary to strategy formulation and decision-making. These include political education, organisation, mobilisation, bargaining and management of conflict. Simone Chambers asserts that society's need to reach closure on issues and make decisions with some degree of efficiency also places constraints on discourse (1995: 255). She finds value in deliberative communication for the purposes of will formation and rationalisation of public opinion. 'Discourse', however, 'is essentially open ended. Decision-making is essentially closed ended.' The closer participants come to closure, she argues, 'the more participants will be motivated to act strategically rather than discursively'. Dialogue leading to mutual understanding is a fundamental part of politics and public diplomacy, but both have non-discourse requirements as well. Scholarly critiques of the Habermasian project are relevant to thinking about discourse as a necessary, but not sufficient, element in public diplomacy.

Manuel Castells

In Castells' (1998: 350) path-breaking account of the information technology revolution and its consequences, all societies are 'penetrated, with different intensity, by the pervasive logic of the network society, whose dynamic expansion gradually absorbs and subdues pre-existing social forms'. Flexibility (meaning constant change, organisational fluidity and reversible processes) is a distinct feature of his information technology paradigm. Networks are more flexible than hierarchies and better able to adapt to interactive complexity in human relationships. For Castells (1996b: 60–65), networks can be liberating or repressive: value judgments are contingent on empirical circumstances, not on technology. Both Doctors Without Borders and Al Qaeda (Kepel, 2004: 70–77, 93–100; Devji, 2005: 84–111; Weimann, 2006) are emblematic of networks capable of adapting to complexity and using information technologies to their advantage.

Diplomacy is no exception to the 'logic of the network society'. Castells' project has influenced public diplomacy as seen in the writings of John Arquilla (1999), David Ronfeldt (2000), Brian Hocking (2002b, 2005) and others. Hocking's concept of 'diplomats as boundary spanners' is leading practitioners to think about diplomats less as gatekeepers between governments, and more as mediators between state and non-state actors on multiple issues with changing patterns of interaction. Diplomacy becomes more about interdependence between state and non-state actors, about questioning the logic of boundary control and hierarchical models and about the increased importance of networks and bureaucratic bargaining.

Walter Lippmann

Public diplomacy owes a debt to Walter Lippmann's (1997) early thinking on public opinion and subsequent scholarship in the social sciences on propaganda, media and communications theory. One reason for this debt is his argument that individuals make sense of a complex external world through stereotypes and mental filters – the 'pictures in our heads' that collectively form public opinion. For Lippmann, informed élites are best equipped to provide meaning and context that help make sense of the external world. Political actors should seek to influence opinions advantageously through communication strategies that enlist the interest of publics; find common ground; establish credible symbols and authority; and create consent. Lippmann's instrumental rationality is goal-oriented and driven by interest-based preferences.

From the opinion-shaping strategies of presidents to the public opinion research of their advisors, Lippmann's thinking continues to inform. John Dewey famously contested the implications of Lippmann's psychological model, and it remains under siege from discourse theorists and civil society activists. For Lippmann's critics, governance is best served through 'bottom up' processes that privilege dialogue and the media. Political legitimacy and fairness in the distribution of public goods are best achieved through open debate. Language that seeks mutual understanding and rational consensus is distinguished from language used instrumentally (and for Habermas, more problematically) to advance interest-based calculations. Lippmann and his successors contribute to an understanding of public diplomacy's 'influence' component, while their critics contribute to an understanding of 'engagement'.

Joseph S. Nye, Jr.

Known for his writings on 'soft power' – the term he invented to describe the ability to shape the preferences of others through attraction rather than the use of 'hard power' carrots and sticks – Nye's thinking (2002, 2004b) has influenced analysis of public diplomacy both in the narrow sense in which governments wield soft power, and in the broader sense in which soft power is gained and lost by societies through their culture, values and practices. His views on power, globalisation and the information revolution are laced with implications for state and non-state public diplomacy actors. Two examples illustrate.

First, what Nye calls the 'paradox of plenty' has changed the relationship between information and attention. In the twentieth century, information was less plentiful; public diplomats (with credible messages and moral authority) found it relatively easy to gain attention. In the twenty-first century, Nye argues, 'a plenitude of information creates a poverty of attention'. Public diplomacy in the highly competitive world of abundant 'free information' is more difficult, because attention is the scarce resource. Power flows to those who 'can distinguish valuable signals from white noise'. Reputations become more important sources of power, and 'political struggles occur over the creation and destruction of credibility' (Nye, 2002: 67).

Second, hard power and soft power relate directly and inversely. They relate directly when hard power acts as a 'multiplier' for political actors seeking to persuade or when soft power reinforces the political will of one's allies or dilutes the political will of one's adversaries. Hard and soft power relate inversely when more soft power means there is less need to invest in the costly instruments of hard power. Because information technologies are changing 'the very nature of states, sovereignty and control', Nye contends, fewer issues can be solved through military power. 'Policy-makers will have to pay more attention to the politics of credibility and the importance of soft power. And they will have to share a stage crowded with newly empowered non-governmental actors and individuals' (Nye, 2002: 76).

Habermas, Castells, Lippmann and Nye illuminate how scholars contribute to understanding concepts of public diplomacy and governance. Insights can be gained also from constructivist theory, media framing studies, social psychology, anthropology, language study, hermaneutics, communications research and other disciplines – especially if scholars put public diplomacy into an analytical focus, and if practitioners pay attention. There is a solid basis for developing academic programs devoted to research and structured sequences of courses on public diplomacy, governance and related subjects. There are also possibilities for collaborative inquiry by scholars and practitioners.

Suggestions for collaborative inquiry

Connecting hierarchies and networks

Reorganisation and process solutions in public diplomacy have a bad name because too often they are default choices of parliaments, officials and practitioners in the business of maintaining the appearance of productivity. Lasting impact on thinking and habits is rare. Because networks are dominant structures in information societies, change is necessary and will be inevitable in the stovepiped systems and dysfunctional practices of governments. While eliminating hierarchies in government is neither desirable nor possible, they can be altered so that they adopt network characteristics and connect more easily with networks.

In public diplomacy, this means greater attention to the practical work of knowledge sharing and building flexible and adaptable hybrid institutions. Knowledge sharing has been central to public diplomacy for decades through government support for academic exchanges, democratisation and civil society initiatives. These activities have advanced state interests and the governance interests of non-state actors. But knowledge sharing also means high level comprehension of the cultures, practices and values of others as a precondition to effective public diplomacy. It means not only thinking about diplomats as 'boundary spanners', but also thinking imaginatively about formidable challenges created by those responsible for 'boundary maintenance', the forces that work to preserve separate identities and barriers between insiders and outsiders both within and between political entities and societies (Fulton, 2007).

Knowledge sharing in this sense means investing more public diplomacy resources in penetrating cultural analysis, foreign language study (especially in Arabic, Mandarin, Farsi, Urdu etc.), social network analysis software, polling and media analysis, and other interpretive tools. Political leaders and public diplomacy professionals too often minimise the difficulty and desirability of such 'listening'. Diplomats tend to think they understand indigenous cultures sufficiently through their own perceptions. Campaigning politicians spend large sums on research to understand voter preferences; then, when in office, they routinely ignore opinion and social network research in their public diplomacy efforts.

Non-state actors share with state actors engaged in public diplomacy a need to understand cultures, languages and social networks, and to appreciate the usefulness of interpretive tools such as media frame analysis and social network software. Non-state actors also need to improve knowledge sharing with each other. Gaps exist between knowledge and practice, and between what is easy compared with what is meaningful. NGOs can act in response to funding and project 'booms' with insufficient empirical research and accumulated knowledge, although analytical literature on state building and civil society assistance is growing (Carothers, 2006: xiii–xiv, 327–337). Humanitarian NGOs do not systematically share information on dealing with private security organisations (Singer, 2006: 109–110). Decisions by NGOs to support local movements typically are based on factors that reflect the NGO's cultural and organisational features, factors which often 'remain unwritten and informal, known by key staff members and enforced by NGO managers' (Bob, 2005: 197).

Improving knowledge sharing among actors in governance is a challenge both for NGOs and states. NGOs are advantaged in doing so by their flexibility and networking skills, and disadvantaged by weak authority structures in a highly competitive global civil society, 'in which hard-nosed calculation of costs and benefits constantly competes with sympathy and emotion' (Bob, 2005: 194–196). States are advantaged by authority structures within and between states, which have the potential to require knowledge sharing, and disadvantaged by inflexible hierarchies traditionally resistant to collaborative approaches to global issues.

Universities, research organisations and NGOs offer untapped resources in knowledge domains, area and language expertise, planning and consultative services, opinion and media analysis as well as evaluation methods. Much can be accomplished in public diplomacy through collaboration with civil society organisations – and through relationships between public diplomacy professionals within and between government departments and embassies. Such collaboration can do more than leverage knowledge and expertise. As intelligence analysts are discovering, it can reduce information costs, foster communities of interest, generate better understanding of what works and create appetites for more collaboration (Cooper, 2005: 54–57).

Imaginative process solutions are needed in building flexible networks and hybrid institutions. Because more of what ambassadors and political officers do involves outreach beyond embassies and government ministries, Canada's diplomats are merging political and public diplomacy career paths. US diplomats could learn from their example. Incentives and penalties in career systems are critical to transforming organisational cultures. If promotions to senior diplomatic ranks are contingent on public diplomacy skills and accomplishments, traditional foreign ministry cultures will change. Public diplomacy training, inter-agency assignments, private sector details and knowledge sharing skills must be seen as career enhancing. Improved software and technology infrastructures will foster network environments. Foreign ministries and public diplomacy institutions need flexible people, continuously adaptable structures and the capacity to connect people and their expertise.

Leveraging technologies and trust

Diplomats can learn a great deal from non-state actors in creative uses of the Internet and other technologies. At one level, this simply means more effective use of interactive tools – podcasts, blogs, text messaging, web chats, DVDs, tailored websites and automated sentiment and social network analysis – for listening, communication and evaluation. Promising academic work is being done, for example, on development and use of multiplayer online games as venues for cultural dialogue. Can shared experiences in virtual games build relationships that facilitate cultural understanding and cooperative values (Fouts, 2005)? Case studies in which activist NGOs have used the Internet to their advantage are numerous and compelling (Barber, 2000; Florini, 2000). Cases in which governments have done the same are hard to find.

Scholars and practitioners also can enhance understanding of the strengths and limitations of technologies for public diplomacy. The Internet hosts countless forums in which people argue, agree, share and talk past each other. Enthusiasts celebrate the deliberative advantages of free public spheres and the influence of citizen groups empowered by web-based technologies (Jenkins and Thorburn, 2003: 1–17). Analysts are exploring the benefits of reputations built through cheap, multiple and redundant information channels and the use of network 'trust technologies'. In blogospheres where millions 'vote' with hyperlink clicks, top bloggers gain 'authority' in their content domains through navigation services that analyse citations and traffic patterns (Evans, 2006).

Sceptics, however, contend that online forums can become 'echo chambers' where people sort themselves into likeminded groups in which conversation 'is specifically tailored to their own interests and prejudices' (Sunstein, 2001: 2). Others point out that the Internet, more than earlier media, 'decontextualizes information from the social frames that give it meaning' (Bollier, 2003: 29). Social context and sender identity on the Internet are not necessarily self-evident – a characteristic used by Al Qaeda and others to advantage. Technologies change not just how we communicate, they change the way we construct personal identities and culture. The Internet is a forum not only for discourse about content, but a place where memories, stories and narratives resonate emotionally: it is a virtual public sphere in which 'boundary spanners' and 'boundary maintainers' contest ideas and use stories to connect with the past and shape the future. Scholars, NGOs and practitioners have ample opportunity for mutually advantageous inquiry into the meaning of Internet technologies for public diplomacy.

Public diplomacy and governance

A third area for collaborative inquiry builds on assumptions about power, strategy and the instrumental role of public diplomacy in governance. These assumptions include: (1) Public diplomacy can advance both hard and soft power strategies; (2) Public diplomacy is one of many persuasive and coercive instruments from which state and non-state actors make choices in formulating strategies to achieve governance goals; (3) Public diplomacy has costs, limitations and strengths, which political actors often fail to appreciate; (4) Effective public diplomacy is contingent on situational contexts and vicissitudes of attraction and repulsion; (5) Public diplomacy involves open communication – it should be credible and persuasive, not deceptive or manipulative. Scholars and practitioners can build on these assumptions in a variety of ways.

First, research is needed on public diplomacy's strategic value and importance to the successful use of other instruments of power. Emphasis on public diplomacy as a soft power instrument neglects its relevance to hard power and to the interplay between the two forms of power. Further, public diplomacy is instrumental in war and peace as well as a range of conflict/cooperation possibilities in between. It can be a means of achieving security as a public good. It can also be a means of achieving health care, economic well-being, tolerant civil societies and many other public goods on which security depends. Analysts should focus not only on public diplomacy *per se*, but also on how it fits in strategic calculations about policy priorities; diverse geographic and social contexts; choices among persuasive and cooperative instruments; and trade offs between short-term and long-term objectives.

Second, empirical research at the interface between diplomacy and governance would increase understanding of public diplomacy by non-state actors and the extent to which their activities fit easily with the core components and time dimensions of public diplomacy as practiced by states. For example, Doctors Without Borders seeks to understand, engage and influence global publics to further a governance goal – health care. Directors of Doctors Without Borders frame perceptions within news cycles through speeches and press conferences. The organisation's *Campaign for Access to Essential Medicines* is a multi-year advocacy effort to lower drug prices and reduce trade barriers to medical treatments. And after decades of international networking, engagement and long-term dialogue are now organisational priorities. Research on these and similar activities by other NGOs would help to establish whether public diplomacy can be understood to include governance activities of non-state actors acting independently of governments.

Finally, scholars and practitioners should take care to separate analytical judgments about political actors and public diplomacy from political and moral judgments about policies and strategies. Both judgments matter, but conflating them is a path to confusion. Non-state actors often challenge the legitimacy of state (and corporate) power, but they do not enjoy political and moral superiority simply because they are non-state actors. Nor do state actors have political and moral legitimacy simply because they are representatives of sovereign states. Political and moral judgments about the actions of both state and non-state actors turn on assessments of the means and ends they employ, not on the perceived taint based on their institutional status in governance.

15
Stretching the Model of 'Coalitions of the Willing'

Andrew F. Cooper

> Wars are best fought by coalitions of the willing... The mission must determine the coalition.
>
> (Rumsfeld, 2002)
>
> To have real impact... means using new methods... to co-opt, not coerce; the power that comes when 'coalitions of the willing' form around shared goals and mobilize support across the international community.
>
> (Axworthy, 1998)

Coalitions of the willing have become commonly linked with the war against Saddam Hussein's Iraq in 2003. Indeed a good deal of the invasion led by the United States was constructed and justified through the use of this mechanism. As evoked by President George W. Bush, when he spoke at a news conference just prior to the November 2002 North Atlantic Treaty Organization (NATO) summit in Prague, a marker was set between those ready to join in this campaign and those unwilling to do so. Choices had to be made by all nations as to 'whether or not they want to participate' (CNN, 2002; Donovan, 2002).

What appears to be a new and exceptional mode of activity can be found, however, to have a far more complex trajectory. The move to locate coalitions of the willing at the core of US strategic doctrine, far from being a sudden and novel response to the exigencies of the moment, may be viewed as an outgrowth of the earlier crises in the Persian Gulf and Kosovo. Even more dramatically, the sense of exclusivity in terms of ownership for this model can be contested. At odds with the familiarity of its tight association with the foreign policy of the dominant global power, coalitions of the willing have an expanded identification as well with an alternative set of projects, ones based on extending a rules-based regulatory system via the introduction of innovative governance practices. Through this alternative format the model of coalitions of the willing is stretched beyond the Iraq invasion to those generated on a diffuse set of issues, most notably in connection with the campaign to prohibit anti-personnel landmines (through the so-called Ottawa Treaty of 1997) and the establishment of the International Criminal Court or ICC (via the Rome Statute of 1998).

At one level, the purpose of this chapter is to simply trace the different models and meanings of coalitions of the willing. Although utilising the same phrase or expression, the dynamics intrinsic to these models are exhibited in highly variant ways and offer divergent insights about how core elements of world politics interact. At another level, the argument is made that notwithstanding the distinctions between the two basic models of coalitions of the willing, they do not exist in solitude from one another. On the contrary, there is a good deal of interaction and blurring with respect to timing, styling and even some elements of substance. Finally, there is some examination of the presence of internal distinctions within the two types of coalitions of the willing. Instead of being cast in a rigid, one-size fits all fashion, both of the models allow for considerable variation in terms of their inner workings as well as external expression.

Towards a typology of coalitions of the willing

The fundamental question posed concerning both models of coalitions of the willing (for the sake of convenience simply termed model one and model two) relates to how, why, with whom and under what conditions they have performed in practice. This exploration allows for a series of snapshots about the nature and extent of the distinctions between the two models.

The first and perhaps the most manifest difference between the two renditions of the coalitions of the willing relates to the contrasting means of organisation. Consistent with a longer pattern of mobilisation the overarching feature of the model one type of coalition is its top-down, hierarchical and asymmetrical framework. The emphasis is tilted strongly – to use the phrase effectively promoted by Richard Haass – toward the sheriff not the posse (Haass, 1997). The primacy of the United States is privileged to the extent that the paramount trait of the coalition is taken to be not the coalitional aspect *per se*, but rather that of US leadership.

Situated in this version of a hub and spoke matrix, the United States as the central pivot is accorded full power of agency with an enormous amount of autonomy provided for its commitments and capabilities. One fundamental issue that can be connected to this theme (although its detailed exploration lies beyond the scope of this work) relates to the way this approach differs from and/or complements US unilateralism. Does a move towards a top-down coalition of the willing indicate a move from alliance leader (with a need for some sensibility to genuine if asymmetric partners) to an imperial project (with subalterns)? (Ikenberry, 2002: 44–60; Michael Ignatieff, 'The American Empire: The Burden', *New York Times*, 5 January 2003, 53–54; Ferguson, 2004). Or alternatively does this shift reflect an anxiety on the part of the United States with over-stretch that has translated into a move towards shifting some of the burdens to others? (Johnson, 2002; Mallaby, 2002: 2–7; S. Hoffmann, 2003) From another angle, does this approach reflect a concern with instrumental delivery or with symbolic legitimacy? Is the emphasis on burden-sharing or on deflecting criticism concerning from widespread perception throughout the international community of the Iraq war as an illegal action? (G. Dinmore, 'Ideologues Reshape World over Breakfast', *Financial Times*, 22 March 2003; J. O'Sullivan 'The End of Unilateralism', *National Review*, 22 March 2004).

Regarded as spokes, the coalition members for the most part have been relegated to background structure in a community of unequals. The United Kingdom, through the robust efforts of Prime Minister Tony Blair in championing the model one type, strove for a higher status as the United States' first follower (International Centre for Security Analysis, 1999). So did Australia on a regional basis. Yet there were risks as well as advantages to buying into this coalitional model. The image of an 'Anglo-sphere' was hardly attractive to those with memories of colonial domination. Prime Minister Howard constantly had to fend off charges by some Southeast Asian states – above all by Indonesia – that Australia was acting as the United States' deputy sheriff within the Asia-Pacific region (Australian Broadcasting Corporation (ABC), 2003).

Consistent with the US-led tenor of this model, the main work of rounding up the coalition of the willing was restricted to Americans, above all then Secretary of Defense, Donald Rumsfeld and Richard Perle, the Chair of the Defense Policy Board. The vocabulary used in this mobilisation effort was culturally rooted within a highly US-centric linguistic tradition, as exemplified by the reliance on such concepts as sheriff and posse.[1] When a large group of British Labour MPs rebelled against their own government's decision to go to war in March 2003 Rumsfeld did not send a signal of support to the government of its key ally, but rather the message that the United States was prepared to fight without the United Kingdom. The fixed image of this model one format of coalitions of the willing was one in which the membership was an extension of the United States with little consideration of any political or cultural attributes that might promote contrasts as opposed to compatibility in outlook and expectations.

The stark distinction in the extent in the type of self-reference and public commentary deemed appropriate for the leader as opposed to the larger membership in the coalition of the willing accents the top-down nature of model one. Every detail of US thinking and operational activity received close scrutiny. By way of contrast the wider array of followers (or posse members) was systematically relegated to being names and numbers on various lists compiled about who belonged to the coalition, such as the Vilnius Eight or the Letter of Ten of Central/Eastern European countries waiting in line to join the Western Alliance. Cases in which countries escaped this group categorisation were rare, the most obvious illustration being the special role accorded to Turkey. Though even in this latter case, the country was eventually treated with less sensitivity than might have been expected, had it been authentically deemed to be a core ally (Wolfowitz, 2003).

Model two, or the alternative formulation for building coalitions of the willing, has a markedly different orientation. In contrast to the tight hierarchical contours of the model one version, the mobilisation of initiatives such as the landmines campaign and the establishment of the ICC, as well as the campaign against the use of child soldiers and small arms and the formation of the Kimberley process on blood/conflict diamonds all operated as fluid networks with a bottom-up impetus in the international system. Although participation took place on a self-selective basis, the focus in this second model has tended to shift towards the collective and not to the individual members. More specifically, this coalitional model was viewed as a variant of a new form of complex and catalytic multilateralism (Cox, 1997: 103–116; Cameron, 1998: 147–165; Schechter, 1998; Benedetti and Washburn, 1999: 1–38; O'Brien et al., 2000). While the diplomatic efforts of individual actors (whether through the high-profile agency of middle powers or individual diplomatic personnel through the use of expertise and reputation) was not overlooked, the main thrust of attention remained on the process of group interaction. As opposed to the command and control structure featured in model one, scrutiny of model two honed in on questions pertaining to issue-specific leadership, task distribution, the ability (or inability) to rotate functional responsibility and the degree to which institutionalisation (most notably, through the establishment in 1999 of the so-called Lysøen Group composed of eleven states and nine non-governmental organisations or NGOs) took place.

Highlighting the networking component of this second type of coalition does not automatically lead to suggestions of a flat structure. In each of the major case studies, whether it is the campaigns on landmines, the ICC or any of the other illustrations mentioned above, a jockeying for stratified positions took place amongst the participants. If it made little difference to the overall campaign whether the location of a meeting or the signing of an agreement/convention was Oslo/Lysøen, Ottawa, Canberra, Vienna, Stockholm or other sites in a wide number of secondary states, it mattered a great deal to the individual actors involved. Nor was the tendency simply to list membership (whatever the degree of commitment) avoided. To give one demonstration, the War Child Landmine Project drew up a list of 'Good Nations', who supported the call for a comprehensive ban on anti-personnel landmines. Paralleling the US-led initiative such dichotomising introduced a measure of 'with us or against us' to the campaign. Kudos for those on side with the campaigns was accompanied by 'naming and shaming' those off side, as exemplified by the appearance of a corresponding 'Bad List' on land mines, a 'Watch List' on children in armed conflict, and the so-called 'Foul Report' on conflict diamonds (a play on the name of the main author of the report, Robert Fowler, Canada's then Permanent Ambassador to the United Nations or UN).

A second major axis of difference extends across the motivations for coalition membership. Power stood at the core of the motivations for the joiners of model one coalitions. The main question was what sort of power? To many of its keenest advocates, the joiners bought into the concept of coalitions of the willing because of the attractions of soft power associated with the United States and the Western Alliance and connected with the power of ideas and the pattern of socialisation (Haass, 2003). The willingness of the Central/Eastern European countries to jump on board, even when they had to openly disagree with France and Germany in doing so, especially stoked this argument. To its detractors, this argument smacked of either hypocrisy or delusion. Playing up the benefits of regime-change in terms of values, whether through the limitations placed on the role of authoritarian states, or respect for individual and collective rights, merely disguised the role of structural determinants related to economic and military power. States joined in not as part of a genuine search for a new just order, but because of the fear of disciplinary pressure and/or the pull of tangible benefits. Through one lens, coalitions of the willing then become transformed into coalitions of the coerced. Through another lens, they become coalitions of the bribed. In either case, the image was one of opportunism in which follower-ship became linked not only to moral commitment or participation in a collective identity, but to a clear set of interest-based quid quo pros whether by omission (avoiding punishment through retaliatory action) or commission (gaining some material advantage through side-payments) (Jim Krane 'Coalition Partners Seek Payback for their Support', *Associated Press*, 27 September 2003; William D. Hartung and Michelle Ciarrocca, 'Buying a Coalition', *The Nation*, 17 March 2003; Phyllis Bennis et al., 2003).

Model two shifts the bias away from structural or situational imperatives to the non-material incentives for voluntarism. Rather than constraints, the lure and expectation that the membership of this type of coalition could make a difference in terms of normative and institutional development (at least on a single issue) served as the trigger for activity. The landmines campaign and the other initiatives were all attractively wrapped in a cloak of good international citizenship, with a focus on the creation of transnational regimes to regulate or judicialise activity. While such claims allowed these alternative coalitions of the willing to both get off the ground and build support from a wide range of participants, it must be cautioned that these benefits did not free this alternative model from some additional problematic baggage. With the promotion of norms came status seeking, as supposedly like-minded states vied with others to show off their credentials within the international system. Whatever the attraction of this appeal on the basis of good international citizenship, moreover, the membership of this variant of coalitions of the willing lacked the clout to alter the preference of the larger actors in the international system. In none of the key case studies of bottom-up multilateralism was the coalition able to change the official mindset of the United States. What is more, the United States was joined by other major players in the adoption of a resistant stance in each of these cases. India, China and Russia opposed the landmines treaty. China and Israel refused to accept the Rome Statute on the ICC.

The third axis along which the two types of coalitions of the willing split relates to the question of actorness. Model one remains resolutely state centric. The approach continues to privilege a framework of unitary states operating on the basis of their perceived interests with little need or appreciation of non-state actors. The pivotal points of decision-making revolve around a small cluster of political leaders namely President George W. Bush, Prime Ministers Tony Blair, John Howard or Silvio Berlusconi. The only exception in the case of the first model, arguably, is in regard to the intrusion of Halliburton (one of the world's largest management and service providers to the oil and gas industries), Bechtel Corporation (a leading multinational corporation in engineering, construction and project management) and other major American companies into the mix of the machinery of government. And even this military/industrial nexus showcases the inter-connection between the US political and economic elites, not the autonomous space carved out by firms themselves.

The actorness on display in the coalitional model two stretches these boundaries beyond recognition. At the state level, two features standout. One is the name recognition established by a number of state officials: most notably through the landmines initiative, ranging from Lloyd Axworthy, then foreign minister of Canada to Ambassador Jacob Selebi, the head of the South African delegation who chaired the conclusive 1996 Oslo conference which produced the landmines draft treaty. The other is the sheer scope of participation. In addition to the amplified role of many established middle powers, including the Nordics, Canada, Australia and New Zealand, an extended group of activist states became involved. Of these countries the 'new' South Africa stands out. Taking a cue from the classic middle power playbook, it played a huge role both on the landmines campaign and within the 'Lifeline Nations', a group of states advocating an independent court and independent prosecutor as opposed to an ICC under the control of the Security Council.

What provided the coalitional model two with its most distinctive brand, however, was not its extended associational pattern at the state level, but its innovative element of partnership between state and non-state actors. The networking style concomitant to the alternative model of coalitions was quite distinct in its horizontal nature and open-endedness. The NGOs engaged with the campaigns on landmines and the ICC shared a coincidence of outlook with the middle powers at the head of these campaigns in terms of both means (a bias to moral arguments) and ends (an enhanced rules-based regulatory machinery). They could also blend their comparative advantages. Working with select 'like-minded' state partners allowed NGOs greater access to decision-making bodies. Harnessing themselves to the NGOs in turn provided these same states not only with some additional sources of expertise, but also with a greater ability to mobilise public opinion through a reframed type of discourse and publicity production.

It was this fundamental division about actorness that has done the most to stretch the models of coalitional activity apart from each other. The US-led model one staked its claim to legitimacy on the willingness of individual sovereign states to join the coalition. Consequently, in operational terms this type of coalition took shape not only via extensive interaction at the apex of power, but through a web of contacts through foreign/defence ministries. Leaders and ministers held joint press conferences and attended meetings to make significant decisions at various times on Iraq. These vertical networks remained not only closed to non-state participation, but to revised assessments concerning the sources of danger on a global scale. Terrorism continued to be treated in state-based terms, whether in response to the Taliban, Saddam's Iraq, or other so-called 'rogue' states.

Model two made a virtue of normative development in the promotion of global governance challenging some conditions of state sovereignty. Links between mixed state and non-state like-minded actors were honed and consolidated, whether through one central group (the International Campaign to Ban Landmines or ICBL) or multiple partners (diverse groups such as Amnesty International, Human Rights Watch, to the Lawyers Committee for Human Rights on the ICC). At the same time, deep inroads were also made into forging informal partnerships in some distinctive arenas of what can be termed the 'un-likeminded'. As a result of the well-known actions of Jody Williams, the Vietnam Veterans of America, and Senator Patrick Leahy, one of the most dramatic elements of the landmines campaign was its penetration into the US political fabric at least at the non-governmental and legislative level. A prominent group of retired US military officers was even persuaded to back this campaign, albeit not on normative grounds as a 'scourge against humanity', but on the basis that these weapons were not necessary in military terms. Notwithstanding, because so much of the alternative coalitions of the willing was directed at and opposed at the US state level, a counter-movement of opposition was easily generated at the non-state level. 'Poke in the eye' diplomacy directed at 'Washington, DC' was not a characteristic exhibited exclusively by middle powers, but also by many prominent American citizens.

The fourth axis of differentiation between the two models is concerned with the triggers for mobilisation. The coalitional model one was linked explicitly with the core priorities of the lead actor that pertained to its hard security agenda. They are driven by a conflation between national interest and a sense of crisis, extending from the attacks on 9/11, to the targeting of weapons of mass destruction and the build-up of 'Operation Iraqi Freedom.'

The mobilisation for the Iraq invasion put a heavy onus on a military doctrine of strategic flexibility and tactical manoeuvrability at the expense of overwhelming force (at least in terms of ground troops), long-term reconstruction planning and an exit strategy. The alternative bottom-up coalitions were an outgrowth of both the relaxation of parameters of activity at the end of the Cold War and the concomitant ascendancy with respect to an extended security agenda. Built into cases such as the campaign to ban landmines and the promotion of the ICC was a strong sense of voluntarism or niche-selection. The activist states, or for that matter the NGOs, taking the lead positions on these campaigns signified a considerable range of choice about the focus of their activity. They also had a longer trajectory to build support for their initiatives.[2] The ICBL initiated its campaign in 1992 and drew inspiration from both visionary principles (the extension of humanitarian law) and practical purposes (the protection of development workers on the front lines of conflict zones). The initiative on the ICC came as a reaction to the deep flaws in the international system as exposed by the crimes and traumas associated with the former Yugoslavia and Rwanda. The campaign pushed for an expansion of international norms to allow for a collective duty to prosecute in cases where individual states hid behind their sovereign rights.

Some blurring of the models

Identifying how the model of coalitions of the willing can be stretched according to this set of criteria is a valuable, but incomplete exercise. As will be discussed below, it neglects the nuances of internal differentiation within as well as between the two models. With reference to their external projection, this depiction overlooks the salience of the temporal condition. The impression that the dominant expression of coalitions of the willing originates exclusively from the 2003 Iraq war has to be reconsidered. A more accurate appraisal is that this model owes its creation to the reactions vis-à-vis two earlier crises. The first of these arises out of the 1991 Persian Gulf War in which the administration of President George H.W. Bush put together a broadly based coalition (variously calculated to be between 28 to 36 states) to engage Iraq after its invasion of Kuwait. In conformity with the coalitional model one, this earlier mobilisation constituted a form of ad hoc coalition building led by the United States. It also featured a blend of material inducements and threats of diplomatic/economic retaliation.

The obvious differences between the two cases, however, dim this sense of lineage. Unlike the 2003 Iraq coalition, the 1991 Persian Gulf coalition received support from the UN Security Council through a number of mechanisms, most decisively by Resolution 678 authorising members to use 'all necessary means' to remove Saddam's forces from the territory of Kuwait. Through the declaratory image of the 'New World Order', Bush Senior provided some positive vision by which the Gulf War coalition could coalesce. Abundant support, including some forms of participation at least by the mainstays of the 2003 'coalition of the unwilling' (Germany, France, Soviet Union/Russia), was thus obtained relatively easily.

The comprehensive prototype for the 2003 Iraq coalition of the willing was established through the US-led coalition's response to the 1999 Kosovo crisis. In the same manner as Iraq, Kosovo blurred the picture between what could be deemed necessary from a humanitarian perspective and what was considered to be correct from the perspective of international law (as reflected in the Kosovo Commission's distinction between illegal and legitimate actions). Consistent with the coalitional model as it was operationalised in 2003 (and unlike the 1991 Gulf war case) the Kosovo campaign constituted an end-run around the UN system, in that the NATO action ('Operation Allied Force') received only retrospective endorsement from the Security Council. Kosovo just as crucially pointed to what should be avoided if this model of coalitions of the willing was to work again in the future. The frustrations generated by the NATO mode of operation in Kosovo, fighting 'by committee', fed into a push for a refinement of the coalition of the willing framework by the time of the 2003 Iraq invasion. That is to say, the constraints imposed by the need for consensus during Kosovo reinforced the perception of US strategic planners that the key to success in the future lay in their ability to free themselves from consultations, so they could concentrate on flexible and ad hoc mechanisms (Richard Norton-Talyor, 'A Lame Duck?', *The Guardian*, 22 May 2003).[3] The application of this lesson was voiced most forcefully in the statement by Donald Rumsfeld, the engineer if not the architect, of the US-led model one as it was stretched into shape through the rationale that the 'mission must determine the coalition' (Rumsfeld, 2002). Yet, the main thrust of this strategic transformation, the notion that the United States should avoid 'talking shop' at times of crisis, was an echo of what General Wesley Clark had laid out during the Kosovo crisis (Clark, 2001).

If the coalitional model one morphed out of the Kosovo intervention, the model two has had a far more diverse trajectory. The campaigns to ban child soldiers and the use of children in armed conflict, together with the initiative to implement a UN-sponsored regime for the certification and regulation of trade in rough diamonds, replicated many of the same compelling features associated with the land mines and ICC initiatives: a concerted push towards an extension of international humanitarian law, a mixed middle state and NGO coalition and a robust public campaign. Yet, as in the model one, it is the variations as much as the commonalities that stand out. On the small arms case the strength of the NGO coalition in favour of a new treaty instrument (encompassing disarmament and arms controls groups, development organisations, and humanitarian and human rights groups) has been countered by strong resistance from the very 'unlike' non-state actor: the US gun lobby, led by the National Rifle Association. The campaign against child soldiers has focused attention on not only the need for a new regulatory framework in zones of conflict, but on practices in the militaries of the developed world (the recruitment by the US military of volunteers under the age of 16 and the treatment of child combatants by coalition forces in Iraq and Afghanistan). The campaign against blood or conflict diamonds stretched the parameters of action in different directions.[4] Unlike the cases of landmines and the ICC in which the business community did not play a distinct role, the initiative on diamonds was constrained by the severe initial tensions between the NGO community (led by Global Witness) and De Beers, the dominant firm in the global diamond market prior to the establishment of the tripartite working group known as the Kimberley Process. Equally though by incorporating an explicit 'name and shame' approach, the campaign on diamonds demonstrated the tendency of middle powers to co-opt tactics developed by NGOs to build momentum on this type of initiative.

Stepping beyond the internal dynamics of the two models of coalitions of the willing, some cases can be located where features associated with the US-led model one and alternative model two commingle. A number of UN authorised operations highlight the emergence of a hybrid model in which elements of both models are filtered into the mix. One illustration of this blending is the format developed in the Italian-led coalition of the willing in Albania (Scognamiglio-Pasini, 2001: 26–27). The 1999 Australian mobilisation of the East Timor intervention also fits with this model (Annan, 2000). So, even more contentiously, does the connection between the US-led coalition of the willing and the UN-sanctioned International Security Assistance Force (ISAF) in Afghanistan with major contributions by countries such as Germany and Canada. In each of these cases, there a strong theme of normative and institutional development, as well as status seeking as featured in the coalitional model two. Yet, in common with the model one approach, each of these initiatives depended on US leadership, resources and co-ordination.

The most striking trait of commonality however, remains not in substance, but in the manner in which they built impetus for their activities. Both types of coalition owe a great deal of their existence and profile to a shared sense of impatience about how the international system works. From the perspective of the model one, US-led type of coalitions established institutions (even one as vital as NATO, never mind the United Nations) had to be circumvented. In the face of strenuous resistance, this effort did manage to mobilise the support of up to three-dozen states on Iraq (a force encompassing at the height of participation some 26,500 non-US troops). Sharing this 'can do' attitude, the model two coalitional type for its part made appeals directly to opinion leaders and the mass public avoiding the caution embedded in the more traditional diplomatic culture. If the time line for the mobilisation of the landmines and ICC initiatives was far more extended than found in their model one counterparts, the burst of intensity at the end of the negotiating process was similar.

These characteristics imparted both coalitional models with a determined style that continued to be a common hallmark feature of their activities. Still, as boundary spanners both variants remained constantly in flux. On top of these problems of encouraging entry to the coalitions, multiple dilemmas have come into play concerning exit options as the risks of participation became accentuated. This exit scenario has come to the fore in the Iraq case. Spain, with the victory of Jose Luis Zapatero's Socialist party, turned from being a steadfast deputy to the United States (with 1300 troops in Iraq) to a member of the coalition of the unwilling with close ties to France and Germany (John B. Roberts, 'Spain in Revolt', *Washington Times*, 18 March 2004). By the end of 2004, Poland opened the door to an exit strategy and became another addition to the ranks of this new 'coalition of the leaving' in terms of its 2,500 personnel. Leszek Miller, the then Polish Prime Minister, stated: 'When people see dramatic scenes in which soldiers are killed, there will be more pressure for a pullout' (David Usborne, 'Iraq in Chaos: Is "Coalition" Unravelling as Rampant Violence Daunts Allies?', *The Independent*, 10 April 2004; Judy Dempsey, 'Poland Unexpectedly Says Troops May Quit Iraq in 2005', *International Herald Tribune*, 5 October 2004). Prime Minister Berlusconi has come under mounting pressure to pull Italian troops (3000 personnel) from Iraq after a number of hostage-takings involving Italian nationals and the much-publicised killing of an Italian senior intelligence officer by US forces (John Hooper, Ewen MacAskill, and Richard Norton-Taylor, 'Berlusconi to Pull Troops from Iraq', *The Guardian*, 16 March 2005).

Nor, it must be added, is the coalitional model two immune from the internal problems related to keeping coalitions together. If there are positive forms of adaptation towards a more inclusive coalitional style unavailable to the US-led variant, rivalries and tensions did pose some difficulties for these initiatives. Competition for status continued at the state level. Moreover, suspicions remained on both sides of the state-societal continuum about whether governments were taking civil society 'hostage' or if states were co-opting NGOs (Cameron, 1998). And as the small arms case reveals splits could appear among non-state actors as well.

Future directions of coalitions of the willing

The attempt to stretch the lines of analysis concerning both models of coalitions of the willing gives rise to very different scenarios about their respective future trajectories. The strong inclination to juxtapose the two models along different and self-contained axes presents them as a micro-cosm of a fundamental chasm located in today's international system; a reflection of a split between those actors that favour a Hobbesian self-help mode of operation versus those that support the expansion of Kantian insti-tutionalism (or in its updated version modern versus post-modern or even a Mars versus Venus contrast) (Kagan, 2003). Reinforcing this notion of polar-isation is the dichotomous language used to describe these coalitions. The UK left-wing weekly *New Statesman* advocates the need for 'new' coalitions of the willing to deal with non-traditional threats dealing with the environ-ment and health issues ('We need a New Coalition of the Willing', *New Statesman*, Vol. 132, 14 July 2003; Ramesh Thakur, 'Rectifying NGO Practice: New Coalitions of the Willing Seek Change', *Japan Times*, 21 March 2004). Elements of the US conservative media have called for narrower coalitions of the trusted for dealing with future crises such as Iraq (Zinsmeister, 2003). Stretching the parameters of analysis even further, some experts point to an extended spillover of this division from the security domain into other spheres of activity. Jagdish Bhagwati, for instance, has expressed apprehen-sion that the United States will tilt its focus away from institutionalised multilateralism towards 'trade coalitions of the willing' in the post-Cancún atmosphere with favouritism towards 'bilateral agreements with "will-do" nations' (Bhagwati, 2004: 52–63).

These dichotomous contours are reinforced by a divergent attitude towards the salience of diplomacy. In the US-led coalition on Iraq, diplomacy remained subordinated to military preparedness as epitomised by Rumsfeld's statement, 'I don't do diplomacy' (US Department of Defense, 2003). From an outward-looking perspective, this attitude mirrored the impatience of US strategic thinkers with institutional constraints. Rumsfeld concentrated his efforts on buttressing the position of the 'willing'(whether in his comments about the virtues of 'New' Europe or in his support for US/coalitional troops on the ground in Iraq) not on converting the 'unwilling'. From an inward perspective, the robust attitude adopted by the Pentagon could be contrasted against the formal 'by the book' approach favoured by the Department of State. Taking up this theme, Rumsfeld's intellectual supporters were quick to point out the ineffectiveness of then Secretary of State Colin Powell's diplo-matic activities. Max Boot pointed out for instance that Powell travelled less than any secretary of state in 30 years (and failed to get key actors such as Turkey on board through high-profile visits) (Max Boot, 'The Legacy of a Failed American Salesman', *Financial Times*, 18 November 2004).

What the top-down model one did not attempt to do was to encourage a wider campaign of public diplomacy on behalf of the coalition.[5] Support by key decision-makers outside of the United States was deemed to be enough. A closed and controlled atmosphere was maintained in terms of getting the message out. On the rare cases where the US Secretary of Defense was con-fronted by critical voices, he sounded confrontational not conciliatory.

In contradistinction, the alternative model two sought effectiveness and legitimacy through an extended form of diplomatic networking. It made appeals directly over the heads of all governments/negotiators through the use of the mass media, information technology and the mobilisation of key change-agents among individual celebrities (Princess Diana most notably on the landmines case) as well as state officials and NGOs. The bottom line throughout the campaign was to transform diplomacy from a narrow confined vehicle of statecraft to embracing a wider and diffuse dynamic.

As rehearsed throughout this chapter, establishing the two types of coalitions as polar opposites draws the dichotomous condition too sharply. Because of the evidence of some blurring of style and substance, the way lies open not to sharp divergence, but rather to modes of functional convergence. Given the philosophical and operational gap between them, accentuated by the changes in personnel within the second administration of President George W. Bush, it is likely though that this process of reconciliation will remain fuzzy, fragmentary and awkward. Yet given the compelling claims of so many non-traditional issue-areas such as disaster prevention and relief and pandemics, there could still be space for some movement towards hybrid styles of coalitions of the willing in a more selective and possibly low-key manner.

With all the repercussions from the Iraq invasion, and the results of the US presidential election, any blended improvisation and merger between the two models are bound to meet with conceptual suspicions, if not outright practical dismissal. The division between them may simply be too far apart to allow for hybridisation. Whatever the future contours of coalitions of the willing, however, it is clear that any variants of coalitions of the willing, or what has often been termed *à la carte* multilateralism, will not be composed or conducted according to one precise script. Nor, despite its high profile use in the Iraq invasion, should this mode of activity be recognised as the property of one owner, even such a dominant one as the United States. The model has been stretched across a far more diffuse normative and practical terrain and needs to be analysed in such contexts.

Notes

1. On the importance of the linguistic connection to diplomacy, see Iver B. Neumann (2003) 'Returning Practice to the Linguistic Turn: The Case of Diplomacy', *Millennium; Journal of International Studies* 31(3): 627–651.
2. On this process more generally, see Sanjeev Khagram et al., eds (2002) *Restructuring World Politics: Transnational Social Movements, Networks, and Norms*, Minneapolis: University of Minnesota Press.
3. For the frustrations of some other NATO members, most notably France on US leadership on Kosovo, see Mark R. Brawley and Pierre Martin (2001) *Alliance Politics, Kosovo, and NATO's War: Allied Force or Forced Allies*, New York: Palgrave.

4. On the role of mixed-actor coalitions in a wide range of emergent issues, see Böge et al. (2006).

5. On this criticism, see Suzanne Nossel (2004) 'Foreign Policy: How America Can Get its Groove Back' (with commentary from Mitchell Cohen, Stanley Hoffmann, and Anne-Marie Slaughter), *Dissent* (Fall): 31–43; See also Joseph S. Nye, Jr. (2002) *The Paradox of American Power: Why The World's Superpower Can't Go It Alone,* Oxford: Oxford University Press.

16
On the Manner of Practising the New Diplomacy

Jorge Heine

"Politics in an information age 'may ultimately be about whose
story wins'".

John Arquilla and David Ronfeldt[1]

Introduction

What do diplomats do in a rapidly changing global environment?

On 25 April 1994, I arrived in Johannesburg at what was then still known as
Jan Smuts International Airport, two days before the election of Nelson
Mandela as President of South Africa. On the previous day, a Sunday, a bomb
had exploded at the very same terminal I landed at, killing two people. I
told myself how lucky I was that the Malaysian Airlines flight from Buenos
Aires arrived on Mondays rather than on Sundays. Welcome to the new South
Africa, I said. Perhaps those who warned me it was a mistake to accept a post-
ing to an African country undergoing a violent transition, instead of a more
comfortable European destination, had been right after all. ('South Africa?
You are mad', a friend had told me. 'Why not Bosnia? You'd be safer there.')

A few months later, a Government of National Unity was fully in place,
Nelson Mandela was President, F.W. de Klerk Deputy President and
Mangosuthu Buthelezi Home Affairs Minister, and the country was on a
roll. Part of the South African transition, of course, had to do with 'transformation', meaning putting new staff – black African, Indian, Coloured – in
the ministries. The Ministry of Foreign Affairs (MFA) too was undergoing
some major changes. These changes affected all structures of the ministry,
but those divisions in charge of regions, like Latin America, of less than
central concern to South African foreign policy took a bit longer to be
restructured than others, and it was not always clear who was in charge of
what.[2]

Several colleagues of mine, very much in the traditional mould, who were
trained to define their function rather narrowly as the art of negotiating

271

agreements between sovereign states and who found that for months on end there was no one in charge of Latin America at the MFA, were rather bewildered and frustrated. Eventually, some of them, in despair, left of their own volition. On my part, my foremost concern was not to negotiate any kind of agreement or to find out who my exact interlocutor at the MFA would be, but to educate myself about and contribute in a modest way to one of the emblematic processes of democratic change in the nineties. I went on to spend an extraordinarily stimulating five years there during the presidency of Nelson Mandela, in a period described by one of my colleagues as 'the springtime of our lives', but also one in which much happened in the relationship between Chile and South Africa.[3]

This perhaps overlong personal vignette illustrates the perspective I bring to bear on the question of how diplomats deal with a quickly changing environment – one in which established procedures and norms do not always apply, domestic governmental structures are in flux, and the distinction between internal and foreign affairs is increasingly blurred.

This particular perspective is that of a professional political scientist from Latin America, who has had the opportunity to spend close to five years as ambassador in South Africa during its transition to democracy, and now two-and-a half years in India, at a time when that country's opening to the world – in the opinion of some, taking it by storm; in the expression of the local press, as part and parcel of 'the global Indian takeover'.[4] I would like to think my foreign relations experience of key countries in the global South that are undergoing what can only be described as cataclysmic changes, has given me a special window on the diplomatic practice of middle powers like Chile and how they can achieve their objectives in an increasingly competitive international system.[5] Drawing on this experience and perspective, this chapter advances some propositions as to how we can best further our understanding of the challenges faced today by diplomats in general, but especially by those from middle powers among the developing nations of the global South.[6]

From the 'club' to the 'network' model of diplomacy

'Globalisation' has become a bit of a buzzword. My own preference is instead to use 'globalism,' defined as 'a state of the world involving networks of interdependence at multicontinental distances'[7] (Keohane and Nye, 2000: 2). Globalisation then is the process by which globalism becomes increasingly 'thicker'. In some ways, globalisation itself is not particularly new. Most observers, however, would agree with the proposition that 'globalism' today is 'faster, cheaper and deeper' than before, and that there is a qualitative, not just quantitative, difference in the flows of goods, services, capital, images, data and general information that today crisscross the planet, as well as in the effects of these flows on international governance and on governments themselves.

What are the implications of globalism for diplomacy and diplomatic practice?

Globalism poses a severe challenge to the nation-state, most dramatically expressed in the financial crises that have bedevilled countries – such as Russia, Brazil, Thailand, and Indonesia – as 'hot money' suddenly flows out of (mostly) emerging markets, often as quickly as it has come, wreaking economic havoc and, in the process, affecting the stability of many other economies, including some far removed from the one originating the crisis.[8] The challenge, however, is not only economic. In the political sphere, globalisation, the increasing number of international interactions, and the rapidly diminishing cost of communications have led to a growing number of actors, both domestic and international – non-governmental organisations (NGOs), private companies, churches, business associations and the always critical 'foreign policy community' – which are making their presence felt and adding layers of complexity to government decision-making and legislation. In short, the model of an international system based purely on independent states has been replaced by one in which the nation-state is still a key component, but by no means the only one.

In the 'club model' of diplomacy, diplomats meet only with government officials, among themselves and with the occasional businessman or woman, and give an interview or speech here or there. By and large, however, they restrict themselves to fellow members of the club, with whom they also feel most comfortable, and focus their minds on 'negotiating agreements between sovereign states'.[9]

As can be seen in Table 16.1, in the world of the twenty-first century, the 'club model' of diplomacy has given way to a flatter, less hierarchical 'network model'[10], in which diplomats engage a vastly larger number of players in the host country – including many who would never have thought of – setting foot in the rarified atmosphere of the salons and private clubs the diplomats of yesteryear used to frequent. More and more, diplomacy is becoming 'complexity management', to a degree earlier master practitioners like Cardinal Richelieu would not have imagined. Yet, although the environment in which diplomacy is exercised has changed drastically, there is a considerable 'lag' between these changes and the adaptive behaviour of

Table 16.1 Club versus network diplomacy

	Number of players	Structure	Form	Transparency	Main purpose
Club diplomacy	Few	Hierarchical	Mostly Written	Low	Sign Agreements
Network diplomacy	Many	Flatter	Written and Oral	High	Increase Bilateral Flows

many diplomats, missions and foreign ministries, which is part of the problem they face.

The advent of the network model has to do not only with increased democratisation and the growing number of relevant actors for policy-making – all of whom must be 'kept in the loop' for 'things to happen' – but also with the increased interpenetration of different societies.[11] As significant a dimension of globalisation as the economic is the social and cultural one. With modern communications and travel, societies can easily take up experiences from other countries and apply them in their own. Ideas travel fast in today's globalised world, but they do not do so by themselves – they need to be shepherded and guided, especially so in the case of small and middle powers.

Diplomats, in their 'labour in exile', as Callières (1963: 65)[12] put it, are ideally placed to communicate to their host societies the ideas, values and significant social and cultural projects that are under way in their home countries. In so doing, they bridge the gap between them, which can often be quite wide, and thus lay the foundation for cooperation across a wide array of issues.

Commentators often consider this new environment in which diplomats operate in terms of 'add-ons' to the traditional diplomatic functions of the old 'club diplomacy'. Far from being mere 'add-ons' to the tried and true ways of practising the diplomatic craft, I argue that the changes brought about by globalism and the forces that are reshaping the international system require a radically new approach.

One would think that the increases in international trade and Foreign Direct Investment (FDI) flows, and the negotiation of many international treaties to facilitate these flows, would lead to a 'golden age of diplomacy' in which the roles of foreign ministries and diplomats would be recognised as vitally important, and translated into increased budgetary allocations and other, more symbolic expressions. That this has largely *not* occurred (in fact, the opposite may be true) leads me to argue that many of the difficulties diplomats and foreign ministries more generally face these days are due to a lack of understanding of these imperatives of change, as the world makes the transition to a much more dynamic and less hierarchical 'network diplomacy'. A traditional line of attack on the 'diplomatic establishment' – and the elaborate structure of resident missions, consulates, pomp, protocol and paraphernalia that goes with it – has been its supposed irrelevance in a world in which presidents and prime ministers meet at summits and instant communications are available.[13] What purpose is served, so the reasoning goes, by having diplomats stationed at great expense in distant lands, when deals and agreements could be struck over the phone or by teleconferencing and the text sent anywhere in the world in fractions of a second?[14]

A second source of vulnerability has been the world's growing democratisation and push for transparency. Whereas a few decades ago foreign policy and diplomacy were considered by many to be beyond the grasp of the mass public, this is no longer so. Television and 24-hour news channels have brought the world to one's living room, and citizens can see quite graphically the effects of their leaders' foreign policy decisions and how diplomats cope with them on the ground – even halfway across the world. That the electorate should therefore develop strong opinions on such matters is not surprising, and politicians must be ready to face the consequences. We are in a different world from the one in which the ordinary elector could be described as 'ignorant, lazy and forgetful regarding the international commitments for which he has assumed responsibility' (Nicolson, 1963: 48).

Transparency is also at play. The media and the public, quite legitimately, want to know what is happening 'behind Embassy windows', at least in terms of how (and if) their interests are being served and furthered, and the demand for diplomatic accountability, something which would have astounded Callières, is very much with us. This expresses itself especially in the many belt-tightening exercises to which foreign ministries and their missions abroad are subjected. Diplomats are thus no longer sheltered from the political give-and-take, at least not as much as they were in the past, and they must respond to these new demands.

And if these 'external' pressures often put foreign ministries and their missions abroad against the wall, much the same could be said about 'internal' ones, meaning developments inside government. The considerable increase in international flows of goods, services, capital, people, images and data across the world has meant that more and more ministries and government agencies are 'getting into the act' with their own 'Office of International Affairs', which conducts a parallel diplomacy of sorts. In some of the bigger countries, an Embassy might have more staff from other ministries than from the foreign ministry – staff over which the head of mission often has little effective control. Often, these other ministries have more resources than the foreign ministry, and many of the more specialised functions, such as trade negotiations, are handled by non-diplomatic experts.

All of this is leading to a progressive 'hollowing out' of traditional diplomatic duties, sometimes leaving the impression of diplomats as mere 'coordinators' of the substantive activities of other agencies – hardly an enviable position, but one that conforms to such cutting remarks as those of Peter Ustinov, some years ago, that 'a diplomat these days is nothing but a headwaiter who is allowed to sit down occasionally'.

Yet, these pressures must be put in perspective.

With some 216 member countries in FIFA (Fédération Internationale de Football Association) and 192 at the United Nations, nobody expects governments to have fully manned missions everywhere, and none does. Microstates, like some of the English-speaking Caribbean islands or those in the Pacific, have only a few missions, and in most countries the foreign ministry's budget is among the smallest of all ministries. In Chile, the hard-currency yearly budget is around US$140 million for some 70 embassies, which comes out at around US$2 million per embassy.[15] For a country that this year is projected to export US$55 billion and that has attracted on average some US$5–6 billion a year in FDI over the past 15 years, this would not seem to be an extravagant amount of money. It amounts to less than 0.7 per cent of the fiscal budget and 0.1 per cent of Gross Domestic Product (GDP).

For all the talk about the inordinate sums foreign ministries spend abroad, with ever-increasing flows of international trade and FDI – when any given successful FDI project a foreign mission generates can mean, at one go, an investment worth ten times the ministry's total yearly budget – the notion that cutting spending at the foreign ministry from 0.7 per cent to 0.65 per cent of the fiscal budget is a productive exercise is doubtful, to put it mildly.

One reason foreign ministry budgets are under seemingly permanent attack is that they have not developed their constituencies or adapted to the new age of 'network diplomacy'. Ministries with much larger budgets – agriculture, health, education – have no such problem, for obvious reasons. Yet, in a world in which more and more jobs depend on international trade and FDI, it should not be too difficult for top foreign ministry authorities, and diplomats themselves, to be a bit more proactive in making clear to the informed public that international markets do not operate on autopilot, that opening markets for one's country's products is not done by an invisible hand, and that it is a tough competition out there to attract multinational corporations and to sign trade and tax agreements.

One obvious route is to generate direct links between missions and their home state's own regions and localities.[16] This can show that diplomats on the ground actually help to generate jobs, something not always apparent to the average citizen. Headquarters will often not approve, as it will feel left 'out of the loop', but it would do well to consider such a strategy as part of its outreach activities. It is certainly needed to counter the strange (and in many ways perverse) foreign ministry cost-cutting syndrome. This is where the ministry with one of the smallest budgets – whose policies often get the best public opinion ratings and which plays a key role in opening export markets and attracting FDI – finds itself permanently operating on a shoestring, closing missions and cutting to the bone of its core activities.

In fact, in today's world, diplomacy, far from becoming redundant, is more important than ever, since there is so much more at stake in international engagement. And the diplomat, as an intermediary between his or her country and the host country – as a 'hinge' of sorts – is critically positioned to make the most of leveraging the opportunities that come his or her way or that are generated through his/her own wits. However, this demands a certain conception that is very different from the traditional view of diplomatic duties.

It requires understanding, above all, that it is no longer enough to count on the good will of the 'Prince', as ambassadors of yesterday were, to get things done and to keep your job. In today's world, to be effective, diplomats must practise 'network diplomacy'. In other words, they must *build up extensive networks at home and abroad* to 'deliver the goods.' Being on good terms with the head of state or government (whom many diplomats today hardly know anyway), the foreign minister or the ministry bureaucracy is no longer sufficient. Yet, as one who has been associated with and has taught at diplomatic academies – especially, but not only, in Latin America – for many years now, I know only too well that the skills required to build, to nurture and to reach out to those extensive networks are hardly among the priorities in curricula filled with courses on international law, protocol and similar subjects, which, however interesting in themselves, hardly speak to the main tasks at hand. Why?

The nature of the problem

The standard template of a diplomat provides the basis for what I have referred to as the 'club model' of diplomacy. There are, naturally, the prescribed rituals, from the elaborate presentation of credentials, through the courtesy calls on ministers and colleagues, all the way to the farewell dinners. But I am not referring here to form, important as it is. I am thinking of the day-to-day behaviour in a job that, at least at the head-of-mission level, is to a large degree self-defined, which is part of its attractiveness but also part of its difficulty.[17]

This template, originally forged in the Italian city-states of the thirteenth and fourteenth centuries,[18] was formalised subsequently largely by French and British diplomatic conceptions and practices. In a highly traditional profession – sometimes called the 'second oldest in the world' – this template provides a ready-made, off-the-shelf manual for many diplomats from African, Asian and Caribbean countries still in the first decades of independent nationhood and the initial stages of developing a foreign service.

It is no coincidence that even a revolutionary state like the former Soviet Union saw fit to translate and publish an edition of Sir Harold Nicolson's book on diplomacy and to distribute it to its legations and embassies. Many diplomatic conventions and customs are still very useful and will stay with us for years and decades to come. But the real question is not about rituals and procedures, important as they may be and in whose absence nothing much of substance could be accomplished. Rather, it is, in today's post-Cold War world – when issues of human security are displacing more conventional ones of state security, when transnational politics and cross-border flows are as significant as state-to-state interactions or even more so – is it still useful to think of what diplomats do in the same old-fashioned way, though perhaps with a couple of 'add-ons'?

Table 16.2   Complexity management in network diplomacy

Levels	Local, Domestic, National, Bilateral, Regional, Global
Scope	Broad array of public policy issues
Actors	Governments, Private Firms, MNCs, NGOs, Trade Unions

Diplomats today are essentially tasked with helping their own countries navigate the perils of globalisation.[19] To some degree, this is done by ministries of finance and of trade and industry, but it is also, and very significantly, undertaken by foreign ministries and their missions abroad. Now, the diplomat's traditional skills of dealing, mostly *in camera*, with a relatively small group of government officials and elite decision-makers are quite different from those needed to engage, often in the open and under the glare of television lights, the many actors that have become relevant in international affairs today – from business associations to trade unions, from NGOs to think tanks, from political parties to farmers' groups and, of course, the media. And, as can be seen from Table 16.2, it is not only the vastly larger number of actors involved that adds complexity to the management of the new diplomacy, but also its much broader scope, and the many more policy levels it entails.[20]

Yet – and herein lies a great paradox – many young diplomats from young countries today are being socialised into a certain way of practising diplomacy precisely at the time when it is becoming obsolete. Perversely, the standard diplomatic template becomes an aspirational goal for many foreign service trainees from the global South just when it is increasingly irrelevant. It is as if we were to put calligraphy and excellence in longhand writing at the very top of our high school priorities just when the IT revolution is hitting us. Elegant handwriting, as with many other expressions of human skill, has its place, but to put it front and centre among the things our youth should strive to master would strike most as a little *passé*. Much the same goes for the standard diplomatic template.

What do diplomats do?

For Nicolson, the tasks of a diplomat are *to represent, to inform* and *to negotiate*. The three have been radically altered by the course of events, with the first two demanding more proactive and discriminating stances, and the third somewhat receding in significance as more specialised officers take their seats at the negotiating tables.

The 1961 Vienna Convention, on the other hand, lists *representing, protecting, negotiating, ascertaining and promoting* as among 'the functions of a diplomatic mission'. They all have a somewhat routine, bureaucratic tinge to them that seems far removed from the different pace we have acquired as a result of the Third Industrial Revolution, launched in 1980. Acknowledging these functions to be somewhat on the passive side, Kishan Rana provides an alternative list, which includes *promotion, outreach, feedback, management* and *servicing*.[21] In an age when high-quality 'service to the public' is expected from government agencies, the latter cannot be ignored. 'Household chores', to which 'management' refers, are, naturally, another *sine qua non*.

Such functions, however, provide only a baseline. They are a necessary, but by no means sufficient, condition for fulfilling the diplomat's duties in today's world. Even the words *promotion* (largely associated with commercial purposes) and *outreach* (implying, in its blandness, the periodical sending of Embassy newsletters to various 'friends of the mission') fail to do justice to the centrality of the diplomatic task: the *projection* of one's country into the host nation.

It is all very well to say that diplomacy is 'the art of negotiating agreements between states'. With more than two hundred independent nation-states, many agreements are signed on a daily basis. But there is a limit to the number of agreements a country can sign. So, for diplomats, in many ways the most critical issue is the signing of agreements that are really worth it, with countries that have something to offer. Indeed, the real task is getting to the negotiations, let alone the signing. This takes some doing, and I am not sure that the traditional diplomatic toolkit has all the necessary instruments that small and middle powers need to get there.

In today's world, the only way this can be done is by *bridging the gap between home and host country* – that is, by attempting to bring the two societies closer. And for this, the development of extensive networks around key issue areas in both countries is critical. Otto von Bismarck's dictum that 'diplomacy is the art of gaining friends abroad' remains valid. What has changed is that the sheer number of friends that need to be gained has increased exponentially. To an important degree, this means taking one's country's case to the public at large, to engage civil society – which leads us to the role of think tanks.

On think tanks and program material

It is one thing to promote exports or one's country as an investment destination; it is quite another to have a 'story', and the moment diplomats limit themselves to the equivalent of used-car salespeople, they do a disfavour to themselves and to their own countries.

And this is where research centres from 'back home' come in.[22] Much has been written about NGOs and research centres as 'independent diplomatic actors';[23] here, however, I am more interested in their role as 'dependent diplomatic actors' – that is, in how they can be enlisted and deployed by diplomats. By definition, their business is to churn out information and analysis on the issues of the day. In doing so, they can become valuable allies of diplomats. By bringing relevant material and, whenever possible, some of the researchers and analysts who are 'thinking one's country', as it were, diplomats can make a lot of difference in 'bridging societal distances' – one of the cardinal objectives of diplomacy these days.

The Big Powers use many such instruments, from Voice of America to the BBC and the British Council, from the Alliance Française to the Goethe-Institut and the Cervantes Institute. High-quality glossies like *Span*, distributed by US embassies, or *Asia-Pacific*, published by the Japanese Foreign Ministry, perform a similar role. Yet, most developing nations have nothing of the sort.

Yet, if much of this can be broadly construed as 'outreach' or 'public diplomacy', I am thinking of something else: relevant public policy experience.[24] Unlike the countries of the North, few countries in the developing world have sufficient resources for international cooperation programs, whether generous or miserly, to engage in what is sometimes referred to as 'South-South cooperation.' But what they do have is experience in many crucial public policy areas that can be valuable to other countries in the South – experience that, in some ways, is much more valuable than that of developed societies. The transfer of that experience, however, is by no means a mechanical or even straightforward process. It needs to be researched and systematised, findings backed up and so on – all tasks for which research centres and think tanks are the natural foci. For those tasks, they could be deployed in a much more energetic and proactive fashion than most foreign ministries in the developing world are willing or ready to do.

In Chile, we still have a long way to go in this matter, but we have made some progress. In the early nineties, a decision was made to get Chile involved in Asia–Pacific Economic Cooperation (APEC). We realised early on that it could not be done without the backup of some research centre. So, in the mid-nineties, the Fundación Chilena del Pacífico was created, funded by both the public and the private sectors. This small but highly effective think tank has played a key role in Chile's Asia–Pacific policy. Chile joined APEC in 1994, the second Latin American country (after Mexico) to do so. The Fundación has provided some basic research and dissemination capabilities at which foreign ministries are not very good, and it played a key role in the November 2004 APEC Summit, which Chile hosted and which was the most significant international conference ever held in Santiago.

In 2007, Chile had more trade with Asia than with North America or Europe – 40 per cent of Chile's exports went to Asia. Chile's top export was China, and three of Chile's top six export markets are in Asia (China, Japan and South Korea). A free trade agreement with South Korea came into effect in 2004, another with China was signed in November of 2005, and I signed a preferential trade agreement with India in March 2006 – all of them 'firsts' between a Latin American country and each of those Asian nations.[25]

Diplomacy in media-driven societies

References to the way modern communications affect diplomacy are not new. The invention of the telegraph and later of the telephone were watershed events that, effectively, brought the foreign mission much closer to headquarters and eliminated much of the leeway that diplomats had in the era when instructions came by post. Hans Morgenthau, in the chapter on diplomacy in his classic 1948 book *Politics Among Nations*, also comments on it extensively. Telex, radio and newspapers, however, are one thing; the Internet and 24-hour news channels – of which there are 36 in India alone, in English, Hindi and Tamil, among other languages – are something else again. The rise of media moguls and empires, considered by some to be much more influential than governments themselves (since in many ways they can make or break governments) is another expression of this.[26]

Yet, it is important not to get stuck on the means of communications themselves and their strictly technological dimension, significant as it may be. The hundreds of television channels available in any one country and internationally, the thousands of AM, FM, short- and long-wave radio stations, the thousands of newspapers – India publishes some 7000 daily, with a circulation of some 78 million copies, in a business that is growing at 7–8 per cent a year with no signs of slowing down – the millions of web sites and not least, the blogs, the latest fad in all this, all of these effectively make us operate in real time, as it were, in one gigantic 'Big Brother' reality show. But we must also realise that the communications revolution is driven by and needs 'content', something to fill the newspaper columns and all that empty air. Yet, most diplomats from small- and medium-sized powers do not know how to fill those needs.

Emblematic of the changing significance of communications for today's diplomacy was the recently strong if ultimately unsuccessful, candidacy of UN Under Secretary General for Communications Shashi Tharoor for the position of UN Secretary General. Tharoor ended up as the first runner up for the position in all the straw polls undertaken in the Security Council, yet only a few years ago it would have been considered preposterous for the communications person in any significant international organisation to be considered for the top job. Such people were often second-rate journalists who got their jobs through political connections or sleek public relations specialists who were great at managing events and producing press releases, but who had nothing to say on substance. Yet Tharoor, an accomplished writer with a PhD in international relations who rose through the ranks to his present position, is precisely the sort of international civil servant who has made a brilliant career in multilateral diplomacy by understanding that, as important as *what* you are doing on the global scene is *to tell your story*. The many opinion pieces signed by Kofi Annan on various issues, from AIDS to the Football World Cup, that crowd the world's leading editorial pages are testimony to that understanding. The same goes for the Secretary General's sheer 10-year endurance, despite many concerted attacks from some powerful quarters, in which the media played a key role. But he gave as good as he got.

What made Tharoor such a strong candidate was not his 28-year experience at the United Nations – after a 10-year stint by the current incumbent, another career international civil servant, this might have been held (and was) against him. Nor was it Tharoor's strong managerial abilities, which he has shown on the ground in humanitarian relief actions in Bosnia and elsewhere. Rather, his strength was his capacity to communicate complex issues in an accessible fashion, orally, but especially in writing. This is not public relations. It is to understand that, in today's world, unless you take your case effectively and convincingly to the many constituencies on which you depend, you will not carry whatever issue you are battling for.

That kind of ability – as opposed to the arcane, convoluted and stilted way of talking and writing that diplomats are often accused of indulging in – is one of the most critical virtues today's diplomats should develop. The notion that diplomats need deal only with a diminutive, elite segment of their host society, for which a facility for small talk and after-dinner conversation is more than enough, is quite wrong. Yet, it is widespread.

To be an effective communicator, the contemporary 'network diplomat' needs both sufficient command of the subject matter at hand, be it nuclear policy or reproductive rights, and an ability to convey it in easily understandable language. This is the only way to make the case for one's country effectively and convincingly, not the diffident, *blasé* pose so many diplomats strike as part of their *dramatis persona*. And key instruments to help build the network the contemporary diplomat needs in the host society are, of course, the media, which not only help set up the network, but also, critically, assist its maintenance, refinement and expansion.

If this is true within the host country, it is also valid for the home turf, where some of the most difficult battles – for resources, for priorities, for high-level visits – are waged. Here, too, and this is especially true for heads of mission, the ability to make one's case persuasively, not just to foreign ministry officials but also to parliamentarians, business leaders, political parties and trade unionists, can be crucial for the success of any given initiative.[27]

From trained observer to proactive
initiator and modern orator

In his classic book, Nicolson refers to the change that took place at some point from the 'orator' diplomat of the Greek city-states to the 'trained observer' of the nineteenth and twentieth centuries, one who sent dispatches of necessary information to let the minister know what was going on in distant lands. In today's globalised world, the question of what diplomats do has in many ways become crucial, but the answer is somewhat different than it was in the first half of the twentieth century. Increasing international flows of all kinds, increasing numbers of interactions among nations and far higher numbers of actors, including many NGOs, have changed the nature of diplomacy and raised the stakes in terms of the results of international engagement. If you get it right, as Singapore or, to a smaller degree, Chile has, you really are in business; if you get it wrong, as many Central and West African countries have, you are marginalised.

With today's communications revolution, many details and analyses of current events happening in the host country are available almost instantly at home headquarters, and there is no need to engage in the extensive reporting about them that was so popular in the diplomatic dispatches of yesteryear. The key, of course, is to identify the major developments that do need an informed opinion, as well as those of significance for the bilateral relationship.

In the traditional model of diplomacy, the functions of a diplomat are to represent, to inform and to negotiate, with national sovereignty as the bedrock upon which the whole system rests. Its attitude is best summed up by Talleyrand's recommendation to all diplomats and heeded, in more ways than one, to this day: '*et surtout, pas trop de zèle.*' This model is, however, no longer relevant.

We need a new approach, one that responds to the imperatives of the age. The intense cultivation of a few key players, so characteristic of 'club diplomacy,' is being replaced by the development of 'network diplomacy', a much more extensive set of contacts at home and abroad built around critical 'issue areas' of special relevance to the mission. These issue areas ought to flow from what the head of mission identifies at the beginning of his or her tenure as the 'central problem' of the bilateral relationship, which may overlap with, but not necessarily mirror, the goals defined in the head of mission's instructions. If properly tended to and nurtured, this network feeds on itself.

In this new model, which demands a radical change in the self-image diplomats have of themselves and their job, negotiation is still present, albeit in a diminished fashion, but the other functions are largely superseded by newer variants. For 'representation,' with its somewhat old-fashioned, slightly passive connotation (one represents by being rather than by doing), I would substitute 'projection', by which I mean conveying what the diplomat's country is and entails to the host society and government. And for 'information', I would use 'analysis and influence' – that is, ways by which a diplomat can actually make a difference for the better in the host society, reflecting the increased interpenetration and interdependence of today's world. In so doing, he or she would in fact be going some way in the direction of bridging the gap between global governance and traditional diplomacy

that has been the core concern of this book, that is between the more flexible, open-ended and normative (but also somewhat diffuse, and difficult to
operationalise) concerns associated with the former and the more rigid,
closed and pragmatic (but also more results-oriented, and often therefore
more effective) manner often identified with the latter.

In other words, the 'trained observer', no longer suited to a 24–7 world of
business process outsourcing and knowledge process offshoring, needs to
become a 'proactive initiator' and 'modern orator'. Twenty-first-century diplomats must actively engage the society in which they reside, not just the
government to which they are accredited. They should look for ways to
project their own nation upon the one they live in, and try to make a difference. They ought to reclaim the tradition of the orators of the Greek city-
states and walk once again into the modern-day equivalent of the *agor* – the
communications media – and speak out. This has its perils; given the motto
of so many civil servants, 'those who do nothing have nothing to fear', one
can understand why it has not happened so far. Yet, it is the only way the
world's second-oldest profession will be able to remain relevant in the
twenty-first century. Above all, ladies and gentlemen, *plus de zèle!*

Notes

This is a revised version of a paper prepared for the conference 'Worlds Apart?
Exploring the Interface between Governance and Diplomacy,' organised by The
Centre for International Governance Innovation (CIGI) and Loughborough
University, at Wilton Park, 23–25 June 2006. The author would like to thank the
conference organisers, Andrew F. Cooper and Brian Hocking, for the opportunity
and Ramesh Thakur for his comments on an earlier version.

1. John Arquilla and David Ronfeldt, *The Emergence of Neopolitik: Toward an American
   Information Strategy*. Santa Monica: RAND Corporation, 1999, p. 53. Cited in
   Joseph S. Nye, *Soft Power: The Means to Success in World Politics*. New York: Public
   Affairs, p. 108.
2. For a recent assessment of South African foreign policy, see Elizabeth Sidiropoulos
   ed. (2004) *Apartheid Past, Renaissance Future: South Africa's Foreign Policy 1994–
   2004*, Johannesburg: South African Institute of International Affairs. See also
   James Hamill and Donna Lee (2001) 'South African Diplomacy in the Post-
   Apartheid Era: An Emergent Middle Power?', *International Relations* 15(4): 33–60.
3. For some reflections of one aspect of that, see Jorge Heine (2005a).
4. Thomas Friedman's (2005) world-wide bestseller *The World Is Flat: A Short History
   of the Globalized World in the Twenty-First Century*, London: Allen Lane, is largely
   inspired by the Indian experience in the development of IT and IT-enabled services. On Indian foreign policy, see C. Raja Mohan (2003) *Crossing the Rubicon: The
   Shaping of India's New Foreign Policy*, New Delhi: Penguin/Viking; Stephen Cohen
   (2001) *India: Emerging Power*, Washington, DC: Brookings Institution; and
   K. Shankar Bajpai (2006) 'India Engages with the World', Speech given at the 11th
   Prem Bhatia Memorial Lecture, 8 May, New Delhi, India. On the Indian Ministry
   of External Affairs, see Kishan S. Rana (2002) *Inside Diplomacy*, rev. paperback ed.,
   New Delhi: Manas Publications.

5. For an analysis of how Chile coped with some key multilateral issues in the government of President Ricardo Lagos (2000–06), see Jorge Heine (2006a) 'Between a Rock and a Hard Place: Latin American Multilateralism after 9/11', in Edward Newman, Ramesh Thakur, and John Tirman, eds, *Multilateralism under Challenge? Power, International Order and Structural Change*, Tokyo: United Nations University Press. See also Heraldo Muñoz (2005) *Una guerra solitaria: La historia secreta de EEUU en Irak, la polémica en la ONU y el papel de Chile*, Santiago: Random House Mondadori. The literature on Chilean foreign policy is extensive, but see especially José Miguel Insulza (1998) *Ensayos sobre política exterior de Chile*, Santiago: Editorial Los Andes; and Alberto van Klaveren (1998) 'Inserción internacional de Chile', in Eugenio Lahera and Cristián Toloza eds, *Chile en los Noventa*, Santiago: Dolmen.

6. The concept of 'middle power' emerged in the nineteenth-century balance of power literature on Europe, alluding to countries that found themselves between the Big Powers and the small nations. It is often used today to refer to countries such as Canada or Australia. But there is also an extensive literature on Latin American 'middle powers', originally encompassing Argentina, Brazil, and Mexico, but to which most observers today would add Chile. See Raúl Bernal Meza (2006) *América Latina en el mundo: el pensamiento latinoamericano y la teoría de las relaciones internacionales*, Buenos Aires: Grupo Editor Latinoamericano, 225–233.

7. Robert O. Keohane and Joseph S. Nye (2000) 'Introduction', in Joseph S. Nye and John D. Donahue eds, *Governance in a Globalizing World*, Washington, DC: Brookings Institution Press. I also draw on Keohane and Nye's excellent essay to develop the theoretical framework for this paper. I am indebted to Robert O. Keohane, whose student I had the privilege to be at Stanford many years ago, for his extraordinarily penetrating insights into the changing nature of world politics.

8. This became evident in Chile, which was affected quite strongly by the so-called Asian crisis, which originally erupted in 1997 in Thailand. Because Chile is so dependent on Asian markets for its exports, after growing at close to 7 per cent for much of the 1990s, it experienced its first negative growth in 16 years when GDP fell by 1.1 per cent in 1999. Ironically, a country like India, a close neighbour of Thailand, was essentially unaffected by the Asian crisis, which speaks volumes about how globalisation works in today's world.

9. An even more restricted type was 'boudoir diplomacy' – 'personal diplomacy at its most intoxicating.' See Harold Nicolson (1963) *Diplomacy*, New York: Oxford University Press, 31–32, on Sir James Harris, Earl of Malmesbury, and his dealings with Queen Catherine the Great of Russia.

10. See Keohane and Nye (2000).

11. The standard work on networks is Manuel Castells (1996a) *The Rise of the Network Society*, London: Blackwell, the first volume of a trilogy on 'The Information Age.'

12. Monsieur de Callières (1963) *On the Manner of Negotiating with Princes*, Notre Dame, IN: University of Notre Dame Press, 65. This little gem of a book, originally published in 1716 by one of Louis XIV's best and sharpest ambassadors, remains to this day an excellent source of advice for diplomats and a good version of the 'royal court model of diplomacy,' which evolved seamlessly into the 'club model' extant today. The title of this paper paraphrases the title of that book. For a commentary, see Maurice Keens-Soper (2001) 'Callières', in

G.R. Berridge, Maurice Keens-Soper, and T.G. Otte *Diplomatic Theory from Machiavelli to Kissinger*, Basingstoke: Palgrave, 106–124.

13. On summit diplomacy, see Jan Melissen (2003) 'Summit Diplomacy Coming of Age', *Discussion Papers in Diplomacy No.86*, The Hague: Netherlands Institute of International Relations 'Clingendael'. Summit diplomacy has become especially widespread in Latin America; on one of their expressions, the Iberoamerican summits, see Raúl Sanhueza Carvajal (2003) *Las cumbres iberoamericanas: comunidad de naciones o diplomacia clientelar?*, Santiago: FLACSO-Chile and Editorial Universitaria; and Francisco Rojas Aravena, ed. (2000) *Las cumbres iberoamericanas: una mirada global*, Caracas: FLACSO-Chile and Nueva Sociedad.

14. See Robert Wolfe (1998) '*Still Lying Abroad?* On the Institution of the Resident Ambassador', *Diplomacy and Statecraft* 9(2): 23–54; and Paul Sharp (2004) 'Who Needs Diplomats? The Problem of Diplomatic Representation', in Christer Jönsson and Richard Langhorne, eds, *Diplomacy* 3, London: Sage Publications, 58–78.

15. Actually less, since a not-insignificant amount of that is spent at headquarters on conferences and *per diem* and other expenses.

16. The Chilean Ministry of Foreign Affairs has recently established a Division of Regional Coordination, whose responsibility is to promote closer links between each of Chile's thirteen Regions and various countries around the world, something in which the Chilean missions abroad are supposed to play a key role.

17. For some recent Latin American perspectives on the diplomatic function, see Eduardo Jara Roncalli (2002) *La función diplomática*, Santiago: RIL ; and Ismael Moreno Pino (2001) *La diplomacia: aspectos teóricos y prácticos de su ejercicio profesional*, Mexico City: Fondo de Cultura Económica.

18. See Garrett Mattingly (1937) 'The First Resident Embassies: Medieval Italian Origins of Modern Diplomacy', *Speculum* 12(4): 423–439. For sixteenth-century and early modern diplomacy, see his 1964 book *Renaissance Diplomacy*, Baltimore: Penguin, 105–256.

19. For Latin American perspectives on how to cope with globalisation, see Claudio Maggi and Dirk Messner eds (2002) *Gobernanza global: una mirada desde América Latina*, Caracas: Nueva Sociedad. On the strictly economic dimension of this coping, see Economic Commission for Latin America and the Caribbean (2002) *Globalización y desarrollo*, Santiago: ECLAC.

20. I am indebted to Ramesh Thakur for this point.

21. See Kishan S. Rana (2006) *Bilateral Diplomacy*, 2nd printing, New Delhi: Manas Publications, 21.

22. See Shankari Sundararaman 'Research Centers as Diplomatic Actors', paper delivered at the conference 'Worlds Apart? Exploring the Interface between Governance and Diplomacy', CIGI and Asia-Pacific College of Diplomacy, Australian National University, 4–5 March 2006, Canberra, Australia.

23. See Andrew F. Cooper and Brian Hocking (2000) 'Governments, Non-governmental Organizations and the Re-calibration of Diplomacy', *Global Society* 14(3): 361–367; see also John English, Andrew F. Cooper, and Ramesh Thakur eds (2002) *Enhancing Global Governance: Towards a New Diplomacy*, Tokyo: United Nations University Press.

24. On 'public' or 'mass diplomacy,' see Pierre C. Pahlavi 'Cyber-Diplomacy: A New Strategy of Influence', paper presented at the Canadian Political Association General Meeting, 30 May 2003, Halifax, Nova Scotia.

25. See Jorge Heine (2005b).
26. Media barons have been around (*and* throwing their weight around) for a long time, as the case of William Randolph Hearst attests. What is new is to have media empires of world-wide reach.
27. On this, as well as a more general discussion of the role of the head of mission, see Kishan S. Rana (2005) 'The Domestic Dimension', in *The 21st Century Ambassador: Plenipotentiary to Chief Executive*, New Delhi: Oxford University Press.

Conclusion: National Diplomacy and Global Governance

Ramesh Thakur

Two of the heaviest lifters in the world of contemporary international diplomacy are the United States – primus inter pares, if ever there was one – and India. One of the most critical challenges in the field of the global governance of international security is the fraying nonproliferation regime.[1] Over the last two years, the above two have intersected with respect to the India-US civil nuclear cooperation deal signed by President George W. Bush and Prime Minister Manmohan Singh in March 2006 and endorsed by the US Congress in December 2006. (Although ratification by the legislature is not required in the Westminster system of parliamentary government in India, the deal ran into rough weather in 2007 because Singh is the head of a coalition government which includes many left and communist party politicians whose anti-Americanism is deeply ingrained.[2]) National diplomats have negotiated over the technical details of the various clauses and agreements, but have had negligible roles in shaping and determining the big policy issues and decisions. Supporters and opponents from the political parties, business sectors, civil society organisations and strategic allies or adversaries have engaged in informational, advocacy and lobbying campaigns to facilitate or block relevant decisions and legislation. Moreover, they have formed ad hoc coalitions of convenience with like-minded actors across territorial borders. Similarly, at one level the decision on whether or not to proceed with the deal will be made ultimately by national governments – India and the United States – through their respective constitutional and political processes. But at another level, the deal has built-in provisions for India, first negotiating special arrangements with the International Atomic Energy Agency and then, with active US diplomatic support, gaining the unanimous consent of the Nuclear Suppliers Group.

At the time of writing, the complex process seems to be in its endgame phase with the outcome highly uncertain. Regardless, the story is a very apt, fitting and timely refutation of the putative divide between diplomacy and global governance. On some issues and in some contexts, they diverge; on others, they come together and need and complement each other.

Reports of a permanent and irrevocable split between them have been much exaggerated.

In this concluding chapter, I will first examine the concept and manifestations of global governance and then look at the changing world of diplomacy and diplomats. An effort will be made to integrate appropriate examples from the chapters in this volume into the discussion.

Global governance

I define 'governance' as the sum of laws, norms, policies and institutions that define, constitute and mediate relations between citizens, society, market and the state – the wielders and objects of the exercise of public power. 'Good governance' incorporates participation and empowerment with respect to public policies, choices, and offices; rule of law and independent judiciary to which the executive and legislative branches of government are subject along with citizens and other actors and entities; and standards of probity and incorruptibility, transparency, accountability, and responsibility. It includes also institutions in which these principles and values find on-going expression. Good governance thus can be considered a normative definition – concerned with laudable standards.

Global governance – governance for the world without world government – refers to cooperative problem-solving arrangements on a global plane. These may be rules (laws, norms, codes of behaviour) as well as constituted institutions and practices (formal and informal) to manage collective affairs by a variety of actors (state authorities, intergovernmental organisations, Nongovernmental Organisations (NGOs), private sector entities). Global governance thus refers to the complex of formal and informal institutions, mechanisms, relationships, and processes between and among states, markets, citizens and organisations, both intergovernmental and nongovernmental, through which collective interests are articulated, rights and obligations are established, and differences are mediated.[3] It suggests, as Christer Jönsson argues, a multi-layered rather than state-centric organisational universe (this volume).

Such global governance faces a fundamental paradox. The policy authority for tackling global problems and mobilising the necessary resources is principally vested at country level, in states, while the source and scale of the problems and potential solutions to them are transnational, regional and global. One result of this situation is that states have the capacity to disable decision-making and policy implementation by global bodies like the United Nations (UN), but generally lack the vision and will to empower and enable their own global problem-solving on issues such as environmental degradation, human trafficking, terrorism and nuclear weapons. Compounding this situation – what Jan Aart Scholte describes as the post-sovereign quality of polycentric governance – is the fact that that even a state with vision and will cannot exercise a singular and ultimate decision-making authority (this volume).

Today's world needs global governance, but most people fear the idea of a centralised, all-powerful world government. Thus the goal of most contemporary proponents of global governance is *not* the creation of a world government, but of various layers of consultations and decision-making. The construction of multi-layered governance networks could establish a genuine global rule of law without centralised global institutions. In this model 'good' global governance would not imply exclusive policy jurisdiction by any one site, but rather an optimal partnership between state, regional and global *levels* of actors, and between state, intergovernmental and nongovernmental *categories* of actors. Given this, in his chapter David Spence deftly outlines the way in which European governance may contribute to global governance through its capacity to provide a normative framework for the resolution of national and regional challenges (Chapter 4 of this volume).

The distinction between law and legitimacy is an old one for political philosophers and intersects with the equally familiar discourse on the grounds of political obedience. Power is the capacity simply to enforce a particular form of behaviour. Authority signifies the capacity to create and enforce rights and obligations which are accepted as legitimate and binding by members of an all-inclusive society who are subject to the authority. If the source of legitimacy is institutions (either formal organisations or recurring and stable patterns of behaviour), then those institutions indicate the existence of an international authority even in the absence of world government. For 'the international system clearly exhibits some kind of order in which patterns repeat, institutions accrete, and practices are stable.'[4]

The UN is the only truly global institution of a general purpose which approximates universality. The size of UN voting majorities, the forcefulness of the language used and the frequency with which particular resolutions and language are recited are important because of the political significance attached to its perception as the closest we are able to get to an authentic voice of humanity. The role of custodian of collective legitimacy enables the UN, through its resolutions, to articulate authoritative standards of state behaviour. It is the site where power is moderated by lawful authority as law and legitimacy come together; or at least they should, in terms of the core identity on which the international organisation was constructed. A community denotes shared values and bonds of affinity. An international community exists to the extent that there is a shared understanding of what constitutes legitimate behaviour by the various actors in world affairs. A gulf between lawful and legitimate international behaviour at or by the UN is prima facie evidence of an erosion of the sense of international community.[5] The UN is the symbol of an imagined and constructed community of strangers who have banded together to tackle the world's problems collectively and to work together cooperatively in the pursuit of shared goals. In this sense the UN is the site where value-maximising national diplomacy and interest-mediating global governance intersect. As Megan Davis points out in her chapter on the establishment of the international legal regime for Indigenous peoples at the UN, this intersection also occurs at the transnational diplomatic level (Chapter 12 in this volume).

Changes in the world of diplomacy and diplomats

The UN was conceived of and fashioned and negotiated by national leaders dissatisfied with the lack of adequate mechanisms of global governance both for muting conflict and promoting collaboration among sovereign states. Was the UN Charter signed in another age for another world? There has been a threefold change in the world of diplomacy and diplomats since 1945:

1. In the *levels* of diplomatic activity, from the local through the domestic-national to the bilateral, regional and global;
2. In the *domain and scope* of the subject matter or content, expanding rapidly to a very broad array of the different sectors of public policy and government activity; and
3. In the rapidly expanding *numbers and types of actors*, from governments to national private sector firms, multinational corporations, NGOs and regional and international organisations.

The business of the world has changed almost beyond recognition over the last century. As Iver Neumann details in his chapter, the cross-border flows of persons and information have skyrocketed in the last century, with obvious consequence for diplomacy being the explosion of consular work (Chapter 1 in this volume). Four decades ago the influential French theorist Raymond Aron argued that 'the ambassador and the soldier *live* and *symbolize* international relations which, insofar as they are inter-state relations, concern diplomacy and war.'[6] Today, alongside the horde of diplomats and soldiers, the international lawyer, the multinational merchant, cross-border financier, World Bank technocrat, UN peacekeeper and NGO humanitarian worker jostle for space on the increasingly congested international stage.

In the classic formulation, the overriding goal of foreign policy was the promotion, pursuit and defence of the national interest. The über-realist Hans Morgenthau defined diplomacy as 'the art of bringing the different elements of national power to bear with maximum effect upon those points in the international situation which concern the national interest most directly.'[7] The four core tasks of the diplomat were to *represent* his[8] country's interests, *protect* his country's citizens visiting or residing in his accredited country, *inform* his own and host government and people about each other, and *negotiate* with the host country.[9] This was conducted in a world of 'club diplomacy' (and occasionally the even more intimate 'boudoir diplomacy').[10] Because of the threefold changes identified above, the overriding goal of foreign policy in the contemporary world is to forge issue-specific coalitions with like-minded actors. China and India teaming up with Brazil and South Africa to ensure that any Doha accord will be a development outcome in reality and not just in rhetoric is a good example.

The matching core task of diplomacy is to engage in issue-specific 'network diplomacy.'[11] The latter has more players than club diplomacy, is flat rather than hierarchical, engages in multiple forms of communication beyond merely the written, is more transparent than confidential, and its 'consummation' takes the form of increased bilateral flows instead of formal signing ceremonies. The motto of new diplomacy could be: networking to promote welfare and security by managing risk and reducing vulnerability in a world of strategic uncertainty, increasing complexity and rapid globalisation.

Those attached to the old world of pomp and pageantry, rituals and procedures, are increasingly detached from the real world of modern diplomacy, and are the less effective for it. Not only can presidents, prime ministers and foreign ministers go over the ambassador's head directly to their counterparts in other countries; often so can business executives, trade union leaders, journalists and NGOs. The bigger departments from the home country's bureaucracy, better staffed and resourced, often place their own personnel in overseas embassies: not just defence, but also agriculture, education, and so on. The agenda-setting capacity of NGOs – Amnesty International, Human Rights Watch, the International Committee of the Red Cross (ICRC), Greenpeace, World Wildlife Fund (WWF), the International Union for the Conservation of Nature (IUCN) – is greater than that of many governments. Moreover, in the instance of the ICRC, Martine Letts and Ivan Cook contend that the organisation's international legal personality allows it a quasi-diplomatic role that is acknowledged by both states and civil society (this volume). If, therefore, the diplomat wishes to escape from Peter Ustinov's withering description as 'nothing but a headwaiter who is allowed to sit down occasionally,'[12] then he and she must learn to engage and communicate with the full range of social, economic and political actors, across all domains of subject matter, and at all levels of interactions.

Ambassadors' lives no longer consist, if they ever did, of equal parts of protocol, alcohol and geritol. New Age diplomacy is increasingly about issue-specific and goal-directed partnerships between different actors. Ambassadors must engage with the host society in which they live, not merely negotiate with the government to which they are accredited. No longer is the ambassador someone sent abroad to lie for his country; prime ministers and presidents manage to do that quite well at home directly. Instead, in attempting to navigate the shoals while exploiting the opportunities of a globalised and networked world, the diplomat must cultivate all manner of constituencies in home, host and sometimes even third countries. Sometimes, as Jorge Heine recounts from his own ambassadorial experiences, these constituencies include those 'who would never have thought of setting foot in the rarefied atmosphere of the salons and private clubs the diplomats of yesteryear used to frequent,' requiring diplomats to engage in 'complexity management' (this volume). However, the cultivation of all relevant constituencies is the key to network diplomacy.[13]

A changed world

The world of international relations – the 'field' in which diplomats operate – has also changed substantially since 1945. We operate today in a global environment that is vastly more challenging, complex and demanding than the world of 1945. The issues and preoccupations of the new millennium present new and different types of challenges from those that faced the world in 1945. With the new realities and challenges have come corresponding new expectations for action and new standards of conduct in national and international affairs. The number of actors in world affairs has grown enormously, the types of actors have changed very substantially, the interactions between them have grown ever more dense and intense and the agenda of international public policy has been altered quite dramatically in line with the changing temper of the times. Eight changes are especially worth highlighting.

The *Cold War* was a global struggle centred on and dominated by two superpowers who were able to structure the pattern of international relationships because of a qualitative discrepancy in military capacity and resources. The end of the Cold War terminated the US-Soviet great-power rivalry, brought victory for the liberal over a totalitarian ideology, and marked the triumph of the market over the command economy model. The elimination of countervailing power to check the untrammelled exercise of US power ushered in a quasi-imperial order in which the reality of inequality structures the relationship between the imperial centre and all others. This poses the biggest challenge as much for diplomacy as for global governance: how to interact with a unipolar Washington that views itself as uniquely virtuous, resistant to 'Gulliverization,' exempt from restrictions that apply to all others, oscillating between neo-isolationism and neo-conservatism. A second and related challenge is how to interact with one another without always routing relations through Washington in a hub-and-spoke model.

One of the historic phenomena of the last century, powerfully championed by Washington in the decade after the Second World War , was the emergence of large swathes of humanity from foreign rule to independence under *decolonisation*, even if for many the reality of oppression did not materially change, or at least not for long. The first great wave of the retreat of

European colonialism from Asia, Africa and the South Pacific was followed by the collapse of the large land-based Soviet empire and a fresh burst of newly independent countries in Eastern Europe and Central Asia. There has been something of a revival of the enterprise of liberal imperialism which rests on nostalgia for the lost world of Western empires that kept the peace among warring natives and provided sustenance to their starving peoples. This is at variance with the developing countries' own memory and narratives of their encounter with the West. There are several resulting diplomatic challenges. For most former colonies, the triple challenge of national integration, state-building and economic development remains imperative. We also need to avoid state collapse and failure and the resulting humanitarian emergencies. Former colonial powers and settler societies have to be sensitive to the foreign policy input of historical trauma, while former colonies must make an effort to escape the trap of viewing current events and motives from a historical prism. One of the clearest examples of the dual danger is in relation to providing international assistance to victims of atrocities inside sovereign borders. The matching global governance challenge is to provide a new and politically acceptable vocabulary for international engagement and transitional administration.

The two come together even more starkly in trying to fashion credible and effective responses to the *changing nature and sites of armed conflict*.[14] The number of armed conflicts rose steadily until the end of the Cold War, peaked in the early 1990s, and has declined since then. The nature of armed conflict itself has changed, with most being internal struggles for power, dominance and resources rather than militarised inter-state confrontations. Battle lines, if they exist at all, are fluid and shifting rather than territorially demarcated and static. Because they merge seamlessly with sectarian divides, contemporary conflicts are often rooted in, reproduce and replicate past intergroup atrocities, thereby perpetuating hard-edged cleavages that are perceived as zero sum games by all parties. Thus all sides are caught in a never ending cycle of suspicions, atrocities and recriminations. The net result is that noncombatants are on the frontline of modern battles. The need to help and protect civilians at risk of death and displacement caused by armed conflict is now paramount.[15] National diplomats, international officials from the UN, World Bank, International Monetary Fund (IMF), and even the ICRC and NGOs will be judged on how well they discharge or dishonour their international responsibility to protect.

The multiplication of internal conflicts was accompanied by a worsening of the abuses of the *human rights* of millions of people. Human rights advocacy rests on 'the moral imagination to feel the pain of others' as if it were one's own, treats others as 'rights-bearing equals,' not 'dependents in tutelage,' and can be viewed as 'a juridical articulation of duty by those in zones of safety toward those in zones of danger.'[16] The origins of the Universal Declaration in the experiences of European civilisation are important, not for the reason that most critics cite, but its opposite. It is less an expression of European triumphalism and imperial self-confidence than a guilt-ridden Christendom's renunciation of its ugly recent record; less an assertion of the superiority of European human nature than revulsion at the recent history of European savagery; not an effort to universalise Western values but to ban the dark side of Western vices like racial and religious bigotry. The challenge for diplomacy is how best to interpret and apply universal values with due sensitivity to local contexts and Asian sensibilities. Far from cross-cultural divisions, the loss of a son killed by government thugs unites mothers of all religions and nationalities in shared pain, grief and anger. The solution is to create and operate international governance institutions whose investigative and enforcement jurisdictions are universal and non-discriminatory. Australian and Canadian ministers and officials can no more condemn Burma and China but remain silent on Guantanamo Bay and extraordinary renditions without loss of credibility and efficacy than can the UN, Amnesty International or Human Rights Watch.

By virtue of their growing influence and power, humanitarian actors have effectively entered the realm of policy making, at the same time as their emancipatory vocabulary has been captured by governments and other power brokers. International humanitarians are participants in global governance as advocates, activists and policy makers. Their critiques and policy prescriptions have demonstrable consequences in the governmental and intergovernmental allocation of resources and the exercise of political, military and economic power. With influence over policy should come responsibility for the consequences of policy. When things go wrong or do not happen according to plan, the humanitarians share the responsibility for the suboptimal outcomes. Human rights have become the universal vocabulary of political legitimacy and humanitarian law of military legitimacy. But rather than necessarily constraining the pursuit of national interests in the international arena by military means, human rights and humanitarian law provide the discourse of justification for the familiar traditional means of statecraft. Much as humanitarians might want to believe that they still hold up the virtue of truth to the vice of power, the truth is that the vocabulary of virtue has been appropriated in the service of power.

The rise of environmental consciousness, the need to husband resources more frugally and nurture our fragile ecosystems more tenderly as our common legacy for future generations, was another great social movement of the last century that contributed greatly to the greening of the agenda of international affairs. The concept of *'sustainable development'* was one of the major norm shifts, with the Bruntland Commission being the midwife.[17] How best to operationalise the concept in concrete policy and actual practice remains intensely contentious and thus a major diplomatic challenge. Nothing illustrates this better than climate change. The failure of major countries to participate in the Kyoto Protocol undermined its effective implementation and delayed the international effort to slow down carbon emissions of the industrial countries. That is, an international governance innovation was made possible by national diplomacy but also effectively gutted by the failure of national nerve and policy in key countries like Australia, Canada and the United States which simply walked away from the Kyoto Protocol. Kofi Annan commented that climate change sceptics are 'out of step, out of arguments and just about out of time.'[18] Effective programs for tackling what may well be the gravest challenge confronting humanity require active partnerships among governments, scientists, economists, NGOs and industry. The traditional paradigm of value-maximising national interest is simply irrelevant.

Its irrelevance has been accentuated also with the rise of the *human security* paradigm which puts the individual at the centre of the debate, analysis and policy. He or she is paramount, and the state is a collective instrument to protect human life and promote human welfare. The reformulation of national security into human security is simple, yet has profound consequences for how we see the world, how we organise our political affairs, how we make choices in public and foreign policy, and how we relate to fellow-human beings from many different countries and cultures. To many poor people in the world's poorest countries today, the risk of being attacked by terrorists or with weapons of mass destruction is far removed from the pervasive reality of the so-called soft threats: hunger, lack of safe drinking water and sanitation, and endemic diseases. These soft threats kill millions every year – far more than the so-called 'hard' or 'real' threats to security. A major diplomatic challenge is to recalibrate the balance between national and human security and reallocate human and material resources accordingly. A major global governance challenge is to prioritise human and international over national security. The two can cut across each other, for example with respect to arms. The pursuit of more, and more lethal, arms leads to the trap of the security dilemma whereby everyone's net security is no better and may in fact be worse; the pursuit of international security may render the world less dangerous yet leave particular countries more exposed to the predatory raids of the powerful.

National frontiers are becoming less relevant in determining the flow of ideas, information, goods, services, capital, labour and technology. The speed of modern communications makes borders increasingly permeable, while the volume of cross-border flows threatens to overwhelm the capacity of states to manage them. *Globalisation* releases many productive forces that can help to uplift millions from poverty, deprivation and degradation. But it can also unleash destructive forces – 'uncivil society' – such as flows of arms, terrorism, disease, prostitution, drug and people smuggling, etc. that are neither controllable nor solvable by individual governments. Because global capital is not self-governing, stability in financial markets requires the judicious exercise of public authority; because world order is not self-governing, it too requires the judicious exercise of international public authority. The challenge of diplomacy is how best to harness the productive potential of globalisation while muting the disruptive forces, taming the destructive forces and protecting (ethno)national identity. The most efficient and effective solutions will lie in a mix of national adjustment policies and global governance regimes that are rule and rule-of-law based.

Thus globalisation entails risks as well as opportunities, and the sceptical dissenters in the streets offer an antidote to the unbridled enthusiasts of global capital in boardrooms and treasuries. International financial institutions have had their feet held to the fire of international accountability by NGOs who claim to be more authentic representatives of *civil society*. The development and evolution of political institutions is an outcome of contested interactions between political, social and economic elites, on the one hand, and social movements challenging the existing distribution of political, social and economic assets and privileges, on the other. Citizens look more and more to civic associations to channel a growing range and variety of social interactions, which in turn need a framework of governance outside the jurisdiction of the state. 'Civil society' refers to the social and political space where voluntary associations attempt to shape norms and policies for regulating public life in social, political, economic and environmental dimensions. There has been an exponential growth in the number of civil society actors, and in the volume of transnational networks in which they are embedded. They play an important and growing role as an information channel, a font of legitimacy and a catalyst to accountability and transparency. They exert pressure in cabinet offices and boardrooms alike in the rich countries to respond to the special needs of developing countries. The net result of expanding global citizen action has been to extend the theory and deepen the practice of grassroots democracy without borders. International society too is becoming more plural and diverse. The threefold challenge for diplomacy is how to counter uncivil society, give voice to civil society, but neither a vote nor a veto to them: for that would be an abdication of responsibility by national public authorities and international organisations to govern on behalf of all citizens and peoples.

Conclusion

In world affairs the focus on form over substance, structure over outcome means that governance is often dislocated from governing. The most common symbol and representation of global governance today is the UN. The most potent agent of national diplomacy is the United States. The relationship between them therefore is the key to mediating any potential tension between diplomacy and global governance.

Authority is the right to make policy and rules, while power is the capacity to implement the policy and enforce the rules. The UN has global reach and authority but no power. It symbolises global governance but lacks the attributes of international government. While lawful authority remains vested in the UN, power has become increasingly concentrated in the United States which has global grasp and power but not international authority. Often it acts as a de facto world government but disclaims responsibility for the distributional outcomes of its actions. The exercise of power is rendered less effective and generates its own resistance if divorced from authority. The latter in turn is corroded when challenges to it go unanswered by the necessary force. Lack of capacity to be the chief enforcer acting under Chapter 7 means that the UN remains an incomplete organisation; one that practices only parts of its Charter.

The United States has found it difficult to comprehend why the UN does not accept the history of the exercise of American power being virtuous in intent and beneficent in results. But authority also is weakened when it becomes just a handmaiden to power. Progress towards the good international society requires that force be harnessed to authority rather than lawful authority being hijacked to pursue the agenda of power politics. Kosovo (1999) and Iraq (2003) underlined widespread perceptions that powerful countries can break the rules of the UN Charter regime with impunity. This has widened the gulf between law and legitimacy. The humanitarian community has had a critical role in this. For how can one 'intervene' in Kosovo, East Timor, Iraq or Darfur and pretend to be detached from and not responsible for the distributional consequences with respect to wealth, resources, power, status and authority? This dilemma is inherent in the structure of interventions and has nothing to do with the false dichotomy between multilateral interventions in one context and unilateral in another. 'The effort to intervene...without affecting the background distribution of power and wealth betrays this bizarre belief in the possibility of an international governance which does not govern.'[19] In all policy choice frameworks, there are winners and losers, virtuous outcomes and horrendous costs. Because the darker sides can sometimes swamp the benefits of humanitarian work, it must be tempered by a sensibility of pragmatism that focuses the searchlight of critical reasoning on the noble goals and aspirations of humanitarianism. That comment is no less applicable to institutions and agents of global governance than it is to officials of national governments.

Notes

1. See Ramesh Thakur, 'Nuclear Weapons, Anomalies, and Global Governance', in *2003–2005 John W. Holmes Memorial Lectures,* Waterloo, Ontario: ACUNS Reports and Papers 2006 No. 1, 21–31.
2. For my views on the deal, see Ramesh Thakur (2007a), 'Is India so weak that it must fear success?', *Hindu,* 4 September, Chennai; (2007c), 'Nuclear double standards', *Times of India,* 15 October, Delhi; and (2007b) 'No time to hesitate: In good faith', *Daily News and Analysis,* 27 October, Mumbai.

3. See further Thakur, Ramesh and Thomas G. Weiss (forthcoming), *Global Governance and the United Nations*, Bloomington: Indiana University Press.
4. Hurd, Ian (1999) 'Legitimacy and Authority in International Politics', *International Organization* 53(2): 400.
5. In a recent article, Amitai Etzioni argues similarly that the greater threat to the European Union is not the so-called democratic deficit, but a 'community deficit, the lack of shared values and bonds' (Etzioni, 2007).
6. Aron, Raymond (1967) *Peace and War: A Theory of International Relations*, translated from the French by Richard Howard and Annette Baker Fox, New York: Frederick A. Praeger, 5: emphasis in original.
7. Morgenthau, Hans J. (1996) *Politics Among Nations: The Struggle for Power and Peace*, 4th edn, New York: Alfred A. Knopf, 135.
8. Women diplomats were a rarity.
9. The classic formulation was, Sir. Harold Nicolson (1939) *Diplomacy*, Oxford: Oxford University Press.
10. Heine, Jorge (2006b) *On the Manner of Practising the New Diplomacy*, Working Paper No. 11, Waterloo, Ontario: Centre for International Governance Innovation, 5–8.
11. Ibid., 2–12.
12. Quoted in Ibid., 10.
13. In 1948–1949, a young Pierre Trudeau set out on a backpacking adventure across Eastern Europe, the Middle East, Asia and the Pacific. He found overseas Canadian diplomats to be aloof, disdainful and condescending – an experience he never forgot and an attitude he reciprocated as prime minister two decades later. See John English (2006) *Citizen of the World: The Life of Pierre Elliott Trudeau. Volume One: 1919–1968*, Toronto: Alfred A. Knopf Canada, 180, 190. A cautionary tale for young consular officials: the ragged and dreadlocked young backpacker seeking your assistance today could be your minister in years' time.
14. See in particular Andrew Mack et al. (2005) *Human Security Report 2005* (New York: Oxford University Press).
15. See Ramesh Thakur (2006b) *The United Nations, Peace and Security: From Collective Security to the Responsibility to Protect*, Cambridge: Cambridge University Press.
16. Michael Ignatieff (2001) *Human Rights as Politics and Idolatry*, edited and introduced by Amy Gutmann, Princeton: Princeton University Press, 163.
17. For a study of the role and impact of international blue ribbon commissions, see Ramesh Thakur, Andrew F. Cooper, and John English, eds (2005) *International Commissions and the Power of Ideas*, Tokyo: United Nations University Press.
18. Annan, Kofi (2006) 'Climate Change to Test Our Adaptability', *Japan Times*, 10 November.
19. David Kennedy, (2004) *The Dark Sides of Virtue: Reassessing International Humanitarianism*, Princeton: Princeton University Press, 130.

References

A World Player (2004) A public relations booklet on the EU's external relations, available from http://europa.eu.int/comm/publications/

Anaya, S. James (2004) *Indigenous Peoples in International Law* (Oxford: Oxford University Press).

Anderson, Kenneth (2004) 'Humanitarian Inviolability in Crisis: The Meaning of Impartiality and Neutrality for U.N. and NGO Agencies Following the 2003–2004 Afghanistan and Iraq Conflicts', *Harvard Human Rights Journal* 17: 41–74.

Annan, Kofi (2000) *The Secretary-General of the United Nations Briefs the Security Council on Visit to Southeast Asia*, 29 February, New York, available from http://www.un.org/peace/etimor/docs/BSG.htm.

——— (2005) 'The U.N. Isn't a Threat', *The Washington Post*, 5 November, A19.

——— (2006) 'Climate Change to Test Our Adaptability', *Japan Times*, 10 November.

ArabicNews.com (1998) 'Crown Prince Hassan: Islamic-Christian Dialogue Important', 3 March, available from http://www.arabicnews.com/ansub/Daily/Day/980423/1998042301.html.

Araki, Ichirō (2007) 'Global Governance, Japan and the World Trade Organization', in Hook, Glenn D., and Hugo Dobson, eds, *Global Governance and Japan: The Institutional Architecture* (London: Routledge).

Arla Foods (2006a) *Arla Affected by Cartoons of Muhammad*, available from http://www.arlafoods.com/APPL/HJ/HJ202COM/HJ202D01.NSF/O/3DE8AAFDECABBA97C12571020061F1C1.

——— (2006b) *Arla Publishes Danish Government's Press Release in Saudi Papers*, available from http://www.arlafoods.com/APPL/HJ/HJ202COM/HJ202D01.NSF/O/F2B3B702FA17AFE4C12571030056C46D.

——— (2006c) *Danish Muslim Call off Campaign*, available from http://www.arlafoods.com/APPL/HJ/HJ202COM/HJ202D01.NSF/O/953BC798FEAA6AE8C1257108002C2C7C.

——— (2006d) *Breakthrough for Arla in the Middle East*, available from http://www.arlafoods.com/appl/hj/hj202com/hj202d01.nsf/O/680DB47E0A10159EC1257148002E22AC.

Aron, Raymond (1967) *Peace and War: A Theory of International Relations,* translated from the French by Richard Howard and Annette Baker Fox (New York: Frederick A. Praeger).

Arquilla, John and David Rondfeldt (1999) *The Emergence of Noopolitik: Towards an American Information Strategy* (Santa Monica, CA: RAND).

——— (2000) *Swarming and the Future of Conflict* (Santa Monica, CA: RAND).

Australian Broadcasting Corporation (ABC) (2003) 'Australia Plays Down US President's "Sheriff" Remarks', *Radio A*, 17 October.

Axworthy, Lloyd (1998) 'Notes for an Address by the Hon. Lloyd Axworthy, Minister of Foreign Affairs [Canada], to the United Nations Commission on Human Rights, Geneva, Switzerland', 30 March, available from http://www.hri.ca/tribune/viewArticle.asp?ID=2501.

Ba, Alice D., and Matthew J. Hoffmann, eds (2005) *Contending Perspectives on Global Governance: Coherence, Contestation and World Order* (New York: Routledge).

Bache, I., and Matthew Flinders, eds (2004) *Multilevel Governance* (Oxford: Oxford University Press).

Bailes, Alyson J.K., Herolf, Gunilla, and Sundelius, Bengt eds (2006) *The Nordic Countries and the European Security and Defence Policy* (Oxford: Oxford University Press).

Bajpai, K. Shankar (2006) 'India Engages with the World', The 11th Prem Bhatia Memorial Lecture, 8 May, New Delhi.

Ball, Desmond, Anthony Milner, and Brendan Taylor (2005) *Mapping Track II Institutions in New Zealand, Australia and the Asian Region: An Independent Study Submitted to the Asia New Zealand Foundation*, available from http://www.asianz.org.nz/files/TrackIIfullreport.pdf.

Barber, Benjamin R. (2000) 'Globalising Democracy', *American Prospect* 11(20), available from http://www.prospect.org/cs/articles?article=globalizing_democracy.

Barker Rodney, (2003) 'Legitimacy, Legitimation and the European Union: What Crisis?', in P. Craig and R. Rawlings, eds, *Law and Administration in Europe: Essays in Honour of Carol Harlow* (Oxford: Oxford University Press).

Barnett, Michael and Martha Finnemore (2004) *Rules for the World: International Organizations in Global Politics* (Ithaca, NY: Cornell University Press).

Barnett, Tony and Alan Whiteside (2002) *AIDS in the Twenty-First Century: Disease and Globalization* (Basingstoke: Palgrave Macmillan).

Barnier, Michel (2006) *For a European Civil Protection Force: Europe Aid*, 9 May 2006 available from: http://www.ec.europa.eu/commission_barroso/president/pdf/rapport_barnier_en.pdf.

Bátora, Jozef (2005a) 'Does the European Union Transform the Institution of Diplomacy?', *Journal of European Public Policy* 12(1): 44–66.

_____ (2005b) 'Public Diplomacy in Small and Medium-Sized States: Norway and Canada', CDSP Working Paper No. 97 (Clingendael: Netherlands Institute of International Relations).

Bátora, Jozef and Hocking, Brian (2007) 'Bilateral Diplomacy in the European Union: Towards "Post-Modern" Patterns?', ECPR/SGIR 6th Pan-European Conference: Turin 12–15 September 2007

BBC News (2004) 'Spain Proposes Cultural Alliance', 22 September, available from http://news.bbc.co.uk/2/hi/europe/3679336.stm.

_____ (2005) 'The Net and Politicians Don't Mix', 16 November, available from http://news.bbc.co.uk/2/hi/technology/4438664.stm.

_____ (2006) 'OIC Denounces Cartoons Violence', available from http://news.bbc.co.uk/2/hi/south_asia/4736854.stm.

Beetham, David and Lord, Christopher (1998) *Legitimacy in the European Union* (London: Addison Wesley Longman).

Benedetti, Fanny and John L. Washburn (1999) 'Drafting the International Criminal Court Treaty: Two Years to Rome and an Afterword on the Rome Diplomatic Conference', *Global Governance* 5(1): 1–38.

Bennis, Phyllis, John Cavanagh, and Sarah Anderson (2003) 'IPS Releases Report on U.S. Arm-twisting Over Iraq War', Institute for Policy Studies, 26 February, available from http://www.ips-dc.org/iraq/coerced.htm.

Berman, Paul (2005) *Power and the Idealists, or the Passion of Joschka Fischer and Its Aftermath* (Brooklyn, NY: Soft Skull Press).

Bernal-Meza, Raúl (2006) *América Latina en el mundo: el pensamiento latinoamericano y la teoría de las relaciones internacionales* (Buenos Aires: Grupo Editor Latinoamericano).

Berridge, G.R. (2005) *Diplomacy: Theory and Practice* (New York: Palgrave).

Berridge, G.R. and Alan James (2001) *A Dictionary of Diplomacy* (Hampshire, UK: Palgrave).

Bhagwati, Jagdish (2004) 'Don't Cry for Cancun', *Foreign Affairs* 83(1): 52–63.

Bicchi, Federica (2006) '"Our Size Fits All": Normative Power Europe and the Mediterranean', *Journal of European Public Policy* 13(2): 286–303.

Bob, Clifford (2005) *The Marketing of Rebellion: Insurgents, Media, and International Activism* (Cambridge: Cambridge University Press).

Böge, Volker, Christopher Fitzpatrick, Willem Jaspers, and Wolf-Christian Paes (2006) 'Who's Minding the Store? The Business of Private, Public and Civil Actors in Zones of Conflict', Brief No. 32 (Bonn: Bonn International Center for Conversion).

Boin, Arjen, Magnus Ekengren, and Mark Rhinhard (2006) 'The Commission and Crisis Management', in David Spence, ed., *The European Commission*, 3rd edn (London: John Harper Publishing).

Bollier, David (2003) *The Rise of Netpolitik: How the Internet is Changing International Politics and Diplomacy*, Report of the Eleventh Aspen Institute Roundtable on Information Technology, Washington, DC, available from http://www.carleton.ca/cifp/docs/netpolitik.pdf.

Bonard, Paul (1999) *Modes of Action Used by Humanitarian Players: Criteria for Operational Complementarity* (Geneva: ICRC), available from http://www.icrc.org/WEB/ENG/siteeng0.nsf/htmlall/p0722?OpenDocument&style=Custo_Final.4&View=defaultBody2.

Bonel, R. (2000) 'HIV/AIDS and Economic Growth: A Global Perspective', *The South African Journal of Economics* 68(5): 820–855.

Brawley, Mark R. and Pierre Martin (2001) *Alliance Politics, Kosovo, and NATO's War: Allied Force or Forced Allies* (New York: Palgrave).

Brok, Elmar (2008) 'Parliamentary Control over European Security Policy', in D. Spence and P. Fluri eds, *The EU and Security Sector Reform* (London: John Harper).

Brower, Jennifer and Peter Chalk (2003) *The Global Threat of New and Reemerging Infectious Diseases: Reconciling U.S. National Security and Public Health Policy* (Santa Monica, CA: RAND).

Bruter, Michael (2005) *Citizens of Europe? The Emergence of a Mass European Identity* (Basingstoke: Palgrave).

Buch-Andersen, T. (2006) *Denmark Row: The Power of Cartoons*, available from http://news.bbc.co.uk/2/hi/europe/5392786.stm.

Building the Information Society: A Global Challenge in the New Millennium (2003) Non-paper of the President of the WSIS PrepCom on the Declaration of Principles, 5 November, available from http://www.itu.int/wsis/docs/pc3/president-non-paper/president_non_paper.pdf.

Bull, B. and D. McNeill, eds (2006) *Development Issues in Global Governance: Market Multilateralism and Private-Public Partnerships* (London: Routledge).

Bull, Hedley (1977) *The Anarchical Society: A Study of Order in World Politics* (London: Macmillan).

Bulmer, Simon and Martin Burch (1998) 'Organizing for Europe: Whitehall, the British State and European Union', *Public Administration* 76(4): 601–628.

Bunker, Ellsworth (1983) 'Introduction', in Martin F. Herz, ed., *The Modern Ambassador: The Challenge and the Search* (Washington, DC: Institute for the Study of Diplomacy).

Burger, Julian (1996) 'The United Nations Draft Declaration on the Rights of Indigenous Peoples', *St. Thomas Law Review* 9: 209–229.

Burt, Richard and Olin Robinson (1999) 'Diplomacy in the Information Age', Discussion Paper No. 58 (Leicester: Leicester Diplomatic Studies Programme).

Burt, Tim (1997) 'US Intransigence Hits Hopes of Treaty Banning Land Mines', *Financial Times*, 12 September, 4.

Bush, George W. (2005) 'President Discusses War on Terror at National Endowment for Democracy', News Release, 6 October, Washington, DC, available from http://www. whitehouse.gov/news/releases/2003/11/20031106-2.html

Caballero-Anthony, Mely (2005) 'Regional Security in Southeast Asia: Beyond the ASEAN Way', ISEAS, Singapore.

de Callières, Monsieur (1963) *On the Manner of Negotiating with Princes* (Notre Dame, IN: University of Notre Dame Press).

Cameron, Maxwell A. (1998) 'Democratization of Foreign Policy: The Ottawa Process as a Model', *Canadian Foreign Policy* 5(3): 147–165.

Caporaso, James A. (2000) 'Changes in the Westphalian Order: Territory, Public Authority, and Sovereignty', *International Studies Review* 2(2): 1–28.

Carbonnier, Gilles and Marie-Servane Desjonquères (2002) 'Corporate Responsibility – What Does It Mean for Humanitarian Action?', *The Magazine of the Red Cross and Red Crescent Movement*, available from http://www.redcross.int/EN/mag/magazine2002_3/corporate_responsability.html.

Carlsson, I. et al. (1995) *Our Global Neighbourhood* (Oxford: Oxford University Press).

Carothers, Thomas (2006) *Promoting the Rule of Law Abroad: In Search of Knowledge* (Washington, DC: Carnegie Endowment for International Peace).

Castells, Manuel (1996a) 'The Information Age', in *The Rise of the Network Society*, Vol. 1 (London: Blackwell).

_____ (1996b) *The Rise of the Network Society*, Vol. 1 of *The Information Age: Economy, Society, and Culture* (Malden: Blackwell Publishers).

_____ (1998) *End of Millennium*, Vol. 3 of *The Information Age: Economy, Society, and Culture* (Malden: Blackwell Publishers).

Cerny, P.G. (1993) 'Plurilateralism: Structural Differentiation and Functional Conflict in the Post-Cold War World Order', *Millennium* 22(1): 27–51.

Chambers, Simone (1995) 'Discourse and Democratic Practices', in Stephen K. White, ed., *The Cambridge Companion to Habermas* (Cambridge, UK: Cambridge University Press).

Clark, Ian (1999) *Globalization and International Relations Theory* (Oxford: Oxford University Press).

_____ (2005) *Legitimacy in International Society* (Oxford: Oxford University Press).

Clark, Wesley K. (2001) *Waging Modern War* (New York: Public Affairs).

Clarke, John N. (2004) 'Conclusion: Directions and Processes of Global Governance', in John N. Clarke and Geoffrey R. Edwards, eds, *Global Governance in the Twenty-First Century* (New York: Palgrave).

CNN (2002) 'Bush: Join "coalition of willing"', *CNN.com/World*, 20 November, available from http://edition.cnn.com/2002/WORLD/europe/11/20/prague.bush.nato/.

Cohen, D. (1998a) 'Poverty and HIV/AIDS in Sub-Saharan Africa', Issues Paper No. 27 (New York, NY: UNDP).

_____ (1998b) 'The HIV Epidemic and Sustainable Human Development', Issues Paper No. 29 (New York, NY: UNDP).

Cohen, Raymond (2001) 'The Great Tradition: The Spread of Diplomacy in the Ancient World', *Diplomacy and Statecraft* 12(1): 23–38.

Cohen, Stephen (2001) *India: Emerging Power* (Washington, DC: Brookings Institution).

Cohen, Y. (1986) *Media Diplomacy: The Foreign Office in the Mass Communication Age* (London: Frank Cass).

Commission for Africa (2005) *Our Common Interest: Report of the Commission for Africa,* 11 March, London.

Commission of the European Communities (2003) 'The European Union and the United Nations: The choice of multilateralism', 9 October, Brussels, COM: 526 Final.

_____ (2005a) 'Communication from the Commission to the Council and the European Parliament on Combating HIV/AIDS within the European Union and in the Neighbouring Countries 2006–2009', 15 December, Brussels , COM: 654 Final.

_____ (2005b) 'Europe 2010: A Partnership for European Renewal, Solidarity and Security', *Strategic Objectives 2005–2009*, 26 January, Brussels, COM: 12 Final.

Community Currencies (2006) available from http://www.ratical.org/many_worlds/cc/.

Cooper, Andrew F. (1997) 'Beyond Representation', *International Journal* 53(1): 173–178.

_____ (2004) *Tests of Global Governance: Canadian Diplomacy and United Nations World Conferences* (Tokyo: United Nations University Press).

_____ (2007) *Celebrity Diplomacy* (Boulder, CO: Paradigm Publishers).

Cooper, Andrew F. and Brian Hocking (2000) 'Governments, Non-Governmental Organizations and the Re-calibration of Diplomacy', *Global Society* 14(3): 361–367.

Cooper, Andrew F. and Thomas Legler (2006) *Intervention without Intervening? The OAS Defense and Promotion of Democracy in the Americas* (New York: Palgrave).

Cooper, Andrew F., Christopher W. Hughes, and Philippe de Lombaerde, eds (2007) *Regionalisation and Global Governance: The Taming of Globalisation?* (London: Routledge).

Cooper, Andrew F., John English, and Ramesh Thakur, eds (2002) *Enhancing Global Governance: Towards a New Diplomacy?* (Tokyo: United Nations University Press).

Cooper, Jeffrey R. (2005) *Curing Analytic Pathologies: Pathways to Improved Intelligence Analysis,* Center for the Study of Intelligence, available from https://www.cia.gov/csi/books/curing_analytic_pathologies_public/analytic_pathologies_report.pdf.

Cooper, Robert (2003) *The Breaking of Nations: Order and Chaos in the Twenty-First Century* (New York: Atlantic Press).

Copenhagen Criteria (1993), available from http://europa.eu/scadplus/glossary/accession_criteria_copenhague_en.htm.

Council of Europe (2001) 'Convention on Cybercrime', 23 November, available from http://conventions.coe.int/Treaty/EN/Treaties/Html/185.htm.

Council of Ministers (2005) Conclusions of the General Affairs and External Relations Council, available from http://www.eu2005.lu/en/actualites/conseil/2005/05/23cagre/index.html.

CSCAP (1993) *CSCAP Charter, Article II*, 13 December, available from http://www.cscap.org/charter.htm.

Cosbey A. et al. (2004) *The Rush to Regionalism* (Winnipeg: International Institute for Sustainable Development).

Cox, Robert W. (1996) *Approaches to World Order* (Cambridge: Cambridge University Press).

_____ (1997) 'An Alternative Approach to Multilateralism for the Twenty-First Century', *Global Governance* 3(1): 103–116.

CSGR (2007) CSGR Globalisation Index, available from http://www.csgr.org.

Cuddington, J. and J. Hancock (1994) 'Assessing the Impact of AIDS on the Growth Path of the Malawian Economy', *Journal of Development Economics* 43: 363–368.

Cukier, Kenneth Neil (2005a) 'Who Will Control the Internet?', *Foreign Affairs* 84(6): 7–13.

_____ (2005b) 'WSIS Wars: An Analysis of the Politicization of the Internet', in Daniel Stauffacher and Wolfgang Kleinwächter, eds, *The World Summit on the Information Society: Moving from the Past into the Future* (New York: United Nations ICT Task Force).

Davidson, William D. and Joseph V. Montville (1981) 'Foreign Policy According to Freud', *Foreign Policy* 45: 145–157.

Davis, Megan (2002) 'The United Nations Draft Declaration 2002', *Indigenous Law Bulletin* 6. 5: 16.

_____ (2005) 'Outwitted and Outplayed: Indigenous Internationalism and the United Nations', *Indigenous Law Bulletin* 6: 4–7.

Davison, W. Phillips (1976) 'Mass Communication and Diplomacy', in James N. Rosenau, K.W. Thompson and G. Boyd, eds, *World Politics: An Introduction* (New York: The Free Press).

Defense Science Board (2001) *Report of the Defense Science Board Task Force on Managed Information Dissemination* (Washington, DC: US Department of Defense).

Der Derian, James (1987) *On Diplomacy: A Genealogy of Western Estrangement* (Oxford: Blackwell).

Devji, Faisal (2005) *Landscapes of the Jihad: Militancy, Morality, and Modernity* (Ithaca, NY: Cornell University Press).

Dickie, John (2004) *The New Mandarins: How British Foreign Policy Works* (London: I.B. Tauris).

Donovan, Jeffrey (2002) 'NATO: Transcript of RFE/RL's Exclusive Interview with US President Bush', *Radio Free Europe/Radio Liberty*, 18 November, available from http://www.rferl.org/features/2002/11/19112002091308.asp.

Doxey, Margaret (1995) "Something Old, Something New': The Politics of Recognition in Post-Cold-War Europe', *Diplomacy and Statecraft* 6(2): 303–322.

Drinkwater, Derek (2005) *Sir Harold Nicolson and International Relations: The Practitioner as Theorist* (Oxford: Oxford University Press).

Duffield, Mark (2001) *Global Governance and the New Wars* (London: Zed Press).

Duke, Simon W. (2002) 'Preparing for European Diplomacy?', *Journal of Common Market Studies* 40(5): 849–870.

Dunn, David H. (1996) *Diplomacy at the Highest Level: The Evolution of International Summitry* (Basingstoke: Macmillan).

Economic Commission for Latin America and the Caribbean (2002) *Globalización y desarrollo* (Santiago: ECLAC).

The Economist (1995) 'Who 'Ya Gonna Call?' 5 August.

Ekengren, M. (2007) 'The Internal-External Security Interface', in P. Fluri and D. Spence, eds, *The EU and Security Sector Reform* (London: John Harper).

Emerson, Michael, Senem Aydin, and Gergana Noutcheva (2005) 'The Reluctant Debutante: The European Union as Promoter of Democracy in its Neighbourhood', Working Paper No. 223, Centre for European Policy Studies (CEPS), Brussels, Belgium.

English, John (2006) *Citizen of the World: The Life of Pierre Elliott Trudeau. Volume One: 1919–1968* (Toronto: Alfred A. Knopf Canada).

English, John, Andrew F. Cooper, and Ramesh Thakur, eds (2002) *Enhancing Global Governance: Towards a New Diplomacy* (Tokyo: United Nations University Press).

Etzioni, Amitai (2007) 'The Community Deficit', *Journal of Common Market Studies* 45(1): 23–42.

Europa (2007) 'European Union at the United Nations', www.europa-eu-un.org, accessed 12 November, 2007.

European Commission (2001a), 'European Governance: A White Paper', COM(2001) 428, 25 July 2001, Brussels, Belgium.

_____ (2001b) 'Building an Effective Partnership with the UN in the Field of Development and Humanitarian Affairs', COM (2001) 231 Final, 2 May 2001, Brussels, Belgium.

_____ (2002) 'A Project for the European Union', COM (2002) 247 Final, 22 May 2002, Brussels, Belgium.

_____ (2003) 'The European Union: the Choice of Multilateralism', COM(2003) 526 Final, 10 September 2003, Brussels, Belgium.

_____ (2004a) *The European Union Confronts HIV/AIDS, Malaria and Tuberculosis: A Comprehensive Strategy for the New Millennium,* available from, http://ec.europa.eu/development/body/publications/docs/HIVAIDS-millenium_en.pdf.

_____ (2004b) *Taking Europe to the World: 50 Years of the European Commission's External Service* (Luxembourg: Office for Official Publications of the European Communities)

_____ (2005) 'The 2005 UN Summit – Addressing the Global Challenges and Making a Success of the Reformed UN', COM (2005) 259 Final, 15 June, Brussels, Belgium.

_____ (2006a) 'EU Concept for Support to Disarmament, Demobilisation and Reintegration (DDR)', The DDR Communication, Approved by the European Commission on 14 December and by the Council of the European Union on 11 December.

_____ (2006b) 'Europe in the World – Some Practical Proposals for Greater Coherence, Effectiveness and Visibility', COM(2006) 278 Final, 7 June 2006, Brussels, Belgium.

European Communities (2007) 'Working for Peace, Security and Stability', *Europe in the World* (Luxembourg: Office for Official Publications of the European Communities).

European Security Strategy (2003) 'A Secure Europe in a Better World', Council of Ministers, 12 December.

European Voice (2006) 'MEPs Vent Fury at Finland over Censored Documents', 19–25 October.

Evans, Philip (2006) 'Perspectives: From Reciprocity to Reputation', *The Boston Consulting Group*, 6 April, available from http://www.bcg.com/publications/files/425_Reciprocity_to_Reputation_Apr06.pdf.

Falk, R.A. (2000) *Human Rights Horizons* (New York: Routledge).

Farrell, M. et al., eds (2005) *Global Politics of Regionalism: Theory and Practice* (London: Pluto).

Favez, Jean-Claude (1999) *The Red Cross and the Holocaust* (Cambridge: Cambridge University Press).

Ferguson, Niall (2004) *Colossus: The Price of America's Empire* (New York: Penguin Press).

Ferrero-Waldner, Benita (2006) 'The European Union: A Global Power?', speech delivered for the George Bush Presidential Library Foundation and Texas A&M University EU Centre of Excellence, 25 September,College Station, Texas.

_____ (2007) 'The Future of the European Union: Managing Globalisation', speech held at Bucerius Summer School, 31 August, Hamburg.

Finn, Edward (2000) 'International Relations in a Changing World: A New Diplomacy?', *Perceptions* 5(2): 144–145.

Florini, Ann M. (2000) *The Third Force: The Rise of Transnational Civil Society* (Washington, DC: Carnegie Endowment for International Peace).

Forsythe, David P. (2005) *The Humanitarians: The International Committee of the Red Cross* (Cambridge: Cambridge University Press).

Fouts, Joshua S. (2005) 'Rethinking Public Diplomacy for the 21st Century: A Toolbox for Engaging the Hearts and Minds of the Open Source Generation', paper presented at the American Political Science Association Conference on International Communication and Conflict, 31 August, Washington, DC, available from http://ics.leedsac.uk/papers/pmt/exhibits/2467/fouts.pdf.

Fraerman, Alicia (2004) 'Spanish Prime Minister Advocates an Alliance for Peace', InterPress Third World News Agency, 23 September, available from http://www.chasque.apc.org/ips_eng/notas/2004/09/23/10:40:40.html.

Friedman, Thomas (2005) *The World Is Flat: A Short History of the Globalized World in the Twenty-First Century* (London: Allen Lane).

Friedrichs, J. (2001) 'The Meaning of New Medievalism', *European Journal of International Relations* 7(4): 475–502.

Fry, E.H. (2006) 'Substate Governance', in R. Robertson and J.A. Scholte, eds, *Encyclopedia of Globalization* (London: Routledge).

Fukuyama, Francis (2006) *America at the Crossroads: Democracy, Power, and the Neoconservative Legacy* (New Haven, CT: Yale University Press).

Fulton, Barry (1998) *Reinventing Diplomacy in the Information Age*, Report of the CSIS Advisory Panel on Diplomacy in the Information Age (Washington, DC: Center for Strategic and International Studies).

_____ (2001) 'Net Diplomacy', *IMP: The Magazine on Information Impacts*; republished in 2002 by the US Institute of Peace, available from http://www.usip.org/virtualdiplomacy/publications/ reports/14.html.

_____ (2007) 'Geo-Social Mapping of the International Communications Environment or Why Abdul Isn't Listening', *The Hague Journal of Diplomacy* 2: 307–315.

Gilboa, Eytan (2001) 'Diplomacy in the Media Age: Three Models of Uses and Effects', *Diplomacy and Statecraft* 12(2): 1–28.

Gilson, J. (2002) *Asia Meets Europe* (Cheltenham: Elgar).

Goldsmith, Jack L. (1998) 'Against Cyberanarchy', *University of Chicago Law Review* 65: 1199–1216.

Gotlieb, Allan (1991) *'I'll Be with You in a Minute, Mr. Ambassador:' The Education of a Canadian Diplomat in Washington* (Toronto: University of Toronto Press).

de Grazia, A. (1968) 'Representation: Theory', in D.L. Sills, ed., *International Encyclopaedia of the Social Sciences*, Vol. 13 (New York: Macmillan and Free Press).

Greener, R., K. Jefferis, and H. Siphambe (2000) 'The Impact of HIV/AIDS on Poverty and Inequality in Botswana', *The South African Journal of Economics* 68(5): 888–915.

Gregory, Bruce (2005) 'Public Diplomacy and Strategic Communication: Cultures, Firewalls, and Imported Norms', paper presented at the American Political Science Association Conference on International Communication and Conflict, 31 August, Washington, DC, available from http://www.georgetown.edu/ cct/apsa/papers/gregory.pdf

Gruber, Karl (1983) 'Common Denominators of Good Ambassadors', in Martin F. Herz, ed., *The Modern Ambassador: The Challenge and the Search* (Washington, DC: Institute for the Study of Diplomacy).

Gudmundsson, Hjörtur (2006) 'Danish Imams Propose to End Cartoon Dispute', *The Brussels Journal*, available from http://www.brusselsjournal.com/node/698.

Guéhenno, Jean-Marie (1995) *The End of the Nation-State* (Minneapolis: University of Minnesota Press).

Haas, Peter M. (1992) 'Introduction: Epistemic Communities and International Policy Coordination', *International Organization* 46(1): 1–35.

Haass, R.N. (1997) *The Reluctant Sheriff: The United States After the Cold War* (New York: Council on Foreign Relations).

_____ (2003) 'Existing Rights, Evolving Responsibilities', Remarks by Ambassador Richard Haass, Director of the State Department's Policy Planning Staff, to the School of Foreign Service and the Mortara Centre for International Studies at Georgetown University, 14 January, Washington DC.

Habermas, Jurgen (1991) *The Structural Transformation of the Public Sphere: An Inquiry into a Category of Bourgeois Society,* translated byThomas Berger (Cambridge, MA: MIT Press [originally published, 1962]).

_____ (2006) *The Divided West* (Cambridge, UK: Polity Press [originally published in 2004, edited and translated by Ciaran Cronin]).

Hall, R. B. and T.J. Biersteker, eds (2003) *The Emergence of Private Authority in Global Governance* (Cambridge: Cambridge University Press).

Halstead, John G.H. (1983) 'Today's Ambassador', in Martin F. Herz, ed., *The Modern Ambassador: The Challenge and the Search* (Washington, DC: Institute for the Study of Diplomacy).

Hamill, James and Donna Lee (2001) 'South African Diplomacy in the Post-Apartheid Era: An Emergent Middle Power?', *International Relations* 15(4): 33–60.

Hamilton, Keith and Richard Langhorne (1995) *The Practice of Diplomacy: Its Evolution, Theory and Administration* (London and New York: Routledge).

Hänggi, H. et al. (2005) *Interregionalism and International Relations* (London: Routledge).

Hänggi, H. and Winkler, T., eds (2003) *Challenges of Security Sector Governance* (Münster: Lit Verlag).

Hardt, Michael and Antonio Negri (2000) *Empire* (Cambridge, MA: Harvard University Press).

Harroff-Tavel, Marion (2003) 'Do Wars Ever End? The Work of the ICRC When the Guns Fall Silent', *International Review of the Red Cross* 851: 465–496, available from http://www.icrc.org/Web/eng/siteeng0.nsf/htmlall/5SQHC8/$File/irrc_851_Haroff-Tavel.pdf.

Havemann, Paul (2001) 'Participation Deficit: Globalization, Governance and Indigenous Peoples', *Balayi* 3: 9–36.

Haworth, Nigel, Steve Hughes, and Rorden Wilkinson (2005) 'The International Labour Standards Regime: A Case Study in Global Regulation', *Environment and Planning A* 37(1): 1939–1953.

Hecht, R., O. Adeyi, and I. Semini (2002) 'Making AIDS Part of the Global Development Agenda', *Finance and Development* 39(1): 36–39.

Heine, Jorge (2005a) 'All the Truth but Only Some Justice? Dilemmas of Dealing with the Past in New Democracies', Sixth Oliver Tambo Lecture, 22 March, Delhi University.

_____ (2005b) 'China, Chile and Free Trade Agreements', *The Hindu*, 22 November, available from http://www.hindu.com/2005/11/22/stories/2005112203881000.htm.

_____ (2006a) 'Between a Rock and a Hard Place: Latin America and Multilateralism after 9/11', in Edward Newman, Ramesh Thakur, and John Tirman, eds, *Multilateralism under Challenge? Power, International Order and Structural Change* (Tokyo: United Nations University Press).

_____ (2006b) *On the Manner of Practising the New Diplomacy*, Working Paper No. 11 (Waterloo, Ontario: Centre for International Governance Innovation, October 2006).

Held, D. et al. (1999) *Global Transformations: Politics, Economics and Culture* (Cambridge: Polity).

Henrikson, Alan (1997) 'Diplomacy for the 21st Century: "Re-Crafting the Old Guild"', Wilton Park Occasional Paper 1.

Herman, Michael (1998) 'Diplomacy and Intelligence', *Diplomacy and Statecraft* 9(2): 1–22.

Hermann, Charles F., James N. Rosenau, and Charles W. Kegley (1987) *New Directions in the Study of Foreign Policy* (Boston: Allen & Unwin).

Hermet, G. et al. (2005) *La gouvernance. Un concept et ses applications* (Paris: Karthala).

Hettne, B. et al., eds (1999) *Globalism and the New Regionalism* (Basingstoke: Macmillan).

Hewison, K. (1999) *Localism in Thailand: A Study of Globalization and Its Discontents*, Working Paper No. 39/99 (Coventry: ESRC/Warwick Centre for the Study of Globalisation and Regionalisation).

Hill, Christopher (1991) 'Diplomacy and the Modern State', in C. Navari, ed., *The Condition of States* (Milton Keynes and Philadelphia: Open University Press).

_____ (2003) 'A Foreign Minister without a Foreign Ministry – or with Too Many?', *CFSP Forum*, 1(1): 1.

_____ (2004) 'Renationalising or Regrouping? EU Foreign Policy Since 11 September 2001', *Journal of Common Market Studies* 42(1): 143–163.

Hill, Christopher and William Wallace (1979) 'Diplomatic Trends in the European Community', *International Affairs* 55(1): 47–66.

Hines, C. (2000) *Localization: A Global Manifesto* (London: Earthscan).

Hirst, P. and G. F. Thompson (1996) *Globalization in Question: The International Economy and the Possibilities of Governance* (Cambridge: Polity).

Hocking, Brian (1993a) *Foreign Relations and Federal States* (London: Leicester University Press).

_____ (1993b) *Localizing Foreign Policy: Non-Central Governments and Multilayered Diplomacy* (Basingstoke: Macmillan).

_____ (1997) 'The End(s) of Diplomacy', *International Journal* 53(1): 169–172.

_____ (1999a) 'Catalytic Diplomacy: Beyond "Newness" and "Decline"', in Jan Melissen, ed., *Innovation in Diplomatic Practice* (London: Macmillan).

_____ (1999b) *Foreign Ministries: Change and Adaptation* (London: Macmillan).

_____ (2002a) 'Conclusion', in Brian Hocking and David Spence, eds, *Foreign Ministries in the European Union: Integrating Diplomats* (Houndmills: Palgrave Macmillan).

_____ (2002b) 'Diplomacy: New Agendas and Changing Strategies', in Barry Fulton, ed., *Netdiplomacy I, Beyond Foreign Ministries*, Washington, DC: US Institute of Peace, Virtual Diplomacy Series, available from http://www.usip.org/virtualdiplomacy/ publications/ reports/14b.html.

_____ (2004a) 'Changing the Terms of Trade Policy Making: From the "Club" to the Multistakeholder Model', *World Trade Review* 3(1): 3–26.

_____ (2004b) 'Diplomacy', in W. Carlsnaes, H. Sjursen, and B. White, *Contemporary European Foreign Policy* (London: Sage).

_____ (2005a) 'Gatekeepers and Boundary Spanners: Thinking about Foreign Ministries in the European Union', in Brian Hocking and David Spence eds, *Foreign Ministries in the European Union: Integrating Diplomats* (London: Palgrave).

_____ (2005b) 'Multistakeholder Diplomacy: Foundations, Forms, Functions and frustrations', paper presented at the International Conference on Multistakeholder Diplomacy, 11–13, February, Malta.

Hocking, Brian and Spence, David (2005) *Foreign Ministries in the European Union: Integrating Diplomats* (Houndmills: Palgrave).

Hoffman, John (2003) 'Reconstructing Diplomacy', *British Journal of Politics and International Relations* 5(4): 525–542.

Hoffman, Stanley (2003) 'The High and the Mighty: Bush's National Security Strategy and the New American Hubris', *The American Prospect* 13(24): 28–31.

Hofstede, G. (1991) *Cultures and Organizations: Software of the Mind* (London: McGraw-Hill).

Holland, M. ed. (2004) *Common Foreign and Security Policy: the first decade*, 2nd edn (London: Continuum).

Hughes, Steve (2002) 'Coming in from the Cold: Labour, the ILO and the International Labour Standards Regime', in Rorden Wilkinson and Steve Hughes, eds, *Global Governance: Critical Perspectives* (London: Routledge).

Hurd, Ian (1999) 'Legitimacy and Authority in International Politics', *International Organization* 53:2 (Spring).

Ignatieff, Michael (2001) *Human Rights as Politics and Idolatry*, edited and introduced by Amy Gutmann (Princeton, NJ: Princeton University Press).

Ikenberry, G. John (2002) 'America's Imperial Ambition', *Foreign Affairs* 81(5): 44–60.

ILO (2004a) *A Fair Globalization: Creating Opportunities for All* (Geneva: World Commission on the Social Dimension of Globalization, ILO).

_____ (2004b) *HIV/AIDS and Work: Global Estimates, Impact and Response* (Geneva: ILO Programme on HIV/AIDS and the World of Work).

_____ (2006) *HIV/AIDS and Work in a Globalizing World* (Geneva: ILO Global Programme on HIV/AIDS and the World of Work).

Insulza, José Miguel (1998) *Ensayos sobre política exterior de Chile* (Santiago: Editorial Los Andes).

International Centre for Security Analysis (ICSA) (1999) *Coalitions with the US: Maximising The UK's Influence In The Formation And Conduct Of Future Coalition Operations*, available from http://www.kcl.ac.uk/orgs/icsa/Projects/coalition.html.

International Committee of the Red Cross (ICRC) (1995) *Statutes of the International Red Cross and Red Crescent Movement*, available from http://www.icrc.org/Web/eng/siteeng0.nsf/htmlall/statutes-movement-220506/$File/Mvt-Statutes-ENGLISH.pdf.

_____ (1997) 'Preamble', *Agreement on the Organization of the International Activities of the Components of the International Red Cross and Red Crescent Movement*, available from http://www.icrc.org/web/eng/siteeng0.nsf/html/57JP4Y.

_____ (1999) 'Humanitarian Diplomacy', *ICRC Annual Report 1999: Operational Activities*, available from http://www.icrc.org/Web/Eng/siteeng0.nsf/iwpList171/DD A65216C42CA572C1256B66005EB2A1#10.

_____ (2004) *What is the ICRC's Position on the Reported Abuse of Iraqi Prisoners by US and UK Forces?*, available from http://www.icrc.org/Web/Eng/siteeng0.nsf/iwpList53 0/40A0CDE4C698440BC1256E8A004B42AA.

_____ (2005a) *Annual Report 2004*, available from http://www.icrc.org/Web/Eng/siteeng0.nsf/htmlall/section_annual_report_2004?OpenDocument.

_____ (2005b) *Being Hard on Yourself*, available from http://www.icrc.org/Web/Eng/siteeng0.nsf/iwpList109/3A6D1E285BAEC107C1257053004AE25D.

_____ (2006a) *Cluster Munitions: ICRC Calls for Urgent International Action*, ICRC Press Release 06/120, available from http://www.icrc.org/web/eng/siteeng0.nsf/html/ihl-weapon-news-061106!OpenDocument.

_____ (2006b) *For the Private Sector: Humanitarian Responsibilities in War-Prone Areas*, available from http://www.icrc.org/Web/Eng/siteeng0.nsf/html/private_sector_responsibility?OpenDocument.

International Committee of the Red Cross (ICRC) (2006c) *International Red Cross and Red Crescent Movement*, available from http://www.icrc.org/Web/eng/siteeng0.nsf/html/movement.

_____ (2006d) *Israel and Lebanon: ICRC Gravely Concerned about the Plight of Civilians Caught up in Hostilities in Lebanon and Israel*, ICRC Press Release 06/78, available from http://www.icrc.org/Web/eng/siteeng0.nsf/html/lebanon-news-130706.

_____ (2006e) *US Detention Related to the Events of 11 September 2001 and Its Aftermath – the Role of the ICRC*, available from http://www.icrc.org/Web/Eng/siteeng0.nsf/html/usa-detention-update-121205?OpenDocument.

International Council of AIDS Service Organizations (2006) *Community Monitoring and Evaluation: Implementation of the UNGASS Declaration of Commitment on HIV/AIDS* (Toronto: ICASO).

Iorns, Catherine J. (1996) 'Indigenous Peoples and Self Determination: Challenging State Sovereignty', *Case Western Reserve Journal of International Law* 24: 199–348.

Jackson, Sir Geoffrey (1981) *Concorde Diplomacy: The Ambassador's Role in the World Today* (London: Hamish Hamilton).

Jacobs, Francis, Richard Corbett, and Michael Shackleton (2007) *The European Parliament* (London: John Harper).

James, Alan (1980) 'Diplomacy and International Society', *International Relations* 6(6): 931–948.

James, Oliver (2002) *They F*** You Up: How to Survive Family Life* (London: Bloomsbury).

Jara, Eduardo (2002) *La función diplomática* (Santiago: RIL).

Jawara, Fatoumata and Aileen Kwa (2003) *Behind the Scenes at the WTO: the Real World of International Trade Negotiations* (London: Zed Books).

Jenkins, Henry and David Thorburn (2003) 'Introduction: The Digital Revolution, the Informed Citizen, and the Culture of Democracy', in Jenkins and Thorburn, eds, *Democracy and New Media* (Cambridge, MA: The MIT Press).

Job, Brian L. (2002) 'Track II Diplomacy: Ideational Contribution to the Evolving Asia Security Order', in Muthiah Alagappa, ed., *Asian Security Order: Instrumental and Normative Features* (Stanford: Stanford University Press).

Johnson, Chalmers (2002) *Blowback; The Costs and Consequences of American Empire* (London: Time Warner).

Jönsson, Christer (1996) 'Diplomatic Signaling in the Television Age', *Harvard International Journal of Press/Politics* 1(3): 24–40.

_____ (2003) 'Governance in International Relations', in Jan Hallenberg, Bertil Nygren, and Alexa Robertson, eds, *Transitions: In Honour of Kjell Goldmann* (Stockholm: Political Science Department at Stockholm University).

Jönsson, Christer and Martin Hall (2005) *Essence of Diplomacy* (Houndmills: Palgrave Macmillan).

Jørgenson, K. E. and B. Rosamond (2002) 'Europe: Laboratory for a Global Polity?', in M. Ougaard and R. Higgott, eds, *Towards a Global Polity* (London: Routledge).

Juste, Carsten (2006) 'Honourable Fellow Citizens of the Muslim World', *Jyllands-Posten*, available from http://www.jp.dk/meninger/ncartikel:aid=3527646.

Kagan, Robert (2003) *Paradise and Power: America and Europe in the New World Order* (New York: Knopf).

Keane, J. (2003) *Global Civil Society?* (Cambridge: Cambridge University Press).

Keck, Margaret E. and Kathryn Sikkink (1998) *Activists Beyond Borders: Advocacy Networks in International Politics* (Ithaca, NY: Cornell University Press).

Keens-Soper, Maurice (2001) 'Callières', in G.R. Berridge, Maurice Keens-Soper, and T.G. Otte, eds, *Diplomatic Theory from Machiavelli to Kissinger* (Basingstoke: Palgrave).

Kennedy, David (2004) *The Dark Sides of Virtue: Reassessing International Humanitarianism* (Princeton, NJ: Princeton University Press).

Keohane, Robert (1988) 'International Institutions: Two Approaches', *International Studies Quarterly* 32: 379–396.

_____ (2002) *Power and Governance in a Partially Globalized World*, London: Routledge.

_____ (2006) 'The contingent legitimacy of multilateralism', in Edward Newman, Ramesh Thakur, and John Tirman, eds, *Multilateralism under Challenge? Power, International Order, and Structural Change* (Tokyo: United Nations University Press).

Keohane, Robert and Joseph S. Nye (2000) 'Introduction', in Joseph S. Nye and John D. Donahue, eds, *Governance in a Globalizing World* (Washington, DC: Brookings Institution Press).

_____ (2001) 'The Club Model of Multilateral Cooperation and the World Trade Organization: Problems of Democratic Legitimacy', *Working Paper* 4 (Cambridge, MA: John F. Kennedy School of Government).

Kepel, Gilles (2004) *The War for Muslim Minds: Islam and the West* (Cambridge, MA: Harvard University Press).

Kerr, Pauline (1994) 'The Security Dialogue in the Asia-Pacific', *Pacific Review* 7(4): 397–409.

Keukeleire, Stephan (2000) 'The European Union as a Diplomatic Actor', *Discussion Paper*, No. 71, Leicester Diplomatic Studies Programme (University of Leicester).

Khagram, Sanjeev, James V. Riker, and Kathryn Sikkink, eds (2002) *Restructuring World Politics: Transnational Social Movements, Networks, and Norms* (Minneapolis, MN: University of Minnesota Press).

Khan, Aamer A. (2006) 'Hidden Motives behind Cartoon Riots', *BBC News*, available from http://news.bbc.co.uk/go/pr/fr/-/2/hi/south_asia/4716762.stm.

Kingsbury, B. W and N. Krisch, eds (2006) 'Symposium on Global Governance and Global Administrative Law in the International Legal Order', *European Journal of International Law* 17: 1–278.

van Klaveren, Alberto (1998) 'Inserción internacional', in Eugenio Lahera and Cristián Toloza, eds, *Chile en los Noventa* (Santiago: Dolmen).

Kleinwächter, Wolfgang (2004) 'Beyond ICANN vs. ITU? How WSIS Tries to Enter the New Territory of Internet Governance', *International Communication Gazette* 66(3–4): 233–251.

Krähenbüehl, Pierre (2004a) *Humanitarian security: 'a matter of acceptance, perception, behaviour...'*, address given at the High-level Humanitarian Forum, 31 March, Geneva, available from http://www.icrc.org/Web/Eng/siteeng0.nsf/html/5XSGWE? OpenDocument.

_____ (2004b) 'The ICRC's Approach to Contemporary Security Challenges: a Future for Independent and Neutral Humanitarian Action', *International Review of the Red Cross* 855: 505–514, available from http://www.icrc.org/Web/eng/siteeng0.nsf/ htmlall/66CM82/$File/irrc_855_Krahenbuhl.pdf.

Krasner, Stephen D. (1999) *Sovereignty: Organized Hypocrisy* (Princeton, NJ: Princeton University Press).

Kurbalija, J. & E. Gelbstein (2005) *Internet Governance – Issues, Actors and Divides* (Malta: DiploFoundation).

Kurbalija, J. & V. Katrandjiev, ed. (2006) *Multistakeholder Diplomacy, Challenges and Opportunities* (Malta: DiploFoundation).

Kurlantzick, Joshua (2007) *Charm Offensive: How China's Soft Power is Transforming the World* (New Haven, CT: Yale University Press).

Langhorne, Richard (1998) 'History and the Evolution of Diplomacy', in Jovan Kurbalija, ed., *Modern Diplomacy* (Malta: Mediterranean Academy of Diplomatic Studies).

Lee, Donna (2001) 'Endgame at the Kennedy Round: A Case Study of Multilateral Economic Diplomacy', *Diplomacy & Statecraft* 12(3): 119–120.

Lee, Donna and David Hudson (2004) 'The Old and New Significance of Political Economy in Diplomacy', *Review of International Studies* 30(1):343–360.

Leonard, Mark, with Catherine Stead and Conrad Smewing (2002) *Public Diplomacy* (London: The Foreign Policy Centre).

Letter by the Muslim Representatives, 12 October 2005, available from http://www.filtrat. dk/grafik/Letterfromambassadors.pdf.

Lippmann, Walter (1997) *Public Opinion* (New York: Free Press Paperbacks [originally published in 1922]).

Lipschutz, Ronnie (2004) 'Global Civil Society and Global Governmentality: Or, the Search for Politics and the State amidst the Capillaries of Power', in Michael N. Barnett and Raymond Duvall, eds, *Power in Global Governance* (Cambridge: Cambridge University Press).

Lisk, Franklyn and Desmond Cohen (2005) 'Regional Responses to HIV/AIDS in Sub-Saharan Africa: A Global Public Goods Approach', paper presented at the Biennial Conference of the CSGR, University of Warwick, UK October.

Lombaerde, Philippe de (ed.) (2007) *Multilateralism, Regionalism and Bilateralism in Trade and Investment*, 2006 World Report on Regional Integration Series: United Nations University Series on Regionalism (Vol. 1).

Lord, Kristin M. (2005) 'What Academics (Should Have to) Say About Public Diplomacy', paper presented at the American Political Science Association Conference on International Communication and Conflict, Washington, DC, 31 August, available from http://www8.georgetown.edu/cct/apsa/papers/lord.doc.

Lowe, David (2003) 'Idea to Reality: NED at 20', *National Endowment for Democracy*, available from http://www.ned.org/about/nedhistory.html.

Mack, Andrew, et al. (2005) *Human Security Report 2005* (New York: Oxford University Press).

Macmullen, Andy (2002): 'Two Concepts of Governance in the European Union: the 2001 Commission White Paper', presented at the Political Studies Association Annual Conference, available from http://www.psa.ac.uk/journals/pdf/5/2002/macmullen.pdf.

Maggi, Claudio and Dirk Messner, eds (2002) *Gobernanza global: una mirada desde América Latina* (Caracas: Nueva Sociedad).

Mallaby, Sebastian (2002) 'The Reluctant Imperialist', *Foreign Affairs* 81(2): 2–7.

Mann, M. (1997) 'Has Globalization Ended the Rise and Rise of the Nation-State?', *Review of International Political Economy* 4(3): 472–496.

Manners, Ian (2002) 'Normative Power Europe: A Contradiction in Terms?', *Journal of Common Market Studies* 40(2): 235–58.

_____ (2006) 'Normative Power Europe Reconsidered: Beyond the Crossroads', *Journal of European Public Policy* 13(2): 182–99.

Mansfield, E.D. and H.V. Milner (2005) 'The New Wave of Regionalism', in P.F. Diehl, ed., *International Organizations in an Interdependent World*, 3rd edn (Boulder, CO: Rienner).

Mathews, Jessica (1997) 'Power Shift: The Age of Nonstate Actors', *Foreign Affairs* 76(1): 50–66.

Matlary, Janne Haaland (2006) 'When Soft Power Turns Hard: Is an EU Strategic Culture Possible?', *Security Dialogue* 37(1): 105–121.

Mattingly, Garrett (1937) 'The First Resident Embassies: Medieval Italian Origins of Modern Diplomacy', *Speculum* 12(4): 423–439.

_____ (1964) *Renaisssance Diplomacy* (Baltimore, MD: Penguin).

Mattli, W. (2001) 'Private Justice in a Global Economy: From Litigation to Arbitration', *International Organization* 55(4): 919–948.

Mazey, Sonia and Richardson, Jeremy (2006) 'The Commission and the Lobby', in D. Spence, ed., *The European Commission* (London: John Harper).

McCormick, John (2007) *The European Superpower* (London: Palgrave).

McLuhan, Marshall (1962) *The Gutenberg Galaxy: The Making of Typographic Man* (London: Routledge & Kegan Paul).

McPherson, M. (2002) 'HIV/AIDS, Human Capacity and Institutions: Sustaining Economic Growth', paper prepared for *USAID Biennial Conference on Strategies for Responding to HIV/AIDS*, Washington DC, February.

Médecins Sans Frontières/Doctors Without Borders (2007) *MSF: USA Homepage*, available from http://www.doctorswithoutborders.org/home.cfm.

Melissen, Jan (2003) 'Summit Diplomacy Coming of Age', *Discussion Papers in Diplomacy No. 86*, The Hague: Netherlands Institute of International Relations 'Clingendael'.

_____ (2005) *The New Public Diplomacy: Soft Power in International Relations* (Basingstoke: Palgrave Macmillan).

_____ (2006) 'Reflections on Public Diplomacy Today', speech at the Ministry of Foreign Affairs, Republic of Turkey, Ankara, 6 February, available from http://www.clingendael.nl/publications/2006/20060206_cdsp_online_melissen.pdf.

Meyer, Michael A. (1996) 'Public Advocacy – Why the Red Cross and the Red Crescent Should Look before It Leaps', *International Review of the Red Cross* 315: 614–626, available from http://www.icrc.org/web/eng/siteeng0.nsf/html/57JNCU.

Michel, Louis (2006) 'Gouvernance et Développement', Session Plénière Journées Européennes de Développement, Brussels, 15 Novembre 2006.

_____ (2007) 'Ce que l'Europe fit, l'Afrique va le faire'. Cérémonie de relance de la Communauté Economique des Pays des Grands Lacs. Bujumbura, le 17 avril.

Michelmann, Hans J. and Panayotis Soldatos (1990) *Federalism and International Relations: The Role of Subnational Units* (Oxford: Clarendon Press).

Ministry of Foreign Affairs of Denmark (2006a) 'Ambassador of Denmark Confirms his Country's Respect to Religion', Embassy of Denmark, 24, January Riyadh, available from http://www.drawings.um.dk/en.

_____ (2006b) 'Danish Churches Appeal', Embassy of Denmark, 10 February, Islamabad, available from http://www.ambislamabad.um.dk/en/menu/News/DanishChurch Appeals.htm.

_____ (2006c) 'Statement by the Danish Prime Minister Anders Fogh Rasmussen Regarding the Drawings of the Prophet Mohammad', Embassy of Denmark, 31 January, Riyadh, available from http://www.drawings.um.dk/en/menu/news/statementbythe danishprimeministerandersfoghrasmussenregardingthedrawingsoftheprophet mohammed.htm.

Mohan, C. Raja (2003) *Crossing the Rubicon: The Shaping of India's New Foreign Policy* (New Delhi: Penguin/Viking).

Moller, Kay (2001) 'ASEAN and the United States: For Want of Alternatives', in Jorn Dosch and Manfred Mols, eds, *International Relations in the Asia-Pacific: New Patterns of Power, Interest and Cooperation* (New York: Palgrave Macmillan).

Moorehead, Caroline (1998) *Dunant's Dream* (London: HarperCollins).

Moreno, Ismael (2001) *La diplomacia: aspectos teóricos y prácticos de su ejercicio profesional* (Mexico City: Fondo de Cultura Económica).

Morgan, Rhiannon (2004) 'Advancing Indigenous Rights at the United Nations: Strategic Framing and its Impact on the Normative Development of International Law', *Social & Legal Studies* 13(4): 481–500.

Morrison, Charles E. (2002) 'Track 1/Track 2 Symbiosis in Asia-Pacific Regionalism', *Pacific Review* 17(4): 547–565.

Muldoon, James P. Jr. (2004) *The Architecture of Global Governance: An Introduction to the Study of International Organizations* (Boulder, CO: Westview Press).

Muñoz, Heraldo (2005) *Una guerra solitaria: La historia secreta de EEUU en Irak, la polémica en la ONU y el papel de Chile* (Santiago: Random House Mondadori).

Murphy, Craig N. (1994) *International Organization and Industrial Change: Global Governance Since 1850* (Cambridge: Polity).

_____ (2000) 'Global Governance: Poorly Done and Poorly Understood', *International Affairs* 76(4): 789–804.

Naim, Moises (2003) 'An Indigenous World: How Native People Can Turn Globalization to their Advantage', *Foreign Policy* 139: 95–96.

Narlikar, Amrita (2003) *International Trade and Developing Countries: Bargaining Coalitions in the GATT and WTO* (London: Routledge).

_____ (2007) 'All's Fair in Love and Trade? Emerging Powers in the DDA Negotiations', in Donna Lee and Rorden Wilkinson, eds, *The WTO after Hong Kong: Progress in, and Prospects for, the Doha Development Agenda* (London: Routledge).

Narlikar, Amrita and Rorden Wilkinson (2004) 'Collapse at the WTO: A Cancun Post-Mortem', *Third World Quarterly* 25(3): 447–460.

National Committee on American Foreign Policy (2000) 'Toward an Effective Policy on Land Mines', *American Foreign Policy Interests* 22(1), available from http://www.ncafp.org/record/2000/feb00ftr.htm.

National Endowment for Democracy (2005) 'Strengthening Democracy Abroad: The Role of the National Endowment for Democracy', available from http://www.ned.org/about/principlesObjectives.html.

Neumann, Iver B. (2002) 'Returning Practice to the Linguistic Turn: The Case of Diplomacy', *Millennium* 32(3): 627–652.

Neumann, Iver B. (2007) 'When did Norway and Denmark Get Distinctively Foreign Policies?' *Cooperation and Conflict* 42(1): 53–72.

Nickles, David Paull (2003) *Under the Wire: How the Telegraph Changed Diplomacy* (Cambridge, MA: Harvard University Press).

Nicolson, Sir Harold (1963) *Diplomacy* (Oxford: Oxford University Press).

Nossel, Suzanne (2004) 'Foreign Policy: How America Can Get Its Groove Back' (with commentary from Mitchell Cohen, Stanley Hoffmann, Anne-Marie Slaughter), *Dissent* (Fall): 31–43.

Notter, James and John MacDonald (1996) *Track Two Diplomacy: Non-Governmental Strategies for Peace*, available from http://usinfo.state.gov/journals/itps/1296/ijpe/pj19mcdo.htm.

Nye, Joseph S. (2002) *The Paradox of American Power: Why the World's Only Superpower Can't Go it Alone* (New York: Oxford University Press).

Nye, Joseph S. (2004a) 'Hard Power, Soft Power and the "War on Terrorism"', in David Held and Mathias Koenig-Archibugi, eds, *American Power in the 21st Century* (Cambridge: Polity Press).

_____ (2004b) *Soft Power: The Means to Success in World Politics* (New York: Public Affairs).

O'Brien, R., A.M. Goetz, J.A. Scholte, and M. Williams (2000) *Contesting Global Governance* (Cambridge: Cambridge University Press).

Odell, John (2005) 'Chairing a WTO Negotiation', *Journal of International Economic Law* 8(2): 425–448.

Oglesby, Donna (2006) Email to the author, 11 June.

Ohmae, K. (1995) *The End of the Nation State: The Rise of Regional Economies* (New York: Free Press).

Ojanen, Hannah (2006) 'The EU and the UN: A Shared Future', Report of the Finnish Institute of International Affairs, No. 13.

Ormerod, Paul and Shaun Riordan (2004) 'A New Approach to the Analysis of Geopolitical Risk', *Diplomacy and Statecraft* 15(4): 643–654.

Ortega, Daniel (2007) The EU and Global Governance, European Institute for Security Studies, Chaillot Paper.

Outhwaite, William (2000) 'Toward a European Civil Society?', *Soundings*, 16, Autumn.

Oxfam (2002a) 'Debt Relief and the HIV/AIDS Crisis in Africa: Does the Heavily Indebted Poor Countries (HIPC) Initiative Go Far Enough?' Oxfam Briefing Paper 25, Oxford and Washington DC.

_____ (2002b) 'TRIPS and Public Health: The Next Battle' Oxfam Briefing Paper 15, Oxford.

Pahlavi, Pierre C. (2003) 'Cyber-Diplomacy: A New Strategy of Influence', paper presented at the Canadian Political Association, General Meeting, 30 May, Halifax, Nova Scotia.

Peterson, M.J. (1997) *Recognition of Governments: Legal Doctrine and State Practice, 1815–1995* (London: Macmillan).

Pilger, John (2006) 'Stealing a Nation', in John Pilger ed., *Freedom Next Time* (London: Bantam Press).

Pohling-Brown, Pamela (1997) 'Mines Controversy Gathers Pace', *Jane's Defence Weekly, International Edition*, 2 January, 5.

Pritchard, Sarah (1998) 'Working Group on Indigenous Populations: Mandate, Standard Setting Activities and Future Perspectives', in Sarah Pritchard, ed., *Indigenous Peoples, the United Nations and Human Rights* (Annandale: Federation Press).

_____ (2001) 'Setting International Standards: An Analysis of the United Nations Draft Declaration on the Rights of Indigenous Peoples' (Canberra: Aboriginal and Torres Strait Islander Commission).

Rabkin, Jeremy A. (2005) *Law without Nations? Why Constitutional Government Requires Sovereign States* (Princeton, NJ: Princeton University Press).

Rana, Kishan S. (2002) *Inside Diplomacy*, rev. paperback edn. (New Delhi: Manas Publications).

_____ (2005) 'The Domestic Dimension', in *The 21st Century Ambassador: Plenipotentiary to Chief Executive* (New Delhi: Oxford University Press).

_____ (2006) *Bilateral Diplomacy*, 2nd edn (New Delhi: Manas Publications).

Raustiala, K. (2002) 'The Architecture of International Cooperation: Transgovernmental Networks and the Future of International Law', *Virginia Journal of International Law* 43(1): 1–92.

Rehn, Olli (2005) 'What's the future for EU enlargement?', Speech at German Marshall Fund of the United States, 25 September, Washington DC.

Reinicke, W. H. (1999–2000) 'The Other World Wide Web: Global Public Policy Networks', *Foreign Policy* 117: 44–57.

Richardson, James L. (2001) *Contending Liberalisms in World Politics: Ideology and Power* (Boulder, CO: Lynne Rienner).

Riordan, Shaun (2003) *The New Diplomacy* (Cambridge: Polity Press).

_____ (2004) *Dialogue-Based Public Diplomacy: A New Foreign Policy Paradigm?*, Clingendael Discussion Paper in Diplomacy No. 95 (The Hague: Netherlands Institute of International Relations Clingendael).

_____ (2006) Thinking About the Future: New Approaches to Geopolitical Analysis, Unpublished, available from shaunriordan2001@yahoo.es

Robertson, R. (1992) *Globalization: Social Theory and Global Culture* (London: Sage).

_____ (2006) 'Glocalization', in R. Robertson and J.A. Scholte, eds, *Encyclopedia of Globalization* (London: Routledge).

Rojas, Francisco (2000) *Las cumbres iberoamericanas: una mirada global* (Caracas: FLACSO-Chile and Nueva Sociedad).

Rona, Gabor (2004) *The ICRC's Status: in a Class of Its Own*, available from http://www.icrc.org/Web/Eng/siteeng0.nsf/iwpList109/522C6628D83A019741256E3D003FC85F.

Ronfeldt, David and John Arquilla (2000) *What If There is a Revolution in Diplomatic Affairs?* (Washington, DC: US Institute of Peace), available from http://www.usip.org/virtualdiplomacy/ publications/reports/ronarqISA99.html.

Ronit, K. and V. Schneider, eds (2000) *Private Organizations in Global Politics* (London: Routledge).

Rose, Martin and Nick Wadham-Smith (2004) *Mutuality, Trust and Cultural Relations* (London: British Council).

Rosenau, James N. (1969) *International Politics and Foreign Policy: A Reader in Researcher and Theory* (New York: Free Press).

_____ (1992 **Gregory and Cooper/Hocking/Maley**) 'Governance, Order and Change in World Politics', in J. N. Rosenau and E. Czempiel, eds, *Governance Without Government: Order and Change in World Politics* (Cambridge: Cambridge University Press).

_____ (1995) 'Governance in the Twenty-first Century', *Global Governance* 1(1): 13–43.

_____ (1997) *Along the Domestic-Foreign Frontier: Exploring Governance in a Turbulent World* (Cambridge: Cambridge University Press).

_____ (1999) 'Toward an Ontology for Global Governance', in Martin Hewson and Timothy J. Sinclair, eds, *Approaches to Global Governance Theory* (Albany: State University of New York Press).

_____ (2003) *Distant Proximities: Dynamics beyond Globalization* (Princeton, NJ: Princeton University Press).

Rosenau, James N. and E.O. Czempiel, eds (1992) *Governance without Government: Order and Change in World Politics* (Cambridge: Cambridge University Press).

Ross, Carne (2007) *Independent Diplomat: Dispatches from an Unaccountable Elite* (London: Hurst & Co).

Ruggie, John Gerard (1993) 'Territoriality and Beyond: Problematizing Modernity in International Relations', *International Organization* 47(1): 139–174.

Rugland, Jurgen (2002) 'The Contribution of Track Two Dialogue Towards Crisis Prevention', *ASIEN* 85: 84–96.

Rugman, A.M. (2005) *The Regional Multinationals: MNEs and 'Global' Strategic Management* (Cambridge: Cambridge University Press).

Rumsfeld, D. Secretary of Defense (2002) *Annual Report to the President and Congress*, 15 August, available from http://www.dod.mil/execsec/adr2002/toc2002.htm.

Ruotsala, Antti (2001) *Europeans and Mongols in the Middle of the Thirteenth Century: Encountering the Other* (Helsinki: The Finnish Academy of Science and Letters).

Sachs, Jeffrey (2005a) *Investing in Development: A Practical Plan to Achieve the Millennium Development Goals* (New York: UN Millennium Development Project).

_____ (2005b) *The End of Poverty: How Can We Make it Happen in Our Lifetime* (London: Penguin Books).

Samassékou, Adama (2003) 'Building the Information Society: A Global Challenge in the New Millennium', non-paper of the President of the WSIS PrepCom on the Declaration of Principles, 5 November, available from http://www.itu.int/wsis/docs/pc3/president-non-paper/president_non_paper.pdf.

Sandoz, Yves (1998) *The International Committee of the Red Cross as Guardian of International Humanitarian Law*, available from http://www.icrc.org/Web/Eng/siteeng0.nsf/iwpList99/7E2A3790156D885FC1256C5400268136.

Saner, Raymond (2006) 'Development Diplomacy by Non-State Actors: An Emerging Form of Multistakeholder Diplomacy', in Jovan Kurbalija and Valentin Katrandjiev, eds, *Multistakeholder Diplomacy: Challenges and Opportunities* (Malta/Geneva: DiploFoundation, 93–105).

Saner, Raymond and Lichia Yiu (2003) 'International Economic Diplomacy: Mutations in Post-Modern Times', *Discussion Papers in Diplomacy*, No. 84 (The Hague: Clingendael Institute of International Relations).

_____ (2005) 'Swiss Executives as Business Diplomats in the New Europe', *Organizational Dynamics* 34(4): 298–312.

Saner, Raymond, Lichia Yiu, and Mikael Sondergaard (2000) 'Business Diplomacy Management: A Core Competency for Global Companies', *Academy of Management Executive* 14(1): 80–92.

Saner, Raymond and Sylvie Fasel (2003) 'Negotiating Trade in Educational Services within the WTO/GATS Context', *Aussenwirtschaft* 59(2): 275–308.

Sanhueza, Raúl (2003) *Las cumbres iberoamericanas: comunidad de naciones o diplomacia clientelar?* (Santiago: FLACSO-Chile and Editorial Universitaria).

Schattschneider, E.E. (1975) *The Semi-Sovereign People* (Hinsdale, IL: Dryden Press).

Schechter Michael G., ed. (1998) *Innovation in Multilateralism* (London: Macmillan).

Scholte, Jan Aart (2000) *Globalization: A Critical Introduction* (New York: St. Martin's Press).

_____ (2005) *Globalization: A Critical Introduction*, 2nd edn (Basingstoke: Palgrave Macmillan).

Scholte, Jan Aart and A. Schnabel, eds (2002) *Civil Society and Global Finance* (London: Routledge).

Scognamiglio-Pasini, Carlo (2001) 'Increasing Italy's Intput', *NATO Review* 49(2): 26–27, available from http://www.nato.int/docu/review/2001/0102-07.htm.

Secklinelgin, H. (2005) 'A Global Disease and its Governance', *Global Governance* 11(3): 351–368.

Shannon, Victoria (2006) 'What's in an 'i'? Internet Governance', *International Herald Tribune*, 3 December, available from http://www.iht.com/articles/2006/12/03/technology/btitu.php.

Sharp, Paul (1996) 'Representation in a Nationalist Era', *Discussion Papers in Diplomacy*, No.15, Centre for the Study of Diplomacy, University of Leicester.

_____ (1997) 'Who Needs Diplomats? The Problem of Diplomatic Representation', *International Journal* 52(4): 609–634.

_____ (1999) 'For Diplomacy: Representation and the Study of International Relations', *International Studies Review* 1(1): 33–57.

_____ (2004) 'Who Needs Diplomats? The Problem of Diplomatic Representation', in Christer Jönsson and Richard Langhorne, eds, *Diplomacy*, Vol. 3 (London: Sage Publications).

Shell, R. (2000) 'Halfway to the Holocaust: The Economic, Demographic and Social Implications of the AIDS Pandemic to the Year 2010 in the Southern African Region' in Konrad Adenauer-Stiftung Occasional Papers, *HIV/AIDS: A Threat to the African Renaissance?* (Johannesburg: Konrad Adenauer Foundation).

Short, Nicola (1999) 'The Role of NGOs in the Ottawa Process to Ban Landmines', *International Negotiation* 4(3): 483–502.

Sidibe, M., I. Ramiah, and K. Buse (2006) 'The Global Fund at Five: What Next for Universal Access for HIV/AIDS, Tuberculosis and Malaria', *Journal of the Royal Society of Medicine* 99(10): 497–500.

Sidiropoulos, Elisabeth, ed. (2004) *Apartheid Past, Renaissance Future: South Africa's Foreign Policy 1994–2004* (Johannesburg: South African Institute of International Affairs).

Singer, Peter W. (2006) 'Humanitarian Principles, Private Military Agents: Implications of the Privatized Military Industry for the Humanitarian Community', *The Brown Journal of World Affairs* 13(1): 105–121.

Sjursen, Helene (2006) 'What Kind of Power? European Foreign Policy in Perspective', *Journal of European Public Policy* (special issue) 13(2): 169–181.

Slaughter, Anne-Marie (2004) *A New World Order* (Princeton, NJ: Princeton University Press).

Smith, Michael (2006) 'Crossroads or Cul-de-sac? Reassessing European Foreign Policy', *Journal of European Public Policy* (special issue) 13(2): 322–327.

Smouts, Marie Claude (1998) 'The Proper Use of Governance in International Relations', *International Social Science Journal* 155: 81–90.

Soesastro, Hadi (2003) 'Globalisation, Development and Security in Southeast Asia: An Overview', in David B. Dewitt and Carolina G. Hernandez, eds, *Development and Security in Southeast Asia, Volume III: Globalisation* (Burlington: Ashgate Publishing Company).

Spence, David (2002) 'The Evolving Role of Foreign Ministries in the Conduct of European Union Affairs', in Brian Hocking and David Spence, eds, *Foreign Ministries in the European Union: Integrating Diplomats* (Houndmills: Palgrave Macmillan).

_____ (2004) 'The Coordination of European Policy by Member States', in Westlake, Martin and Galloway, David, eds, *The Council of the European Union* (London: John Harper).

Spence, David, ed. (2006) *The European Commission*, 3rd edn (London: John Harper Publishing).

Stearns, Monteagle (1996) *Talking to Strangers: Improving American Diplomacy at Home and Abroad* (Princeton, NJ: Princeton University Press).

Sternberg, Rolf (1968) 'Legitimacy', *International Encyclopaedia of the Social Sciences IX* (New York: Macmillan and Free Press).

Stewart-Harawira, Makere (2005) *The New Imperial Order: Indigenous Responses to Globalization* (London: Zed Books).

Stiglitz, Joseph (2002) *Globalization and its Discontents* (London: Penguin Books).

Stiglitz, Joseph and Andrew Charlton (2005) *Fair Trade for All: How Trade Can Promote Development* (Oxford: Oxford University Press).

Stone, Diane (2002) *Getting Research into Policy?* University of Warwick, available from http://www.gdnet.org/rapnet/pdf/Beyond%20Economics%20Stone.pdf

_____ (2005) *Think Tanks and Policy Advice in Countries in Transition*, paper prepared for the Asian Development Bank Institute Symposium: 'How to Strengthen Policy-Oriented Research and Training in Vietnam', Hanoi, 31 August, available from http://www.adbi.org/book/2005/12/01/1686.policy.research.vietnam/think.tanks.and.policy.advice.in.countries.in.transition/.

Stone, Diane, Simon Maxwell, and Michael Keating (2001) *Bridging Research and Policy*, paper presented at a International Workshop Funded by the UK Department for International Development, Radcliffe House, Warwick University, 16–17 July, available from http://www.warwick.ac.uk/fac/soc/csgr/research/keytopic/other/bridging.pdf/.

Stopford, John M. and Susan Strange (1991) *Rival States, Rival Firms: Competition for World Market Shares* (Cambridge: Cambridge University Press).

Strange, Susan (1996) *The Retreat of the State: The Diffusion of Power in the World Economy* (Cambridge: Cambridge University Press).

Sundararaman, Shankari (2006) 'Research Centers as Diplomatic Actors', paper presented to the conference 'Worlds Apart? Exploring the Interface between Governance and Diplomacy', CIGI and Asia-Pacific College of Diplomacy, Australian National University, 4–5 March, Canberra.

Sunstein, Cass (2001) *Echo Chambers: Bush v. Gore, Impeachment, and Beyond* (Princeton, NJ: Princeton University Press).

Tallberg, J. (2000) 'The Anatomy of Autonomy: An Institutional Account of Variation in Supranational Influence', *Journal of Common Market Studies* 38(5): 843–864.

Telò, Mario (2006) *Europe: A Civilian Power? European Union, Global Governance, World Order* (London: Palgrave).

Thakur, Ramesh (2006a) 'Nuclear Weapons, Anomalies, and Global Governance', in *2003 2005 John W.Holmes Memorial Lectures* (Waterloo, Ontario: ACUNS Reports and Papers 2006 No. 1).

_____ (2006b) *The United Nations, Peace and Security: From Collective Security to the Responsibility to Protect* (Cambridge: Cambridge University Press).

_____ (2007a) 'Is India So Weak That It Must Fear Success?', *Hindu* (Chennai), 4 September.

_____ (2007b) 'No Time to Hesitate: in Good Faith', *Daily News and Analysis* (Mumbai), 27 October.

_____ (2007c) 'Nuclear Double Standards', *Times of India* (Delhi), 15 October.

Thakur, Ramesh and Luc van Langenhove (2006) 'Enhancing Global Governance Through Regional Integration', *Global Governance* 12(3): 233–240.

Thakur, Ramesh and Thomas Weiss (2007) *The UN and Global Governance: An Idea and its Prospects* (Bloomington, IN: Indiana University Press).

_____ (forthcoming) *Global Governance and the United Nations* (Bloomington, IN: Indiana University Press).

Thakur, Ramesh, Andrew F. Cooper, and John English, eds (2005) *International Commissions and the Power of Ideas* (Tokyo: United Nations University Press).

The Economist, 'Britain: New Blood', London: 6 March 1999, 350: 8109, 54, 2.

Todorova, Zdravka (2003) 'HIV/AIDS in Heavily Indebted Countries and Global Finance', *Oeconomicus* 6: 101–112.

de Torrente, Nicholas (2002) 'Humanitarian Action Must Remain Independent in Conflict Zones, Says Doctors Without Borders Exec', News Release, *Stanford University Graduate School of Business*, February, available from http://www.gsb.stanford.edu/news/headlines/detorrente.shtml.

Trevelyan, Humphrey (1973) *Diplomatic Channels* (Boston: Gambit).

Triggs, Gillian (1999) 'Australia's Indigenous Peoples and International Law: Validity of the Native Title Amendment Act 1998 (Cth)', *Melbourne University Law Review* 23(2): 372–415.

Turkish Press (2006) 'Two Killed in Pakistan as EU Tries to Defuse Cartoon Row', 14 February, available from http://www.turkishpress.com/news.asp?id=108160.

Tusa, John (1996) 'Diplomats and Journalists – Sisters under the Skin', *The World Today* 52(8–9): 217–221.

UNAIDS (2006) *Report on the Global AIDS Epidemic: A UNAIDS 10th Anniversary Special Edition* (Geneva: Joint United Nations Programme on HIV/AIDS (UNAIDS)).

UNAIDS/WHO (2005) *AIDS Epidemic Update-December 2005* (Geneva: Joint United Nations Programme on HIV/AIDS (UNAIDS) and World Health Organization (WHO)).

UNDP Report (2003) *Thinking the Unthinkable: From Thought to Policy. The Role of Think Tanks in Shaping Government Strategy: Experiences from Central and Eastern Europe, Bratislava* (New York: UNDP).

UNICEF (2006) 'The Global Fund', Information Sheet, 10 July 2006 (New York: UNICEF).

United Nations (1982) Economic and Social Council Resolution 1982/34 of May 7, 1982 authorizing the establishment of the Working Group on Indigenous Populations.

_____ (1986) 'The Problem of Discrimination Against Indigenous Populations', Jose Martinez Cobo, special rapporteur E/CN.4/Sub2/1986/7 and Addenda 1–4.

_____ (1993) 'The Vienna Declaration and Programme of Action UN Document', A/Conf. 157/23 of 12 July 1993: Part II, B, 2, para 32.

_____ (1994) Draft UN Declaration on the Rights of Indigenous Peoples, adopted by the Sub-Commission on Prevention of Discrimination and Protection of Minorities 1994/45.

_____ (1995) 'Conclusions Review of the Existing Mechanisms, Procedures and Programmes within the United Nations concerning Indigenous Peoples', Report of the Secretary General Sub-Commission resolution 1995/39.

_____ (1998) 'International Decade of the Worlds Indigenous Peoples', GA Resolution 52/108.

_____ (2000) 'Establishment of a Permanent Forum on Indigenous Issues', E/RES/2000/22.

_____ (2001a) 'Declaration of Commitment on HIV/AIDS', UN General Assembly Special Session on HIV/AIDS, 25–27 June, United Nations, New York.

_____ (2001b) 'Human Rights and Indigenous Issues', CHR Resolution 2001/57.

_____ (2002a) Press Release '"You have a home at the United Nations" says Secretary-General, as Indigenous Forum concludes First Session', SG/SM/8249 (24 May 2002).

_____ (2002b) 'Sub-Commission on the Promotion and Protection of Human Rights, International Decade of the Worlds Indigenous People', Resolution 2002/19.

_____ (2003) 'Building an Open, Empowering Information Society Is a Social, Economic and Ultimately Political Challenge, Says Secretary-General at World Summit', Press Release SG/SM/9070 PI/1535, December 10, available from http://www.un.org/News/Press/docs/2003/sgsm9070.doc.htm.

_____ (2004) 'Human rights and indigenous issues Commission on Human Rights Resolution', 2004/62.

_____ (2005) 'Secretary General Announces Composition of High-Level Group for Alliance of Civilisation', Secretary-General SG/SM/10073/Rev.1, 2 September, available from, http:www.un.org/News/Press/docs/2005/sgsm10073.doc.htm.

United Nations (2006) '"Delivering as One": Report of the Secretary-General's High-Level Panel on UN System-wide Coherence in the Ares of Development, Humanitarian assistance, and the Environment', Final Draft to Co-Chairs, 17 October 2006, New York: United Nations.

United States (1977) 'Public Diplomacy and the Future', Hearings before the Subcommittee on International Operations, Washington, DC: House of Representatives.

United States (2005a) 'Comments of the United States of America on Internet Governance', 15 August ,Washington, DC: Department of Defense, available from http://www.state.gov/e/eb/rls/othr/2005/51063.htm.

_____ (2005b) 'No New Oversight for Internet Management, Summit Agrees', 16 November, Washington, DC: Department of Defense, available from http://usinfo.state.gov/eur/Archive/2005/Nov/16-685260.html.

US Department of Defense (2003) *Secretary of Defense Address to Town Hall Meeting*, 30 April, Baghdad, Iraq, available from http://www.defenselink.mil/transcripts/2003/tr20030430-secdef0139.html.

US Institute of Peace (1997) *Virtual Diplomacy Initiative*, available from http://www.usip.org /virtualdiplomacy/index.html.

Wade, Robert Hunter (2003) 'What Strategies Are Viable for Developing Countries Today? The World Trade Organization and the Shrinking of "Development Space"', *Review of International Political Economy* 10(4): 621–644.

Wagner, W. (2006) 'The Democratic Control of Military Power Europe', *Journal of European Public Policy* (special issue) 13(2): 200–216.

Wallace, Helen (1993) 'Deepening and Widening: Problems of Legitimacy for the EC', in Soledad Grecia, ed., *European Identity and the Search for Legitimacy* (London: Pinter).

Wallace, William (1998) 'Ideas and Influence', in Diane Stone, Andrew Denham, and Mark Garnett, eds, *Think Tanks Across Nations: A Comparative Approach* (Manchester: Manchester University Press).

Walzer, Michael (2004) *Politics and Passion: Toward a More Egalitarian Liberalism* (New Haven, CT: Yale University Press).

Wanandi, Jusuf (1995) 'ASEAN's Informal Networking', *The Indonesia Quarterly* 23(1): 56–66.

Watson, Adam (1982) *Diplomacy: The Dialogue Between States* (London: Methuen).

Watson, Graham et al. (2007) *The Case for Global Democracy: Advocating a United Nations Parliament* (Langport, UK: Bagehot Publishing), available from http://www.alde.eu/fileadmin/files/Download/UNPA.pdf.

Weimann, Gabriel (2006) *Terror on the Internet: The New Arena, The New Challenges* (Dulles: Potomac Books).

Weiss, Linda (1998) *The Myth of the Powerless State: Governing the Economy in a Global Era* (Cambridge: Polity).

Weiss, Thomas G. (1975) *International Bureaucracy* (Lexington, MA: Lexington Books).

Wight, Martin (1977) *Systems of States* (Leicester: Leicester University Press).

Wilkinson, Rorden (2000) *Multilateralism and the WTO: The Architecture and Extension of International Trade Regulation* (London: Routledge).

_____ (2006) *The WTO: Crisis and the Governance of Global Trade* (London: Routledge).

_____ (2007) 'Building asymmetry: concluding the DDA', in Donna Lee and Rorden Wilkinson, eds, *The WTO after Hong Kong: Progress in, and Prospects for, the Doha Development Agenda* (London: Routledge).

Willetts, P., ed. (1996) *'Conscience of the World': The Influence of Non-Governmental Organisations in the UN System* (Washington, DC: Brookings Institution).

Williamson, David (1993) 'What sort of Community in the year 2000', 4th Brandon Rhys Williams Memorial Lecture (London: European League for Economic Cooperation).

Wiseman, Geoffrey (1999) ' "Polylateralism" and New Modes of Global Dialogue', *Discussion Paper*, No. 59 (Leicester: Leicester Diplomatic Studies Programme).

Wolfe, Robert (1998) *'Still* Lying Abroad? On the Institution of the Resident Ambassador', *Diplomacy and Statecraft* 9(2): 23–54.

Wolfowitz, Paul (2003) *Deputy Secretary of Defense Wolfowitz Interview with CNN*, 6 May, available from http://www.defenselink.mil/transcripts/2003/tr20030506-depsecdef0156.html.

World Bank (2000) 'Intensifying Action against HIV/AIDS in Africa: Responding to a Development Crisis' (Washington DC: World Bank).

World Trade Organization (2001) 'Doha WTO Ministerial 2001: Ministerial Declaration', WT/MIN/01/Dec I (Geneva: WTO).

Zinsmeister, Karl (2003) 'It's Time for New Allies', The American Enterprise Institute for Public Policy Research (AEI), 28 October, available from http://www.aei.org/publications/pubID.19359,filter.all/pub_detail.asp.

Index

CPSIA information can be obtained at www.ICGtesting.com
Printed in the USA
LVOW041503090113

315046LV00001B/1/P